Spoonhandle

RUTH MOORE

Spoonhandle

A NOVEL

BY THE AUTHOR OF

THE WEIR

NEW YORK

WILLIAM MORROW AND COMPANY

MCMXLVI

Originally Published in 1946
By William Morrow & Co.
Reprinted December 1986 By Blackberry
ISBN 0-942396-49-9

© Ruth Moore, 1986

Blackberry Books
Chimney Farm
Nobleboro, Maine 04555

Printed in the United States of America

Cover photo by Beth Leonard

To

Any American Town

Spoonhandle

PART

I

AGNES STILWELL FLYNN was on her way to see her brother. She walked briskly up the shore path from her house, her compact figure black against the overnight thin sprinkling of snow. Where she crossed the Salt Pond footbridge, the prints of her goloshes showed black against the white wet planks, neat as a cat-track, without any blurring at the heels.

The sun getting ready to rise had turned the southeast sky into a flat plate of light beginning to glitter at the horizon. The ocean was slate-black against it, the trees on Spoonhandle tar-black. The Salt Pond Water had already taken on a clear light from the sky, but under the bridge the tide slid like a dark pouring of liquid glass.

If she had been with somebody, Agnes would have mentioned how pretty the sunrise was and would have stopped to look at it. The view from Salt Pond footbridge was the finest on Big Spoon Island, overlooking the Fore Harbor and the channel ledges to Spoonhandle and the miles of open sea. The summer people admired it and Agnes always told them that the time to see it was November sunrise, when the sun notched the low land on Spoonhandle and rose straight out of the water. Being alone this morning and in a hurry to catch Pete before he opened his store to customers, she did not give a sideways glance at the view.

She did pause for a moment to study the cove at Little Spoon Island where her younger brothers, Horace and Willie Stilwell, moored their lobster-boat. The mooring was empty, she was pleased to see. She'd been pretty sure she'd heard the boat go down the harbor before daylight. The hollow whanging of Willie's old engine was unmistakable. Not that Willie would think it was funny if he saw her talking to Pete, Agnes thought, but there, she had gone to quite a lot of trouble to get up here early to be sure Pete would be alone.

As she passed Mag Snow's Come On Inn, Uncle Tilberry Seavey, peering from his rocker in the kitchen window, said, "Warner Brothers' corsets."

"Who, Tilburry?" Mag looked up absently from the spiderful of bacon she was frying for breakfast.

"Aggie Flynn. All dressed up. You'd think she was goin t' New York."

"Maybe she is. But you know Aggie—she'd dress up to go to the backhouse." Mag came over and bent down to look past the stiff starched curtain. A broad grin spread across her face. "Got a new winter coat, I see. What kind of fur would you say that was, Tilburry?"

"I d'no. Ain't nothin like it in the catalog."

"I bet she never gut *that* out of a catalog." A smell of burning bacon sent Mag scurrying back to the stove. She slid her cooking fork under the crisp strips and laid them on a paper bag to drain. "The way she goes round with her nose in the summer people's placket-hole, probly one of them's sent her a cast-off."

Uncle Til cackled, the thin *heh-heh-heh* of age. "Like to see it on some little red-head with pretty laigs," he said.

"You old hellion," said Mag affectionately. She set the plates of bacon and eggs on the kitchen table oilcloth, and filled two big cups with steaming coffee. "Come'n hev your breakfast."

Uncle Til had his neck craned and his craggy old nose flattened on the windowpane. "Ain't she steppin it off!" he remarked. "You know, Maggie, she always look's if she'd just seen a bedbug."

"Not in her house," said Mag, through a mouthful of bacon. "She can sweep the whole thing from suller to attic and not git nothin but a straw off the broom. My God, I forgut my east-rolls!"

She hurled herself across the room and yanked open the oven

door. The rolls, done to a golden brown, sent a subtle aroma of
fresh bread over the bacon smell, thick in the room, and Uncle Til
unmistakably twitched.

"I'm comin. . . . She's gone into Pete's," he reported. He began
to scrabble himself together to get up, thrusting heavily on his
cane.

Uncle Til was tiny and frail, his body bent at almost a right
angle to his legs. He moved slowly, with infinite care, as if afraid
his joints might come apart at the slightest jar. He was ninety-two
and his arthritis seldom left him free from pain.

"By joppy, Maggie, you do put out a spread!" He ate rapidly
for a moment before his face clouded over. "I don't know what
would a become of me, I swear I don't. Every time I set down t'
your table, I thank God."

"You better thank me that does the cookin," Mag said with a
wink at him. "Tch! I've forgot your napkin, Tilburry. Here, tuck
it under your chin."

He was a very clean old man, his suit unspotted, the skin show-
ing pinkly through his snowy hair and beard. Mag saw to his
cleanliness and she was proud of him, as he was of her. Three years
ago, when the selectmen had seen nothing to do for Uncle Til but
put him on the town, Mag Snow had simply taken him in. It was
a part of her care of him not to let him worry about it.

"Aggie's up to somethin," he said presently. "She don't go nippin
up to Pete's this early, if she ain't."

"P'raps she wants to show him her new coat."

"More like she's found out you've took out a license to sell beer,"
said Uncle Til sagely. "She ain't goin t' like that, Maggie."

"No," said Mag. She took a bite of doughnut and washed it down
with a lusty swig of coffee. "She ain't, Tilburry."

*

From the town landing below the store, Horace Stilwell saw his
sister go along the road. He, too, grinned, but his grin was wry.

He was resting his spare length against the cheeserind of his boat, waiting for Willie to come back from Pete's with some crackers and a new set of spark plugs. On the way out to the fishing grounds the engine had started to miss. They had decided that the old spark plugs couldn't be depended on to last through another day, especially since a clear, still morning like this was likely to turn out a weather breeder. They had put back into the harbor to buy a new set of plugs, and Horace remarked that since Willie was going to the store anyhow, he'd better stock up on crackers.

He watched Agnes go up the snowy steps into the store and waited, his grin slowly fading, for Willie to come out. Willie came, almost instantly, sidling out the door, and not so much hurrying as walking with long strides down the incline to the landing. His face was flushed, and he jumped aboard, not bothering with the last two rungs of the ladder.

"Pete have the plugs?" Horace asked.

"Ayeh. Charged me twice what they was worth, too."

Horace nodded. "Wasn't expecting that, I spose." He tore open the brown paper wrapper. "Nice plugs, though. Hope they do some good."

His fingers, skillful and sure, began moving over the engine, putting in the plugs. "They ain't all that's wrong with this enjun, Willie, my son."

He could see that Willie was upset, the way he fumbled around with the paper bag of crackers, turning it over and over before he finally laid it down on the engine box.

"Pete had some a that good cheese," Willie said, not looking up. "I gut a couple pounds t' go with the crackers."

"Have some of it, Willie."

"B'God, I will!" He unwrapped the cheese, broke off a generous chunk and chewed earnestly, looking off over the harbor. Horace said nothing, waiting for his brother to eat enough cheese and be comforted.

"What's bitin her?" he asked presently. "She get after you about Witherspoon?"

"No," Willie said. He swallowed and took another bite. "Kind of twitted me, that's all," he said finally.

Willie had been picking up his bundles when Agnes came into the store. For a moment she was too annoyed to speak. Then she said sharply, "I thought I heard you go out this morning."

Willie said, "Engine trouble," and as he passed her, went on with an effort at cordiality, "See it fin'lly got round t'snow."

Agnes did not reply. He paused for an answer, then went on to the door.

Then she had said, "I guess you really need some new gear, don't you, Willie?"

*

Pete was building a fire in the store airtight, piling in kindling and soft wood chunks, and Agnes walked at once into the little back room he called his office. It would be warm in there, she knew, for Pete always got his own fire going first. She unbuttoned her new coat and sat down to wait for him.

Agnes loved to sit in Pete's office. Here he kept his files, his rolltop desk, the fat iron safe that had been Grampa Stilwell's. It made her think of how far and firmly back her family went, of the three generations who had kept this store—first Grampa, then Papa, and now Pete. She enjoyed the atmosphere of important transactions that hung over the office almost like a smell—as if the crisp greenbacks and checks which through the years had changed hands here, had left an aroma all their own.

For Pete, like Grampa and Papa before him, was a man with irons in the fire—storekeeper, first selectman, real estate agent, dispenser of advice on anything from buying land to hiring a rowboat.

The room was full, but in spite of the office fixtures and the row of straight chairs for the selectmen's meetings, it looked bleak. Perhaps this was due to the big triple window in the wall beside the desk, which gave on to a bare white field sloping down to a rocky pasture. Some nice curtains would help it, Agnes reflected. It was a shame Pete never would let her put some up. You'd think that Minnie would tend to things like that, but there, poor Minnie, Pete's wife, she never bothered much about the little, nice things. Perhaps being deaf the way she was, she didn't feel the lack of them.

The only decorations were Pete's grade school diploma framed and hung over his desk—he had a business college one tucked away in his drawer which, he said for good reason, he never showed people; and a rope company calendar on which, amid festoons of bright yellow manila, a square-rigged ship sailed briskly on a blue air-brushed sea.

But anyway, Pete's office was no place to sit and pass the time of day. People who came to see him stated their business and went their ways. Even she, his sister, Agnes thought with a little rush of pride, respected his time. So it didn't really matter about the curtains.

She took out of her pocket the two letters she had come to talk over with him and laid them on the desk. The one from Stilwell, her son at the university, wouldn't take long; but Mr. Witherspoon's was important.

Watching Pete's neat back through the open door of the office, Agnes thought how too bad it was that Horace and Willie had to be so different from him. You wouldn't know unless somebody told you that the three men were brothers. Pete was stout and blond, somewhat stoop-shouldered, with a pink round face and blue eyes mild and bland-looking behind his steel-rimmed spectacles. It couldn't be denied that Horace and Willie had the looks—they took after Mamma's side of the family, and the Frame menfolks had always had height and leanness and mops of black hair. Some said that the Frames had Indian blood, but she'd certainly never believed it. Nevertheless, she thanked goodness every day of her life that she and Pete took after the Stilwells.

Once, she reflected, she had been proud of Willie's good looks, and Horace's, too. But now they both went around all the time in those old work clothes. Not that there was anything wrong with work clothes for *work*, but Papa had always insisted on the boys dressing up for supper and Sundays. She herself would have had some say about it, in the old days when she ran Papa's house for him after Mamma died. She had seen to it that the boys, even to Pete, toed the mark with their manners.

Willie, of course, was a lost cause now, shiftless and a ne'er-do-well. He had never had much promise, and the little he'd had he'd lost during the years he went to sea. But up until Papa's death, she'd thought sure they were going to make something of Horace. She and Pete had been grateful for the education Papa had offered to pay for—hers at normal school, Pete's at business college. Willie had refused schooling or to train himself for anything except fishing. And, in addition, she thought, tapping her foot on the floor, he'd gone out of his way to corrupt Horace.

The year Papa had passed away, Horace had been in his junior year at the university, doing well too, at his engineering course. But the day after the funeral, he had packed his things without a word to a soul, and had gone down to live with Willie on Little Spoon Island. He hadn't, she was sure, opened a book since, and he was twenty-six now. She sighed. Willie must be thirty-seven. That made Pete forty-five, and herself, of course, forty-six. My, it didn't seem possible. Thank goodness the Stilwells didn't turn gray.

Pete came in through the office door, dusting his hands and the front of his jacket with his handkerchief. He cleared his throat resoundingly, took the cover off the small sheet-iron stove and spat, and sat down in his swivel chair.

Agnes winced. Pete knew better, of course, just as he knew better than to sit down in the house with his hat on, or to use the same kind of grammar as the other people on the island. His everyday manners were a part of the front he put on for the summer people, who liked to think of him as a character. It was good business to let them think so, but Agnes did wish he wouldn't spit in the stove when they weren't around.

"Kind of short with Willie just now, wasn't you?" he asked.

Agnes could see he wished she hadn't been, and she wondered

why. Maybe it wasn't smart to make Willie any stubborner right now, but what did Pete know about it? After all, Mr. Witherspoon had written to *her*.

Pete explained. "Witherspoon's been in touch with me about buyin Little Spoon Island," he said. "I see he's wrote you, too."

Agnes was taken aback. Here she'd been agog, and Pete knew all the time. She recovered almost at once. Apparently Mr. Witherspoon felt that Pete couldn't handle this alone. "He wrote me the loveliest letter." She picked up the envelope from the desk. "Pete, did he tell you how much he offered Willie for that island?"

"Yup. Three thousand."

"It isn't worth that, is it?"

"Willie's whole shebang down there ain't worth five hundred."

"Well, I'll read you the letter. He says here he—"

Pete reached over and plucked the letter out of her fingers. "Read it m'self."

He held it sideways toward the light and she could see the engraved letterhead on the thick, creamy paper:

CHESAPEAKE HEMP AND MANILA CORPORATION

"Why, Pete," she said, noticing suddenly. "That's like your calendar!"

Pete glanced up at the calendar with a dry smile. "Ayup," he said.

The letter itself Agnes knew almost by heart:

November 1, 1936.
MY DEAR MRS. FLYNN:

My wife joins me in sending you the season's greetings. We have often thought of your peaceful little island off the beaten track and of our all too short visit there last summer. We did appreciate so much the efforts of you and all those good people to make our stay a pleasant one.

We have always dreamed of the time when we could own a little piece of land, preferably a small island, in some quiet place by the sea, and we feel that this year, at last, we are able to make our dream come true. In a lifetime of travel all over the world, as well as the United States, we have never seen a place so beautiful as Little Spoon Island, and I think, and my wife thinks, too, that there is just the place for our "wee hoosie."

Pete let out a snort. " 'Wee hoosie,' for Godsake! What'n hell's that?"

Agnes laughed. "Why, Pete, you know *that!* That's Scotch for a 'tiny house.' "

"H'm." He went on reading:

I spoke last summer to your brother, William Stilwell, with regard to buying Little Spoon Island, the deed of which I understand is in his name, although the property was originally a part of the Stilwell estate. He, it seems, does not feel that the price I have offered him—$3,000—is adequate, though I am quite sure that, taking into consideration the values of island real estate at the present time, it is more than a fair one.

My wife suggested that, in view of your kindness to us, you might be persuaded to talk to your brother, perhaps persuade him to accept my offer and assure him that, alas, I cannot increase it. Mrs. Witherspoon would be heartbroken if we were unable to buy the one place we have loved above all others, after so many years of fruitless search for it.

With our thanks and best wishes,

Sincerely yours,

Nelson Witherspoon.

P.S. My wife suggests that if we are able to buy the island we change the name from "Little Spoon" to "Witherspoon" Island, an interesting play upon words! She is, incidentally, sending you a coat, hoping you may know someone who might use it. It was new only last fall, but is a trifle small for her now and she thought of you as a possibility. N.W.

Pete laid the pages down and sat regarding them. "Wants to 'own a little piece of land,' does he?"

"Well, it's natural to," Agnes began.

"The bugger owns half of Baltimore, Maryland. Got a big summer place over to Bellport, too." He glanced over at Agnes. "That the coat?"

"Yes, and it's lovely. I can't find a worn place on it."

"Probly ain't a worn place on it."

"Pete, how'd you know he's got so much money?"

He jerked his head toward his file cabinet. "Had him looked up. Income taxes, so on. He's got quite a business in Baltimore—some other places, too."

"Then he could afford to pay more for the island, couldn't he?"

"Hell, yes."

"Well," Agnes said thoughtfully, "if he's offered three thousand to start—"

"He never. He begun by offerin Willie five hundred."

Agnes gasped. "He did! My land, I didn't know Willie had it in him!"

"M'm," said Pete. "Willie just says he don't want to sell."

"Why, that's all foolishness," Agnes said sharply. "What surprises me is that he had the sense not to take five hundred."

"Well, you know Willie. If he'd wanted to sell, he would have. Says Little Spoon Island's his home and he likes it. I was talkin with him when you come in."

His glance said that he might have got somewhere if she hadn't appeared and scared Willie off.

"You can't tell just by talking to him," she said, bridling. "The way he always says one thing and means another. I'd better see him."

"You stay out of it, Aggie." Pete tapped a pencil on the desk for emphasis. "You git his back up and the' won't none of us git a cent."

"I'd like to know why not. Papa's will said that if any part of the estate was sold, we'd share and share alike."

"Sure. But 'tain't sold, yit. Besides, I aim to write Witherspoon that the money has t' be split four ways, and it's too bad, but Willie doesn't feel it's worth his while."

Agnes was silent. Of course she'd go and see Willie. Not that she wanted to against Pete's advice, but there, once in a while Pete was wrong. She'd go down to the Spoonhandle and take Willie and Horace a cake, or maybe one of her fresh apple pies. After all, two bachelors living alone couldn't get very much good home cooking.

Pete seemed to be studying Witherspoon's letter. The light struck sideways across his glasses, making a blank glare of his eyes. All at once he said, "Aggie, you know Mag Snow's took out a license to sell beer?"

Under the smooth fur of the new coat, Agnes seemed to swell. "No!"

"Yup."

"Pete, she wouldn't dare to. Not in this town that's always been dry! Why didn't you stop her?"

"Roosevelt legalized beer, didn't he?"

"I wish you hadn't sold her that salt marsh property! Papa never would have split up the estate. He took such pride in owning the whole western end of the island, and I was thinking this morning what a shame we don't own that lovely view from the Salt Pond footbridge any more!"

Pete looked at her quizzically, and one skimpy blond eyebrow moved almost imperceptibly. "Papa never got offered two thousand dollars for fifteen acres of swamp."

"Well, anyway, now she's right between your place and mine, and running a rig like that! Papa would roll over in his grave."

"Well, ne'm mind that. She paid cash on the barrelhead and you gut half of it, remember?"

Pete paused, considering. It was true that he had divided the sale price for the swamp land between himself and Agnes, instead of splitting it four ways to include Hod and Willie, as he would have had to do if he'd followed the exact wording of the clause in their father's will. The clause, which the old man had apparently forgotten when he'd revised his will to cut out Willie, read, "In the event of sale of parts of the estate, or land belonging to the original estate, monies received in payment for same to be divided equally among my four children."

But Pete had an argument all ready for Willie, in case he should come inquiring. He meant to point out to Willie that their father'd made his intentions clear enough the day he'd deeded him Little Spoon Island, and had said the island was all he'd get. Knowing Willie, Pete guessed the argument would carry weight. Willie was a great hand for believing in a man's spoken word. But so far Willie hadn't come around inquiring, and after a while Pete had put the matter out of his mind. He supposed Willie'd have a legal case there, though, if he wanted to press it. Not that he would.

Pete grinned a little, thinking of Willie's horror at the idea of a court of law. He went on meditatively to Agnes: "You better talk Mag Snow over with some of the neighbors feels the same way you do about beer. I gut to git busy now. Salesman comin." He got up, then seemed to see for the first time the other letter Agnes had brought. "What's Stil want—money? Leave it, I'll send him a check."

Stilwell's education was being paid for out of funds left by his grandfather for him. Pete had the handling of the money, though sometimes Agnes wished she had, for he was careful, and sometimes he let Stil run so short that she herself had to make up his spending money.

But there, she thought, we ought to thank our lucky stars he *is* careful. It means so much to all of us.

Divided between indignation at Mag Snow and relief at not having to argue about Stil's check, Agnes let herself be ushered out the door.

*

Pete went back into his office and sat down at his desk. He didn't, actually, have a salesman coming, but there wasn't any more to say to Agnes. Dragging Mag Snow across her path, he could see, hadn't done a mite of good. Before the day was out, or as soon as she could be sure Willie was at home, Agnes would be down there to see him.

Kind of too bad to sic her on to Mag, he thought, leaning back in the swivel chair. After all, Mag had a business to run, and it wasn't any use to keep a transients' place nowadays unless you served beer. Personally, Pete didn't give a hoot what she served—

arsenic and ground glass tea, for all of him. So long as Mag's inn attracted customers, his own store down the road would come in for extra trade. That was what he'd had in mind when he'd sold her the salt marsh property to build her place on.

The main road ran right past her door, and since the PWA had surfaced it and rebuilt the bridge to the mainland—at God knows what cost, Roosevelt didn't care what he spent—the summer people could drive their cars down on the island. Big Spoon Island had always been a backwater, compared to the summer resorts along the coast, largely because of the rickety wooden bridge across John's Reach. A quarter of a mile long, it had been laid on piles driven into the clamflats. Cars could and did cross it, but the rattle of its loose planks and the creaks of its timbers were hardly an invitation to strangers.

Now it was replaced with a wide stone- and cement-reinforced structure, and last summer—the first year it was opened—the summer people had started to come, not in droves the way they came to Bellport, but enough so that Pete could see possibilities ahead if normal times ever came back. And maybe if they didn't; because the big fellers, while they'd dropped money in 1929, hadn't gone under by any manner of means. Last summer, according to a list Pete had kept, cars from twenty-eight states had stopped in front of his store, some of them pretty shiny ones, too.

If a man like Witherspoon bought land and built a big summer cottage, others like him would be sure to come. They all wanted a place not picked over and handled by other summer people who had got there first. And Big Spoon Island certainly was that. Except for the land he had sold Mag Snow and some bits here and there, island property hadn't changed hands for five or six generations. The great-great-grandchildren of settlers who had come there first still lived on land originally bought from Massachusetts.

Some progress, Pete said under his breath.

He leaned forward, the swivel chair squealing under his solid weight, and unlocked a drawer in his desk with a key from his watch chain. He took out a roll of brown paper carefully tied with tape. It was a neat, surprisingly complete map of Big Spoon Island, sketched to scale in ink, with property boundary lines and the names of owners meticulously lettered in his precise round hand.

The map showed Big Spoon to be a small island, roughly shaped like an elongated horseshoe, some four miles long and three miles wide. It lay in a gulf between two shoulders of mainland, almost touching on the north side at the bridge; on the south separated by a two-mile channel. It had been a part of the mainland once, before the sea had eaten out the narrow inlet that was now the salt marshes and clamflats of John's Reach. From north to southeast, the shore line of rugged cliffs and boulders looked to the open sea; on the west out over a wide, shallow bay.

The hole in the horseshoe was a natural harbor, landlocked on three sides—just as good a place for summer people's boats, Pete thought, as it had been for fish-boats, for generations. The Inner Harbor was tidal, but in the Fore Harbor seagoing yachts could and sometimes did anchor with plenty of room. To be sure, the channel was tricky—island-studded, with now and then a ledge out of sight at high water—but the fishermen knew it, and if a colony got going, there'd be some good jobs for the natives running the summer people's boats.

Witherspoon had already made inquiries about getting Horace to run his—said he liked his looks—but of course Hod was so damn touchy you never knew what you could promise.

Pete leaned over the map, rolling the chair back a little on its casters so his ample stomach could ease against the desk. His own land and most of Agnes's in the West Village, he wasn't interested in. The west shore of the island was mostly clamflats and mud, and along his west and south boundaries the state road ran to the bridge. Summer people wouldn't care for that. They wanted to be away from the natives and they wouldn't like to be too near the Come On Inn. Hallet Romer owned a little piece on the foot of Agnes's land that looked out over the channel and might be picked up cheap. Hallet might listen to reason if he didn't get wind of anything. Of course, there was that fine view from the Salt Pond footbridge, but nobody'd want to build a summer cottage in a salt marsh.

The rest of the west side was hopeless, and that was too bad, because between them he and Agnes owned two hundred acres. Willie, of course, after his fight with the old man, hadn't got any of the estate except Little Spoon Island; and the will had stated that Horace wasn't to receive his share until he was old enough and responsible enough to handle property. So far as Pete could see, that day hadn't come yet, and he doubted if it ever would.

Pete ran his eye along the boundaries of his neighbors' lands. Sam Grant, next to him, had twenty acres, with a quarter of a mile of shore; Paris Freeman had ninety, and on his shore line were the best places for summer cottages for miles around—Apple Cove and the Head Cove, High Head, looking out on the two dangerous rocks known for generations as The Grinders. Why, it was a selling point you couldn't beat, the stories about the vessels wrecked on The Grinders. There was even a section of ship's keel, eaten by sea-worms, wedged into the rocks at the foot of High Head.

Cat Cove on Bill Pray's shore was another sightly place. Deepen it a little and put in a breakwater, and you could have a safe summer anchorage for a boat. Bill Pray, though, watched Pete like a hawk. The first notion he got that Pete wanted to buy in land, he'd kite his price out of all reason. Have to go easy, Pete reflected. There ought to be some way to get at Bill. He owned Murre Point, too, and Neighbor's Backside Ledge and Cove—

Pete pulled up short and peered down at the name. Funny, he hadn't thought of that—he was so used to saying it that it never occurred to him. Bill's father had been known, in his lifetime; as "Neighbor" Pray. The cove on the back side of his land and the ledge adjoining it had always been called "Neighbor's Backside Cove," and "Neighbor's Backside Ledge."

Won't do, Pete thought. Not for the summer people.

He pulled out his fountain pen and crossed out "Backside" from both names.

Mary Mackay and Nick Driver didn't have any back shore privileges; their property faced west and wasn't anything he cared to buy. Myron Osgood's twenty acres was problematical, too. But young John Pray owned half the Spoonhandle and Joe Sangor owned the other half. These were fine places. Have to clean them Portygees out of there first, though.

And in the end, there was Little Spoon Island, willed irrevocably to his brother, which Willie, the damn fool, said he wouldn't take any amount of money for.

Fine thing, that that half-baked chump should hold the key to the whole situation.

Pete sat back, and the map, released from his hands, snapped back into a roll and flopped to the floor. He did not pick it up at once, but sat looking out his window and down the snowy slope to the pasture.

Snow was meltin, he said to himself. Well, 't wan't much of a fall, and not likely to stay long.

After a moment, he pulled an inkwell toward him, took out a school tablet of rough, lined paper, with "Big 5" printed on its red cover, and answered Witherspoon's letter:

Nov. 6.

FRIEND WITHERSPOON:

In reply to yrs would say that 3000 is to much for Wm.'s place it ain't worth it. He ain't willing to sell because the place is in his name but any land sold from what was the old Stilwell place the money has to be splitt four ways between my sister my to brothers and self that's the way it was left in the will. I talked with Wm. he figurs it aint worth his wile what hed git out of it hes put an afful lot of work in on that place. Thats the way it is with hareship propity even if you can git a clear title to it theys always something els to fud around with. So I guess you better give up and that has my reggrets because wed like to have you for a nabor and a fine thing for the town.

As ever

PETER STILWELL.

Pete read the letter carefully, took his pen and crossed an "s" off the word "guess," then folded the sheet and put it into an envelope.

There, he said with a chuckle. That ought t' fetch him.

The other letter, to his nephew, Stilwell Flynn, at the university, was short and to the point. Pete did not bother to read Stil's letter to find out how much money he wanted. He enclosed a check for five dollars with a sheet of tablet paper, on which was written: "Take it easy or you'll have us all broke."

*

The new spark plugs had helped the ignition, but they sure hadn't cured what was wrong, Horace thought, listening to the engine with a practiced ear. He ran the boat halfway down the harbor, then spun the wheel and headed for the mooring in Spoon Island Cove. He didn't need to say anything to Willie. He and Willie were so used to each other that half the time they conversed without talking.

"Sounds like it might be a burnt-out bearin," Willie said. He made no further comment, since he and Horace both knew the overhauling job and the lost time that would mean. As Horace slid the boat alongside the punt tied to the mooring, Willie merely gaffed in the buoy and went forward to make fast. He got at once into the punt and started ashore, taking for granted that Hod would want to stay and work on the engine.

Horace watched him go soberly, his eyes crinkling with affection. To an outsider, Agnes's comment might have sounded harmless enough; but he and Willie knew what she meant. They did need new gear—not only a new engine, but a new boat. Each year for the past four they'd hoped to get enough ahead for replacements; but each year fishing had been bad and lobstering worse. What Agnes had really said was that if Willie were hard up, he could sell his house to Witherspoon.

And a lot he'd have left after she and Pete got their claws out of the sugar-bowl, Horace muttered, beginning to take the top off the engine box, so he could get at the old Kermath.

He remembered well the day their father, in a frothing rage, had deeded Willie Little Spoon Island, throwing it in his face as something too worthless to keep.

"Take it and live there like a damn tramp, if you want to," Amos Stilwell had roared. "And don't look for no more out a me, for it's all you'll git."

And Willie had taken it and put into it a half-lifetime of slow careful work—the kind of work Willie did when he was let alone. Now it was all he had to show for his share of the Stilwell property—the money and the rest of the land had gone to Agnes and Pete.

Little Spoon Island had always fascinated Willie. It was a tiny place, an eighth of a mile or so long, connected with Big Spoon by a mussel bar which was under water at high tide. On the north and east the narrow curved peninsula of Spoonhandle protected it from gales and the sweep of the sea, though through the cleared gash on Spoonhandle Neck he could see the open ocean. To the south was the mainland, across a two-mile stretch of water.

Years ago, a Norwegian sailor, looking for a place to settle down after a lifetime at sea, had built a shack on Little Spoon Island, assuming squatter's rights on Grampa Stilwell's land. The old man, knowing no other earthly use for the land—unless you cut the spruces for wood—had let him stay. The Norwegian had lived there for a long time, and after his death, his shack had settled back into the ground to rot.

Willie had been fourteen when he had first started to replace its shingles and windowpanes, and had taken his first licking for wasting time "down in that God-forsaken hole." His father, Amos Stilwell, figured he had better use for a boy's time.

There had been other lickings for the same, and other, reasons, as the years went by, until the quiet, slow-moving youth had got too big to lick. Then one summer Willie had packed up and gone to sea—fishing on the Grand Banks, his family heard, months later. Horace remembered his own grieving, at seven, because Willie had gone away; and how Agnes had got tired of it and had taken a strap to him.

Willie was gone four years. When he returned, still quiet and slow-moving at twenty-two, he had told his father he wanted to live down on the Little Spoon Island place. Horace remembered the row that had taken place, and the curious look of stubbornness around Willie's mouth when the old man had practically thrown him out of the house.

Willie had a better place now than the Norwegian's shack. If he didn't want to swap it for money, Horace didn't blame him; though it was a lot of money—and more to be offered, unless he was mightily mistaken. He had sat in on some of the talks Witherspoon had had with Willie in September.

"Three thousand dollars is a lot of money, Stilwell. You could buy any place around here for that."

"Don't know's I'd feel to home in any place, Mr. Witherspoon," Willie had said.

"Nonsense." The summer man, affable, made a wide gesture with his arms. "With money, a man can feel at home anywhere."

Willie's smile, meant to be polite, was only painful. "I'd have to think that over."

"Well, let me know. I'll expect a letter from you."

Horace chuckled. So far as he knew, Willie had written only one letter in his life and had forgotten to mail that. Horace had it, tucked away in his billfold. It was to him, and it read: "Hod, if you want to cum home, you can live with me."

Four years ago, after he had come home to live with Willie, he had found the letter, dated the previous fall, stood carefully against the clock in Willie's kitchen—in plain sight so Willie would be reminded to send it.

Hod laid out his wrenches and began to loosen the nuts on the carburetor. The Kermath had been a good engine in her day—ten years ago. Now it was all he could do to keep her running.

And if I can't, he thought gloomily, nobody can. If she played out on them this winter, he didn't know but they might have to take Witherspoon up on some of his offers. It was a temptation.

The old boy certainly knew how to make them sound good. Hod recalled the letter which he himself had received a few weeks ago:

If your brother sells me his place [it read in part] and I build on Little Spoon Island, I shall want a good man to run my cabin cruiser. The job pays $200 a month, uniforms and found. Of course it's only for four months, but I hope you'll think it over.

It was a darned sight more than he could make fishing, Hod thought ruefully, with the gear he and Willie had. Even if the price of ground fish and lobsters were to go up, they didn't dare to take the rickety old boat offshore, or out in anything but mild weather. They got by, with nothing ahead for emergencies. This year, they had about two thousand pounds of live lobsters stored up in a car—their fall's work—which they'd been holding for a better price. But that was their winter's living. It would just about take them through till spring and buy new rope and stuff for next year's work.

If they only had a decent boat they could fish through the winter. And it sure would be good to get his hands on a real engine again. There wasn't actually very much about engines he didn't know. Diesels had been his meat, with some solid grounding in the gasoline, or garden variety; he'd had three years of a sound engineering course behind him before he'd quit college. He wished, in a way, he'd stuck it out and got his diploma; but the way he'd felt then, they'd taught him about all he needed to know, and another year would be just stalling around. He'd been wild to get out from under Agnes's domineering and his father's continual nagging about money.

She'd always kept at him about what a wonderful thing an education was; and maybe she was right. She considered that she herself was educated. What she actually had brought home from school was a knowledge of how to make frilly pillows and raffia baskets, to read Tennyson's poems in a high, affected voice, and to be, generally, what was called in the village "nicey-nicey." Maybe a woman like Agnes had to have a lot of education or none at all. A little of it, it seemed to him, had turned her into a regular damn fool.

He'd got to wondering, in those days, if education wasn't doing the same thing to him. He knew enough, he felt, about engines. The kind of life Willie had was what he felt he wanted. Fishing was tough and exciting. But the last year or so it had been hard to keep their heads above water; and another thing—a thing Hod told himself he didn't give a damn about—people seemed to think of him and Willie as a couple of eccentrics, living apart, shiftless and just a little ridiculous. Agnes was partly responsible for that, he knew, and Pete, too. They'd always talked it around to everyone what a queer duck Willie was, and since he himself had gone over to Willie's side, he supposed they talked the same way about him. What Agnes and Pete said carried weight in the community. After all, they were the only solid members left of the Stilwell family, and the Stilwells had been somebody, in their time.

The engines in some of those modern cabin jobs, Hod thought, mopping grease off the Kermath's sludgy carburetor, weren't engines, they were power plants. Witherspoon probably had a honey, damn him.

Hod wished he could put his finger on why the thought of Witherspoon always made him see red. He guessed it might be the man's manner to Willie—the automatic assumption that Willie was a kind of hired man, or something—anyway, not so good as Witherspoon. "Stilwell," he called him. Not that it mattered a lot; but Hod grinned, wondering what Witherspoon's reaction would have been if Willie had called him "Witherspoon."

Maybe I'm jealous of his dough, he said to himself. I guess I'd be jealous of any guy with dough, right now.

But it was more than that, he knew, and suddenly he gritted his teeth. Among other things, none of them could ever hire a man to run a boat without sticking him into a blue serge uniform with a white monkey cap.

Oh, the hell with him. Him and his Christly money. Hod knelt broodingly over the ancient Kermath. "Ah, you old bag," he said aloud, thumping the flywheel with his knuckles. "What's wrong with you now?"

*

Willie rowed the punt ashore, shoving her along backward with short, choppy strokes. He hauled her up on to the landing, went up the short ladder and along the wharf to the door of his house.

The wharf, sunned to grayness, wet now with melting snow, was the front porch of Willie's house. It was one of the first things he had built after he got the shack cleaned out and livable, and had started to carry out his idea of having a room that opened out on the water.

Through the years, working at first alone, later with Hod's help, he had driven protecting piles out from the shore and dumped boatloads of rocks to make a small breakwater. The wharf had to be solid, for the tide in the cove rose and fell from nine to twenty feet, and in winter, the salt water ice rose and fell with it.

The wharf was built out now to a little below high-water mark. It was made of spruce timbers driven down into the mud, braced with·crossties and anchored with stones. He hoped, some day, to extend it far enough into the cove so he could come in there at any low tide in his boat and walk along it directly into his house. He liked, he always said, to have things handy.

The house now, outside and in, was as taut as a ship. At first Willie had merely cleaned the shack and made it weather-tight; then he had begun to build. A barn for cows and chickens; a shed for wood; then he had torn out both ends of the shack and lengthened his one room. Later he had built on a bedroom for himself and one for Horace.

The central room, which he called his kitchen, was compact, neat to bareness. Willie scrubbed the old pine floor once a week with a wire brush fitted to a handle. He would empty a bucket of suds on it, scrub with his brush, then sweep the dirty water out the side door and rinse off with a clean bucketful. It was surprising how neat you could keep a floor that way. The pine planks were bleached white and furry with cleanness.

The kitchen table, covered with a blue oilcloth, stood between the two wide front windows. When they ate, Hod and Willie could see across the channel ledges—Aunt Hat's Ledge, Black Ledge and Spider Island—to the western hook of Big Spoon and the open bay beyond. If they had wanted to use the spyglass for that, they could have picked out their sister Agnes when she sat on the porch of her house in West Village.

Back of the house were Willie's garden and hayfields, the soil sweet and deep on them, transformed by years of careful fertilizing from sour pasture land into good growing ground. Beyond them was his wood lot, the trees tended, replacing themselves from year to year.

Willie went into the barn and gave the chickens a measure of grain—not because they needed it, they had had their breakfast, but because it was a cold day. A lean, scrawny hen with a round, featherless bottom like a ripe tomato, made a dive past him to get out as he was closing the door. Willie blocked her off with a swing of his rubber boot. The hen flew at his boot with ruffled feathers and an angry "Scra-a-w." Willie chuckled.

"Git, Bertha, you fool," he said. "The snow underfoot'd ruin you."

The cow had messed in her stall and he cleaned it out and put down fresh straw. He spoke to the cow, and she made a rumbling response from deep within her vitals. His cat came from the hay-mow, rubbing herself with pleasure against his boot.

There were plenty of chores to be done. He'd putty that loose pane of glass in the shed, Willie thought, and he'd wheel up some more rockweed to finish banking the house. He'd cut some brush to lay over it. If there were any time left, he'd split some wood. As he came out of the barn, he saw that a small alder bush in the shade of the spruces had kept its outline of snow; every twig showed black and wet on the under side; on top the snow followed in delicate and sure design the pattern of the bush.

With anticipation, he started his day, unexpectedly taken off from fishing. Witherspoon had lain, a nagging worry, in the back of his mind, but presently Willie forgot him.

*

At noon Willie rowed off in the punt with Horace's dinner. "I thought maybe you'd rather not knock off to come ashore," he said. "I made a chowder. Seemed kind of too bad not to use that haddock today." He handed over the tin dinner bucket and the steaming pail of stew. "You ain't cold off here, are you, Hod?" he went on, noticing his brother's dejected look.

"Hell, no. Not after what I've been wrastling with." Hod indicated the dismantled engine. "She's going to have to go to the shop, Willie. Look at that."

Willie surveyed the cracked cylinder head. "Funny we never thought of that. Water in her, huh?"

"Mmphm."

"Hell," said Willie simply.

"Going to hang us up two weeks, to say nothing of the dough. We'd better get busy and sell the lobsters, price or no price."

"Ayeh," Willie said. He sat down on the cheeserind and regarded the toe of his rubber boot. "We need some new gear, all right." Two weeks' delay would take the heart out of the time left before winter weather set in.

It was characteristic of Willie that he did not rail nor argue with bad luck. Faced with unpleasant facts, he put up with them, thought of the next thing to do and did it.

"Well," he said, "you eat, Hod, and then you might's well come ashore with me. I'll go up to Myron's and call up Josh Hovey, see if the boatyard can take care of it."

Hod had been scrubbing himself up as well as he could with cold salt water applied with engine waste. He opened up the buckets and ate morosely, while Willie sat thinking, still staring at the toe of his boot.

"Might almost haul her up now and be done with it," he said

at last, "if 'twasn't for them traps settin out there, and of course we can't let the engine stay full of water all winter."

"Why not let the damn thing sink at the mooring?" Hod said resentfully. "I've sure had a bellyful of an old boat."

Willie looked at him mildly. "Why, I'd'no b't that'd be an idea. Only next spring we'd be kind of inconvenienced, wouldn't we?"

"Oh, what's the use? We'll keep on using the old tub till she sinks under us, anyway. What in hell ails us, Willie? Other men seem to be able to afford a decent rig. Why can't we?"

"We could, if we had one to begin with," Willie said.

"Ayeh, so it makes a circle. If we had a good boat, we wouldn't need to lose half a season's work every year, so then we could buy a good boat." Hod banged the tin covers back on the dinner buckets and dropped them with a clang into the punt. He jumped into the punt himself, sending a bucketful of water over the side as the light boat tilted under him.

"No need t' sink her," Willie said. He got in silently and took up the oars. He shoved toward shore, his eyes looking out and beyond Hod. "Don't let it bother you any, but we got company."

"Company?" Hod whirled in the seat and groaned. "Oh, my God! That's just what we need."

Standing on the end of the wharf and waving gaily to them was their sister Agnes. As the punt drew in closer, Horace saw with pleasure that she had gone over her goloshes crossing the muddy mussel bar between the two islands.

"Well!" she hailed them. "I certainly had a time getting here. I forgot the mud was so deep on that bar, or I'd have worn a pair of Stil's boots."

"You ought t' said this mornin you wanted to come over," said Willie. "We could've brought you in the boat."

"I know—I wish I'd thought of it then. But I was so haired-up this morning, I couldn't put my mind on anything. I guess you thought I acted funny, Willie, but really I was thinking of something else. What with the way Mag Snow's carrying on, I was about crazy."

"Why," Willie said, "I didn't notice you acted dif'rent 'n usual, Agnes." He backed the punt up to the float and held it for Hod to jump out. Then he tossed over the anchor and climbed out himself. "What's Mag doin?" he asked, coming up the ladder to Agnes.

"Oh, she's started to sell liquor, and you know what that leads to. It was a sorry day she ever came back here from Portland and opened up that roadhouse."

Good for Mag! Hod thought. She had told him last week she was going to have to take out a beer license, because without it she couldn't make a living. All summer she'd barely broken even—as soon as her transients found out she didn't serve beer, most of them had gone somewhere else.

"Nothing but beer, is it?" he said.

Agnes bristled. "Nothing but beer! Why—" She caught herself up. "I hadn't been down to see you in a long time, so I thought I'd bring you one of my apple pies. Aren't you going to ask me into the house to dry my feet?"

"Oh, sure. Sure. Come on in, I'll poke up the fire. I d'no b't it's gone out, though." Willie led the way up the wharf.

Following them, Hod thought, Why couldn't she, just for once, say "a," "an," or "the," instead of "my"? Anyone else in the world would have said, "I've brought you an apple pie." But that was the way she always talked about anything remotely connected with herself. The trees in her wood lot, for instance—"My trees," and often "My lovely trees." "My view. My lovely view."

Hell, I'm unreasonable, Hod thought. A little thing like that. But he could feel the gall come right up into his throat.

Agnes took off her goloshes and her shoes and sat in her stocking feet in front of the oven. Her fur coat she spread out carefully across the back of a chair. "Horace," she said pleasantly, "haven't you got something you want to do? I do so want to talk to Willie alone."

It was the way she used to speak to him when he was ten years old, Horace thought. "Why, no," he said. "Go ahead and talk, Aggie. We all know what you want."

For an instant annoyance dimmed Agnes's bright gaiety. Then

she spread her hands and let them fall in her lap. "Well, of course," she said, "I don't want to antagonize either one of you boys. This Witherspoon business means so much to all of us I—"

Hod sat forward in his chair. "Just what," he demanded, "has it got to do with you?"

Her glance at him was one he had known well—the justified anger, yet forbearance, of an adult dealing with a child. As a little boy, it had sent him weeping into his bedroom or into the hayloft to sulk it out; as a youth, it had sent him raging out of the house. "Willie," he said softly, "if this was twenty years ago, just about now would be when Aggie would get out her strap."

Willie flushed. He, too, remembered Agnes's power in the motherless household. "Hod," he said painfully, "honest, you better go off somewheres and let Aggie talk to me, if she wants to."

"Hah!" Hod exclaimed. "You know what she wants to talk to you for. She's only going to try to get around you."

"I'm sure I'm not trying to get around anybody," Agnes said. Even in her stocking feet she contrived to look untouchable. "We're all the same family, the same family ties. Willie feels the same way I do about that, don't you, Willie?"

"Why . . . haanh . . ." said Willie, clearing his throat. "I guess I do."

"And I'm only trying to make him see what's best for him and best for us all."

"I asked you once before," Hod said, "what Willie's selling his place has got to do with you."

"You know we're all concerned." Her voice, explaining facts to a child, was falsely gentle. "Now you remember, Papa's will said—"

"That we share and share alike when property was sold. Why should Willie bother with that? Pete didn't, when he sold two thousand dollars' worth of the estate to Mag Snow."

"Oh!" Agnes cried. "So that's what you're holding out for. So that's it!"

Willie moved nervously away from the stove where he had been fiddling with the lid-lifter. "Ain't no use for people t' fight, is the'?" he said.

"Well, I certainly didn't come here to fight, Willie. I just came to make you see a little reason, and to tell you how worried I am, the way you're letting yourself go down. If you had a little money ahead and could live like other people, you'd get back your self-respect, Willie, I know you would. It just breaks my heart, that's all, to come here and see you living the way you do."

Horace ground his teeth, but before he could speak, Willie said, "I ain't plannin t' sell this place, Aggie."

"Don't gi' me that! I know now why you're holding out. Pete takes care of the land, pays the taxes on it, and when by his own work and effort he sells a little piece, you expect to share and share alike! Well, I—"

"Oh, get your duds on," Hod said, getting up, "and beat it out of here. Willie and I both put in our time when we had to listen to you. Now we don't."

Agnes stood up, too, in her stocking feet and faced him. "Ah, I've had enough of you, Horace Stilwell," she said. "You ne'er-do-well, you failure! You couldn't make your own living to save your life, and you're scared to death Willie'll sell, so you'll lose your soft little nest with him. Ah, I'm sick to death of you," she went on, sitting down and beginning to worry her wet shoes on. "I did my best to bring you up a decent man, and for years I've squirmed with disgrace every time I've thought of you. A Stilwell, I've thought, making just nothing out of his life, and spending his time drinking beer with a disreputable old Portygee!"

"Portygee?" Horace said. She was, he knew, taking a crack at him for his friendship with Joe Sangor. "Joe and his family have a better time than you do, Aggie, don't you forget it."

"Well, I wouldn't doubt *that*," snapped Agnes. She stood up and put on her coat, buttoning it with quick furious jabs of her fingers. "I just wish you could *hear*," she said, "some of the things I hear about you from the neighbors, the kind of a name you've got around the town. Little did I think when I was working my fingers to the bone bringing you up, that I'd live to see the day when the whole town referred to sons of my father as 'those shiftless Stilwell boys.' "

Hod stood leaning against the table. His face was dead white. "Why, Aggie!" he said in a tone that managed to sound normal. "You've got a big patch of mudflats right on the back of your coat."

"What!" she gasped in dismay. "My lovely coat!" She squirmed her head over her shoulder, and failing to see, whipped out of the coat and held it up to the light. For a moment she stared anxiously, then her lips tightened. "A child's answer is just about what I'd be likely to expect," she said. "That was just exactly the same kind of a trick you used to pull when you were fifteen years old. Well, if you haven't grown up at twenty-six, I don't suppose you ever will. Willie, I'll thank you to row me back across in the punt. I can't be expected to wade through that mussel bar again, and over on the other side, maybe you and I can talk in peace."

Willie made as if to go, but Hod blocked the way. "No, you don't," he said. "I'll row her."

In dead silence he rowed her across the inlet, held the boat for her to get out, and watched her dignified back pass out of sight along the wood path to the road where she had left her car.

She had always been able to grind the courage out of him, he thought, knowing there had been arguments to answer her and that he hadn't been able to use them. His only comeback, as she had said, had been a childish trick to make her mad, and she was right. If one person could be what was wrong with another one, she was what ailed him. Remembering her, with her foolish values, her way of looking at things, he hadn't finished college, wondering if the schooling she'd had was what had wrenched her out of shape the way she was. It had always seemed to him that Willie was the one who saw things with reality, with honesty; yet Willie was looked down on in the community. Agnes was respected.

She had a sure and never-failing instinct for applying her pincers to the sensitive spots.

Maybe we're wrong, Willie and I, Hod thought. But it seemed

to him that for a man to live a simple, honest life, not breaking his neck to get money, not kicking his neighbors in the face for it the way Pete did—it seemed to him that that was Willie's life and that it was good; that it was his own life so far as he could live it, and that he admired that way of living. Yet every time he looked at Agnes, he saw the face of his failure.

Willie, watching with anxiety from the kitchen window, saw the punt drifting slowly toward the head of the island, and at last went out and called, "Hod! Hey, Hod! Tide's settin. You'll have a pull back if you don't come in."

Hod waved his hand. "Okay, Willie." He sculled slowly ashore, coming in through the door to meet his brother's concerned eyes. "It's all right. Don't worry."

"She don't care what she says when she's mad, you know that, Hod. Half of that stuff she makes up out of whole cloth."

"She hit the nail on the head a couple of times, though," Hod said.

"I always used to think so, too. Now I don't. It ain't no sense to, Hod. What people think, whatever 't is, she and her clapper-mouth is responsible for, you know that. Hey! Where you goin with that pie?"

The apple pie, still wrapped in a virgin napkin, had been on the kitchen cupboard where Agnes had left it. Hod, catching sight of it, had scooped it up and was making for the door. "Off the dock," he said tightly.

"My God, boy!" Deftly Willie lifted it out of his hands. "That's the best pie in Hancock County. You throw that off the wharf, you'll go in after it."

For a moment Hod glared at him, then he relaxed and grinned. "Okay," he said. "I'll have some too."

"Damn fool if you don't," said Willie. "Look, I d'no b't I'll take a run over by Cat Cove and see 'f the's any coots flyin. Might git one, later on tonight."

"Sure," Horace said. They both knew that there would be no birds flying until after sunset; but they both knew, too, how much

Willie needed to be by himself. Alone, he built up resistance, repaired defences that had gone down. Sometime after dark he would come back feeling all right again. Hod wished that he himself knew of a way.

"Don't hurry back, Willie," he said. "I'll milk and feed up."

Forlornly he watched his brother take down his shotgun from its hooks over the door and go down the path to the punt landing.

*

Donny Mitchell crouched behind a boulder. His body shook a little and his hands, bare on the stock of the shotgun, trembled with cold and excitement.

The flock of old squaws had come over the low beach that separated Cat Cove from the ocean, scaling in so fast that in the dusk he had almost missed seeing them. He had had his head stuck up from behind the boulder, staring at some black specks off on the water a good ways, wondering if they might be ducks. It was hard to tell, with that funny white light the sunset had left, and there was an old swell off there that heaved glassily into crests and troughs. The specks might be lobster buoys; but he couldn't make out any colors. He caught the movement of the old squaws out of the corner of his eye and glanced around just in time to see them zoom across the cove and brake into the water like a fleet of little seaplanes. Caught off guard, he ducked his head with a jerk and then swore at himself for moving quick like that.

Damn! he said under his breath. I bet them birds see me.

But as he waited, thrusting his knobbly thirteen-year-old's body against the rough hollows behind the rock, he heard the old squaws beginning to talk—the soft nasal gabbling that sounded like old women's voices too far off to make any sense. They hadn't seen him!

Donny took off his cap and peeked carefully over the rim of the boulder. In the still November twilight, the cove lay like a sheet of milky glass, rippled in the center by the swimming birds. As he watched, the flock up-tailed and dived, leaving a lone male on the surface, who hesitated, looked around for a second, then went under too. Before the vague ripple had closed around his smooth tail-feathers, Donny was out of his hiding place, tearing down the shore of the cove in a scrambling run. The shore was made up of boulders, jumbled every which way. His rubber boots, too big for him, clumped and skidded on the rough surfaces. He fetched up behind a jutting shoulder of ledge and lay at full length, his cheek pressed against a ridgy rock.

He hadn't been a moment too soon. The old squaws appeared on top of the water, emerging with an air of casual magic—one moment they weren't there; the next, twenty birds were swimming around gabbling like the Ladies' Aid. Even though you were watching the very spot, you never could seem to see them come up.

Donny gauged the distance he would have to creep before the birds would be in range of his gun. It would take two runs, maybe three, across those rocks. Better count on three, he thought, noticing a high ledge he'd have to scramble over. He looked for cover for his next run and fixed on a big driftwood log, up-ended against two boulders. Just room under an end of it to squat down, he decided.

The flock disappeared again, the male lingering.

Doggone you, Donny whispered. I could make it a lot faster if it wasn't for you. Go *wan*, dive, you ole—

He tensed as the male vanished and ran, stumbling, to the log. It wasn't such good cover as he'd thought. Have to freeze behind it, with his head and shoulders showing.

The old squaws, this time, when they came up, seemed a little nervous. They didn't gabble and they swam about for a long time before diving again. When they reappeared, Donny saw they were farther out from his edge of the cove. Even if he did get to the water's edge without scaring them, it would still be a long shot for Artie's old gun.

Oh, darn, he whispered. Darn, darn, darn. He watched the birds with a longing that made moisture come into the corners of his eyes and a surging feeling in his chest. He was close enough to see their queer-shaped almost triangular heads, the white and black on their smooth sides and wings. If he could only shoot one, just one. . . .

His last run brought him to the shore of the cove. He did not lie down this time, but stood and steadied his gun on a flat ledge-top. When the old squaws broke water, he let go with both barrels. The charges of birdshot plowed into the water at least ten feet on the near side of the flock.

The cove exploded into rags and tatters of foam as the birds churned for headway, standing on their tails. Then they were off, streaking in all directions for the sea, out the narrow cove entrance, over the top of the beach.

Donny stared after them, not hearing the quick ripples their frantic flight had made, nor even the echo of his shots that died with a hushing sound against the woods and the opposite shore. Slowly he unfroze from his stance, broke his gun at the breech and ejected the empty shells. He blew down the barrels to free them of smoke, his breath coming in a sharp hiccough.

It wouldn't happen to a dog, he muttered. Not to a dog with a litter of pups.

He kicked violently at a pebble, relishing the sharp crack it made as it flew against a ledge.

Nothing ever went right with him any more. Not school, nor his plans, nor the new home he'd had such hopes of. Not even gunning. Cap'n My Mitchell, his great-uncle, had always said that however long it was a-comin, change in a man's luck was all he could be sure of; but since Cap'n My's death, it seemed to Donny there'd been nothing but bad luck and hard times.

He had lived with Uncle My at Bear Harbor, a town some twenty miles down the coast. His mother had died before he had known her; his father, shortly after, had been lost at sea. Uncle My had died two years ago, when Donny was eleven. The old man hadn't owned his place and the sale of his few things had brought hardly enough to bury him. For a while, Donny had stayed with some neighbors. Then they had turned him over to the State Welfare. He was wild, they said; he didn't act right, didn't appreciate what was done for him. Better, they said, for somebody with some authority to take him before it was too late.

The State Welfare sent Donny to Foxcroft to board with a town storekeeper. He was to help with chores and be a part of the family. Maybe, in time, the storekeeper would adopt him.

Donny hated the store. He hated the storekeeper and his tight-faced wife. Foxcroft was inland; it seemed to him he couldn't stand it so far away from the water. What was there to do for fun, with nothing around you but flat plowed fields, woods, and a State high-way running through the middle of the town?

The storekeeper expected a certain amount of work from him, and, heck, Donny thought, the State was paying his board no matter whether he worked or not. So why couldn't he be paid, even just a little money, for what he did, not have to go around forever without a cent in his pants? After a while, the rest of the boys got to know you never could pay your way anywhere.

Besides, Donny couldn't help having daydreams. He knew from the movies that whenever orphans got adopted, it was by some big shot with a Cadillac roadster—not by a stingy, two-for-five store-keeper who smelt like moldy crackers.

He stuck it out for six months and then ran away. The State cops picked him off a freight train outside of Portland.

In the past year and a half, Donny had had three foster-homes; it didn't look to him as if this last one with Mis Mary Mackay was going to be much different.

Mis Mackay was an old lady, a widow, living alone, who needed someone for company and to do her outdoor chores. She served him good meals and she was nice enough, except when he didn't mind her or slacked on his work.

What the heck, if she needed a hired man, why didn't she hire one and pay him fair wages? The trouble with all these people who got State boys to board, they wanted something for nothing—a boy to do their work and the State to pay them board besides.

Cheap skates, Donny muttered.

Mis Mackay would raise the deuce when he got home. He'd sneaked off without doing the afternoon chores, and now he couldn't even take home any birds. She might have been easier to handle if he could have. He'd had it all planned out. He'd come into the kitchen and hold up five-six sea birds, and say, "I know I run off without milkin or fillin the woodbox, Mis Mackay, but I done it to get these birds for us."

But what was the use? She wouldn't know that evening chore-time was just the time when the birds were flying; or that he'd planned for days to borrow Artie Osgood's gun and that today was the only day Artie'd let him have it. All she'd think about was her cussid old chores.

He hadn't even got what he'd hoped to out of going gunning. He'd thought he might get back some of that happy feeling, have the same kind of fun that he and Uncle My used to have, when they went gunning off the rocks together at Bear Harbor. Uncle My had taught him an awful lot about gunning.

With him here, Donny reflected, we'd of had five-six of them birds. I'd just like to know what it could have been that I done wrong.

They'd had a pretty good time, he and the old man, living in that busted-down farmhouse, working when they felt like it and doing as they darn well pleased. Those were the days before the neighbors horned in on him, and everybody in the world all of a sudden had a say in how he had to live his life.

But gunning, now, wasn't the same.

He went slowly back to his first hiding place to get his cap, and then, turning, stopped in his tracks. Someone in a ragged old hat was moving on the other side of the cove. As he watched, Willie Stilwell climbed up across the ledges and walked toward him. Startled, Donny watched him with narrowing eyes.

What was *he* doing, sneaking around like that? Did he, maybe, have some ideas about that lobster car?

A week or so before, he and Artie Osgood had tried to swipe some lobsters out of Hod and Willie Stilwell's car. Artie had had the idea, saying that they could have a feed on the shore, and then sneak the rest of the lobsters over to Bellport somehow and sell them to Connie's Diner. Artie had it all planned out, how they could wrap the lobsters up in bundles and hitch a ride over to Bell-port on one of the bread trucks that called at his father's store. But the lobster car had been locked with a padlock, and while they were figuring how to get it open, Hod and Willie had come in from fishing, so they'd had to give it up. It had been fairly dark, just after sunset, but Donny wasn't sure whether they'd seen anything.

Then, as Willie came closer, Donny saw that he had his shotgun cuddled in the crook of his arm, held close to his body so he hadn't noticed it at first, and two ducks slung across his shoulder. Willie had been gunning, too.

Donny's alarm changed to bitterness as he realized that Willie had got two birds. "Well, no wonder," he said. "I knew somethin scairt my old squaws."

"I don't b'lieve I did, did I?" Willie said amiably. "I shot these ducks a long time ago, before them old squaws ever thought of comin into the cove."

"Well, somethin scairt em," said Donny darkly. "I know I never."

Willie stood his gun against a rock, sat down and pulled out his pipe, which he began to tamp full of tobacco with a horny thumb.

"Nobody scairt em," he said companionably. "They was feedin out. I see you creepin up on em, and it was a darned smart job."

"Fat lot of good it done me," Donny grunted. But he was molli-fied. Ole Willie might not be quite all there—in the village they said he wasn't—but he sure had the name of being a smart gunner. When it came time for birds to fly, they always said around the store and the fishwharf, "Ask Willie Stilwell. He'll know where they'll light. He ain't got nothin else t' do but study out birds."

If Willie said it was a good job of creeping up, it probably had been.

"Wouldn't done you no good if you had shot one," Willie went on, "without you'd had a dog or a boat. The's a kind of a whirl-pool out there in the cove at this time of the flood tide. They'd have just floated out there and twizzled round and round."

"If I'd got one," said Donny fiercely, "I'd of swum out there and brung him in."

"Go into that cold water?" Willie eyed him with a mild disbelief. "Nobody but a crazy man'd do that."

"Hunh!" Donny thrust out his lower lip. "I been in water colder'n this."

Willie puffed at his pipe. He appeared to be considering.

He sure is funny-lookin, Donny thought, with that ole sheepskin coat and them patched pants. He crushed back a giggle, noting that one of Willie's rubber boot-tops was higher than the other.

Actually, the sheepskin was only well-worn, like almost every other coat in the village; Donny himself had on a pair of patched pants; and the tops of long-legged rubber boots quite often sagged unevenly.

But in the two months since he had come to East Village, Donny had heard a lot of gossip about the Stilwell "boys," especially Willie. A rich man had offered Willie a lot of money for his camp —some said as much as fifty thousand dollars—and Willie wouldn't sell. It was about what you could expect, people said, from somebody who hermited-up the year around. When Donny had arrived in town, people who for years had been used to Willie and Hod were in the process of raking up a lot of old stories and speculations, as a basis for the yarn about Willie and Mr. Witherspoon.

Both of the Stilwell boys, Donny had learned, were "peculiar." Hanging around the village, or huddled over his homework in Mis Mackay's kitchen while the neighbors gossiped, Donny heard that the Stilwell family in West Village were somebody—they had money and big houses. But Willie and Hod wouldn't have a thing to do with them. They'd gone off by themselves to an old camp on an island.

"Willie's a good man, he never told a lie in his life nor done nobody harm, but he's got a screw loose. And Hod, I guess, would be like other folks, if it warn't that Willie's influenced him. Anyway, that's what Aggie Flynn says. Their own sister."

Artie Osgood, the boy Donny liked best of all the kids in school, had told him a lot about Willie and Hod, the night they tried to break into the car. Artie was Myron Osgood, the East Village storekeeper's son. He had three older brothers in high school, and he never seemed to have any spending money either. It had seemed kind of natural for Donny and him to go around a lot together.

"Willie and Hod won't hurt nobody unless they get mad," Artie said. "But they say if they get mad, they're an awful sight. You look close, sometime, you'll see they got a kind of a wild light in their eye. Him'n Hod's the best-lookin and the strongest men around here, too. They say down on the wharf once, Hod lifted a two-hundred-pound engine block, just for the hell of it."

Looking at Willie, Donny couldn't detect anything unusual in his eye. He would be kind of good-looking, tall like that, and wide-shouldered and easy-moving, if it wasn't for them slouchy old clothes. Donny felt his own superiority grow.

Glancing up, Willie nodded, as if to agree with him. "Now me," he said, "I'm a cold man in the water. Never go into it, even in the summer. You're a swimmer, I take it."

"I always swum out after the birds when I went gunnin with Uncle My."

Willie looked up again, quickly. "That wouldn't be Cap'n My Mitchell down to Bear Harbor, would it?"

"What's it to ya?" Donny said brashly.

"Nothin to me. I just don't recollect ya." Willie glanced at him, surprised.

"I stay to Mis Mackay's. Mitchell's my name."

"Why," said Willie, with pleasure. "You're Cap'n My's great-nephew. I heard you was comin to stay to Mary's, and I've seen you up around the wharf, but I never made the connection. I knew Cap'n Myron Mitchell well. Went to the Banks two seasons on his vessel."

"You did!" Donny was excited. "I didn't know you was ever away from your camp down there. The way I heard it was—" He stopped, surprised to find himself embarrassed.

"You can hear anything around here." Willie got up, stretching his legs leisurely. "Well, well. Cap'n My Mitchell! I knew your pa, too. He was a great gunner."

"That's what Uncle My always said. He was always braggin about pa." In his gratification, Donny forgot his scorn of Willie. "That's why I learnt to swim off after birds. Uncle My said my father used to do it." His face darkened. "I guess you and me's the only ones left that care anything about that now."

"Shucks!" said Willie. "Lots of folks remember Granville Mitchell. Joe Sangor, lives down on the Point, does, I know for a fact. When Joe first come over from the Cape Verde Islands, he went fishin on the Banks. He was aboard the vessel your pa was lost off of. You ought t' go down and see him."

"That Portygee?" Donny asked stiffly.

Willie cleared his throat and spat on the ground. He regarded Donny with a keen, cool eye. "Your pa," he said, "nor your Uncle My neither, never let nobody tell them whether a man was a decent feller. They found out for themselves. Joe's a heck of a good guy. He could tell you a lot about your pa I bet you don't know."

Willie stuck his shotgun-stock in his armpit and started off down the path. Suddenly he stopped and turned. "I was thinkin," he said, "Hod and me's got a chowder to finish up, and I don't b'lieve I can use these ducks. You like to have 'm?"

"Well, gee, I . . ." Donny was taken aback. Suddenly he grinned and his eyes shone. "Gee, I sure would." He scooped up the birds Willie held out and raced off down the path.

Watching him go, Willie shook his head. The poor little duffer, he muttered. I don't know's I ever see anyone so lonesome. Unless, he mused, starting slowly along the path, it might be Hod.

*

Donny hustled, but it was dark by the time he had returned Artie's gun, listened to Artie's congratulations about the ducks—he didn't say he had shot them himself, but then, he didn't say he hadn't, either—and had run the quarter of a mile back to Mis Mackay's house.

As he came up the driveway, panting, he could see Mis Mackay through the lighted window, eating supper, her gray head bent over her plate. The clean shining milk-pail, bottom up on the back of the range, told him that she had done the milking herself. She had lugged the wood and cut the kindling, too, he saw, glancing at the full woodbox and basket.

"Well!" she said, eyeing him as he came through the door. "I'd give you up for lost."

Somehow in the face of her clear gaze, the story he had fixed up seemed pretty foolish. What were two bedraggled old birds, and why would he think she'd want them? Oh, the heck with it, he thought. Let her go ahead and jaw.

The warm kitchen was a nice place to come into, or would have been, he thought, if there'd been somebody there who liked you. It was full of the smell of hot biscuits and cooked meat, and he saw, with the water starting along his tongue, that she was having pork chops and potatoes and peas and apple pie. In the lamplight, the food laid out on the clean white tablecloth looked wonderful to him.

"Hurry up and wash and have your supper," Mary Mackay said. "I can't wait all night to clear away. Where on earth you been?"

"Gunnin," Donny said briefly. "I got two birds. You want em, or will I throw em out?"

"Of course I want em. They'll go good. Oh, Lord, not in the sink! Hang em on a high nail in the shed, so's the cat won't get at em." She chewed and swallowed a hearty mouthful, her wrinkled, good-natured face troubled, while Donny splashed briefly at the washbasin and sprawled into the chair across the table from her. She shook her head firmly as he piled his plate with three pork chops and four potatoes and hunched over it to gobble, shoveling huge mouthfuls.

"Donny," she said. "You put one of them chops and two potatoes back on the plate. If you want a second helpin, you can have it. No, not with your fingers. Here's a clean fork. Now you set up straight and stop gobblin."

He was, she thought with a sigh, a pretty do-less youngone, and she wished she knew how on earth to handle him. If one of her own boys had ever acted that way at the table, she'd have snaked him bald-headed; but she'd tried jawing Donny and it seemed to make him so wild she hated to do it. After all, living with that dirty old man so long, and being handed around from pillar to post, wasn't likely to have taught a boy manners. Things like that would come in time. But she didn't know how she was going to teach him. Talking didn't do one mite of good.

If only I was a better talker, she thought. But she wasn't, she knew. Even in the days when her own family had filled the house, she'd always been the one who was content to listen. Bob Mackay and the three boys had roared talk around this table, while she'd sat like a rock with water washing over it, enjoying every minute, just so long as she didn't have to think of words to say.

With Bob dead and Paul and Dave and Benjamin grown up and gone, she'd thought that another youngster around the house would be the very medicine for her lonesomeness. He with his chatter and his friends and his doings would fill up the empty spaces in the house where she rattled around. But Donny never spoke unless he was spoken to; and he didn't seem to have any friends except that Artie Osgood.

It's sure one on me, Mary thought. Two silent ones in the same house. I swear, I don't see how we'll ever make a go of it.

She noticed, as she sat thoughtfully eating, that Donny's ears were red and that his frantic mouthfuls had slowed down.

Waiting for me to open up on him, the poor little scamp, she said to herself. I'd just like to get my tongue on the kind of people he's been with. I bet I could talk then. I'd blister em.

Well, he'd have to have a talking-to, but she'd let him finish his supper in peace.

"I guess you was pretty hungry," she said, and even to herself her words seemed to sound sarcastic.

"Uh," said Donny. He ducked his head closer to his plate.

Silence fell.

"Where'd you get the birds, down to Cat Cove?" Mary went on at last.

"Uh-huh."

"You must have had to borrow a shotgun."

"Uh-huh."

Mary cut a piece of chop and swallowed it. She took a drink of tea and tried again. "Look like nice fat birds. How'd you want em cooked? Roasted or stewed?"

"I don't care."

"Well, how *do* you like em?" She felt her patience snapping. "After all, they're your birds."

"Baked, I guess," Donny mumbled. He'd just like to see her squat down over a fire on the beach, roasting birds on a stick with a piece of salt pork wrapped around their middles, the way he and Uncle My used to do.

Mary cut herself a piece of pie and a generous piece for Donny, and set the rest of the pie where he could reach it.

"Anyone else out gunnin?"

"Just Willie Stilwell."

"Oh . . . Willie." Mary gave a little laugh. "He's always out gunnin, this time of the year. Nothin else to do. He have as good luck as you did?"

The sideways, suspicious look he gave her startled Mary. What on earth was there in that to upset him?

"He's a funny one," she went on. "Didn't you think so?"

"Well . . ." Donny said. "Well, Mis Mackay . . ." He turned red and his voice, never very stable these days, squeaked into an upper register. "I don't 'low nobody to tell me whether a man's a good feller. I find out for myself."

"Why!" said Mary, astonished. "That's a good idea, Donny, only you don't need to make it sound quite so sarsy."

Donny pushed back his chair from the table. "My father and my Uncle My was like that," he went on, more loudly than he needed to, "and I figger it's a good way to be." He reached for his cap.

"Donny, you set right back down there." Now she'd have to do it. Yet how would she? A boy as sensitive as Donny, if he lost too much face in a place, he wouldn't be able to stay. And she just couldn't seem to scold him, the way she would have her own boys, without sounding a lot madder than she was. With her own boys, it occurred to her, she'd never bothered to think whether she sounded mad or not. She'd just let go with what was on her mind, and let the boys take it or leave it.

Donny had stopped in mid-stride toward the door and was standing looking at her.

"Now, see here. You ain't goin out anywheres tonight, with tomorrow a school day." In spite of herself, her voice sounded harsh and she tried to soften it. "It warn't very nice to go off and leave me with the chores. You could at least have told me."

He stood looking at her.

"With a thing like gunnin," she went on, "my own boys used to go a lot, and I know that you have to be away just at nightfall. Once in a while I don't mind doin your outdoors work, but I want you to tell me ahead of time."

His outdoor work, Donny thought. Who owned the damn wood and the damn cow, anyway?

"Okay," he said sullenly, waiting for the rest of it.

"I think you ought to wipe the dishes for me tonight," she said. "Seeing I did your milking and lugged your wood."

Donny was taken aback. This was the first time he'd out-and-out run away from his chores without telling her, and he'd expected much worse. He wiped the dishes in a kind of lather of relief.

"Well, thanks." Mary snapped her snowy dish towel in the air to take out the wrinkles. "That certainly was a help. I was so tired tonight I don't know's I'd have been able to get em done alone." Actually, all she meant to do was to thank him and let him know he'd been a help to her.

But to Donny, it sounded as if she were still bearing down on him for letting a tired-out old lady do work that he was supposed to do. Sure, he thought, keep on rubbin it in. "That's okay," he said aloud.

"I was thinkin," Mary went on, ignoring his sullenness. She was maybe making a little headway with him, she told herself. "It'd be awful handy to have a mess of birds off and on this winter. Why don't you use my boy Dave's gun, that's packed away in the closet upstairs?"

She saw the flare of joy in his eyes, quickly hidden. Oh, Lord, she thought. Dave was fifteen before he had that gun.

"Why, I dunno," Donny said carefully. "What kind of a gun is it?"

Mary was already regretting her impulse. That gun had been the apple of Dave's eye.

"All I know is, it's a good one," she said brusquely. "Dave spent all his newspaper route money on it one fall. If you use it, Donny, you mind me now, you'll have to be somethin awful careful of it. It's got to be kept clean and greased and hung up every time you use it. And you'll have to remember, it ain't yours, it belongs to my boy Dave."

He had been moving slowly across the sitting room while she was talking, and now he stood at the hall door, waiting for her to finish. He opened the door quietly and closed it behind him. Then she heard him go tearing up the stairs two at a time.

A moment later he called desperately down the hot-air register, "Mis Mackay! Oh, Mis Mackay! Which closet?"

*

Walking down the Spoonhandle to Joe Sangor's in the early morning, Hod hunched his big shoulders into his sheepskin coat. The glassy weather-breeder yesterday had heralded a southerly; not yet a storm, but taking its beginning from a cold dripping fog-mull that had buttoned down over the coast sometime between midnight and morning. Daylight had been only a slow smudging light growing on the windowpanes, and the spruces around Willie's clearing were blurred triangles against soft impenetrable gray. Under the thick stillness that hung over the island, the sea was beginning to stir uneasily. The foghorns had set up a drowsy chunking, as if through sleep.

Josh Hovey at the Bellport boatyard had told Willie over the phone that, sure, he could work on the engine if they brought the boat over right away. At any time now Josh was planning to start overhauling a dragger, a job that might take a week or more, but the fellow hadn't brought the dragger in yet, and today and tomorrow Josh might have some time.

"My Lord, Willie, that ain't that same old Kermath?" Josh boomed. "Last time I had her in here I performed a maracle. I d'no what we can do if she's cracked, but bring her in. I gut another one here prit' near's old's she is. We might shuffle em together and git somethin, but I wouldn't dast to guess what."

Hod didn't think twice about taking a boat to Bellport through the fog. He had done it too many times in worse weather; and it was said of him in the village that he steered by the taste of his shirt-tail, anyway. But he'd either have to borrow Joe's boat to tow his own, or persuade Joe into coming along himself.

He doubted if he could get Joe to show his face outside the house this morning. In spite of the years he had spent in a northern climate, Joe was a sunny weather man. On the Cape Verde Islands, where he came from, the sun shone hot and forever. Cold and wet Joe didn't understand. People in the village said, untruthfully and unkindly, that he and his family holed up like squirrels from November to April, and it was true that they went out as little as possible in cold weather; except Joe's two oldest kids, who had to go to school.

Hod knew if Joe wouldn't go, it would mean he'd have to tinker for a while with the odd collection of strings, wires, bolts and old iron that made up the engine in Joe's lap-streak boat. Joe could run it without much trouble—from practice he knew where everything connected; but anyone who didn't was likely to have to do some studying. And after yesterday, Hod felt he'd had about enough of an old engine. He strode along crossly, his rubber boots squelching in the mud left from yesterday's melted snow.

The walk down Spoonhandle was about three-quarters of a mile, most of it through thick spruce woods which butted solidly on each side of the narrow path. People said it was a shame to let that lovely old wood road grow up; when Grampa Pray owned the land you could drive a horse and team clear down to Spoon Point. But Joe didn't own a horse; his wood he cut near his house, and he had no need of hauling, for he brought his supplies from town in his boat. The low land on Spoonhandle, cleared four generations ago for pasture, was kept open and nibbled down by John Pray's cows. But the rest of the peninsula was slowly going back to the way it had been when Grampa Pray's grandfather had settled there in 1765. All down the narrow strip of land, in some places not more than a hundred yards wide from shore to shore, the spruces and their undergrowth were thrusting tough roots down into the neglected land.

She was-a too bad, Joe said, those land she'd been hard to clear; but what could he do, a busy man with a family? Besides, he went on, with his broad sunny grin, the thicker those tree she grew, the less likely people in town would be to complain about his dooryard.

Joe's dooryard, Hod thought, coming out of the woods directly into it, was pretty cluttered, but no worse except from the point of view of variety, than some he could name in town. The thing was, Joe didn't bother with a neat lawn. He liked his things around handy, and his kids felt the same way about theirs.

The house was an old low-gabled Cape Codder, built by an early Pray, but it had had so many sheds and lean-to's added that its original shape was hardly recognizable. Out of these sheds and lean-to's bulged and tumbled the possessions of Joe. They dribbled across the yard, leaned against outcropping ledges and ended in a crazy toppling pile beside his door.

An old sofa dripped springs and stuffing over by the woodpile. On it Joe had piled his year's salvage from around the shore of old lobster traps, odds and ends of rope, logs and buoys. This was topped off with an aged fish-flake covered by a ragged quilt. The structure made a kind of rickety cave, apparently used by the children for a playhouse, for inside it Hod could make out some rusty pans and bits of china. Pieces of wood, glass toggles and rags lay about the yard—a broken kerosene lamp, some oil drums, a Sears, Roebuck catalog trampled into the mud by children and chickens, and behind a bush at the corner of the house, a rusty kitchen stove, complete with pipe.

There'd been a story going around the village about that stove. Someone made up the yarn that it was Joe's water-closet; that the Portygees just lifted off a lid and sat down, and on windy days when there was too much draft for comfort, they closed the damper in the stovepipe. It was the typical kind of story which nobody really believed, but it was the kind, also, that people loved to tell about foreigners, so it went the rounds. Joe himself, as a matter of fact, had heard and retold it, roaring laughter.

Joe said his dooryard didn't bother him; when he was out in it he was either busy or looking at Africa, anyway. The house sat high up on the tip of Spoon Point; on the north side spruces gave it a little shelter, but on the other three sides the windows looked out over water. On a clear day, Joe assured people, he could see the Cape Verde Islands, and if he used his spyglass, he could make out his relatives and tell what they were doing.

And on some days, looking out over the magnificent plain of water, empty to the horizon, it did seem as if anyone might be seeing all the way across the world to some continent fabulous and far-away.

Hod made a great stamping and scraping on the stoop, as if he were getting the mud off his boots. It wasn't a custom of the country to knock, and he didn't want to walk in unannounced on Joe's family. From inside came a little squeak and a scurry—somebody, apparently, hadn't been quite dressed—and Joe opened the door.

He was a tremendous man, topping by a couple of inches Hod's six-foot-one, his bulk filling the doorway and dwarfing the small kitchen behind him. He was dressed to meet the weather, his sheepskin vest buttoned tightly over a red-plaid wool shirt, his thick pantlegs thrust into the felt tops of a pair of felts-and-rubbers. But even so, he flinched as the raw wind met him, and his very mustache, winged out in fine style from the middle of his pleasant, butternut-brown face, seemed to recoil.

" 'Allo, 'allo, Hod, come in queeck!" He shut the door behind Hod with a tooth-jarring slam. "Goddam, she's a cold day! Take off your coat. Have coffee, hnh?"

"Sure," Hod said. "If Mary's got some to spare, it'd go good." He grinned at Joe's youngest, Manuel, a baby of two, who sat, clad in a skimpy undershirt and nothing more, in the middle of the floor on a stout comfortable chamber pot. "He's a better man than you are, Joe."

"Hanh?" Joe regarded the baby, his head on one side. "Oh, Manny he's born-a this place. He's a Yankee. I cold, me!" He pulled a clean cup from the cupboard and filled it with steaming coffee from the big pot on the stove. "You lik' a New Bedford coffee cake?" He roared toward the bedroom, his rich voice like a fog-horn, "Mary! Where's-a coffee cake?"

In spite of his twenty-odd years in America, Joe still had a good deal of trouble with English. He tried hard and his wife tried hard to help him—she who had been to the school in New Bedford— but Joe never could seem to concentrate on it. He understood simple talk, if it didn't go too fast, but his own was pretty primitive and likely to remain so. This was in some ways strange, because when Joe, through emotion or other stress, broke into his own tongue, it was evident that he was an eloquent man.

His wife came from the bedroom, tying her apron-strings. "Coffee cake!" she said, regarding him with great good-nature. "You et it all, you fat Cape Verde puffer. All the time he eats, Hod, and his kids is just like him. I can't keep a thing in the house."

Mary Sangor had been a New Bedford girl, Portuguese like her husband, but a generation further away from the Islands. Her father had married a New Bedford woman and Mary's skin was the clear color of cream darkened a little by the sun. She had a cloud of thick black hair which she wore cut short at the back of her neck, a wide serene forehead and dramatic black eyebrows, like small neat bird-wings over her dancing merry black eyes. At thirty, and after four children, she had not even begun to get fat. Joe said that was just what he liked. He liked to watch her move around, he said, she walked like a wave of the sea. He thought she was very beautiful, and he was not far wrong.

She had gone into her pantry and presently she came out with a platter which she put on the table with such vigor that it bounced. On it was a huge loaf of sweet bread, thickly candied over with burnt sugar and crusted with raisins and nuts. "This's all I got, and it ain't fit to eat."

Joe let out a bellow of delight. "Goddam, Mamma, where you keep-a those? Maria! Joey! Leon! Come queek and see what the Mamma she's-a made!" He sat down, thrusting his legs under the table with gusto. "Where's-a coffee? Where's-a cream? Where's-a sugar?"

Joe's two older boys came whooping from the bedroom, where they had been getting ready for school, followed by Maria, his four-year-old. They all fell upon the bread, which Joe broke off in big chunks with his hands. Hod came in for a generous piece, which he ate with enjoyment, washing it down with gulps of hot coffee. In less than five minutes, nothing, not even a crumb, was left on the platter.

"Can you beat it?" Mary said. She stood, her hands on her hips, wagging her head in wonder. "Three times a day I see that happen and I still can't believe it. Now you kids kite off to school. You'll miss the bus, and besides, Hod wants to talk to your papa." She shooed the boys into their wraps and out the door, then whisked the baby, throne and all, into the bedroom, like a good wife leaving the men to talk their business and also, like a good wife, to listen to it.

"Yas, Hod, whassa matter? Whassa on your mind?" Joe took a last comfortable *soop* of coffee and breathed out a long-drawn "Aaah!" of enjoyment.

"Our engine's played out," Hod said. "We need a tow to Bellport."

"Oh. Gee. Thassa shame." Joe waggled his head in sympathy. "You want take-a my boat, hanh?"

"Can't you come, too, Joe? You know I can't run that boat of yours, short of a week to study her out."

Joe groaned. "Oh-h, she's-a too cold. I freeze, me. You take-a the boat, hah, Hod?"

"Sure you can't?" He hated to persuade Joe, knowing that he did feel the cold. But it wasn't too bad a day, not like winter. "I'd like to get over soon's I can. Hovey ain't got too much time, he says."

"Sure, he'll go." Mary came out of the bedroom, with the baby, dressed in a clean playsuit, on her arm. "I need a lot of things from the A & P. If we get em to Pete's, they'll cost us double." She stopped short with an embarrassed glance at Hod.

"You can't hurt my feelings," he said quickly. "I know Pete as well as you do."

But he could see Mary was afraid she'd said too much. She broke into a spatter of Portuguese, shouting at Joe—persuading him to go, Hod guessed, because Joe scowled and looked stubborn and began arguing back.

In spite of the years he had known Joe and Mary, there were still times when they all at once remembered they were Portygees and he wasn't. Not that he blamed them. After the way they were looked down on and made fun of in the village, it wasn't surprising that they were careful how they trusted anyone. He supposed he and Willie were the only people on the island who ever came, easily, in friendship, to see the Sangors, or sat down to eat at their table.

Willie had been responsible for it, he had to admit. Joe was an old friend of Willie's from the days when they had gone to sea together. When Joe had wandered north, looking for a place for himself and his wife to settle down—for some land they could buy with their few hundred dollars of savings—Joe had remembered Willie and had stopped at the island to see him. Willie had dickered with John and Bill Pray to sell Joe twenty acres off the end of

Spoonhandle. He and Joe picked right up where they had left off so long ago; Willie seemed tickled to death that Joe hadn't forgotten the name of the place where he lived.

Left to himself, Hod wouldn't have thought of making friends with the Portygees. Not that he felt about it one way or the other— it just wouldn't have occurred to him. But he found out quickly that that kind of indifferent stand-offishness was one of the few things that could make Willie see red.

"Now you look here, boy," Willie said, "if he wasn't a Portygee, you'd *want* to find out what kind of a man a neighbor was, wouldn't you? Well, you hop down there and get acquainted with him. And if I ever catch you doin a thing like this again, I'll knock your jaw right out through the back of your head."

Hod remembered his astonishment at this violence from Willie, of all people.

Now, he thought suddenly, he wouldn't swap Joe Sangor for any five or ten men he could name.

He slipped his arm around Mary and gave her a hug. "Mary," he said, "quit jabbering that gabble and let me in on this. Poor old Joe don't have to go if he don't want to. You give me your list, I'll get the stuff over to Bellport."

Joe suddenly threw up his arms with a roar of laughter. "My God, he comes-a in here, he eats-a my bread, he makes-a love to my wife, and what I do? I *go!*" He flung to the closet and began hauling out overcoats, which one by one he proceeded to put on, tying the whole bulky structure around his waist with a thick piece of rope. "Mamma, have-a the hot brick in the bed when I come back! I don't die in a cold bed, me!"

*

Josh Hovey took one look at the remains of the dismantled Kermath and let out a howl. "Holy fried cat, Hod, what'd you expect me t' do with that?"

"I d'no," Hod said soberly. "Looks like a goner, don't she?" He didn't feel much like kidding back and forth with Josh, even though he knew Josh expected it, especially about Willie's old engine, which was a byword at the boatshop. It had taken him nearly three hours to tow the boat from Spoon Island to Bellport, with Joe's engine wheezing and gasping and occasionally dying altogether, and Joe doing practically the same thing from the cold. If Josh couldn't fix the Kermath, he and Willie were sure out of luck.

"I swear, I d'no why you bother," Josh said, his head and shoulders out of sight inside the engine box, so that all Hod could see was the round of his ample stern. "Throw good money after bad, that's all. Cylinder head's cracked, I guess you know that. What you need," he said, popping his broad red face up so abruptly that Hod jumped, "is a whole new engine block. Three hun'd dollars, best I can do."

"That so?"

"Ayup." Josh squeezed out past the engine box and sat down on the cheeserind, letting his weight come to rest with a moan. "I can fix her, Hod, I'll start in if you say so, but I tell you right now, she ain't worth the powder."

"Well, she's all we've got," Hod said sullenly. He was trying to do some mental arithmetic. Two thousand pounds of lobsters at thirty cents . . . if they got forty . . . He wished he'd insisted on Willie's coming along.

"How old's this boat, anyway?" Josh asked. Without waiting for an answer, he knelt down and took up the trap in the platform over the bilge. Reaching in at arm's length, he began to tap with his Stilson wrench. "Everywhere I tunk she sounds punky," he announced. "You got some rotten timbers in there, Hod."

"Hell!" Hod exploded. "I know she's got rotten timbers. I've been expectin her to sink any time, for the last two years."

"H'm." Josh regarded him with his keen little blue eyes. "That ain't good, is it? Happen you fetch up on the hard side of a comber, some choppy mornin? Well, what say? Want me to start the boys to work her?"

"I don't know. I'll . . . have to think it over."

"Ain't no hurry. Take quite some time t' git a new block down from Bath." Moaning, Josh got to his feet and began to lever his big frame slowly up the ladder of the boathouse wharf. Since it was low tide, he had quite a climb and he was purple in the face and wheezing by the time he reached the top. "You thank God you ain't got asthma," he gasped. "I sure ain't built for stuff like that any more." He eyed Hod's long hard body enviously. "You ain't got much meat on you, Hod."

"No. Not much."

"I gut more'n I need, I d'no b't. Come on down here a piece. Want t' show you somethin." He led the way along the wharf and turned down into the boatyard, ducking laboriously past the sleek bows of cabin cruisers and yachts hauled up on rockers and snugly housed over for the winter. In normal times, Josh's boatyard did a rousing business with summer people's boats, and it looked to Hod as if some of his trade, at least, were beginning to come back. He mentioned this to Josh.

"These don't look much like depression, Josh."

Josh stopped to get his breath again, leaning against the polished stern of a mahogany speedboat. "Hell, no! Ain't nothin to what 't used t' be, but you know, Hod, the's a lot a them big fellers made money on the depression. Hell, they caused it!" He was off on his pet subject, and he enlarged on it as they moved on through the yard. Hard times, it seemed, were planned, one every twenty years or so, so's a few big fellers could get fat out of starving out all the little fellers.

"That Witherspoon's one of em," Josh wheezed. He had worked himself into quite an excitement, but he cooled down suddenly and said in a normal tone, "That's his hooker over there. The one named the 'Northwest Wind.'"

Hod glanced at the big cruiser, intending his look to be casual, but in spite of himself his eyes went back in admiration to the low-slung hull, the powerful lines, the clean sheer of the flaring bow.

"Nice, ain't she?" Josh said. "I happen to know she cost him fifteen thousand dollars. Hear tell he wants you to run her for him next summer, Hod."

"You could hear tell I was goin to have a baby, but it might not be so," Hod said sourly.

"Shouldn't think likely." Josh glanced at him sideways. "She's got a power plant in there that would alarm you. Want to see it?"

"Hell, no."

"You ain't goin t' take the job, then?"

"Not if I can help it."

"Why?" Josh had sat down on a barrel, turned sideways, and was regarding him with interest.

"Kind of like to keep on calling my soul my own as long's I can manage it. You bring me down here to show me Witherspoon's boat, Josh?"

"Oh, no, no. Somethin else entirely," said Josh, scrabbling hastily to his feet. "She's over here on the slip."

"She" was a thirty-five-foot dragger, partly hauled up on the ways, her bow high, her stern still in the water.

"Feller from Calf Island brought her in here last week," Josh said. "Come in here so gosh-dang mad and swearin so's I could hardly tell what he wanted. Don't seem's so I ever see the air burn s' blue round a man's head. When he fin'lly cooled off enough, I found he was goin t' sell his boat. Seems he was draggin offshore and his dragnet gut hung down. He's gut one a them old-fashioned rigs aboard there, donkey-engine ain't got no reverse on it, steel cable, and he couldn't git loose. Said he'd a been there yet if it hadn't come on to blow and busted the cable. He lost the works, net, cable and all. He come right in here before he et and sold me his boat, wouldn't take no for an answer."

"That so?"

"This whole rig, here, cost me a thousand dollars."

"You don't say!" Hod had been taking in the lines of the dragger, his eyes going over her from bow to stern. He had to admit she was a pretty nice boat, not new, but not old either, and she looked as if she'd handle in weather. "Kind of a fool to sell her for that, wasn't he?"

"He was roarin mad. I paid him cash and he took the bus right out of here for the west'ard. Said he was goin to git him a job, and I'd hate t' repeat what he said 'd have to happen t' him before he ever went fishin again."

"Well," Hod said, "you got a bargain all right." He turned as if to go. "I've got to round up Joe. He went somewhere to eat and get warm. Got to start back before the weather kicks up too stiff for that hooker of his. I'll talk with Willie and phone you about starting the repair job."

"Oh, *pickle* the repair job," said Josh impatiently. "You can go home in this boat here. I c'n hev her in the water in fifteen minutes."

Hod spun on his heel. "What in hell you talking about, Josh? I can't buy a new boat, if that's what you've been working up to."

"You c'n take her out of here for the down payment of what it'd cost you to have your old one fixed up," Josh said. He pursed his lips and shot a stream of tobacco juice at a knothole in the wharf. "She's the kind of a boat you can go offshore in. You can fish all winter when prices are high and make some money, instid of layin up until spring."

Hod looked from Josh to the boat and back again, with narrowed eyes. What was Josh up to? He hadn't the name of being an easy man in a deal.

"I'd have to talk it over with Willie," he said.

"Sail her home if you want to. Bring her back if you don't like her. Won't cost you a cent. The price is twelve hundred dollars, all the time you want to pay it in. She's gut a Redwing engine in her, ain't but two years old."

"Josh, what is this? This boat's worth two thousand—maybe twenty-five hundred. How come?"

"We-ell, no," said Josh, running an appraising eye along the boat's hull. "She might be, in good times, or if anybody, right now, had the money t' buy a dragger. What it is, Hod, if I haul her up, she'll set there forever rottin, and I'll lose money on her. Or if I want t' sell her, I'll have to build her over into somethin the summer people'll buy. Either way, I won't make no more'n if I sell her to you just as she stands for twelve hundred."

"It still sounds like kind of a charity deal to me. I'd still like to know how come."

"Put it I growed up with Willie, if you want to," Josh said slowly. "Went to school with him."

"Oh," Hod said, his bewilderment growing. Josh, he could see, was beginning to get a little mad.

"My God, do I have t' spell it for ya?" Josh howled. "Boats come in here all the time from Spoon Island. I hear a lot of talk. Bound to. I ain't one of them that thinks Willie's a screwball, if you're intrusted. I know the kind of deal he gut from Pete and the old man. I gut an idea of the spot he's on, right now, or will be if he don't have no boat t' work with."

Horace began to see. He started to speak, but Josh cut him off.

"And what's more, I ain't one t' set around and see a man have to sell his place, if he don't want to. Or, if you want plainer talk, to see another one have t' take a job sailin one a them cussid summer boats, if he don't feel like it. I've dealt with the summer people for twenty years. Some's all right, I guess, but some of em's barstids." Josh had been working himself up, but now, having delivered his climax, he went on in his normal tone. "You sail this boat home. She ain't no somethin-for-nothin, the way you figger. I'm 'lowin you three hundred on your old boat, and you pay me nine hundred, on time."

The old feeling of not knowing what to do, so familiar to him all through his boyhood and youth, came flooding over Hod. He wished with all his heart he had brought Willie along. He almost wished for Agnes, who in the old days had made all his decisions for him.

"I've got to go eat, Josh," he said slowly. He ran a hand along the boat's sleek planking, feeling her solid and taut, not punky the way Willie's old boat was. God, he wanted her. "I'll be back."

Josh turned away. He was hurt, Hod could see.

"Well, make up your mind," he grunted. "I can't keep her here on the ways forever, and if you don't want her on them terms, the's others that'll jump at her."

Hod didn't blame him. It had been a favor, freely offered by Josh, who wasn't known for any tendencies to do free favors for his fellow man. Josh must have been pretty deeply stirred up by something, Hod thought, making his way out of the boatyard and along the sidewalk of Bellport's Main Street. Probably something out of the past between him and Willie.

Josh looked after him with narrowed eyes. "Gosh sake," he said to one of his helpers, stopping to talk as he went back up the yard. "That boy looks enough like his grandfather, old Joel Frame, to be him. You rec'llect old Joel Frame, Nat?"

The helper, an oldish man with gray hair, looked up with a kindling eye. "Over to Spoon Island? Sure, I do. Big, thin old man, looked like a red Injun. Easy-goin, every day, but if he ever gut mad, he'd tear hell out of a situation."

"That's him. Well, this kid, this grandson a his, he's limper'n a clamworm. Ain't that too bad, though?"

Nat, judiciously, nodded his head up and down a few times. "You don't say. Is that a fact, now?"

"Ayup. Just like his name that that cussid fool of a sister of hisn give him the day after his mother died. *Horace!* My God, Nat, ain't that a name t' saddle down on a pore little bit of a defenseless baby?"

"By God, 't is, you know it?" Nat said.

"Ayup." Josh drew in his breath cautiously and finding that he no longer wheezed, let it out with a relieved "hah!" "But, God, you know, Nat, them Stilwells, they'd take the gimp out of most anybody."

"They never took it out of Joel Frame," Nat pointed out. "Old Joel, he was one jump ahead of Frank Stilwell till the day he died."

"That's right," said Josh. "Well, it's too bad the old man couldn't of passed his inwards down to his grandson, along with his looks, ain't it?"

*

The place where Spoon Islanders usually ate when they were in Bellport was Connie's Diner. Connie's food wasn't anything to write home about, but her prices were low, and she didn't double them for the summer trade, the way other Bellport restaurants did. Connie's real business, anyway, was in the winter, when most of the other restaurants were closed down. Her clientele, summer or winter, stayed about the same, local working people and fishermen from the islands. Summer people bored Connie. She said she'd go out of business before she'd put doilies on her tables; the sight of a lace doily, anyway, she said, made her want to puke.

Connie had been quite a girl in her day, but she was getting old now, and lame, and fairly often she had had a few drinks. She suffered agonies with her feet. Alcohol, nine times out of ten, would ease the pain, and Connie wasn't the woman to hold back. If people didn't like her, or her diner, they could eat somewheres else, she said. She had enough to do, without a lot of starving people coming in on her three times a day, anyway. Nobody knew, quite, how Connie managed to get by, but she seemed to, year after year. At least, the diner, and the food, stayed the same.

Hod always ate there when he happened to be in Bellport at mealtime, partly for the reason that other people he knew did, but more than anything because he liked Connie. She was bleary-eyed and shabby, and sometimes not too clean; but there was something indomitable about her that appealed to him.

Today he read the menu through twice before he took in the fact that fried haddock and baked potatoes was the meal of the day. He asked Connie to bring it without saying hello to her, and he was too absorbed in his problem to notice the way she bridled and sniffed. When she brought his order, he sat without eating, still not looking up.

He and Willie did need a good boat. With this one Josh had, they could go offshore, stay out on overnight hauls if they needed to, make sets where the fish were likely to be instead of just where they dared to go in Willie's boat. They could earn three times what they earned now, if they had even ordinary luck.

On the other hand, twelve hundred dollars was a big debt. Willie had a horror of debt. The old boat was Willie's; Hod had no right to turn it in on a deal. Agnes would hit the ceiling. Pete would be sardonic and sarcastic. Pete's first question would be "How much did you give for her?" and when he found out, he would say something like "And what kind of a tree d' you think you'll find money like that growin on? You ain't made enough to keep you, the last five years, hev ya?" Well, Pete could go climb a tree, Horace thought angrily, and feeling at the same time the familiar sense of helplessness. If Pete had ever wanted to do the right thing, he'd have turned over the share of his father's estate due Hod when he became of age.

All the arguments against getting the new boat churned over in Hod's mind. He even thought of the way Willie liked that old hooker—the way he liked all his seasoned possessions.

Hod felt himself sweating and realized he hadn't taken off his hat and coat before he had sat down. As he slid out of his jacket and tossed his hat at the hook over the table, an amused female voice said, "I wondered how long it would take you to remember that."

"Eh?" said Hod, startled. He glanced sheepishly at the occupant of the next table, whose presence he had realized before only as a vague blur. "Why," he went on, with pleasure. "It's Ann Freeman."

"Mm-hm." The girl nodded. "And I'd have known Hod Stilwell if I'd just have seen a man come in to eat and then forget to."

Hod blushed. "Haven't changed much, I guess. But you sure have."

It had taken him a second or so to place her as Ann Freeman, daughter of his neighbor, Paris Freeman, over on the island, and someone he had known all his life. He had gone to grade and high school with her, and they had graduated together; but afterwards she had gone somewhere away to college, and then had settled down, he had heard for good, in New York. He guessed she had been home once or twice for short visits, but he himself hadn't seen her for over six years. There had been talk about her being a writer—stories for magazines and some sort of a book, he recalled.

Willie had gone to the trouble to get the book from the Bellport Library, but, Hod remembered, with embarrassment, he himself hadn't got around to read it. He'd meant to, but what he read, mostly, was technical stuff, and after a while the book had been due at the library and Willie had taken it back.

Ann was different now from the leggy high school girl he had known, he thought, remembering how revolting her frizzy hair had looked over the top of the seat in front of him. He wondered what in thunder she had done to her hair. She wore it short now, waving back from her forehead in crisp gold-brown curls.

No, not gold-brown, he decided. Amber-colored.

She was bareheaded and wore a brown-and-white plaid wool shirt and woolen slacks tucked into the tops of a capable pair of fur-lined boots. A warm brown leather jacket was neatly folded on the chair next to her. Hod caught himself wondering with an inward grin what old Paris Freeman was going to say when his daughter turned up at the island in a get-up like that. And not only Paris, but all the assorted neighbors. So far as he himself was concerned, Hod thought admiringly, she looked darned nice.

Ann saw his appraising look and grinned ruefully. "I know," she said. "The island'll hit the ceiling. But I traveled all night on the day coach, and this was the only warm rig I had with me. Pa'll die when he finds out I rode on the train all the way from New York in pants."

"That's right." Hod grinned. "When you travel on the train you're supposed to wear a hat with a veil."

"And a dark blue suit with laced oxfords," she said. "Well, I started out all right, but the car was cold, so I changed. Are you going back to the island this afternoon, Hod? Can I bum a trip across with you?"

"Sure, if you don't mind Joe Sangor's old boat. Ours was played out, so I had to come over with him."

"I wouldn't mind a bait-bucket, just so I get over today," she said. "I thought I'd be stuck here till night, waiting for the night mail-truck. How about bringing your dinner over here and eating with me, so we won't have to yell at each other?"

"Sure." He began ineffectually to gather up his dishes, wondering, now that he was committed to talk to her, what on earth he'd find to say.

"That's certainly a tired-looking piece of haddock you've got there," said Ann, as he set his plate down on the table. She tapped briskly on her water glass with her knife to attract Connie's attention.

Connie had been lurking crossly by the kitchen swing-door. "Was you doin that at me?" she asked, with fire in her eye.

"My friend got to thinking and let his food get cold," Ann said, smiling up at her. "Would you get him some hot, and hot up his coffee for him?"

Connie muttered something about if people et their food when 'twas set before them, without moonin at it, 'twouldn't git cold, but she took Hod's plate and stumped away with it to the kitchen.

"It's the pants," Ann said. "She thought I was a hussy when I came in and now, to cap the climax, I've gone and picked up a man."

"Oh, Connie's all right," Hod said. "She's picked up a man herself, in her time. Her feet probably hurt."

Ann glanced at him quickly. "I'm sorry," she said. "I guess I'm acting like the efficient type. I hope you don't mind."

"Oh, no." He grinned at her again. "Besides, she probably thinks you're a late variety of summer people. She don't like summer people."

"Oh, gosh!" Ann groaned. "Well, tell her the difference, will you?"

"Well—better not monkey much with Connie today. Sometime I will. I was just thinking how much you'd changed," he finished flatly.

"For the better?"

"Lord, yes! I mean—" Hod floundered and stopped, but Ann burst out laughing and he found himself laughing with her.

"A lot can happen in six—or is it seven?—years," she said. "I know more now, too." She regarded him. "Speaking of looks, if you will bring that up, you're still the handsomest man I ever saw. Are you still one of the nicest?"

"My God!" Hod said, astonished. He felt the color flood into his face.

She looked at him with a little smile. "That was for that crack about summer people. What have you been doing all these years, Hod? Did you get to be an engineer, the way you wanted to?"

"Well, no." He decided he liked the way she smoked a cigarette, as if she enjoyed it. "At least, I got to be two-thirds of an engineer. I had three years of it before I quit."

"What happened?"

Her eyes, he saw, were warm amber-brown, carrying out and deepening the color-scheme of her hair.

"Oh, I got an idea I was getting to be an educated damn fool," he said. The words were out before he thought. She wouldn't be likely to understand a thing like that. If what he had heard about her were so, Ann Freeman had worked like a dog to put herself through college. But to his surprise, she nodded.

"Some do. I'm beginning to have doubts about myself," she said.

"That so? You don't act like one."

"Good. I'm glad it doesn't show." She looked at him soberly, and he saw she meant what she said. She really had doubts. The idea startled him a little.

"I'm awful educated, Hod," she went on. "I had four years at Bates and one at Columbia School of Journalism. I worked on a newspaper in Hartford for a while, and on one in New York. This year I sold some short stories and wrote a book. It was published last spring."

"I heard about it," he said. "What are you kicking about?" He thought briefly of his own aimless existence, the unachieving years of living down on the island. In comparison with hers, his own career seemed drab. He must be pretty dull for her to talk to, too.

"Skip it," she said softly. "I think of the kind of life you have, and it seems to me that some people get all the luck. You might say, all the wisdom."

"I'll be darned!" He stared at her incredulously. She didn't need to try to make him feel better. But was she? She sounded as if she meant it.

Connie came flat-footedly from the kitchen and slapped his plate and his coffee down in front of him. She stood a moment, her hands on her hips. "You want anything else?"

"No, I guess not, Connie," Hod said. The piece of haddock had not taken well to its warming-over. It was burned around the edges and had the smell of an ancient lardy frying-pan. He began on it dubiously, turning it over with his fork.

"Ought t' hev et it in the first place," Connie said. "God knows, I lug enough of that Christless haddock around, without havin t' lug it twice."

"I'm sorry," Ann said. "I didn't mean to make extra work for you."

Connie spun on her. "And if you're intrusted, Miss Pants," she said, "my feet *do* hurt. I've got very coarse veins you could anchor a punt with." She stumped away and the swinging door to the kitchen shut behind her with a long wheezing sigh.

"Oh!" Ann said. "The poor old thing! She must have heard us."

Connie thrust her head part way through the diamond-shaped small window in the door. "This winder," she snapped, "ain't gut no glass in it, the way most folks thinks it has."

Ann looked at Hod ruefully. "Oh, darn," she whispered. "I could kick myself. Hod, I could howl!"

Most people, he reflected, would have thought old Connie was funny. Unless he was mistaken, Connie had quite a load of whisky aboard today.

"Never mind," he said. "She'll forget all about it the next time she sees you. That's just the way she is."

"And I was going to come home and start right off making a lot of friends," she said.

"I wouldn't judge by old Connie, if I was you. She'll like you all right, some day when she's sober."

"Oh," Ann said. "Oh-h."

The coffee, Hod decided, had a definite taste of flats-mud, and the way Connie was feeling, he wouldn't put it past her to have chucked some into it. He made up his mind not to drink it. If he got hungry, he could stop by Mag Snow's on the way home. Better get started, too, he thought. But he still had to make up his mind about Josh's offer. What was he going to do about that? Talking with Ann, the matter had gone into the back of his mind, but it was still there, heavy and uncomfortable, not yet resolved. Talking to Ann, it occurred to him suddenly, was the most fun he had had in a long time. Other things could wait.

She was sitting frowning down at the ashtray, making a long job of putting out her cigarette. Hod put both elbows on the table and regarded her with approval.

"What you home for, Ann? Just a visit or going to stay?"

"I thought I might stay." She looked at him soberly. "I've made enough money to live on while I write another book."

"What's your book about?"

She shrugged. "I'd hate to tell you."

Hod looked uncomfortable. "I read a lot of technical stuff," he began, "but—"

"Oh, never mind. You didn't miss much."

"You don't sound as if you like it."

"I thought I did, when I was writing it. Now I'm not so sure. I didn't put enough time on it, for one thing. When I have a job besides, I don't write very well. For another thing, I didn't know enough."

The way she felt about her work, he thought, was just the way he himself felt about a boat or an engine. Their performance might not be so good, but that depended on you. Or it might be darned good, and that depended on you, too.

"To tell you the truth," she went on, "I was sitting here with a fine case of the jitters when you came in."

"You were? You didn't look it. What about?"

"I was all right until I got off the train this morning. I had a lot of fine foolish rapture about living simply and doing good simple hard work. But this morning . . . well, I saw how bleak the countryside looked, and then, to underline it, I came in here and saw—" she lowered her voice—"your friend Connie."

"What's Connie got to do with it?" Hod was puzzled.

"I'm scared of this part of the country, Hod. It's bleak and unyielding."

"But it's wintertime, now."

Seeing his bewildered look, she went on. "No . . . what I mean is . . . unprotected people are pretty defenseless."

"I thought in the city . . . that is—" he began.

"In the city, it's impersonal. Here, people start to go down for the third time, and everybody knows it, but nobody does anything. I remember, now. I'd forgotten it."

"Good Lord," he said, staring at her.

"Sounds neurotic," she said, smiling at him. "Doesn't it? Well, that's what your friend Connie made me think about. In the city, you've made a place for yourself, you know your way around, you can go out and get a job—well, I've chucked my job. I've got money to live for a year. After that, if the stuff I write doesn't sell—"

"You've got your folks," he reminded her.

"M'm. A comfort. You've got yours, too, haven't you?"

"Ayeh." He nodded slowly. "I see what you mean."

She meant a lot more than just being stranded without money, he could see that. If your folks supported you, they had too much of a say in what you did, but that wasn't all. Ann hadn't been away so long but she remembered Agnes and Pete; and her own father, Paris Freeman, too, whose domineering had overshadowed her childhood and youth. Hod suddenly remembered about Paris.

When people supported you, you lost not only your pride, though that didn't matter so much, but also an inner privacy that was needful—that rightfully should be no concern of anyone's but your own. About Connie, what she meant was that Connie was doing the thing that most unattached and unprotected women around here did—plugging along at a tough, woman-killing job, and going under doing it. And nobody, actually, gave a damn.

"So," Ann said, looking at him with a smile, "I got to thinking of the chances I'm taking, and it got me down. I'm glad I ran into you. Talking about it's made me feel better. I'm snapping out of it." The smile spread to her eyes. "I don't usually feel like talking about myself. But we aren't exactly strangers."

"We sure aren't!" He had a feeling that he knew her better than he had in all the years of casual acquaintance of their youth, and that, suddenly, it was a fine thing. "Don't worry about taking a chance. A lot of people do and come out all right." He took a deep breath and plunged. "I was about deciding not to take one myself, when I came in here."

"You were? I knew you had something on your mind, the way you were walking around blind. What's yours?"

Quite easily he found himself telling her about the boat, about Witherspoon and Willie and himself and the wornout engine, about Josh Hovey's offer.

"So there it is," he finished. "Everybody'll be on my neck if I take her, and if I don't Willie and I are sure out of luck."

"They'll be on your neck whatever you do," Ann said. "They always were." She looked at him with a glint in her eye. "If everything flops, we might be beachcombers."

Hod grinned. "Don't know but what we might."

"What's easier than to go tell Hovey to drop the boat into the water? And see what comes of it?"

If she could take a chance, he could.

"Nothing, I guess. I better do it, before I change my mind." He pushed back his chair and reached for his hat. "Hey, Connie! What do we owe you?"

Connie's face, its eyes red-rimmed and bleary, appeared at the window. "You don't owe me a cent," she stated nastily. "I feed the fruits for nothin." She pushed open the door and came in, rolling richly as she walked. "A dollar'll cover it. And don't leave no tip. If I ever found a tip, I'd drop dead."

Hod had already seen Ann slip a folded bill under her plate, and he knew better than to argue with Connie in her present mood. He spread a dollar from his billfold and laid it on the table.

"Fruits?" Ann said, as he closed the door behind them. She looked at him with her head on one side.

"Well, I'm afraid that's local for summer people," Hod said. "Since your time."

After they had gone, Connie found the bill under the plate and, without unfolding it, carried it out and dropped it in the swillpail. Later she got to wondering how much it was, reconsidered, and fished it out. It was a five dollar bill, she saw, to her amazement, and she tacked it carefully to a shingle and dried it in the oven.

*

The fog had not cleared when they left Bellport in the dragger, and as they rounded the can-buoy at the entrance to the harbor, Hod saw that the southerly had piled up some sea since morning. Out in the channel, the big swells were coming in long and green and wide apart, and on the western shore of the narrow harbor he could hear the rote smashing against the ledges.

Hod would have preferred to get the feel of the new boat in weather a little less strenuous, but he didn't much care. He knew the course back to the island as well as he knew his name, and besides, this boat had a built-in compass with a magnet adjusted to compensate for deflection caused by steel in the engine.

It wasn't much like Willie's temperamental old compass which was off nearly a degree anyway and which had a tendency to creep off still farther if you accidentally got metal within shooting distance of it. Hod recalled with a grin Willie's story of the time he had taken a summer lady as passenger over to the island in a fog and had gone aground on Spud Ledge. No one within the time of man, let alone Willie, had ever gone aground on Spud Ledge; but it seemed the summer lady had on corsets with steels in them and she had sat down too near the compass.

No danger of a thing like that with this baby, Hod thought, giving the wheel a little spin to see how she handled. So far as he could tell, she was good and steady and she rode the swells like a duck. He couldn't try her out the way he wanted to because he had Joe's boat towing behind, and he wasn't sure just how much the old lap-streak would stand. Hauled along even at half-speed, she had her nose three-quarters out of water. Joe himself was below in Hod's cabin, hunched up as close to the engine as he could get for warmth. Alone in his own boat, Joe would have had a long wet trip home, and Hod had figured it was better to tow him.

Josh hadn't said much when Hod appeared back at the yard and told him he would take the boat. He'd just grinned, in a pleased kind of way; then he and his helper had started the donkey to haul the dragger down the ways. Now, holding the wheel and feeling the boat's smooth response, Hod wondered how on earth he could have considered not taking her. He felt a kind of exaltation driving her into the cross-chop, with the spray knifing back on either side of her sturdy bow, and he gave Ann, standing in the coop beside him, a wide joyous grin.

"This is wonderful," she said, returning it. "This is one reason why people like you have all the fun. Can you get any more speed out of her?"

"Sure," he said, "but I don't know how Joe's old hooker will stand it. She's pretty well up on her tail." He advanced the throttle cautiously, and the lap-streak thrust her nose a little higher, as if in outrage.

Joe, watching through the open hatch door, gave a shout of delight. "First time she don't stop on me if she want to!" he yelled above the thrum of the engine. "She don' lik' it, hnh?"

The southerly coming on with the night wasn't yet as bad as it would be; the green rollers coming up the bay from the open sea were only forerunners. But the cross-chop was exciting, and with growing appreciation Ann watched Hod getting the feel of his boat. She might as well have been a bait-tub, she thought, for all the attention she herself got. He held the wheel lightly, his head cocked a little as if listening; he seemed almost to sense, a split-second before his hand on the wheel could have felt, the stress of each jerking plunge and climb. When the boat needed it, he eased her, letting the bow fall off slightly into the foaming troughs as they flashed by; when she could take it, he drove her, head-on. The big engine sang steadily. The glass of the wind-screen was blind and streaming.

She was seeing, Ann realized, more than ordinary precision in the use of a rather fine instrument. The boat, to Hod, was something more than a means of transportation to take him home quickly. It seemed to her, watching his absorption, and the awareness of his long brown hands on the wheel, that he was trying to establish some relationship between himself and the boat—between his own skill and the shaped wood, the bolted metals, which by themselves were nothing.

She groped a little after the idea, wondering if she weren't reading into Hod's performance something of her own conviction about the almost mystic experience of the good workman who realizes the potentialities of his tools. After long self-discipline, she had come to realize it only dimly herself; though in her case the tools were words.

She did feel better, she realized, since she'd talked to someone; for the experience getting off the train that morning in Bellport had shaken her more than she cared to think about. In the city, and motivated by a savage, contributing reason, she had felt eager to get home. Hard, simple work, a chance to think without being driven, had seemed good medicine to take for discontent and emptiness. She told herself, bleakly, that it was for these, too, she had given up her newspaper job and come away—not just to escape seeing Cary Bennet every day. But on the Bellport station platform in the early daylight, seeing the naked frozen countryside, the silent, indrawn faces of the people, she had felt something almost like terror; and if she could have called the train back, she would have got on it and gone to the end of wherever it was the train was going.

What was she doing here, in a place she had fought to escape from? What would there be to do here—and who to talk to when, emptied out by a day's hard work and effort, you needed companionship and conversation? And if her work failed, where would she go, what do, when her money was gone?

Now, watching Hod sail his boat, his ears turned to the sound of the water and the drum of the engine, she felt a loneliness in herself go out to meet what must be a similar loneliness in him; and, not speaking, she felt comforted.

In Joe's boat, or in Willie's old one, it had taken Hod two hours and a half to go to Bellport. Today, even with the dragger throttled down because of the tow, he made the trip back to the island in an hour. He circled to the eastern shore of the harbor to drop Joe off at his mooring, and then went up the twisting channel to leave Ann at the town float.

"You hungry?" he asked her, as the boat slid alongside the float.

"I'm starved," she said. "Connie's haddock doesn't seem to stay by you."

"Let's go down to Mag Snow's."

"Where's that?"

"Mag's? Oh, I guess that's new since your time. Mag used to live here—Mag Averill, remember?"

"Yes—she was a nurse, away, wasn't she?"

"Mm-hm. Came home three years ago and bought the swamp from Pete, Lord knows why, unless she likes swamps. Anyway, she put all her savings into it and into a place for transients. The Come On Inn, it's called. Mag's quite a gal and her food's swell."

"Okay," Ann said. "I ought to go home first, but—sure, I'll go."

Hod jumped out on the float and made fast with bow and stern lines. The flat platform, supported in the water by empty oil drums, was beginning to sway a little with the offshore swells, but not enough to worry about and not enough to chafe a boat's planking if she didn't stay there too long. He thought he had noticed a cork fender in the cabin, and he dug it out, fixing it carefully over the side between the float and the boat's white paint.

He stood back a little, running his eye along the dragger's lean lines, and his face took on a look of pride. "I don't know but I've bought me a bargain," he said. "Lots of stuff down there, too, that feller left aboard. Going to be kind of fun pawing through it."

Ann smiled at him. "You like boats," she said.

"Ayeh, I do."

"I noticed you did, coming over. When you were seeing what she'd do in a heavy sea."

"Wasn't a very heavy one," he corrected her. "What I want to have her out in is a nor'wester coming in from The Rock, with the wind smokin in and the tide runnin out." He grinned. "Then I'd find out if I'd got me a lemon."

"But you know you haven't. Don't you?"

He nodded. "Sure haven't. She's all right."

As they climbed the cleated walk to the wharf, someone in rubber boots came clumping down the planking toward them. It was Pete Stilwell, dressed in the long raincoat he kept at the store for bad weather, and slouching along slack-shouldered, so that the skirts of it almost dragged on the ground.

"Oh-oh," Hod said. "He must have seen me from the store window." Anyway, he went on to himself, he's come down to find out whose boat that is. His heart sank a little; then he recalled that Pete would have his say, and it might as well be sooner as later. Only Hod wished that Pete had waited until Ann got out of the way.

Pete had his mouth open as he hove to in front of them, but Ann spoke first.

"Hullo, Pete," she said. "Remember me?"

His eyes, shadowed by the brim of his sou'wester, were vague. "Hud-do," he answered. "The Freeman girl, ain't it?" He flopped her hand up and down and withdrew his own, without cordiality. "Knew ya by the look of your ma. Quite a stranger, ain't you?"

"Yes. I haven't been home for a while."

Pete's gaze slid over and beyond hers to Hod. "Been to Bellport," he said, the words halfway between a statement and a question.

"Ayeh," said Hod.

"I thought that looked like a Bellport boat. I see her come in and I thought I'd better come down and tell the owner of her that she's too big to lay to the slip in a southerly. What did you do, have to hire someone to bring ya home?"

"No."

As first selectman and harbormaster, it was part of Pete's job to look after the town slip, but since he had seen the boat come in, he must know quite well that there had been no one on board of her but Hod and Ann. Hod felt his nerves coil with anger at the way in which, without asking outright, Pete had trapped him into telling what he was doing with a boat like that. His impulse was to pick up the pudgy man and drop him over the side of the gangway into the water. At the same time, seeing Pete's eyes on him, impersonal and blank, Hod felt the familiar, deadening sense of nervousness and apprehension.

Pete turned his head and regarded the boat with a leisurely stare. His eyes traveled over her from bow to stern. "You borrowed her, I take it," he said.

"No," Hod said again. He waited a second, steeling himself. "I bought her."

Now that he had actually committed himself, he felt an almost malicious pleasure at the way Pete's eyes, their vagueness gone, swiveled around and concentrated on him.

That rocked him back on his heels, Hod thought.

But Pete merely said, "That so?"

"Ayeh."

"Looks like a pretty good boat."

"She is a good boat." Hod felt the palms of his hands, thrust into his pants pockets, grow clammy. He hoped that Ann wouldn't notice his nervousness, and he made an effort, balling his hands into tight fists.

"What'd you give for her?" Pete asked with the ghost of a grin. "Soap coupons?"

"How'd you guess?"

" 'T wan't hard."

"Borrowed from an old man with a long green beard," Ann said suddenly. It was rude, she knew. She'd meant it to be. It was the rudest thing that, offhand, she could think of.

She had been standing between the two men, unable on the narrow railed runway to go either up or down, unable not to listen to what was said, and getting madder by the moment. Hod was trying hard, she could see, to fight back, using Pete's own methods—as the shy, somewhat indecisive boy she had known in school would never have dared to do. But he was still no match for this round, harmless-appearing man who looked like a whiskerless Santa Claus. She could see the pride and the self-respect going out of Hod; and it seemed to her, all at once, that she couldn't bear it.

"Wan't askin you," Pete said. His tone was neither polite nor impolite, merely impersonal. It ignored her as a meddling person of no consequence, and as he had doubtless guessed it would, it made her furious.

"Mind moving over and letting us by?" she asked shortly.

"Oh, sure, sure. The gangway is kinda narrer with me on it, ain't it?" Pete flattened himself against the railing, as far as his pursy stomach would allow. He went on, however, in his leisurely way to Hod. "You go to the bank for money, Hod, or did Willie fin'lly decide to sell the place?"

"Neither one." Hod started to follow Ann past Pete, but Pete's next comment stopped him in his tracks.

"The reason I seem nosey is that if you need money, you might better come to me."

"What good would that do?" In spite of himself, Hod's voice shook a little.

Ann went on up the walk to the top of the slip. She had a feeling that if Hod lost his temper now, let Pete get the better of him in front of her, he wouldn't be able to stand it—that she wouldn't see him again for a long time. "Hod," she called down to him, "let's skip the lunch. I ought to be hustling home anyway."

He looked up at her and she saw the misery in his face. She saw, too, Pete's faint sarcastic grin appear again briefly and vanish.

"Okay," Hod said. "See you later."

He watched the brown shoulders of her leather coat and the clean-cut back of her head go out of sight behind the fish-sheds, and felt miserable with disappointment. He hadn't realized how much he'd been counting on spending some more time with her. Still, in a way, he was glad she had gone.

"Don't learn em down to college not t' stick their nose in other people's business, do they?" Pete said. He hawked and spat over the side of the gangway into the water.

"They don't teach that anywhere," Hod said angrily. "That's something you learn yourself."

"Might," Pete agreed. He regarded Hod noncommittally, his eyes gone carefully vague again. "I'm still keepin your share a pa's money, you know. You might better come t' me, before you go messin around gettin in debt with the bank." Pete turned and went back up the walk, the flimsy planks buckling under his weight.

"I'll be damned!" Hod said, after him. So far as he could remember, this was the first time in his life that Pete had ever mentioned his father's legacy—except to make pointed remarks about his being too scatterbrained to handle the few thousand dollars it consisted of.

What's it about? he wondered, going slowly down to the boat. His nervousness hadn't come from anything Pete had said, but from the steeling of himself to meet what Pete was going to say; and in the end he hadn't said anything. Was he up to something, or had he suddenly decided to be decent? Ten to one, it wasn't the latter. Bewildered, Hod mulled the matter over in his mind all the way across the harbor to the mooring in Willie's cove.

It wasn't until he had made the boat fast and was closing the cabin-hatch against the night's weather, that he saw Ann's suitcases standing beside the companionway. She'd forgotten them. He realized, with a little jerk of exultation, that he'd have to take them to her, and soon, because she'd be needing them.

*

Ann walked between the narrow, dilapidated fish-sheds on the weathered wharf and along the hard dirt path to the main road. The spruces bordering the ditches were dripping with fog-drops and their tops were beginning to lash in the wind. Fog made a blurry outline of Pete's store, as she passed it, and of the white, clapboarded house and barn belonging to Sam Grant, her father's next-door neighbor. Under her feet, the road was sloppy with half-frozen mud and puddles.

I sure picked an attractive day to arrive home, she thought.

The fat man, with his cool, expert meddling in Hod's affairs, the neat way in which, with three words, he had turned her into a silly interfering female, had made her angry—but something else, too. It had been a long time since she had encountered indifferent disregard of herself as a thinking human being, so long that she had almost forgotten how it felt.

I'd better begin to remember it, though, she said to herself wryly. I don't expect pa's changed much.

If you had any sense of humor left, it might be funny to arrive home, and the moment you set foot on shore be treated as if you were the gawky girl who went away.

Well, what's the matter with me? I asked for it, didn't I? And it isn't as if that fat slug mattered a hang.

It hadn't much to do with Pete Stilwell, the reason she suddenly found herself fighting back tears, her sense of security with Hod gone completely.

She'd expected it—that was the way the men here were to their women-folk; you couldn't count on any change. She'd had it, and fought it, all through her childhood and youth. What it had done was to make her try hard, discipline herself, train her mind into a tool that would give her back some self-respect.

What it had done, too, Ann mused, walking fast along the tarred highway, was to make you wonder if there weren't some common ground on which human beings could meet without trying to wrench each other out of shape. If you took the trouble, couldn't you find out and understand the inner stresses and strains that made people need to interfere with other people, most often the ones they knew best and loved?

She'd thought, nearly seven years ago, when she'd left her father's house, furious and humiliated by her final battles with him, that, with parents, it was because they wanted you to grow up on their terms, not on yours; unwilling to see that what you had new to add might be just as much credit to them as if you made yourself into a carbon copy. She'd carried that idea around with her resentfully through the college years, which hadn't been easy— Paris Freeman hadn't helped, though Myra, her mother, had sneaked a little cash to her off and on through the mail. And then, when she'd started to learn to write, concentrating on the impact, the effect of human beings on one another—for that, in essence, was what you tried to do—she'd begun to understand a little better the insecurities, the frustrations that made a man like her father feel and act the way he did. She'd thought, long before she'd decided to come home, that she might be able to get along with him better now.

But I'm not so sure, she thought, angrily wiping away her tears.

She'd given the theory a pretty good test with Cary Bennet. Suppose you did go more than halfway to find out what made a man's wheels go round; suppose you were willing to change, in the ways he wanted you to, even though the change violated some inner integrity? It hadn't seemed hard after the first wrench to live Cary's life instead of her own; to come down out of the ivory tower of work and follow his light-hearted procession about the city.

Cary was a newspaper man, not much different from others she knew on the paper's staff, brittle and merry, mostly here today and gone tomorrow. When he wanted to, which seemed fairly often, he could turn out brilliant copy. He'd told her she was one of the few bright girls he'd ever seen who was beautiful, too. For a long time she hadn't fallen for that bewhiskered old line. Then he'd told her one night—and she remembered, suddenly, how his hair, rumpled and standing on end, had seemed endearing—that she had a rare gift of understanding.

And that, Ann said to herself, did the trick, damn him!

That had been last September. It was still hard to get over, particularly when you'd thought you might iron out the relationship between two people if only you tried hard enough. She'd come away partly to make the break complete, and partly to see if she couldn't do some honest writing.

Her published book she hated to think about; it had been mostly reporting anyway, possibly, she hoped, a good yarn. It had sold enough to give her a year without a desk job, if she were careful.

No, she thought, turning into the path that led to the side door of her father's house, Pete Stilwell didn't have a lot to do with the way she felt. His manner to her had only made her mad; his treatment of Hod had made her think again of the way one person could violate the being of another, particularly someone defenseless.

Maybe Hod wasn't defenseless, though. There was a lot bottled up there, if only he found it out, or if someone he liked took the trouble to tell him. With her hand out to open the door, she suddenly remembered that she had forgotten her suitcases aboard his boat.

Her mother was standing by the stove, doing something to a soup kettle with an iron spoon. Myra glanced up absently. Then her mouth fell open and she stood for an instant as if galvanized by an electric shock. The spoon fell to the floor; both Myra's hands went into the air as high as they could go and she screamed.

"Ann Mary Freeman! My Lord of heavens!"

She launched her tiny body across the room, her wisps of gray hair flying, and fetched up with a thump against her tall daughter.

"Where on earth did you come from and on a day like this!

Why didn't you let us know? I never was so glad to see anybody
in all my born days!"

Ann, hugging her, realized with affection and with eyes again
a little moist, that it was the same now with her mother as it always
had been—in any crisis involving excitement, whether of joy or
sorrow, her hair, every bit of it, fell down.

*

Willie heard the deep thrum of the boat's engine coming into
the cove. Through the fog, now sliced and tattered by driving rain,
he saw the unfamiliar outline slide up to the mooring and Hod go
out on the bow to make fast.

He had not expected Hod back much before night, thinking he'd
probably stay and help Josh work on the engine. But the weather
was making up into a bad storm and Hod had likely borrowed a
boat to come home in before it got too rough. Might be Joe's boat
had broken down, too; you sort of expected Joe's boat to break
down.

So Willie speculated, while he set a pot of fresh coffee on the
stove to brew and made sure the beans in the oven were hot and
browning.

Hod came into the warm kitchen on a gust of wind which
slammed the storm door behind him with a crash.

"Gosh!" said Willie. "Blows, you know it? Better git out of
them wet oil-clo'es and have somethin hot."

"It's a wicked one, all right," said Hod briefly. He shed his
streaming oilskins and sou'wester and hung them behind the stove
to steam dry. The wood fire felt good and the kitchen snug and
warm with Willie's comforting presence.

"Be some traps stove up tonight," Willie went on. "Good thing
we left most of ours in deep water. The's them four we set off High
Head, they're probly goners, but I should think the others'd be
all right."

"Willie," Hod said. He sat down heavily in the rocker behind the stove and began rolling down his rubber-boot tops. "I guess I've gone and done it. As usual."

"Why, I d'no's I'd put it that way." Willie was setting the table with his quiet, deft movements. "I ain't never found no reason to question your judgment. What's the matter—can't Josh fix the enjun?"

"The engine's shot to hell, and Josh says so's the boat. Look, Willie, I know you liked that old boat, you'd had her a long time."

Willie grinned. "Ayeh," he said. "Had her since I was twenty-three. No sense latherin up because a thing's wore out, Hod. Sure, I liked her. She was a good boat in her day, and I was used to her. But she wan't safe t' go lobsterin in. Set down and eat your supper and tell me how much this new one's goin t' cost, and then we'll figger out how we can pay for her."

It was like him, Hod thought, with a sudden flash of affection. Already, he knew, Willie would be wondering how on earth he'd learn to handle a new boat, and a big one at that, knowing it would take months before he'd really feel at home in her. And the money —that was another thing Willie would worry over.

Well, he would, too, Hod said to himself. And how!

But with Willie, unless you knew him pretty well, you'd never guess he was worried. Doubt and worry were things he kept to himself.

"We can go offshore in her all winter," Hod began. He was going on talking, for after the meeting with Pete, he needed to convince himself all over again, but looking up, he saw the expression on Willie's face. In Willie's kind, keen little eyes were humor and understanding, and Hod knew he didn't need to explain.

The beans were succulent and Willie's biscuits crisp. Hod ate three, thick with butter, and two plates of beans before he leaned back in his chair feeling better.

"Ann Freeman's back home," he announced, knowing Willie would want to hear news from the village and, also, feeling a need to talk about Ann. "Brought her over with me from Bellport."

"She is? Thought she had a writin job, away."

"Uh-huh. She's come home, she says, to write a book."

"I thought she wrote a book."

"That's right." Hod chuckled inwardly, knowing that to Willie the production of one book was an accomplishment to last a lifetime.

" 'T wan't a bad book. At least, I liked it. That girl was always a smart little tyke," Willie said. "I remember I hauled her out of the mudflats, once, when she was ten. How'd she turn out?"

"Swell," Hod said briefly.

"H'm." Willie glanced over at him and went on with his beans. "She pretty?"

"Pass in a crowd, I guess. I took her up to the slip," Hod said, changing the subject quickly. "That was how I happened to run into Pete."

"Oh, you see Pete, did you? More like he saw you, ain't that so?"

"He met me at the slip."

"I'll bet he did," Willie said under his breath. He had been wondering what had ailed Hod. Getting a new boat had been quite a step, but after all, there wasn't anything about it to knock a boy's pins out from under him. Willie chewed a moment in silence. "You with a new boat and a new girl ought t' give him and Agnes enough to fill their ditty-bags for quite some time," he said finally.

Hod blushed. Trust Willie. "Well, I don't know about the girl. But Pete was all ready with a mouthful about the boat."

"Mean, was he?"

"He's got me all balled up. He started out to be sarcastic, and then turned right around in his tracks. Willie, why would he bring up the money pa left me, right now? Said to drop by the store and we'd talk over using some of it to pay for the boat."

Willie glanced out of the window into the lashing rain. "Aggie brought us a pie," he said absently, as if to himself.

"Oh." A light dawned on Hod. He might have known. "They're trying to get around us about selling the island."

"Might be they figger they can ketch more flies with sugar than they can with vinegar. I wouldn't say," Willie went on thoughtfully, "that 't was a good time, right now, to owe Pete money, would you?"

"No, by God!"

"When it comes a time I can't tell what Pete's up to, I'll begin to worry." Willie sighed. "Might be he'd pay you that money, Hod, lettin on it was yours, and then later on make out you owed it to him. He don't figger I'd let you lose your boat. He's on to all them legal tricks, and we ain't. I'd stay away from him, I d'no b't."

"Well, I sure will. I'd just as soon monkey with a buzz saw."

"Ne'm mind," Willie said. "We can make twice the money, and if b' some chance it turns out we can't meet Josh's payments, why, hell, boy, the' ain't nobody dead, is the'?"

*

Joe Sangor was in the shed off his kitchen, replacing the torn heads in some lobster traps. He had a fine fire going. The thin sheet-iron stove was crammed with seasoned hardwood chunks and glowing a hearty red. Joe was comfortable; as he laced the white twine heads into the gray-brown traps, he sang—not a song of words, but a deep baritone grumble down in his throat, a song of well-being and serenity which required no concentration.

She was old, those trap, the barnacle had specked her white, and along her laths the small seaworm he had made the home. But with those new head, fine twine, all strong, she would last one, two month, maybe till spring. When the trap she was gone, he would make the new one. It was all the same to Joe.

The movers from the Bellport Furniture Emporium, headed by the store's deputy bill collector, advancing into the clearing, saw Joe's silhouette against the shed window, and one of them tapped on the glass.

Joe sang out, "Whoosa there?" He laid down his twine needle and came to the door. Opening it a crack, he thrust forth his fine beak of a nose. "Yas? Whoosa there?"

"You Joseph Sangor?" asked the deputy.

Joe instantly withdrew his nose and closed the door. Strangers looking for Joseph Sangor could only be those unpleasantly concerned with money. Joe had no bills that he could think of; yet there might be some that had gone out of his mind. He went back to his bench and picked up his needle, trying to recall. He was standing with his eyes closed, concentrating, when Mary came out into the shed.

"There's some men to see you, Joe."

"Whoosa?" Joe said, rolling his eyes at her.

"I d'no—unless you've been running up the bills behind my back. You haven't, have you, you bum?" she asked, looking at him with affection.

"N-nh," said Joe. "You talk-a them, Mary."

"The man of the house, they want. That's you."

"That's-a me," Joe agreed, puffing out his chest.

"Joe, you did make a payment on the piano, didn't you?"

Joe rared back at her and blew out his cheeks until they turned purplish-red. "The piano she's-a paid for!" he roared. "How manny times I tal you?"

Mary shrugged and shook her head. She did not seem overly frightened of him. "Well, go talk to em. They look like trouble to me."

"N-nh."

"Go on." She gave him a little push.

As he passed her, she spanked him once lightly on the stern, and Joe, with a delighted bellow, caught her around the waist and kissed her with a resounding smack.

"I don't see no collector of the bills, me," he said, his rich baritone sounding through the house. "Me, now, I make-a the love to my wife."

She looked very fine today, did Mary, in the blue wool dress from the Sears and Roebuck. The necklace of small polished yellow shells Joe himself had given her. It had been his mother's and he had brought it from the Islands. Mary had worn it on their wedding day and, ever since, the wearing of it had become a kind of unspoken code between them—whenever she put it on, she knew that night Joe would make love to her.

Mary said nothing, merely looked at him from beneath her long-lashed heavy lids and Joe followed meekly after her into the kitchen.

He liked to watch her moving away from him, her supple back, the dark contour of her head, the lovely relaxed motion when she walked. It was in his mind to tell her that she walked like a wave of the sea, but he would keep that for later, he decided, coming into the kitchen to face his unexpected guests.

The deputy, with his four men back of him, was standing squarely in the middle of Mary's red hooked rug. Maria, Joe's four-year-old, was standing bolt upright a few feet away from him, staring at him angrily with wide black unmoving eyes. Manny, the baby, was playing on the floor, and Mary went over and scooped him up and took Maria by the hand. "You come with Mamma," she said.

"Aw right, now," said the deputy to Joe. "Give. Where's that piano?"

Joe looked at him, dignified and quiet. "What you care?" he asked civilly. "She's-a my piano now. She don't belong to you."

"The hell you say! You've made two payments on it and not a cent for—" he looked at some papers in his hand—"four months. This here's a warrant to repossess. Where is it?"

"Hah?" Joe said, bewildered.

If a man talked slowly, he could understand the English words. Mary wished him to speak English—she who had been to the school in New Bedford—and she always made a point of speaking it with him. No matter how much he loved his own tongue, it must be kept for emergencies when she and he must speak together quickly, and, of course, for making the love. He must learn all the English words, she said, first as a courtesy to his neighbors, and second so that in practical matters he would understand everything that was said and thus would not allow himself to be swindled. And Joe had tried hard, but he had not the head for the many words; they would not stay inside it. Besides, this man talked too fast.

"They've come to take it, Joe," Mary said. "They can, you know, if you didn't make the payments."

"I pay fifty dollars and fifty dollars," Joe pointed out. "And the piano she's-a still not mine?"

"No, she ain't yours." The deputy's voice was heavy with sarcasm. "No use arguin, boys. It's probly in the other room. Go git it."

"No!" said Joe, shaking his head. With a fine show of courage he backed up against the sitting room door-jamb, doubling his fists.

He had not been a fool about the payment for the piano, believing, as the salesman had told him, that you paid cash only the matter of fifty dollars and the piano was yours. It had seemed, later, that there was no end to that salesman and his desire for fifty dollars; and if, in the end, an honest man who considered himself swindled and who needed his money elsewhere, ceased to pay, still there was little reason for angry people to come and take away the piano without permission from his house.

"It ain't no use t' make trouble," the deputy said. He hadn't expected a fight and didn't want one. "If you don't let us take it, we'll only have to git the sheriff down and put you in jail."

"Joe," Mary said warningly, in Portuguese, "let them have the piano and you come over here beside me."

Joe undoubled his fists and went at once. She understood these things. When she spoke to him in that tone, he knew at once that the situation was dangerous and out of his hands. Not that he couldn't have handled any situation, he, Joe Sangor, if he had only been able to speak the English. He stood by her and she put her hand on his arm, while the men filed into the sitting room and started taking the legs off the piano.

At once they began to talk in loud voices, and the deputy came back into the kitchen. "What in hell's happened to it?" he demanded. "It ain't even saleable now, with all them hacks taken out of it. I spose you know you'll be held legally responsible."

"We will pay," Mary said levelly. "How much will be due?"

"How much?" he howled. "Two hundred dollars, the rest of the payments, that's what you'll have to pay."

"Then if we are to pay the full price," Mary said, "why aren't you leaving us the piano?"

"Because you've defaulted, that's why!" He started back to the sitting room, then turned on her again. "I don't know what you damn guineas think, comin here from away, and buyin stuff without payin for it. For God's sake, don't livin around with white people learn you nothin?"

"You take your piano," Mary said, "and you get out of my house." She took a step toward him, and he backed hastily away.

"Come at me like a snake," he said, telling the story later. "Yessir, flattened her head back, just like a damn snake."

It may have been that Mary gave some such impression.

Joe stepped protectingly in front of her and began to make a speech. He was sorry, he said, that he had to speak in his native tongue, but he had not the English. The scorpions were eating his manhood that his wife must speak for him in the matter of these unpleasant things. These men had come unbidden into his house. If the piano belonged to them, they might have had cause to point out with loud voices the places where the small boy, Leon, had chopped with his kindling hatchet. But it was his, Joe Sangor's, piano, bought by him in good faith for his wife. At least, he had thought so at the time.

The deputy listened to a few sentences and then said, "Oh, for chrissake!" He went into the sitting room to help with the dismantling, turning his back on Joe, who followed him, still speaking eloquently in Portuguese.

If the real price of the piano were three hundred dollars, he said, and the fifty only a single payment, why had not the salesman made this clear to him at the time? That was the only thing about the matter that had been dishonest, and, Joe pointed out, it was not he, Joseph Sangor, who had done this. If he had been a fool, it was because sometimes he did not understand the words and the customs of this country where he had so long tried to make his home.

It was a fine piano, Joe went on to say, and he remembered with pleasure the times he and the kids had sung loud and long while Mary played it on the summer evenings. But now he did not wish to have it, and he would ask them please to hurry up and take it away, and to go themselves, for neither his wife nor he wished to have them longer in the house.

While the flow of meaningless jabber went on, the deputy and his moving men grinned and jerked their heads at each other. But once outside the house and faced with the job of carrying the piano up the rough, narrow wood-path to the top of the Spoonhandle, where they had had to leave their truck, they were fighting mad. They had not thought of taking it off in a boat, lowering it over the cliffs with a block and tackle, the way Joe had landed it.

"Kuh-riced!" one said throatily. "What can you do?" And the deputy went back and said through the open kitchen door, "You'll be damn lucky if we don't have the law on you!"

Joe closed the door and at once his fine eloquence deserted him. Mary was sitting in the rocker. The baby had gone back to his play, but Maria was by the window watching the men take away the piano, her eyes still motionless, wide-open and dark with wonder.

Joe went over and knelt down beside Mary. He put his bristly face into her soft neck.

"Never mind, Joe," she said mechanically. She looked out over his head, her own eyes icy with a cold, quiet rage.

They had come too far afield, she and Joe, she was thinking, wanting their own place and having too little money to buy it with. Land had been high near New Bedford, but someone had told Joe it was cheaper to the north.

It's lonesome here, Mary said, but not to Joe. The words formed themselves silently in her mind. I'm homesick for my own people. We haven't done well here. And, poor Joe, he'll never learn anything about money.

"I am the greatest fool in the world," Joe mourned, his voice muffled against her, and presently she cupped her hands around the back of his head, rocking him gently back and forth with the motion of the chair.

"No, Joe," she said, and the sound of his native tongue was like a low music in his ears. "You are not a fool, but a brave man who stood up like a lion to five men at once, courageous to protect his home and his wife. I *shook* when I saw you standing there. I am proud of you and—" she pulled his head away from her bosom and flashed to her feet—"and today I have on my yellow beads!"

*

Seated at his desk in his Baltimore office, Nelson Witherspoon read Pete Stilwell's letter for the second time. A slight frown creased the smoothness of his large forehead. Pete's eccentric spelling had at first made him chuckle; now that the morning's business routine was out of the way and he had time to consider the letter again, he did not smile.

At sixty, Mr. Witherspoon looked younger than his years, an illusion carried out by his uncreased cheeks and his thick, reddish blond hair only beginning to turn gray. A tall man, he carried his shoulders erect and unceasingly exercised his stomach muscles. He had deep-set convictions about wholesome living: A man of great responsibilities had no right ever to take chances with health; when so much and so many depended upon him, he would be unworthy of his trust if he did not make of a few wise, simple daily rules almost a sacred duty.

Thus Mr. Witherspoon neither drank nor smoked, and he saw to it that his wife maintained for him a healthy diet, consisting of plain meats and vegetables, with no desserts except a little fruit. He insisted, of course, upon the best cuts of meat and the best fruits and vegetables in season. Many were the noble standing rib roasts of beef and thick tender steaks which had gone to make up his fine solid flesh. They were, he claimed, along with plenty of exercise and fresh air and sleep, the reason for his prolonged and vigorous health. He was in the pink of condition; in fact, his office subordinates sometimes referred to him behind his back as "Old Pinky."

The Witherspoons had always been plain people, enjoying plain living, and he was no exception. His great-great-grandfather had been one of the first settlers of the Chesapeake Valley. An astute man, this ancestor and founder of a fortune had bought in at a very reasonable price some ample sections of wild land which was later to become a prosperous city. His money, transmitted through the careful hands of sons and grandsons, had become a power in the land in the time of Nelson's father. Now, as chief inheritor and the holder of the chalice, Nelson Witherspoon was a wealthy man.

For his own career, he had as a young man not followed the traditional family professions in real estate and banking. He had taken over a neglected and nearly moribund fiber and rope company belonging to his father, and had built it up into an important business, with, of late years, foreign subsidiaries. Now, Chesapeake Hemp and Manila was almost a household word in any region where rope was used and known. It had become so, Nelson Witherspoon felt, through his energies and his alone—through his investment and his vision. So perfectly, now, did his great organization function, that he could go away for months on end, if he wished, not even leaving word where he would be. In his absence, capable hands would mesh the gears, keep the massive cog-wheels turning.

Now that he was no longer bound to his machinery—his "beehive" years over—he had made plans for other, different, years to come. Quiet and contemplation had never been his, nor an opportunity to enrich himself from the fundamental simplicity of his fellow man. In the give-and-take of modern industry, the mind was merely a tool—a fine tool, of course, but stripped and streamlined toward a single purpose; and the relationships with men were functional, never partaking of any fundamental simplicity. Mr. Witherspoon had had in mind now for some time a niche for himself in some place where men were simple.

But looking at the cheap tablet sheet of Pete Stilwell's letter, he blew out his breath, puffing his lips impatiently. It's amazing, he said to himself, how you see it creeping in, even in the most remote spots.

After a moment, he pressed the button which summoned Gerald Bundy, his secretary.

"Take a look at this, Gerald," he said, "and tell me what you think of it."

The young man read the letter through with a noncommittal expression, darting a side glance at his chief to see how he was expected to react. His eye faltered a little over the unaccustomed crudeness of the sentences and the handwriting, and when he finished he went back and read the letter over to make sure he hadn't missed anything. Nelson Witherspoon, when he asked for an opinion, expected a comprehensive one.

"Seems straightforward enough," Bundy began tentatively. "Fellow's something of a rough diamond."

"Rough diamond be damned!" snapped Witherspoon. "He's one of the shrewdest business men in his part of the country. I've had him investigated and he's well off—that is, compared to his neighbors. Nobody's rich down there, you know. He's first selectman of his town and a graduate of a business college."

"Then what gives?" Bundy glanced at the letter, mystified.

"He's fixing to hold me up." Witherspoon reached for the letter and laid it on the desk in front of him, smoothing out its creases. "He thinks I'll take this letter as hearty friendliness from a not-too-bright good man, who has my best interests at heart."

"Certainly seems that way," agreed Bundy. "Do you want the property?"

"Of course I want it. I merely thought I could get it for about what it's worth."

"Looks to me as if you'd have to pay through the nose."

"I suppose I will—if I buy, and I certainly intend to. You know, Gerald," he went on ruminatively, "when I first bought my place in Bellport, those people down there had hearts of gold. Simple and kindly—you never saw such hospitality as there was in those fishermen's cottages." His expression tightened. "It's a shame the way the Bellport country people have been ruined."

"Is that so, sir?"

"Now if you hire one of them, he expects to be paid three times what the job's worth, and if you buy anything, the over-charge is anything the traffic will bear."

Witherspoon's voice had risen richly as he talked, and Bundy waited for a pause into which he could insert a few words of agreement. He had heard this grievance before, though generally with regard to labor unions. Mr. Witherspoon believed that the workingman should be fine and upstanding and the backbone of the country, but, also, should know his limitations as to material possessions.

"I bought a hundred acres of shore property in Bellport in 1915," said Mr. Witherspoon, "for fifty dollars an acre. Land had been in one family for generations. But the old fisherman I bought it of was perfectly satisfied—thought he had a fortune. He did, too. He was the salt of the earth." He stopped, tapping the desk with his fingers.

Bundy judged that now was a good moment. "My wife and I notice the same thing in Connecticut," he said. "The rural sections all over the country seem to be changing a good deal. What do you think causes it, sir?"

Witherspoon whacked his hand flatly against the desk-top. "Automobiles and the radio!" he exploded. "And every other damned kind of gadget these people think they have to have. Before the depression, and even during it, every yokel in the country was abused if he didn't have at least one automobile and one radio. Take these fishermen—half of them mortgaged their houses to get the cash for a car. If the common people of this country had had the brains to save their money for a rainy day, instead of blowing it on luxuries they didn't need, there never would have been any depression!"

"The automobile and radio people would hardly go along with

you there, sir," said Bundy, and bit his tongue almost before the words were out of his mouth. Oh, hell! he thought.

Witherspoon had stopped in full course and was staring at him. "You seem to be a little seedy this morning," he observed. "I wish you young fellows would find a way to keep your hangovers out of the office. You know, Gerald, hangovers are generally the only result, when a man wastes his spare time on nondescript acquaintances. That'll be all. Send in Miss Simpson, will you?"

"I'm afraid she's out to lunch," Gerald said.

Witherspoon gave a start of annoyance and glanced at his watch. It was time, he saw, for his own lunch to arrive. Doyle, his chauffeur, was a little late. "Well," he said, "if she manages her personal affairs so as to get back before two-thirty, send her in then. If not, I'll have Miss Foster."

"Certainly, sir."

Doyle arrived, bringing the discreet brown wicker basket, neatly packed with salad, light sandwiches and milk in Witherspoon's own kitchen. Mr. Witherspoon did not like restaurants. The food in them, even in the best ones, wasn't fit to put in a man's stomach.

"You're late, Doyle," he commented, as the big Irishman set the basket on the desk and turned to go.

"Yes, sor." Doyle grinned. "Sally waited for the Persian melon to put in the basket. She was fit to tie, sor."

Witherspoon himself smiled, thinking almost with tenderness of the temper of Sally, his cook, when faced with a delay in the production of his dinner. There was nothing wrong with Sally and Doyle, he thought, starting to take the cover off his lunch. They had served his family for years with a touching and unquestioning loyalty.

"You tell Sally that was very thoughtful," he said, "and that I enjoyed the melon tremendously."

"Thank you, sor. That I will," said Doyle. He closed the door behind himself quietly.

It was these young people, not the older ones, Witherspoon thought. Gerald was a case in point. He must remind himself, soon, to have a long talk with Gerald. From reports, the boy was running with a peculiar crowd—not reds, exactly, but it might be a little off-color. Some friends of his wife had mentioned it. It would be too bad for Gerald to get started on the wrong foot, when, Witherspoon said to himself, I've been like a father to him.

He was accustomed to his own opinions, was Nelson Witherspoon, and few people in his life ever crossed him. He considered that there were few people who had the right to cross him. Democracy, after all, was a chance for the best to rise to the top; and when the best had risen, was that not sufficient proof that the country contained none better? He felt this with a good man's pride in honest achievement, about himself, his family and their equals in money and position.

The feeling was so automatic that it seldom emerged on the surface of his mind. It was like a protective coloring, inherited from many generations and so ingrained that to question it would never even have occurred to him. He and his were the best. The cream, as in nature, had come to the top of the bottle.

Yet one thing, these later years, had troubled him. He wished with all his heart to be appreciated by all classes of men, by those who had not made the most of their opportunities. The creed was simple. Any American child could find it in his schoolbooks. You worked, you achieved; and the rest of the world, the lesser world, looked up to you, as your just reward. True, he had not earned all his fortune by the work of his hands; but he had done something greater and more constructive.

He had seen how to convert available resources into a thing of tremendous and world-wide benefit. Because of him cargoes moved, plantations hummed; opportunities were made for thousands of capacities and skills. Money poured in at the top fanned outward and downward, as through an inverted funnel, leaving creation in its wake—the jobs, the finished products, the prosperous towns— until, coming to a final resting place in the hands of the people, it bought shoes, clothes, food for children. This was what he had done, like the sacred keeping of some tremendous faith.

And yet, it seemed to him that respect for great works was dying out of the world. Instead of rewards for achievement, you received dislike and suspicion. He sometimes caught a look that was not reverence in the eyes of his office and factory workmen—as he had in Bundy's that morning. It was nothing you could put your finger on, or he could have spoken and stopped it. It was like the ghost of a smell in the air that alerts the nostrils just before it becomes bad—something that did not assail, but questioned, the faith in him of his fellow man. The man in the street was changing, and the idea shook Nelson Witherspoon, threatening some security that he had thought unshakable.

He did not wish for great power—leave that to the politicians and the Democrats. What he wanted now, more than anything, was to be the center of some small world, where simple, kindly people looked up to him—not because of money or favors they could expect, but sincerely. Bellport was too full of his own kind, of too many who wished to be looked up to, some of them able to command more respect than he. The little place on the island was to be a kind of manor house, with himself in it, through the mellow summers of his declining years, dispensing jobs and advice—not money, at least not often, for loan oft loses both itself and friend and borrowing dulls the edge of husbandry.

When he had looked at Willie Stilwell's small white buildings between the green clipped grass and the brooding spruces, with the sound of water hushing them all day, he had felt a strange sense of quietude, almost of homecoming, as if here was something he had known once and had not thought to know again. He had set his heart on having Little Spoon Island, and he meant to have it, come hell or high water. When the stenographer came, he dictated two letters, one to Pete and one to Willie Stilwell, offering them eight thousand dollars.

In his letter to Pete, he said:

I did not realize that the property was so tied up in your family. This is, of course, unfortunate for me. But I surely do not wish anyone to be aggrieved or slighted when the sale takes place. I expect to spend the Christmas holidays in your vicinity, and perhaps we could arrange to conclude the deal at that time. Incidentally, since most of the Bellport hotels will be closed, perhaps your sister, Mrs. Flynn, would put me up for a couple of days.

Eight thousand, he reflected, was too much, but he was tired of haggling. And two thousand dollars apiece would give the Stilwells something to get their teeth into.

*

Agnes Flynn's house, on the western hook of Big Spoon Island facing the harbor, had been built for her by her father the year she married Albert Flynn. Amos Stilwell had believed in old-fashioned big houses with plenty of room for children. He foresaw that a daughter of his would have many children, and Agnes, if a little doubtfully, had agreed with him. It was not her fault that she had failed to fulfill Papa's hopes, to which her big house was the only remaining monument.

Albert had been "from away"—a willowy stranger, who, word had it at first, was the son and heir of a shoe manufacturer in Lawrence, Massachusetts. The origin of the rumor was never traced down, and when, later, it came out that he was not a son and heir, but merely a salesman of the shoe firm, no one knew whether or not Agnes had believed it when she married him. Albert had been a good and a convincing talker; he let it be known from the beginning that he had come to spend an idle summer by the sea to write and to recuperate from a wound received in France, where he had been a lieutenant in the A.E.F. Before the summer was out, not only Agnes, but everybody in town had heard and re-heard Albert's stories of his war exploits. They made good listening, too, for he told them well.

After a time, the byword around town about anyone who blew his own horn without, it might be, sticking quite to the letter of the truth, got to be that "so-and-so could tell a story good as Albert

Flynn." Yet when Albert died, quietly, two months before Stilwell, his and Agnes's only child, was born, it turned out that what had killed him actually was an old shrapnel wound and that he had possessed an Army pension. So the village gave up and said you'd just have to draw your own conclusions about Albert Flynn.

Whatever Agnes may have thought of him while she was married to him, she remembered him now as the beautiful boy who had wooed and won her with poems of his own making; it was the pride and joy of her life that Stilwell, to her way of thinking, looked and was exactly like his father.

Agnes's house had twelve rooms, not counting the woodshed chamber. In it, since Stil's departure for the University, she had lived alone.

It stood at the top of a gently sloping meadow that ended in sand beach and a pebbled shore and its view looked out across the harbor to the open sea. In summer the meadow was thick with hay, starred with daisies and devil's paintbrush. After the hay was cut, a second crop always came up of a peculiarly silky and delicate green grass. Agnes's spiraea hedge divided this grass from her lawn, but seen from the harbor the hedge blended back against the house, so that in August the whole meadow seemed to be lawn. The two immaculate gables, painted white with green blinds at the windows, had austerity and beauty against the wide leisurely space in front and the dark spruces of the wood lot behind. They could be seen for miles at sea and fishermen for years had used them as marks for fishing grounds.

You sailed southeast, said the fishermen, until the north gable of Aggie Flynn's house showed over the tip of Spoonhandle and Hardwood Island Light came in line with Catlett's Head, and you were on the Enoch Shoal, a famous underwater ridge where every fall cod and haddock in abundance were taken.

The twelve rooms, though Agnes would not have put it in so many words, had been her life-work. For years she had added carefully to her possessions—a mahogany bedroom set for the upstairs front bedroom, sets of fluffy bath towels with her monogram in colors, inlaid linoleum for the pantry and kitchen. Her special pride and joy was that, except for the kitchen, Papa had gone to the expense of hardwood floors throughout the house. These, each year, she had Hallet Romer, who did her heavy work around the house and farm, revarnish and re-wax, so that now they shone unmarred, with a clear and deadly yellow under her many rugs of various sizes and colors.

In her five upstairs and three downstairs bedrooms, the windows and beds were hidden under clouds of starched and spotless ruffles. Each room had its own material of matched and harmonizing colors —dimity, cretonne, lace, gingham, or chintz. She was clever with her needle and crochet-hook—in school, the sewing class was what she had done best in—and the ruffles were all put in by hand with thousands of tiny tucks.

Her masterpiece, however, was her upstairs front bedroom, done in lavender and white chiffon. The mahogany bedroom set was stained a shiny, purplish black, and for its twin beds she had crocheted spreads in lavender and white squares. Upon these spreads she had put thin chiffon overspreads, with lavender ruffles to the floor. Window curtains, bureau and commode scarves, even two virginal little square pillows, one in the exact center of each bed, were all frilled with lavender and white chiffon.

The room was a wonder to the wives of the village who came to knit and sew, when it was Agnes's turn to entertain the Ladies' Aid. In a way, the whole house set a town standard for interior decoration, so that several upstairs front bedrooms in the community were more frilled than they need have been. But no one could come up to Agnes, for none of the ladies had her money and most of their houses were furnished, as well, with large families of children. The wonder, sometimes, was mixed with lip-biting, as on the Aid afternoon when Lucy Osgood, whose four boys in their time had "gone through" three sets of furniture, remarked right before Agnes that she'd like to know what it would do to a room like that if anybody's kids ever slept in it. Agnes had observed icily into the silence that she thanked heaven she'd never had a moment's trouble with Stilwell so far as rowdy behavior was concerned.

It was true that Agnes had little company, and nobody ever did sleep in the room. Hallet Romer told the story—which some believed—of how once when he had been waxing the floor and Agnes had been away visiting, he had taken off all his clothes and lain down on one of the twin beds, just to see how 'twould be. It was like laying down in the middle of a marshmallow, he declared, and he bet if he hadn't been so scared and could've gone to sleep there, he'd have had some good dreams. But he had kept thinking what if *she* came home unexpectedly, and after a few minutes he had climbed down, and put his clothes back on again. But he wasn't, he said, a mite of good the whole rest of the day.

The story had gone the rounds, not, however, reaching Agnes's ears.

The day after the southerly blew itself out was not Agnes's Aid day, but she had telephoned to the Aiders around town and had asked them down. As president, she felt it was her duty to appoint a committee to visit Mag Snow and protest her opening a saloon.

Left alone, it would not have occurred to more than one or two of the Aiders that there was anything sinful about selling a little beer. Beer, after all, wasn't like gin and whisky, and the years of prohibition, when there had been a good deal in the Bellport paper about how silly it was to pass laws against people doing what they wanted to, weren't too long forgotten. But November was a dull time on the island—not much going on—and the Aiders, knowing Agnes, scented a scrap. They turned out in a body.

Seated in Agnes's company parlor, whose wide windows, nearly covered with brocade drapes and ruffled scrim, opened out on the magnificent spread of the harbor, they sewed and listened while she addressed the meeting. The wind of the storm had gone down, but the breakers still pounded on the beach at the foot of the meadow, and Agnes had to raise her voice now and again to be heard above their tumult.

"It's of special importance to those among you whose boys are growing up or are young men," she finished. "We never have had a saloon in this town, and I don't propose to stand by with my hands folded while somebody irresponsible brings one here. I'm throwing the meeting open to discussion, and I'd like to hear what you ladies think."

She sat down, feeling she had made an especially effective talk. She did not realize that by the simple phrase "among you," she had put most of her listeners' backs up. If she had said "among us" and thus included her own son, Stilwell, with those boys who might have moments of weakness, no one would have given the matter a second thought. At her subtle distinction, several mothers made up their minds that Aggie wasn't going to get her way this time—not without working for it.

She wouldn't admit that young hellion ever done a thing out of line in his life, Lucy Osgood sniffed to herself.

Lucy's youngest boy, Artie, had been in bad trouble several times, but never, she thanked heaven, with liquor. At least, not that she knew about. But my goodness, she thought, I *admit* it! She was about to mention her opinion when Henny Pray, Bill Pray's wife who had sons of sixteen and seventeen, spoke up.

"I don't believe the's a thing we can do," she said. "Mag's got a permit from the gov-munt. If she wants to sell liquor, she'll sell liquor."

"Nonsense," said Agnes briskly. "There're any amount of things we can do."

"I should say so," chimed in Sara Romer. Since her husband Hallet got most of his living from the work he did around Agnes's place, it was to be expected that Sara would agree.

Tiddy Driver, too, whose husband ran the gasoline scow and bought lobsters on a concession obtained from Pete, showed quickly where she stood. "We could call a special town meetin. If the town don't want liquor, all it's got to do is vote dry."

"I ain't so sure we got any right to," said Myra Freeman. She bit off a thread and laid the garment she was making across her knee while she made another knot. "Mag's got a livin to earn and her business ain't very brisk. She's got to have somethin to bring in the public."

"From all I hear, Mag's got plenty to bring in the public without botherin with beer," Sara said significantly.

There was a moment's silence while the ladies considered the hearsay reputation of Mag Snow. Nobody knew it for sure, but there had been some speculation, with all those salesmen and transients who stopped at the Come On Inn in the summertime.

"When a rig like that starts running in any town, it usually isn't long before it turns into something worse," said Agnes. She was surprised that there should have been any dissenting opinion. "I don't understand why we don't all see that. What you've got to consider is the morals of the young men of the town."

There it was again, that infuriating "you."

"Well, I don't know's the growin boys of this town are as bad as all that," said Henny. "I'm sure I'm not that worried about mine."

"Nor I about mine," put in Lucy Osgood. "The day I can't keep *my* boys out of a saloon, just because there happens to be one in town, I guess I'll go out of business."

Two bright red spots glowed in Agnes's cheeks. There was little doubt as to what the ladies meant. The way they'd slanted it, she was trying to close down Mag Snow because she wasn't quite sure she trusted Stilwell.

Why! Agnes thought. I never heard of anything so hateful! She might have expected some such opposition from Lucy, on principle. Her husband, Myron Osgood, ran a grocery store on the other side of the harbor from Pete. Of course, it was small, and it didn't begin to get the trade Pete's did, but still the two stores were in competition. She did wish Lucy wouldn't let jealousy blind her better judgment.

"All I've got to say is any mother can't be too careful," Agnes said. "If temptation is in the way, there'll always be *some*"—she glanced at Lucy—"who'll try it out just to see how it is."

"My Sam tried it out," said Myra Freeman comfortably. "He and a couple of Bellport boys got hold of some kind of stuff over

there, I'm sure I don't know what, but somethin a little stronger
than beer, I guess. My land, Sam come home sick's a dog, in bed
and throwin up for two days."

Agnes looked at her in horror. "I think Stilwell would die rather
than let a drop of the dreadful stuff pass his lips," she said in meas-
ured tones.

Myra chuckled. "Well, you know, that's just exactly the way
Sam feels now," she said.

Lucy Osgood had not missed the side-glance nor the significant
stress Agnes had put on the word "some." "Sam never got it at
Mag Snow's, did he?" she said triumphantly. "The point is, if boys
are goin to try on a rig, they'll try it on. The farther away from
home they are, the better they like it." I guess that'll hold her, she
thought, seeing Agnes's underlip caught briefly between her teeth.
"You don't plan to dry up Bellport, do you, Agnes? Or do you?"

"I'm concerned with the wellbeing of my own town," snapped
Agnes. "I must say I'm astonished that others aren't."

"Well, I certainly am," said Tiddy. "I move we put it to a vote
right now and vote liquor out of this town forever."

"I don't think we're *quite* ready to vote, are we?" Agnes glared
at Tiddy and Tiddy subsided, her lips opening and closing with
a slight gobbling motion. "What I mean is, there are some here
who haven't given an opinion. What do you think, Mary? From
all I hear, you've got a problem on your hands with that State boy.
How are you going to feel if there's a place handy where he can
get liquor?"

Mary Mackay had been sitting in the background listening, as
she always did when other people were willing to talk. She had not
had it in mind to take a strong stand either way, but she didn't
know that she particularly cared for Agnes's bland assumption that
Donny would drink if he knew where he could get beer.

"Why," she said, flushing a little, "I don't know's I've got any
special problem. Donny's lively, the way any boy is, but I don't
think he'd drink. I've known Mag Snow since she was a little girl.

From all I can say first-hand, she runs a clean respectable place and I don't believe she'd sell beer to minors."

"But after all," said Agnes, "we don't really *know* what kind of a life Mag Snow's led in all the years she was away from here, do we?" She glanced around the room. "My *dear* friends, I do hope you're all looking at this matter seriously enough. This is a beautiful little village and it's always been kept respectable and clean. I think it's up to us womenfolks to be on our guard. You know about what you can expect from the men. When the opening wedge of liquor gets into a town—"

"For goodness' sake, Agnes," interrupted Lucy. "First you say the town's kids ain't moral and now you're implyin the menfolks ain't. As for liquor, Bellport's had saloons wide open for years, even when it wasn't legal. It certainly hasn't gone to the dogs."

"I certainly said nothing of the kind," said Agnes icily. "And I was under the impression that I had the floor."

"You can have it back." Lucy waved her hand airily. "I've said my say."

The ladies, more or less covertly, glanced at each other. They were beginning to enjoy themselves in a totally unexpected way. Ordinarily, it wouldn't have occurred to them to vote against one of Agnes's projects. She had been the acknowledged leader of the Aid for too long—hardly one of them could remember when she hadn't been president. She had got their backs up several times in the past, but never in such a way that they could be certain they all sided against her—except for Tiddy and Sara, of course, who didn't dare to express a different opinion.

When a question came to actual vote, there had always been three or four faint-hearts who didn't quite have the nerve to buck Agnes. But the morals of children were a sensitive point. The ladies were quick to sense their unanimity and the wholesome satisfaction that comes from being part of a solid front. If Agnes got mad at one individual, that was one thing—she could certainly make life miserable for her—but what good would it do her to get mad at the whole Aid?

"I move we stop havin it over and vote," said Nell Pray. Nell, John Pray's wife, was younger than most of the others. Her two children were small, and she wasn't particularly concerned about their drinking habits, except to keep plenty of fresh milk available. Besides, she considered the whole discussion a bore and a tempest in a teapot. She and John liked an occasional can of beer—in fact, John had already brought some home from Mag Snow's on one or two occasions, and they'd both enjoyed it. "I move that we let Mag Snow alone to earn her livin."

"I second the motion," said Lucy Osgood.

"Very well," said Agnes sulkily. "I object to having such a deadly serious matter referred to in that particularly irresponsible way, but I've no choice than to put the vote. Those in favor raise their right hands."

There was a prompt showing of a large majority of hands. In fact, the "Nays" were represented only by Tiddy and Sara and Agnes herself.

"The motion is carried." Agnes got up. "I'm sure I hope you all realize what you've done. I never thought I'd live to see the Spoon Island Ladies' Aid vote in favor of liquor. I see I'll just have to go alone to reason with Mag Snow."

She stalked out into the kitchen to fetch the refreshments, customary at the end of an Aid meeting.

The ladies looked at each other. Ordinarily, some of them would have gone out and offered to help Agnes, but nobody, today, wished to be the first to start. They sat in their seats, and the fruits of the solid front tasted heady and sweet.

In the kitchen, Agnes stood for several moments motionless and stiff. On the table sat the three caramel layer cakes she had made that morning for refreshments. They looked, and were, delicious. The recipe was a secret one, known only to Agnes's grandmother, her mother and herself, and she was famous for her caramel cake. After a moment, she picked up the cakes, one by one, and thrust them out of sight into the cellarway.

Two days ago, she had experimented with a recipe from one of

the women's magazines for making blueberry muffins out of pre-
served blueberries and ginger. It had sounded good, but the muffins
had not come out very well. She had mixed and baked three batches
before she had given up. She had meant to put them into the gar-
bage for Hallet to feed to the hens, but they had been out of sight
on the cellarway shelf and she had forgotten to do it. They were
there now, cold and soggy with two days' damp from the cellarway.

Her lips tight together, Agnes piled plates high with the muffins,
set coffee cups and the coffee she had had percolating on trays, and
carried the whole into the parlor.

The Aid ate the muffins with gusto and a concealed hilarity. Such
jokes as were told were laughed at more heartily than they need
have been, and the conversation was gay and spirited. At the usual
time, they said good-by with usual cordiality and went their various
ways home. But it would be many the long day before the village
forgot the time that Aggie Stilwell got so mad at the Aid that she
fed them on soggy blueberry muffins.

*

Mag Snow put down her fountain pen and gazed thoughtfully
at the page of her account book where she had balanced up the
month's business. Since the summer trade had stopped, she had
steadily gone behind; but this month it looked as if she had come
out on top by nineteen dollars and eighty-two cents.

She had had the Come On Inn for going on three years, and
each year she had barely managed, by hook or by crook, to break
even. Sometimes she wondered if she hadn't made the mistake of
her life to put all her savings into this land and buildings. Three
years ago, when she had bought the land from Pete Stilwell and
had had the old ice-house and sheds remodeled into the Inn, it had
seemed like the fulfillment of a dream. In actuality, it had been.
Mag had originally been an Island girl, but twenty of her forty-
three years she had spent in Portland as a practical nurse, living
frugally and saving all the money she could toward some day
having a transients' place of her own.

In the course of those years, Mag had been married three times, but her marriages never seemed to take. Two of her husbands had died; the third, Philander Snow, had been a drunk and she had divorced him. And good riddance, she told herself. Being married always did make her feel twitchy.

She had been quite aware when she bought the old Stilwell swamp that the land was worthless, and that Pete had soaked her too much for it. But Mag remembered the swamp of old. It was a secret and a private place where nobody went. All her life she had thought of it, off and on, most especially when she had a difficult patient, some sick and unlovely person, whose querulous demands never left her a minute's peace.

There in the back of her mind would be lying, quiet and cool, a picture of the old Stilwell swamp, its ferns and its moss and crooked tree roots, its black pools edged with green, the alders thick as a man's leg growing between the aisles of the spruces. She remembered the Salt Pond Water, emptying and filling with the tide twice a day; and the lookout from the footbridge and the soft sound of the ebb and flood under it. Some days, she told herself, thinkin about such things was about all that kept her a-goin.

Well, she owned it now and Pete Stilwell had her bedpan money. Bedpan money was what she, for years, had called her savings, put away dollar by dollar as she finished case after case. She couldn't recall how many sick people she'd taken care of. That part of her life was over now—except now she had Uncle Tilberry Seavey. He took quite a lot of care, but she thanked her stars every time she thought of him that she hadn't let the selectmen put him on the town. He was the pluckiest old man she had ever known, and in her life she had known a lot of ailing old people.

She only hoped she'd be able to support him for as long as he needed it. For the past months, sometimes she'd wondered, seeing how poor business was, and how, as the days went by, the bills went up and she got further and further behind. It wasn't as if she had a backlog to pull and haul on. Sometimes she got panicky, thinking that if only she hadn't bought the swamp, she'd have had enough with what she could earn at nursing, to be a comfort behind her for the rest of her life.

It seemed queer, not to have those few thousands of savings in the bank; but, she told herself, it was more than worth it to have your own place, paid for, with even a little money passing through your hands. Sometimes, when she got uneasy, she had to put on overalls and boots and go out and walk in the Stilwell swamp. After a while, she'd be able to say to herself, "Well, it's my swamp now," and she'd feel it was worth it again.

It had been worth it, too, to get a license and put in beer, she thought, looking at the figures which said she'd made $19.82.

Uncle Til, sitting in his window and dividing his attention between her and the muddy, rutted road outside, just in case anyone might come along whom he could watch out of sight, saw that she had come to a stopping-place.

"How'd we make out, Maggie?" he asked anxiously. "How'd we do?"

"Well, I may be a little mite crazy," Mag said, "but it looks as though we'd better'n broke even. Nineteen-eighty-two. How'd you like that?"

"You don't say!" His face crinkled into a grin of relief. "Ain't that good, though?"

"Good! It's a cussid maracle. At that rate, I'll git my linoleum in about sixty years, and in about three months, you a new 'lectric heatin pad, Tilburry. But anyway, we're not goin behind." She shut the book with a snap and was about to put it away in the drawer where she kept it when Uncle Til said wistfully, "You sure you ain't made no mistakes?"

"Well, there!" Mag crossed over to him at once carrying the account book and the fountain pen. "I was so took aback over comin out above instid a below the line that I clean forgut I ain't gut no head for figures. Maybe I better not crow till you've gone over em for me, Tilburry."

The accounts, she knew, were right, as they always were, but she always let Uncle Til check them, sometimes even making a mistake or two for him to find.

He had always been proud of his ability to figure, either in his head or on paper. Laid away in the battered trunk in his room were his own account books, started when he was twenty and containing the records of his financial transactions for nearly seventy years. Sums paid him for odd jobs, for lobsters and hake, for herring during the forty years he had been a weir-fisherman—everything, incoming and outgoing, had been set down, even to, in 1900, the entry: *For casket and funeral of wife, $77.00,* and in parenthesis under that (*Paid the minister, $7.00*).

Uncle Til sometimes had Mag get his books out for him, so he could show her the neat way he had kept them, or point with pride to some year when he had come out ahead of the game.

"Now, here," he would say, with one frail, misshapen finger touching a faded figure ruled off with neat blue lines, "here was a good year, Maggie. December 31, 1899, I come out with $322.76, clip and clean, no debts back of me. I caught an awful lot of herrin that year. I remember in the spring we shingled the house and Neeley wanted me to buy another cow, only we didn't because that was the year she begun to go down the line."

His tremulous voice would go on, annotating the dim figures with his memory. Neeley, his wife, was dead, and his house had burned down in 1914, but for a moment these lost riches would be plain to him, returned to the world by the "figger" set down in the years of their splendor. He had kept his books up until three years ago, and though he had not shown the last entries to her, Mag had seen them, looking over his shoulder one day.

Cash on hand, they read, *12 cts. Paid out to Paris Freeman's boy Sam, for bringing medicine, 12 cts.*

Uncle Til, in seventy years of profit and loss, of taking in, paying out, setting down and "figgerin," had come out exactly even.

So Mag let him check her own accounts to make him feel as if he were a part of things again, and to give him responsibility as the man of the house taking care of a woman's casual figuring.

Today she had had it in her mind that he wouldn't feel like bothering. It was one of his bad days, when pain shifted in and out of his twisted joints with the ruthlessness of a rock-crusher. He wouldn't say anything—Uncle Til took pride, and he had a feeling about pain as if it were something to be ashamed of—but Mag could tell from a breathlessness that had come behind his voice and from the occasional, meticulously careful movements he made in his chair.

It grabbed him again, just as he started to reach for the fountain pen, and his fingers, which he couldn't straighten out anyway, curled helplessly and convulsively back into his palms.

"I don't b'lieve I'll need the pen, Maggie," he said after a moment. "I feel today as if I'd like to practice doin a little arithmetic in my head."

Mag, who had laid the account book open across his lap and turned away as soon as she saw he wasn't going to be able not to let the pain show, spoke from the other side of the room. "Well, I'm sure I don't know what I'd do without you to straighten me out, Tilburry. You see'f I'm right about that nineteen eighty-two, while I git that lazy sod upstairs's breakfast for him. I don't b'lieve he'll sell many candy bars, if he lays a-bed till eleven o'clock every place he stops." Glancing out of the corner of her eye at Uncle Til, she saw he was sitting motionless, his head bowed over the book on his lap. "If I ain't right about that little bit of profit," she went on tentatively, letting her voice become lower and die away, "I'm goin to be almighty sorry I even thought of puttin in beer."

He made no answer and she saw that he had dropped off into one of the quick, exhausted naps he sometimes took after a spasm of pain.

The "lazy sod upstairs" was a candy salesman from Portland, whose route eastward twice a month included Bellport and some of the islands. He never stayed at Mag's unless he had to, preferring the livelier hotels and brighter lights of Bellport. This time, however, he had been shy of cash, and also, it had been almost dark when he had got through taking Pete Stilwell's bi-monthly order for penny goods. Stopping at Mag's, he had been entranced at the information that he could get beer, so he had decided to spend the night. Harry Hersh was his name. Mag couldn't stand the sight of him.

"The's somethin about men named 'Harry,'" she informed Uncle Til privately, "that gives me fur on my tongue," and Uncle Til had said with a chuckle, "His name ain't what you don't like about *him*, Maggie. He's a feeler. You keep your eye on him. He's got his on you."

"Oh, poo!" Mag said. "My day's over, Tilburry."

Yet she knew Uncle Til was right. She was forty-three, but in a lifetime of hard work she'd never had time to sit down and lose her figure. This Harry Hersh, unless she was mistaken, was going to make known what he wanted before he went his way. As a matter of fact, he hadn't left much doubt in her mind last night when she had served his supper to him.

Hearing him now moving around upstairs as he got dressed, Mag started her pancakes and bacon, and when he came into the kitchen in his shirtsleeves, she had his breakfast on the table.

Hersh was a fattish man of forty-five or so, bald and blond, with a shiny skin. In his shirtsleeves and with his rather wrinkled mulberry-colored pants hanging over his paunch from his belt, Mag thought with an inner chuckle that he looked like a man she remembered from the funny papers when she was little—a fat character named Opie Dildock. She greeted him with cool politeness.

"Mornin, Mr. Hersh."

"Morning to *you*," Hersh said, with a bright, false heartiness. "Breakfast on the table, hunh?"

"All ready," Mag said. "Set right down. Strong or weak coffee?"

"Strongest you've got." He rubbed his hands together and fell to on the pancakes, his eyes following Mag as she went back and forth from stove to sink.

"Nice place you've got here," he volunteered finally.

"I like it."

"Business kind of slow fall and winter?"

"I make out."

He chewed for a while, then tried again. "Might make out better if you was a little more sociable," he pointed out. "That's a swell bed you got upstairs. Good springs. I'll have to plan to stop here often."

"You'll always get good meals and a comfortable bed."

"That's all?"

"That's all," she said, her back to him.

"Well, shan't you die!" said Hersh. He took a final swallow of coffee, wiped his mouth with the back of his hand, and stood up. "How much do I owe you?"

"That'll be two dollars."

"Ain't that kind of steep? Seems as though I ought a git a little more for my money." He took a step or so toward her, reached around her shoulders and cupped his hands over her breasts.

Mag moved like a cat. The bowl of eggs she had used in making the pancakes still stood on the cupboard. She reached for an egg, and half-turning, slapped him full across the nose with it.

"There's a little more for your money," she said venomously. "Only now it'll be two dollars plus five cents for the egg."

Hersh stood aghast with the egg running down his face onto his shirtfront. "You bitch!" he said furiously.

From the rocker by the window came a high-pitched cackle. Uncle Til, his head thrown back as far as his humped shoulders would let him, was laughing at the top of his lungs.

Hersh glared at him, his face turning slowly purple. Mopping with his handkerchief, he made a dive for the door and up the back stairs. Almost at once he came down with his coat and suitcase, dropped two one-dollar bills sullenly on the table and went out. They heard his car start in the driveway with a roar of racing engine.

Uncle Til gasped. He wheezed and lost his breath, and Mag hurried across to his side. She bent him forward over her arm, using the other hand to thump him on the back until he breathed again.

Lying helplessly across her arm, he looked up at her, his eyes merry, his cheeks streaked with tears.

"Tilburry, you mustn't! I thought you was a goner for sure. How you feel now?"

"By joppy," he said, between breaths. "That—was the—comicalest thing—I ever see. Maggie, I felt so bad this mornin I thought I was goin to die. Now, I betcha I live ten years."

But against her wrist she could feel the thin, uncertain flutter of his heart.

"You're goin t' bed, Tilburry," she said firmly. "Lay back now and le'me lug you."

"Shucks, Maggie, I ain't— Who's that comin?" His head craned inquisitively past her shoulder toward the window. "By joppy. It's Aggie Flynn!"

Mag straightened up to look, then turned back to him, and for an instant their eyes met, silently.

"You ain't goin t' make me miss this, Maggie."

"I'll leave the bedroom door open," Mag said grimly.

But before she could pick him up, Agnes came up the steps and in at the kitchen door, shutting it behind her with a firm click. "I'd like to know what kind of people you put up with staying here," she said angrily. "That car that just went out would have run over me right in the driveway if I hadn't jumped. As it was, he's spattered me all over with mud."

She had on her fur coat and her goloshes, but Mag could see no mud spatters, except for a small irregular patch on her stocking just below the hem of her skirt.

"That was Mr. Hersh, the candy salesman," Mag said civilly. "He oversleep, and I guess he was in a hurry. I've got to put Tilburry to bed, Agnes, he ain't feelin well, but if you'll set down a minute I'll give you a damp rag t' clean the mud off with."

"I feel all right now," Uncle Til said hurriedly. "You give her the rag now, Maggie."

"*Mr. Hersh* was probably drunk," said Agnes pointedly.

"No. I don't think so." Seeing it would do Uncle Til more damage now to go to bed than to stay, Mag moved away from him and across the room to the sink.

"And I don't need any of your 'damp rags,' " Agnes said, her voice putting the two words into quotation marks. "If I want my clothes cleaned, I can send them to Bellport to the dry cleaners."

"Suit yourself," Mag said. There might be a difference between the people who cleaned spots off their clothes with a damp rag and those who sent to the dry cleaners, but, it occurred to her, she didn't believe it was quite that much.

"I never thought when I went to school with you, Mag Snow," Agnes went on, "that I'd ever have to come into your house for any such reason as I've come now."

"Feelin the way you feel, I shouldn't think for any reason," said Mag. "Besides, you've gut to remember, Aggie, it was only grade school." There was in her voice a suggestion of mincing richness, reminiscent of Agnes's own, and Uncle Til, by the window, began to cough.

"And I never thought I'd have to call a special meeting of the Aid to condemn you for starting a saloon in this village."

"No. I'd hardly have thought so, either."

Agnes drew herself up. "I knew I was wasting my time when I came in here, but—"

"That's right."

"—but I'm certainly going to let you know first-hand just what the whole town thinks of the rig you run here with this—this—"

"Flophouse?" supplied Mag ominously.

"If that's what you like to call it, yes. Language like that is just about what I'd expect."

"All right," said Mag. "Now you've told me, why don't you go home?"

"I'm not going home until I've—"

"Oh, yes, you are. You're goin flyin out a here right now. You'll be lucky if you leave tracks." Mag came purposefully across the kitchen, and Agnes gave ground a little. "I ain't got no more time t' waste. I've got my livin to earn, and hungry people comin in to eat a meal I've put on the table. You think about that when you go home to that plush-lined palace you live in—hungry people comin in, three times a day. I've known you, Aggie Stilwell, ever since you was the queen of the sixth grade. If you'll remember, I warn't never one of them that come bowin and kneelin."

"Well!" Agnes said. She made a grab for the doorknob and opened the door. "I never in all my life heard—"

"You hear it now. I mind my business and I'll thank you t' mind yours, if you've gut any that ain't stabbin your neighbors in the back. When you can put your finger on some actual harm I've done, by sellin beer or anything else, you come back here and I'll listen to you. I've gut friends on this island, too, and I know all about what they think of me, without hearin any more of your claptrap, you filthy-minded old flounder!"

"You," said Agnes furiously, "will hear about this from the selectmen."

"I'll wait till I do. If you mean Pete Stilwell, don't you forget for a minute that when my trade's good, his is. Now you beat it out a here, or I'll cut that rabbit-skin coat off'n your back. And the holes won't be in the coat, neither!"

So far, Mag hadn't raised her voice, but having thought of this juicy threat, she couldn't resist letting go with it a little. The blast silenced Agnes and set her, forgetting to be dignified, out through the door, leaving it open behind her.

Mag shut the door firmly and turned to Uncle Til. "You all right, Tilburry?"

He nodded without speaking.

"Oh," she said remorsefully. "There I was botherin to fight with that old hen-coop, while you—"

"I'm all right," he whispered, with the ghost of a grin. "By joppy, you—are, too!"

He wasn't hard to lift. The shrunken old bones with the skin tight over them lay light in her arms, as she carried him to his bed. She undressed him gently and left him warmly covered and surrounded with hot water bottles.

"There, now. I'll go make some good hot tea for us. We've had about enough for one mornin. You and me both."

As she turned to leave him, he opened his eyes. "You feel bad, Maggie?"

"About her? No, I don't. But I'm mad, Tilburry. By the Lord of heavens, am I *mad!*"

*

Agnes went very fast, almost running, down the driveway. Henny Pray, who happened to be going into Pete's, saw her, and in telling the story as she did almost immediately afterward to Prilly Grant, up the road, she used the word "scuttle."

"I see her scuttle out of there," Henny said, agog. "I'd give somethin t' know what happened, wouldn't you?"

But as Agnes rounded the corner of the driveway and came out into the road, her back was as straight as ever. She walked toward home with her usual steps, dignified and neat.

For a little while, as she walked, she was too angry and too shocked to think coherently, beyond the words "cheap," "awful," and "vulgar." But as she came along the hedge that separated the lawn at the back of her house from the road, she saw Hallet Romer standing on the walk beside a wheelbarrow. The wheelbarrow was full of manure, and Hallet was spreading it on the lawn, tossing it as far as he could reach with a dung-fork.

"Well," Agnes said, conversationally. "I guess it's a good thing I came home just when I did, Hallet, isn't it?"

Hallet was an indefinite-colored little man of forty-five or so, with a crumpled brown pleasant face and round blue eyes. His eyes, as he looked at her, took on a slightly frightened expression, and opened wider and rounder.

"Why, yes, Mis Flynn, I guess 't is," he said uncertainly, looking around to see what was wrong.

"I don't believe you remember that I asked you to do that job after the ground was frozen, do you?"

"Well," Hallet said, "it was froze this mornin, Mis Flynn." His eyes wandered first to the wheelbarrow, then across the brown expanse of thawing lawn, covered with indefinite blobs of dung.

"Because of the smell, I told you, remember?" Agnes went on pleasantly. "And because I didn't want you to spoil the lawn by wheeling a loaded barrow across it when it was wet. But I guess you don't remember, do you, Hallet?"

"But I ain't. I been throwin it from the aidges in!" he protested. "An I can't wait till it freezes too hard, because if I do, the dung'll be froze, too, and you can't spread froze dung!"

Agnes gave a start and the pleasant look left her face. "And I'll thank you to remember the times and times I've asked you to watch your language," she said. "Oh, dear, Hallet, I did so hope you'd try to deserve a raise this Christmas."

"You want I should rake it up?" Hallet asked.

Agnes sighed. "No. You'll only do more damage than you've done. Only don't put any more on until the weather's the way I told you." She went into the house and closed the door, leaving him standing there.

Hallet carefully laid his dung-fork on the depleted load, picked up the handles and trundled the barrow back to the barn. As soon as he was out of sight of the house windows, he gave the whole thing a flying shove and sent it toppling into a heap, the upside-down wheelbarrow on top.

And I wisht she was under it! he said to himself. Crisake, what'd she expect me to call it? "It," I spose, the way she does.

Then he sighed, and went to get a rake to clean up the mess before she came down and saw it.

*

Inside the house, Agnes was feeling almost herself again. It was dinnertime, she saw, looking at the kitchen clock, but my goodness, after you'd been through such an unpleasant morning, it would be a living wonder if you could eat anything. She'd poach herself an egg—something light, that was just what she needed.

But as she sat down at the corner of the kitchen table to eat the egg, there was something about it sitting there on its neat brown

slice of toast—something about the empty table, with one place set
—that made her feel uneasy.

Hungry people coming in to eat a meal you've put on the table,
she heard Mag Snow's voice say; and in an instant Agnes was mad
all over again.

Well, I've certainly done my share, she said angrily to herself,
losing my husband the way I did, and bringing up a fine boy like
Stilwell to manhood. Which is more than she ever did, and probably
that's what's the matter with her. Jealousy! she thought. Half the
world's troubles came from jealousy—people wanting things other
people had, that they hadn't the brains nor the gumption to get for
themselves.

There it was, she couldn't eat. She might just as well give up
trying. She'd go upstairs, that's what she'd do, and work on her
Christmas presents. Doing things for others, there was nothing like
it to make you forget unpleasantness.

She scraped the egg into the garbage-can, washed her few dishes,
and leaving the already immaculate kitchen a little neater, she went
up through her silent house to the front room, where the presents
she had for people were spread out ready for wrapping.

My, they do make a roomful! she thought with satisfaction, stop-
ping in the door to look.

The things were heaped on the bed, on the chairs, even on the
bureau, commode and mantelpiece. She had gifts for almost every-
one she had ever known or heard of.

She was one who believed in being forehanded with Christmas.
A few weeks after one Christmas was over, she always started in to
accumulate and prepare for the next one.

I just have to, she told herself, picking up scissors, bright tissue
paper and string from the heap at the foot of the bed. There, if I
didn't, the whole of December would be just one rush, rush, rush.
I have so many friends.

*

Mary Mackay came up the cellar stairs with short purposeful
steps, setting her feet down hard. Her lips were pressed tightly

together, and her own family, if any of them had been around, would have known at a glance that she was mad. She went through the shed and out around the house where Donny Mitchell had been sawing cordwood sticks into stove lengths and was now splitting them. He was going at it with great effort, lifting up the ax and letting it fall on a tough spruce butt, so that the blade barely pierced the bark each time and bounced off ineffectively. He glanced around at her with no expression, and then leaned on the ax-helve, as if its support were the only thing that kept him upright.

"Donny," said Mary Mackay, "what's become of that root beer I made and put down suller?"

"I d'no what's become of it," Donny said. "I never touched it."

"Well, somebody's touched it. Somebody warn't satisfied with drinkin it all up, they even went to the trouble to fill up the bottles with water, so's I wouldn't notice 't was gone."

"Maybe the yeast didn't work," said Donny hopefully. "There was a place I was to, up-country, Mis Mackay, they made root beer and it all just turned to water. I know that for a fact. I was there."

"I guess if you was there, the' was a reason why it turned to water, wasn't the'?" Mary said, eyeing him grimly. "Donny, I'm sick and tired of your doin underhand tricks and then lyin out of it. You drunk up that beer and you filled those bottles with water."

"I never!" Donny's voice went up a shrill note. "How do you know who might of broke into that suller some dark night when we was sleepin?"

"Oh, fiddle! Of all the foolish yarns! You've got to stop this business, Donny, hear me? I've stood all of it I'm goin to."

"That's right, blame me! That's all you ever do, jaw and blame me for stuff I don't know nothin about." Moisture appeared in the corners of Donny's eyes and his Adam's apple worked with a dull gulping sound.

It was true, he had drunk up the root beer and had spent some long careful moments refilling the bottles, not spilling any water on the cellar floor. But the explanation he had worked out seemed perfectly reasonable to him. Somebody *might* have broken in. The outside cellar door was never locked. The fact that Mis Mackay refused to consider this logical possibility and preferred to blame him was only further proof that she leaned over backwards whenever she could to pick on him. He felt deeply wronged, and, suddenly, alone in the world, and a fat tear rolled down his cheek and splashed against the front of his work jacket.

"Who'd want your old root beer anyway?" he said with a hiccup. "I'll bet it wasn't any good."

"I don't imagine 't was," Mary said tartly. "Root beer's terrible when it's flat, and that needed to work before anybody drank any of it." She stared sternly at his figure of woe, and suddenly sighed deeply and sat down on a corner of the woodpile.

"It ain't the root beer I care about, for goodness' sake, Donny," she said. "Remember, I told you I made it for you and you could have all you wanted when it was ready. Why did you bother to act like you was stealin it?"

"I never! It wasn't me that done it!"

"It's the same way with the cookies and the pie in the pantry," Mary went on. "I try to keep the cookie jar full and plenty of sweet stuff baked up, and I've told you you could help yourself any time. I spose you think I don't know how you come sneakin downstairs in the middle of the night and lug stuff up to hide in your bureau drawer. Why, the bottom of your drawer is covered with old stale crumbs and globs of punkin pie! And it's all foolishness. The stuff is there for you, free as air. You don't have to steal, and besides, it tolls the mice!" The neat housewife in her awakened with a sense of outrage, and she was mad all over again. "If you don't stop it, Donny, I'm goin to lock the pantry door. I've got a key and a good place to hide it, and so help me, that's what I'll do if you don't mend your ways."

She got up and went into the house, leaving him standing there by the woodpile. It wasn't a bit of use to get mad at him, she told herself, and she just couldn't seem to get over being mad in a hurry, so she'd better wait awhile before she said any more.

Well, he'd cried for her, Donny thought, and he hoped she was satisfied. He hadn't done that before, but she'd çaught him when he was feeling kind of bad and couldn't help it.

He waited until she was out of sight behind the corner of the house. Then he picked up the ax and flung it furiously into the middle of the woodpile. He followed the ax with the bucksaw and saw it land with a satisfactory, vibrating crash against a spruce butt. Let her try to catch him on her gimpy old legs, the nosy old hen, he thought, starting down the shore road on a dead run. The idea, her thinking she could snoop around his private things in his bureau drawers!

His rage at being caught about the root beer was nothing, compared to the way he felt at finding out she'd known all the time about his coming downstairs to the pantry at night.

He couldn't, if he'd wanted to, have explained the deep thrill and sense of accomplishment he got out of creeping down the stairs, feeling out with his bare toes the creaky treads and boards that gave a little in the floor. For weeks he'd made a study of the noisy places and had filed away in his mind a neat diagram of stairs and floor, with X-marks where he mustn't step. There was something satisfactory about having a supply of pie and cake stored away in his room; but, in addition, to swipe it at night without anyone knowing, gave him a sense of getting his own back, taking away from someone who had plenty something that would be actually his.

The trouble was, he didn't own anything, even his clothes. The woman from the Welfare came around every few months to check up on his wardrobe, and later sent him what she thought he ought to have. She never said, "Donny, how would you like a red sweater?" or "What kind of a cap do you want?" She just made notes in a little blankbook she carried, and when the clothes finally arrived they'd be just the same old stuff, only maybe a little bigger. He never had any spending money, unless Mis Mackay got soft-hearted and doled him out thirty-five cents to go to the movies with. Then she always gave him just exactly thirty-five cents, so that if he did go to the movies he never had anything after the show for treat, the way the rest of the boys did. Even the shotgun which was the pride and joy of his heart she hadn't given to him outright. She was always reminding him it was her boy Dave's gun, which she was letting him use.

Donny began to dawdle as he came to Osgood's store down by the wharf. He sidled through the door, closing it quietly and carefully behind him, the way Mr. Osgood, Artie's father, liked to have it done. It was suppertime and nobody was in the store; but Donny could hear the wheeze of the hand pump on the kerosene barrel in the storeroom, which was where Mr. Osgood must be. He darted a quick glance around, reached out his hand and took a package of Camels from an open carton on the counter, stowing it away in the front of his blouse where the bulge, under his sweater, wouldn't show. When Mr. Osgood came in, carrying a filled kerosene can, he was waiting by the counter, whistling a tune between his teeth.

"You want something?" the storekeeper said, eyeing him. Myron Osgood wasn't at all sure Donny was lightfingered; but a couple of times lately after the boy had been in, he'd wondered. You couldn't be sure about a handful out of a loose box of candy, for instance, or that there were only six packages of cigarettes left in a carton where you'd thought you'd had seven. It was only that Myron's eye was trained to estimate quantity and told him, as if with a sixth sense, that something was missing.

Besides, Myron had it in mind anyway to keep an eye on Donny. Them State kids were pretty tough customers; their families were hardly ever all they ought to be. If they had been, they'd have seen to it that their kids had a decent home, not turned loose for the State to spend the taxpayers' money on. Of course this kid was almost local folks. His father had been a pretty good man, but from all Myron had heard, his mother wasn't any better than she might have been, and old Cap'n Mitchell who'd brought the boy up, everybody knew was as shiftless as they come.

"Mis Mackay wants a package of pilot bread," Donny said. He knew Mr. Osgood didn't have any pilot bread, having heard him say so to a customer earlier in the day.

"She's lucky my shipment came in this afternoon then," Myron said. "It ain't unpacked, though. If you'll wait a minute, I guess I could pry the cover off a case of pilot bread."

"Oh, never mind," said Donny hastily. He thought with discomfort that he hadn't a cent in his pockets. "She don't need it till tomorrow."

"No trouble," said Myron. He picked up a hammer from the counter, and then hesitated, as it occurred to him that the newly arrived crates were in the storeroom and that he'd rather not leave Donny alone in the store. "You come on out and hold down the box," he said.

"It's okay." Donny started toward the outer door. "Don't bother. I'll be by tomorrow." He turned the knob and to change the subject, asked over his shoulder, "You don't happen to know where Artie is, do you?"

"If he's where he ought to be, he's home eatin his supper," said Myron shortly. He didn't like the idea of Artie's hanging around so much with this boy.

Funny actin kid, he thought, staring meditatively after Donny. 'T wouldn't taken me a minute to open them crackers. He glanced again at the carton of cigarettes. Six packs left—that was right. And he was almighty sure there'd been seven.

Donny slouched along the shore road, slack-shouldered, his hands driven deep into his overalls pockets. Where would he go now? he asked himself. Everybody in the world was eating supper in a nice warm room with their folks. All except him; he didn't have any folks—at least, not what you could call folks. He wouldn't go back *there*, not till good and late, anyway. Let her wonder and worry about him for a while.

The shore road ahead of him dipped close to the bleak slate-gray water. The sun had set, leaving a streak of clear amber yellow close down on the horizon; the rest of the sky was lowering with heavy, bluish-dark clouds. It was early lamplighting time, only down this far on the Spoonhandle road there weren't any houses and no lights. Donny glanced over his shoulder at the yellow warmth streaming from Myron Osgood's store, at the spark from John Pray's house snugged in by the road. The next house back was Mary Mackay's, but he wouldn't look at her light. Not much, he wouldn't!

No use to go down the Spoonhandle, he reflected, stumping solidly along the rutty road; nobody down there but the Stilwells in their camp and that Portygee family. The thought of the Portygees recalled to him what Willie Stilwell had said about Joe Sangor's knowing Donny's old man. There, now, would be a place to go. Maybe the Portygee would tell him something about his father he didn't know, and maybe, too, the woman would give him some supper, if he arrived just at the right time. Still, from what Artie had told him, people like them lived awful dirty. You might not be able to stomach it to eat off of Portygee dishes. It would be a long walk, and a dark one through the woods, though. But what of it? He'd get back plenty late and no one would think of looking for him down there.

The wood road was rocky and rough with roots. After a while, the long shadows among the trees made him feel scary, and more lonesome than ever. By the time he came out into the clearing above the mussel bar that led to Willie's island, Donny had given up his project. It was too far to Joe Sangor's and he was too tired and hungry. For a while the idea of talking about his father with someone had seemed like a lamp in a nice warm room at the end of a cold cheerless tramp through the woods; but talking wouldn't give him any folks to go home to when he got ready to go back again.

Might as well go home, he thought listlessly, slackening his stride. The old lady'd jaw, but she'd at least have to feed him.

As he made his way slowly along the rocks, he caught sight of a small white punt hauled up in the jog where the mussel bar met the beach. Somebody, either Willie or Horace, had rowed over from the island. They weren't around though. Since he hadn't met anybody on the way down from Myron's, he guessed that whoever it was had gone on, some time before, up to the village—maybe to the post office. If that was the case, it would take him quite a while to get back.

Donny went down the beach cautiously and looked the punt over. If only he had a line and some bait, he could take her and go off and catch a pollock or a flounder. He and Uncle My had often made a supper off of fish like that, cooked on a board by an open fire and salted with sprinkles of sea water.

There was no line in the punt—only a bucket which had a few scraps of lobster bait dried to its bottom.

Darned if he was hungry enough to eat that. But the bait made him think of lobsters, and all at once he narrowed his eyes and studied carefully the cove on the opposite shore where Willie and Hod kept their lobster car. He and Artie Osgood had looked over the ground pretty carefully the other night. The car was locked, but he bet he could pry the padlock off with an oar handle.

Carefully, so that the pebbles grating under the punt's bottom would make as little noise as possible, Donny shoved her off the bar into the water and rowed silently across to the cove. Most of the way he was able to keep the punt in the dark water along the shadowy side of the bar.

The staples on the padlock, he noted with satisfaction, were big ones. He stuck the hand grip of one of the oars through one and pried, and felt it give with a punky splintering of water-soaked wood.

Willie, coming back with his shotgun through the woods from Cat Cove, heard the splintering sound and wondered what it was. Something from out in the harbor, maybe. Sounds carried far on a still night like this. Coming out on the shore where he had left his punt, he saw with surprise that she was over by the lobster car. Through the dusk he could make out her white sides and see the dark outline of someone who had the car trapdoor open, feeling around inside and pulling out lobsters. For a moment Willie thought it must be Hod; but Hod had taken the boat and gone up to the town slip to carry the Freeman girl's suitcases to her. He couldn't possibly be back yet.

Willie slipped silently behind a boulder and crouched down. He felt a deep sense of bewilderment and shock. He would never have believed that there was anyone living who'd be mean enough to swipe a man's lobsters out of a car. Why, people kept their lobster cars around all over the place, and some of them weren't even locked up. Willie was tempted to let fly with his gun and sprinkle the marauder with birdshot, but he hadn't the heart. Birdshot didn't kill at that distance, but they might make nasty painful little wounds that, like as not, would get infected.

Donny rowed silently ashore and hauled up the punt as he had found it. When he went past Willie's boulder, his windbreaker thrown sack-like over his shoulder and bulging with lobsters, Willie shot out a hand and grabbed him firmly by the collar.

For an instant Donny froze still with fright. Then, seeing who it was, he dropped the lobsters and began a silent, terrified struggle to get away. Willie merely held him, fending off the flying fists and letting Donny's wild kicks thud harmlessly against his thick rubber boots.

"It's you, is it?" Willie said finally. "I swear, boy, I wouldn't never of believed it."

"You le'me go!" Donny threshed his arms and legs in a flurry. "You dirty ol' bastid!"

"That'll do," Willie said.

Donny twisted his head and did his best to bite Willie on the wrist. Failing, he let go with a mouthful of words that made Willie wince.

"I said, that'll do." He tightened his grip a little and Donny squeaked and let himself go limp. Willie regarded him meditatively. "You come along over here with me," he said.

Still holding Donny by the collar, he fumbled in his pocket for his jackknife and opened it with his teeth. Donny gave a squawk of terror, but Willie merely reached and cut from the bushes a short, limber cane.

"If 't wasn't that I remember what a good man Cap'n My

Mitchell was," he said, "I wouldn't bother with this. I'd take you to Bellport and hand you over to the sheriff."

The cane landed with a *thwack!* in the proper place. Donny let out an outraged yowl.

"That's better." Willie grunted with effort. "Anyway, it sounds better to me."

He did a thorough job. When he was through, he thought Donny would probably take out and run, but the boy merely stood blubbering, with both fists stuck into his eyes.

"What did you think you was up to, stealin lobsters?" Willie asked. "My Lord, boy, don't you know that's a state's prison crime?"

His voice sounded reasonable and kind, not wild mad, the way Donny had thought he was. "I was just hungry. I only wanted a few to cook for supper."

"You had a lot more there than you could eat," Willie pointed out. "I guess you run of an idea that what you couldn't eat you could sell somewhere, didn't you?"

"Yes," Donny admitted. "I guess so." He couldn't imagine why he was telling on himself this way. But somehow he didn't want to lie; he just wanted to let his tears run and keep on feeling better. He'd done a rotten bad thing and he'd been thrashed good and hard for it. For the first time in months Donny felt uncomplicated and simple, as if things had straightened out for him. They had begun to straighten out too just as soon as he found out Willie wasn't mad.

"How come you was hungry? Don't Mary Mackay feed ya?"

"Sure. She feeds me all right." Donny let his breath go in a hiccup. "Only, tonight, see, we had a fight."

"Oh." Willie nodded his head. He looked keenly at Donny and then turned and started down the beach toward the punt. "You want to come with me and put them lobsters back in the car?" he asked over his shoulder. "After it's done, we'll go over to my camp and have some supper."

"Eyeh." Donny rubbed his sleeve across his eyes. He picked up the windbreaker full of lobsters, ignored by Willie as he had passed it, and brought it down to the punt. He helped Willie launch the punt and held her while Willie climbed in.

"Be a favor t' me if you was to row," Willie said. "I been bankin the house today and I'm tired."

"Sure." Scrabbling in over the side, Donny's feet splattered water all over the rowing thwart. He sat down in it gingerly, but his stern still stung royally from the licking, and the cold water felt good. He took the oars and dug manfully, sending the punt flying across the cove.

"You handle a punt pretty good," Willie said. "I guess Cap'n My learnt you how to row."

"Yes, he did. He learnt me a lot of things about a vessel, too. His idea was that maybe I'd be skipper of a vessel sometime. Only—" Donny stopped.

"Only he died before he got you learnt, that it?" Willie said. "You know, I could use a boy that knows some of the things about the water that Cap'n My knew. I'd pay twenty-five cents an hour. What d' you do with your spare time after school and Sat'd'ys?"

Donny looked sullen. "I help out Mis Mackay with her work. She don't pay me nothin."

Willie nodded. "She probly can't," he said. "Your board from the State's about the only cash money Mis Mackay's gut comin in, don't you know that?"

"I don't b'lieve it!" Donny said, shocked. "She's got a lot."

"Maybe you know that for a fact," said Willie. "But I heard diff'rent. Oh, her boys send her a little, off'n on, but they can't spare much, either."

He didn't know it for a fact, Donny realized. He'd just taken it for granted that because Mis Mackay had a nice house and plenty to eat she had plenty of money as well. Maybe she didn't. If she didn't, well, then she wasn't stingy.

"You think it over," Willie said. "After we eat, I'll walk home with you and we'll ask her if she can spare you part of your time to help me."

The punt moved across the still cove in the gathering darkness. Where the oars dipped, small bubbles of phosphorescent light winked dully and disappeared, and the V-shaped wake behind slid glassily outward to vanish in pale ripples of light.

"I see a fifteen-foot shark in this cove one night," Willie said. "Went right under the boat. Like to scairt me to death."

"You did!" exclaimed Donny. His mouth opened slowly and he stared at Willie, awestricken. "You see a *shark* in here?"

Willie nodded gravely. "He was after a school of herrin and mack'rel. On nights when the sea fires, one a them sharks goin under the boat leaves a trail thirty-five, forty feet long. Looks like a whale."

*

Mis Mackay, Donny could see, as he came in through the entry door with Willie, was still mad. She didn't look up and she didn't notice Willie until Willie lifted up the storm lantern with which he had lighted them through the woods, and blew it out. Then she jumped a little and said, "Oh! It's Willie Stilwell. Good evenin."

Willie said, "Evenin. I brought your boy back. He's been down to supper with me."

Mary Mackay still did not look at Donny. "It's a good thing he et somewheres," she said. "For I certainly didn't save him any supper tonight." She was mending a torn pillowcase, and she bit off her thread with an angry little snap.

"Well, now," Willie began. He was, as always, ill at ease in the presence of a cross or a positive woman, and uncertain of what to say. Mrs. Mackay had not asked him to sit down, but in his embarrassment he did so, in a straight chair across from her rocker, his ragged old hat balanced across his knees. "I knew he'd run off," he went on, "but I was eatin supper and he was hungry, so I fed him. I hope I ain't kept him too long."

"Well, if he hadn't come when he did, I'll tell you," she said, "I was just about ready to call up the State Woman and tell her to drive down tomorrow and take him away." She looked at Donny for the first time, a stony glance which seemed not to see him.

"Donny, if you've had your supper, you go up to bed. I'll talk to you in the morning."

"But Willie's—but he's got somethin to ask you," Donny said desperately. He had to know whether she was going to let him go down to Willie's in his spare time. He and Willie had had a wonderful supper of fried eggs and potatoes and preserves. Willie had let him cook most of it, and afterwards had shown him a lot of things in an old sea chest—a real swordfish sword, and some silver pirate earrings he'd bought in New Bedford, a long time ago. There were a lot more things to show him, Willie said, only they'd better take him home or Mis Mackay'd be so mad she'd never let him come again.

"Ne'm mind, now," Willie said. "We'll talk it over later on. You run along to bed, like you're told."

"I got to know." Donny stood stubbornly.

"What is it you've got to know?" Mis Mackay eyed him. "I spose you know you smashed up that bucksaw, throwin it around, don't you?"

"Well—so I was mad when I throwed it. I—"

"He was figgerin out a way he could pay for it," Willie cut in smoothly. Misery in someone defenseless always put him on his mettle, and now the conversation had shown him a way to go. "I told him I could use a boy sometimes after school and Sat'd'ys and Sundays, pay him a quarter an hour. He said he'd like to have the job, only he had chores to do for you."

"That's right, he does," said Mary tartly.

"I wouldn't want to cut in on your time," Willie added in haste. "Only thing is, he wants to buy you a new saw. Maybe earn a little of his own expense money as time goes on."

"The way he does now he ain't a mite of use to me," she said. She sounded mollified in spite of the sharpness of the words, and Donny took a deep breath. "At least, I'd know where he was part of the time."

"That's fine." Willie got up as if the matter were settled. He picked up his hat and his lantern. "First day she can spare you,

you come on down, Don." He paused in the entry door and looked back with a smile. "Good night."

Something in the quality of Willie's smile surprised Mary Mackay. She wouldn't have called it sweetness if she had had to describe it—she would just have said that he had a nice smile. She had known him for a long time, but not very well. He never came to see people in the village and, in the last ten years, she might have met him half a dozen times, either casually at the store or at the hall on Town Meeting Day. For years she had taken for granted the neighbors' gossip that he was a hermit and kind of peculiar-acting. But certainly tonight he'd behaved like anybody else, and in some ways a lot nicer than most.

If Donny had been her own, she would have felt pretty doubtful about letting him go to work for Willie. You never knew how much there might be in talk, and where there was smoke there must be some fire. Not that, thinking it over, she could remember any specific thing that people said was wrong with Willie. As a matter of fact, when you came right down to it, most people always said he was an awful good man. Just peculiar.

Seeing she was responsible for Donny, she ought to be careful. But there, perhaps a job—any job—would straighten him out a little. She didn't seem to be able to do it. The State was just going to have to take him back if something didn't change him, that was all. Myron Osgood had stopped in tonight to bring her a box of pilot crackers she hadn't even ordered. When he'd told her how he came to bring it and what he suspected about Donny, she'd been worried out of her life.

She doubted if a man with a smile as pleasant as Willie Stilwell's could do much harm to Donny. Be the other way around, like as not, she thought grimly.

She turned to tell Donny he could take Willie's job if he didn't skimp on his chores for her, and discovered that he had slipped silently away to bed. The way he'd taken to vanishing, as if he'd melted away, she'd like to shake the shirt off him!

Upstairs, in the room that had once belonged to Mis Mackay's

boy Dave, and still did, Donny paused in the act of pulling over
his head the sleazy nightshirt provided by the State. It was too nar-
row even for his thin shoulders, and he felt the cotton cloth rip as
he tugged at it. In sudden exasperation he yanked it in two, balled it
up and tossed it into the corner. Creeping raw between the cold
sheets, he was warmed almost instantly by the thought that Willie
had promised he could go out fishing some Saturday with him and
Hod in their big new boat.

*

Hod had got back from his trip to the village, Willie saw by the
lighted window as he came up from the landing after taking Donny
home. Couldn't have stayed very long at the Freemans', Willie re-
flected. Anybody'd think that after a fellow had gone to the trouble
of luggin up them heavy suitcases, the girl could at least have
entertained him for the evenin.

"You're back early," he said, coming in the entry door.

Hod was sitting in the rocker by the table, reading the daily
paper, which he had brought from town. "Ayeh."

As a matter of fact, he had not seen Ann at all. Myra Freeman
had thanked him for bringing up the suitcases and had asked him
to sit down. "I don't know where Ann is," she said. "She might've
gone for a walk. But she'll be awful glad to git them bags. She
ain't had a stitch to wear but what she had on her back, and them
pants a hers has about drove her father crazy. I thought she looked
real good, them browns go nice together, but you know Paris." She
looked at him with a twinkle in her bird-bright blue eyes.

"Oh, sure," Hod said. "She looked okay." He had always liked
Myra Freeman. In the old days, he remembered, she had often
stood between Ann and the wrath of her father. Myra believed in
letting people live their lives and she had a warmth and sweetness
that went strangely with Paris Freeman's temper.

"I meant to have the bags up here before," he went on. "Only
every day it's poured rain, and seemed too bad to get em wet."

"My Lord, I know it!" Myra's voice made drama out of the
spell of bad weather. "Did you ever see such a southerly in your

life! I woke up Paris bout twelve o'clock that first night and made
him git up and go down and fasten the windows. I thought they
was goin t' blow right into the middle of the kitchen. The' was one
while there I didn't know but we'd have to take the matrusses off
our beds and batten the windows with them."

"That's right. Pretty bad storm." Hod fidgeted a little on the
straight kitchen chair. "How's Ann getting along?"

"Pretty good," said Myra cheerfully. "Her and her pa's had
some set-to's, but no more than I thought they might. She spends
most of her time up in the woodshed chamber, pickin away on her
typewriter. Writin another book," she added proudly.

"So she said."

"She's fixed up a stove so she won't freeze to death up there,"
Myra said, "but I d'no b't Paris'll have a hem'ridge over her
burnin so much extry wood. He's always a one, you know, to
count every stick in the woodpile, and I guess he had it figgered
down pretty close how much it'd take to git our two stoves through
the winter. I told him, shucks, 't wouldn't hurt him to cut a couple
cords extry this year, but there, he always has to make just so much
fuss. Then when she offered to buy some wood, he like to died."

Myra spoke without rancor, with the air of one to whom Paris's
fusses were an old and accepted story.

"Well," Hod said, getting up, "you tell her I brought the suit-
cases?"

"I certainly will," said Myra heartily. "I'm sure I thought she'd
be right back. You ain't goin so soon, Horace?"

"Guess I better get back and put the boat on the mooring before
it gets too late," he said.

She followed him to the door. "Well, you be sure to come again,
sometime when she's home. My, it's got dark, hasn't it? These
November days are so short I can't git one thing done, and seem's
so the nights are a lot darker than summer nights. How's your
brother gittin along? Someone said he was goin to sell his place to
the summer people. Is that so?"

"He hasn't said," Hod replied briefly. He started down the steps, then waited politely for her to finish.

"There, now, you can hear anything around this town," Myra said. She had been dying to ask Hod that question ever since he'd come in. There had been a good deal of speculation among her neighbors, and no way to find out the truth of the matter, for one so seldom saw either of the Stilwell boys. "People's been sayin Willie's place was sold, for an awful sum of money. They say the's quite a lot of summer people wants to buy places on this island. Be a wonderful thing for the town, if only they did start to come here more, wouldn't it?"

"Would be if you like summer people." Hod took another step.

"Well, of course, nobody *likes* em." Myra settled herself in the doorway for a longer chat. "They have t' be waited on hand and foot, and frigged with, and they act like they was God Almighty. But they do bring a lot of money and work to a town."

"There you are, then." Hod grinned at her. "If that's what you want. Good night, Myra."

"You come again!" she shrieked after him, and heard his muffled acceptance as he turned the corner. My! she reflected, he's some close-mouthed about that place bein sold. I bet there's more to that than meets the eye.

Thinking it over, Myra decided that Willie Stilwell was certainly going to sell his island, but was keeping quiet about it, probably on account of the big price he was getting. Well, if there was big money going around, she and Paris had better keep their eyes open. After all they owned ninety acres of land, some of it nice shore property with a handsome view.

*

Hod went down the path to the town slip, stopping on the way at the post office. There were two letters, both for Willie, and the Bellport paper. As he was buttoning them inside his coat, Nick Driver, the postmaster, stuck his head out through the wicket.

The post office was only a fourth class one, and Nick found time for it between his other jobs as lobster buyer for Pete and tender of the gasoline scow. Tiddy, his wife, managed to be around to tend office when he couldn't. "Lobsters gone up ten cents," he remarked. "Forty cents now. Lucky you never sold. Goin to bring yours in?"

"Tomorrow," Hod said. This was wonderful news. He couldn't help thinking how pleased Willie'd be.

"Any time," Nick went on. "Use all you got. I see Willie's got a letter from that Witherspoon."

"You see more than I do, then," Hod said briefly. He went out the door, leaving Nick with his mouth a little open. He supposed he was abrupt, but, for the love of God, the whole village was minding Willie's business for him.

He didn't suppose they could be blamed. When summer people came into a town, it did mean money and work, particularly if the summer people were wealthy, like the ones who had settled at Bellport.

He thought of Bellport—once a sleepy fishing village and now, in summertime, a thriving town, with its golf links, its country club, its swank hotels, and the branches from Fifth Avenue exclusive shops lining its streets. Along the shores for miles at Bellport, the big summer estates lay hip to jowl, enclosed by fences or stone walls, with neat signs—sometimes plain, sometimes quite ornate—saying, "No Trespassing," or "Private Property," or sometimes merely "Keep Out."

There had been a story about a Bellport millionaire who had had his no trespassing sign made by quite a famous artist in wrought iron and had paid a thousand dollars for it. Horace grinned, not believing the story—at least the amount of money involved.

At no place along the Bellport shore line could a man who did not own property there get down to the water except at the public wharves; for the land was all summer people's property and it was all fenced or posted.

No one living in Bellport now did very much except cater to the summer trade. The men had jobs on the estates as gardeners, or as boatmen or handymen; the women were kitchen workers, house-

keepers and maids. For four months of bonanza in Bellport, prices
went sky high. Business flourished and the town hummed. The rest
of the year the town slept, boarded up.

Well, what's the matter with it? Hod grunted to himself.

He was halfway home, and the big boat slid sweetly through the
November night, making phosphorescent patterns in the glassy
water.

It's honest work and pays better than fishing. You can't blame
people.

Yet he knew quite well what was the matter with it and why he
winced at the idea of such a summer colony starting up at Spoon
Island. The summer people acted like royalty, with royalty's gra-
cious, condescending manners, and the local people took it for
granted. Hod recalled the Bellport housewife whose talk he had
overheard one day in a store.

"Why, Colonel Swansley told me," she was saying with pride,
"that I was the only housekeeper he ever had whom he considered
worthy to mingle with his guests."

She was pretty silly, Hod had thought at the time, and she was
probably lying for the benefit of her listeners, but it was the state
of mind behind what she'd said that had made his stomach turn
over. Bellport, from a village of independent fishermen and farm-
ers, their own men who took nothing from anybody, had become a
townful of domestic servants.

At home and unfolding the paper to read, Hod thought over
his disappointment at not seeing Ann. He grinned at himself a
little wryly. Well, she'd be around all winter.

She was apparently having her troubles with Paris. The old son,
Hod could imagine just how mean he was being about that fire-
wood. The thought gave him an idea, which he was mulling over
when Willie got home.

"Letters for you," he said, jerking his head at the mail lying on
the table. He had some other news, good news, too, but he knew it
was no use throwing it all at Willie at once.

Willie picked up the letters and looked at one of them with a

kindling eye. He slit the envelope, pulled out his glasses and set-
tled himself at the end of the table where he got good light from
the kerosene lamp. The letter seemed to be a circular of some sort.

"This is the catalog from that hen-farm up-country, I was
tellin you about," he said to Hod after an absorbed five minutes.
"Tells all about them white pullets. They're a cross between a
White Leghorn and a Plymouth Rock, seems like, and somethin
else I never heard of. Meat on em ain't so heavy for eatin as 't is
on a Rhode Island Red, but seems they're hell for layin aigs."

"That so?" Hod lowered the paper and looked at him with
amusement. "Letter for you there from Witherspoon."

"Haanh," said Willie. He regarded Witherspoon's envelope.
"Hell. Him and me's said all we got to to each other." He took the
letter in his hand and turned it over once or twice. Then he reached
up and slid it unopened behind the clock. "Read it bime-by, maybe.
You know, Hod," he went on, turning a page of the circular, "I d'no
b't I'll send for five-ten a them hens."

"Five or ten won't do much good," Hod said. It was all he
could do to keep from rocking back and forth and shouting with
glee. It seemed to him that never before had he loved Willie
so much. "Send for a flock of twenty and kill off some of those
old tomato-bottoms you've got out there now. You need some
new hens, anyway. Some of yours remember the Civil War."

"Two dollars apiece," Willie mused, doubtfully.

"What of it? We'll be fishin all winter. Lobsters have gone up
ten cents." Hod paused to observe the effect of his good news. "I
saw Nick."

"Forty cents?"

"Nick'll take all we've got for that. All right with you?"

"You know 't is." Willie rubbed his palms together with satis-
faction. Thirty cents was all he had hoped to get for the lobsters. He
glanced again at the circular. "I'd sure like t' have a couple of white
rabbits, too," he said. "Five dollars, it says here, for a buck and two
does. If they breed the way it says they do, we could sure have some
nice rabbit stews, 'long about spring."

"Well, get em, why don't you? They and the hens'll pay for themselves, give em time. I sure do like rabbit stew, too."

"By God, I will." Willie got up and went to the desk to make out his order blank to the chicken farm. He paused, after a moment, and chewed the end of his penholder. "You know, Hod, I don't believe I want to kill any of them hens. They ain't what you could call old."

"Bertha, for instance?" Hod eyed him with a grin.

Willie grinned back. "Oh, well . . . Bertha. She is kind of old. But she's half human, not to say she's got a disposition just like Bertha Cummins. I wouldn't kill Bertha for ten dollars."

His pen scratched laboriously for a few minutes. Then he folded the order blank and tucked it in an envelope. "I sure do make heavy weather out of writin any kind of a letter," he commented. "I'll git a money order made out at the office when we go over tomorrow to sell them lobsters. Hod," he went on, after a moment, "you got any objections t' havin that Mitchell kid around once in a while? The one 't's stayin to Mary Mackay's?"

Hod lowered the paper again. "He's a little hellion," he said doubtfully. "Him and that Artie Osgood's been makin quite a team up around the fish-wharf."

"I kind of like him," Willie said, pulling out his pipe. "He don't seem t' be a bad kid. Been kind of mistreated, I think."

Hod got up to fetch his own pipe from the shelf over Willie's head. "Willie, my son," he said, "anything you like is all right with me." In his exuberance, he brought his hand down with an affectionate crack between Willie's shoulders.

Willie grunted. "God, boy, you don't want to hit a man. Another one a them, my backbone'd come flying out through my stomach."

"Okay. I won't." Hod went back to his chair and stoked his pipe, smoking meditatively. "Now, what *I* need, Willie, is a couple cords of wood."

"That so?" Willie regarded him over his glasses. "Kind of wood? Stove lengths or cordwood sticks?"

"Stove lengths."

"H'm." He thought for a moment. "The's the tail-end a that woodpile I made out b' the southeast corner of the barn. Bout two cords in that, I'd judge, soft 'n hardwood mixture, mostly maple. You can have that. I was lookin at it the other day and thinkin it was liable t' git dozy before we could use it up."

"Thanks. I'll take it."

It was like Willie to give him what he wanted without even a question as to what it was for. After a moment Hod told him.

"I need it," he said, "for a present to give to my girl."

*

Donny Mitchell's alarm clock went off at half-past two Saturday morning. For a moment, numbed with sleep, he heard the raucous waves of sound breaking over him without knowing what it was. Then he pawed wildly around on the stand by the bed, found the clock and shut the alarm off. The bedroom was icy cold, full of thin frosty light from a late moon. He shivered, thrusting his arms quickly under the quilts again. In a minute he'd get up. In a minute . . .

Someone was calling to him from far away, calling and banging two bars of iron together.

"What?" he mumbled vaguely.

The banging became intolerable. It was somebody rubbing a stick down thick metal slats just inside his ear.

"What's the matter?" he shouted wildly, sitting up in bed. "What is it?"

It was Mis Mackay calling and rattling with a broomhandle against the underside of the hot-air register.

"Donny! *Don-nee!* Your clock went off ten minutes ago. You don't want to miss your trip."

"Okay. I'm up." He came suddenly wide awake. This was the day he was going with Willie and Hod to make a set of trawls outside Hazlett's Rock. Willie had said three o'clock. Here it must be twenty of three already!

He tore out of bed, into his clothes and down the stairs. In the sitting room he was brought to a full stop by a white, stocky ghost moving toward him across the patch of moonlight from the window. His hair started to crinkle before he realized that it was Mis Mackay in her long flannel nightdress. She flipped hastily past him and into the dark open door of her bedroom.

"My land, there!" her embarrassed voice floated out to him. "I didn't expect you'd be down quite so quick. I built a fire and started some coffee, Donny. You eat a good breakfast, now, I don't want you goin off hungry. And I put out a warm sweater of Dave's. You put it on. It's an awful chilly mornin."

"Okay," he said, fidgeting, waiting for her to finish. Her and her boy Dave!

The kitchen clock said ten minutes to three. The fire was hot and roaring up the chimney, but the coffee-pot wasn't even warm. If he ran all the way, it would take him ten minutes to go down to Willie's landing by the mussel-bar, where they were going to pick him up in the punt. Willie had said three o'clock sharp.

What did she have to put in *her* oar for? It was nice of her to get up and call him, he appreciated it, but he wasn't hungry, he didn't need breakfast.

He pulled on his rubber boots and jacket, settling his cap firmly over his uncombed bristly hair. Teetering from one foot to the other in front of the stove, he grew more and more nervous. She'd be sore if he went without the coffee, but, heck, it would take forever!

At last Donny made up his mind, tiptoed across the kitchen floor, unbolted the door and closed it softly behind him. Then he went tearing down the driveway as fast as he could go. The moonlight made his small leaping shadow grotesque on the frosty grass.

Mis Mackay heard him go and got out of bed with a creaky sigh of weariness and impatience. He hadn't shut the back draft in the stove—she could hear the fire still roaring up the chimney. Well, it had to be shut. No sense having the chimney catch on fire.

She padded out across the icy floors in her bare feet. He'd left the kerosene lamp burning, too, and she saw with a little "Tch!"

of annoyance that he had taken neither Dave's sweater nor the dinner bucket she'd packed so carefully for him the night before.

And not even a thank-you out of him, she thought. Oh, dear, I spose he'll learn, but it's an uphill drag.

The coffee was beginning to bubble and smell good. It was a shame to waste it. She sat down to have a good strong cup of it before going back to bed. Sitting there, she was suddenly homesick for her own family—for Bob and the boys whom she had understood and who had understood her.

The place was going to rack and ruin, slipping back to wild land. Every day she could see some new repair that needed to be done to house and buildings. She did what she could, but that wasn't anything, lame as she was. Nobody'd care if the house fell right down. Donny, *he* wouldn't, just so it didn't fall on his head.

It ain't no use, she said, rocking a little while she sipped her coffee. There's no one can ever take the place of your own.

Donny had meant to take the sweater and he had meant to take the dinner bucket. In his desperation over being late, he had forgotten both.

Willie was waiting for him at the landing. In the moonlight, the punt's white sides showed up a long way off. Frost crystals on the planks made them whiter, sparkling and gleaming. It was nearly high tide. The channel was a wide pale-gray soundless flat, with the white path of the moon slashed across it.

"Cat's sake," Willie said, as Donny pounded up and tumbled into the punt. "No sense bustin a guzzet. I heard your feet thumpin the road all the way down from Mackay's."

"My alarm never woke me up very good." Donny panted, getting his breath. "I hustled so's you wouldn't go off and leave me."

"Well, I wouldn't go off and *leave* you," Willie explained. "Not just because you was late. I'd a hat to go in a minute, on account of catchin the low-water-slack off the Rock to haul the trawls on."

"Well, I got here," Donny said, relieved. Willie wouldn't have gone off and left him unless he'd had to. He wouldn't take it out on you because you were a few minutes late, the way a lot of people would. Donny had the feeling that Willie wouldn't have wanted to go without him; if he'd had to, it was because of a good, solid *man's* reason—because he'd had to catch the tide.

"Hod's pickin us up at the foot of the island," Willie said, heading down the channel. "Save time that way and we can anchor the punt and pick her up on the way in t'night."

For all he was in a hurry, rowing with short, choppy strokes, Willie's oars made very little sound. The blades hit the water cleanly and came out feathered just right for the next stroke. Lines of silver drops cascaded down them making tiny craters in the water, and the punt slipped along with a soft rushing whisper. As they came past the foot of the island, Donny could hear the slow *thunk-thunk* of an idling engine, and presently he made out the white cutwater and side of the big dragger as she slid toward them.

"Hi," Hod said briefly, as they clambered aboard. He kicked the gear lever ahead and swung the boat in a wide slow circle, long enough for Willie to straighten out the punt's painter and drop the anchor overboard. Then he opened the engine wide open and headed down the channel for the long, three-hour run to the fishing grounds off Hazlett's Rock.

"Calm's a clock, ain't it?" Willie said, easing himself to a seat on the gunnel beside Donny. "Don't know when I've seen a prettier night."

"Some breakfast'd be prettier," Hod said over his shoulder. "How about that?"

"Why, I d'no," said Willie. "You hungry?"

"I could eat a clunk of raw horse," said Hod cheerfully. "How about you?" He glanced at Donny.

Donny had been feeling a little uneasy about Hod. He didn't know him very well—not the way he felt he knew Willie. He'd seen Hod often around the fish-wharf, and had even admired in secret the width of his shoulders and his lean, rangy height. But Hod never had very much to say to people; most people felt he was pretty unsociable. Donny had been wondering what it would be like, aboard a boat with him for a whole day. But now he could see it was going to be all right.

"I sure could eat," he said, grinning.

"You can't have no horse," said Willie. "The horse is all for the skipper. You'n me'll have t' make do with fried ham." He started for the cabin. "Come on down and help me wog it up."

At the mention of ham, Donny felt the slow drool start along his tongue. He was beginning to remember Mis Mackay's dinner bucket that he'd come off without. He was also wishing he'd brought the sweater. The warmth of his run had cooled on him, and the big boat roaring down the channel was making her own penetrating wind in the frosty air. Willie was probably kidding about the ham, but he'd have something down there to eat, Donny thought, going down the companionway steps to the cabin.

"Hod's got it fixed up down here like a lady's buddwa," Willie said. "He pokes a couple wires down inside the engine and look what comes out." He clicked something, and the cabin was lighted up by a small electric bulb set in the ceiling. "Ain't that a myst'ry, though?"

"Gee," Donny said. "You got a stove down here. Bunks, too."

"Ayup. So's we can stay out on all night hauls, if we need to. Think you could build up a fire while I dig out some grub? Wood 'n kindlin over there in the locker."

The tiny camp stove was wired to blocks nailed on the top of a locker, its insulated pipe set out through a hole in the boat's deck. Donny put in paper and shavings and some pieces of lath and hunted in his pockets for a match. With satisfaction he heard the flames begin to crackle inside the firebox as he replaced the covers.

"We most always eat breakfast like this on the way out," Willie said. "Saves time. And darned if it don't taste better aboard the boat, too."

Willie finished filling an iron spider with thick slices of ham and set it on top of the stove. "Keep an eye on that, will ya, and don't let it burn? Better shed your coat, hadn't you? You'll be cold when you go on deck. She heats up down here, with the stove goin."

"Oh, my gorry, that smells good," Donny said. He unbuttoned his jacket and dropped it on the locker. He was warm now. The cabin was filling up with the rich smoke from the frying ham. Nothing had ever smelled so good, not even wild ducks roasted on the beach with Uncle My.

He tended the ham with absorption, afraid it would burn or cook too dry, turning it oftener than he needed to with the point of Willie's jackknife. He was relieved when it came out all right, pink in the middle and crisp brown around the edges.

"Guess we'll have to ship you steady as cook if you can fry eggs like you can ham," Willie said.

Hod and Willie liked their eggs fried hard, Donny learned, so he had his that way, too. He ate three and two big slices of ham, washed down with strong hot coffee sweetened with condensed milk. Everything tasted wonderful.

He and Willie ate first. Then they went back on deck to steer while Hod came down to have his breakfast in the warm cabin.

"I d'no b't you're goin to need a set of oilskins, ain't you?" Willie said, as they came out into the cold air again. "Mis Mackay, she ain't goin t' think much of it if you come home beglammed with bait. You take the wheel while I go down and see 'f the' ain't an extry set in the locker."

He did not wait for Donny to say whether he could steer the big boat. He just left the wheel and went below, taking it for granted that he could.

Donny braced up to the wheel, feeling its icy smoothness through his mittens that seemed to send a chill of excitement and apprehension down his back. Jeepers, he thought, what if I whang her onto a lobster buoy or a rock?

He peered tensely out past the boat's steady bow, beginning to rise and fall a little now in the smooth, offshore swell. For a moment it seemed to him that he couldn't see anything, that it was all a gray blur. He wouldn't know, he thought with a little clutch of fright, if they *were* going to hit anything. Then he realized that he could see better. The gray blur became a wide stretch of smooth water, shimmering a little under the moon, giving off a pale light that was almost lavender.

The way they were heading, there was no land. The white horizon came down to meet the water, blending with it until it looked as though, if you kept on going, you'd sail right off the water on to the sky. Yet if you didn't look right at it, more out of the corner of your eye, you could see the line where one stopped and the other began.

Jeepers, he thought, it's big.

For the first time he was conscious of the deep, steady drone of the engine and of the power that lay under his hand to direct and control. He moved the wheel a little and felt the boat swerve; looking back, he saw a delicate beautiful curve appear in the straight creamy moonlit wake that stretched back out of sight the way they had come.

"Here's your oilskins," said Willie's voice at his elbow. "Shove em on."

"Can I steer some more?"

"Be a favor to us if you would," Willie said. "The's a couple trawls left to bait, and I was wondering how we'd manage if you didn't know how to steer."

"You could tell me the course," Donny said, struggling into the oilskins. "Uncle My, he showed me how to read a compass. I never steered a boat by one, but—"

"Sou'sou'east," Willie said briefly. "Slide the cover off the binnacle, there, and le's see how you make it. Here—le' me roll up them sleeves so they won't be in your way."

The oilskins were too big for him by inches, and he looked, it occurred to Willie, a little like the two-eyed jack in a deck of cards, standing there, with the coat shoulders so much too wide for him and the moonlight giving him height and breadth, but no thickness.

Well, he'll be warm, anyway, Willie thought. Ain't nothin so warm's a suit of oil-clo'es.

With some jockeying and a few tries, Donny found the south-southeast bearing on the compass, lined it up with the snubby mooring post on the boat's bow and held it there. The wake, which had done some snaking around, straightened out and stayed straight.

"You say you never steered by a compass before?"

Donny jumped. He hadn't heard Hod come on deck.

"No." His voice started to go up a little, but he caught it before it broke. "Just Uncle My, he told me—"

"That's a good job then," the big fellow said. He turned away and he and Willie began to break out the trawls and the bait barrels. Working, they paid no further attention to Donny.

The moon sank in the west and turned red, leaving big quiet stars in a whitening sky. The light glistened on the wet planks of the platform, on the piles of silver herring dumped on the bait boards, on the absorbed faces of the men and the enchanted face of the boy. Presently, while the big boat thundered south-southeast, to the exact delicate mark of the compass bearing, the tip of the sun appeared on the deepened line of the horizon, like a small rim of a bright gold dish coming out of the water.

Hazlett's Rock was a rugged table-topped ledge, half an acre long, thrusting out of deep water twenty-five miles from the coast. It was, actually, the peak of a set of underwater ridges, the only one that showed above any tide. Its submerged sides fell sheerly into ninety fathoms—"bold water," the fishermen called it, when water lay so deep up against the land. Gulls nested on The Rock and a few shags, making the ledges white and sour with their dung; but no one ever landed on the lonely place or would want to, because of the steep shore and the fierce undertow.

"You can run in quite close if you want to." Hod had finished baiting on his tub of trawl and he came to stand by Donny's elbow, dragging on a cigarette. "The water makes off deep."

"How close?" The Rock was coming nearer fast. Donny was beginning to feel a little shaky.

"Well—" Hod glanced casually at the narrowing strip of water. "Keep her as she is. Nice, isn't it," he went on, "the way if you keep her true sou'sou'east, you hit The Rock right on the nose?"

"It's an awful good thing t' know in a fog-mull," Willie said, coming up behind them. "Hod, you sure can wipe my eye out baitin trawl."

They flashed by within twenty feet of the black rockweed-covered ledges and the creamy surge of the rote that boiled up on them. For a moment, above the sound of the engine, Donny could hear the purposeful swash and globber of the water.

Willie reached into the bait tub for a handful of herring and threw them high into the air. They fell, twisting and turning, their bright sides sparkling in the sun; and as they landed on the rocks, a cloud of white birds thundered up out of the crevices and fell on the fish. Briefly, on the ledges, there was a milling cartwheel of wild threshing wings, fierce fighting yellow-beaked heads borne up and disappearing. Then the herring were gone and the gulls flew up again, thousands of them in a great web, weaving and screaming over the boat.

Something spatted down and Willie made a dive for the shelter of the steering coop.

"Pete's sake," Hod said, grinning. "Don't you know better?"

Willie, leaning out warily, dipped a bucket overboard and sloshed salt water along the shoulder and sleeve of his oil-jacket.

"I spose so," he said, looking sheepish. "Only I kind of like to. Quite a sight, them birds. They don't pay ya back very grateful, though, do they?"

The underwater peaks known to the fishermen as The Ridges began a quarter of a mile or so outside The Rock. Near The Rock the water was called The Ninety-Fathom Deep, but it shoaled rapidly to thirty and twenty fathoms, in places to as little as ten.

If you knew where each ridge began and where it ended, it was possible to set trawls in the shallower water where most of the fish were. But if you miscalculated, or missed your marks, you sometimes flopped a trawl overboard into one of the Deeps, which meant a grueling haul to horse it up again, with, like as not, a parted ground-line and the loss of your gear.

Willie explained these things to Donny, taking the wheel while Hod threw over the first trawl-buoy with its fluttering, faded marker-flag.

Donny was glad to have Willie take the wheel. He wouldn't want the responsibility, seeing he didn't know his way around out here. Why, he'd be likely to steer her slap off over the edge of one of The Ridges and maybe make them lose a whole trawl! Even Willie, with all his experience, had to keep his eyes open and watch like a hawk.

The engine, barely ticking over, drove the boat ahead slowly. The ground-line of the trawl with its hundreds of baited hooks paid out steadily from the tub and disappeared astern. Hod guided it with deft rhythmic taps from a smooth tapered stick, lifting the loaded hooks over the gunnel and tossing them a little, so that they floated free and untangled away from the ground-line. For a moment they seemed to lie motionless on the water; then they sank slowly, the bait gleaming at first and growing dull as it went deeper into the water.

If you just looked at the top of the water, Donny thought, you wouldn't realize how deep it was. But that line, with the bait going deeper and deeper into the green, showed you how it really was.

The big swells, smooth as cream, lifted the boat without a ripple, passing under her soundlessly and letting her drop into their troughs with a smooth, sleepy, gliding motion. Donny thought for a while as the sun rose and made a strain against his eyes, and began to cook a rich fishy smell out of the bait, that he might be going to be seasick. But the feeling didn't get worse and after a while he forgot it.

They set nine tubs of trawl and then let the boat drift while they waited for the low-water-slack and had a mid-morning lunch. Then it was time to go back and haul the first trawl.

As they slid alongside the buoy and Hod gaffed it in, Donny felt a mounting excitement. Hod and Willie were excited, too, he could tell. The next few minutes would tell the tale.

If there were any fish on The Ridges today, the boat might go home with kidboards loaded down. Or the hooks might come up full of trash—sea-cucumbers and whore's eggs—or fouled up with something almost as worthless, like dogfish or skates.

"By gorry," Willie said suddenly, "I wouldn't swap my job, right now, for any other job you could name."

"I would." Hod grunted. He was hauling the trawl with wide sweeps of his big arms, his shoulders straining at the weight. "Go ahead and talk," he went on, grinning at Willie over his shoulder, "with me doing the work. You can haul the next one. Then you'll swap."

"Nup," Willie said. "Right now I feel like a harvester, a treasure-hunter *and* a gambler. Ain't I a cussed fool, though?" He leaned against the side of the coop, where he could watch the line coming aboard, and winked at Donny. "He feels the same way, only he wouldn't let on—not if he was t' ketch the solid-gold Old Man a the Sea, with eyes a diamonds."

"Right," Hod said. "Gambler, did you say, Willie? Have a look."

The first hooks were coming in, carrying nothing but some shreds of sea-flea chewed bait.

"H'm," said Willie, and said no more.

Looking down into the water, straining out over the side until Willie, afraid he would fall overboard, reached out and clutched the baggy seat of his oil-pants, Donny could see other bare hooks coming up in slow procession.

The entire trawl was empty, except for one lone skate, which Hod slatted off the hook so hard that its teeth, jawbone and all, came out and floated away, looking like somebody's set of uppers incongruously lost and bobbing around in the ocean.

"Too bad the' ain't no other way t' git one a them cussed things off a hook," Willie said thoughtfully.

"What would you do—ask him to spit it out?" Hod wasn't mad, only disappointed. He stowed the trawl under the stern by simply giving the tub a shove along the slippery platform with his foot. Actually, there wasn't any other way to get a skate off a trawl-hook.

The next trawl, which Willie hauled, was more of the same— empty hooks and sea-fleas—and the third one started out to be no different. Then, halfway up, the heavy ground-line took a sudden lunge into the sea. Hod tried to hold it, giving line slowly, and Willie, suddenly watchful, said in a low, excited voice, "Let him run, boy!"

He grabbed a bait-knife out of its leather sheath on the washboard, and began as fast as he could to cut the hooks off the trawl. Donny thought he had never seen hands move so quickly. But even with Hod paying out as little as he could, the line began to burn through his hands so fast that Willie couldn't catch the hooks. For a moment there was a flurry of flying line and gangions, broad shoulders and backs and slipping rubber boots, and Donny, huddled into a corner of the coop to be out of the way, couldn't see what was going on. Then Willie stepped back. The neat coil of trawl that had been in the tub was nearly all paid out again. Hod had an ample length of it in his hand, but it seemed to be slack in the water.

"He gone?" asked Willie tensely. "He didn't hook you, did he?"

Hod shook his head. "I'm almost scared to start hauling," he said. "I can't tell if he's there or not." He began to take in steadily on the line, and as it came aboard Willie methodically cut off its hooks. The line stayed slack for what seemed to be a long time. Then suddenly it straightened out and cut through the water with a *z-zing*.

"No, by God, he ain't gone!" Hod shouted. He braced back and held the line, this time not having to bother about the hooks. Slowly he horsed it in, now gaining, now losing line, but in the end gaining more than he lost.

"Want a spell?" Willie asked, after a time.

Hod started to say something, but at that moment the line decided it was going back to the bottom of the sea, and back to bottom it went, grinding toughly between his clenched fists.

"Gorry!" Willie said. "No wonder the' warn't no ground fish on The Ridges today, with that feller around. What'd you think 't is, Hod?"

"Haul's like a halibut," Hod said, panting. "If it's a shark, it's a jeasly big one." He took a breather, holding the line taut, and then began to haul again. This time it came up more easily, yielding itself in a series of hard jerks and rushes.

"He's drownin out some," Willie said. He picked up a stout-handled gaff and moved over to the gunnel beside Hod, peering anxiously down into the water. For a moment he stood watching. Then his whole body tensed up with excitement.

"By God, I can see him! It's a halibut bigger'n the top a Hazlett's Rock!" He went on talking, as if to himself, in a voice that was half whisper and half croon. Poising the gaff at the surface of the water, Willie said, "Easy, boy. E-e-easy, there. Let him run a little, haul up his head. Oh, you sonova, you great big beautiful sonova— Look out!"

Donny, unable to stand inaction any longer, slipped out of his corner and climbed to the roof of the coop. From there, lying on his stomach, he could look past Hod's shoulders and into the water. Deep down, swirling in the green-black light, he could see something that looked as big as the bottom of the ocean, now dark, now white, as it turned back and belly upward to the pull of the line.

"Dong him in," Willie crooned. "Git him up here just once where I can whang this gaft into his gills. Easy, there. E-e-easy. Dong him in!"

The flat monstrosity, feeling doom with the surface of the water, started down, and Hod lost twenty feet of line. He was breathing hard and the sweat was running down his face. He got the lost line back, felt it give a little. With a tremendous lash of bubbles and foam, the head of the halibut broke water.

"Put the gaft to him," croaked Hod, and Willie put the gaft to him, sinking it deep into the vulnerable soft gills. Together they heaved upward. The great gasping head appeared at the gunnel.

Creatures of different worlds, the three looked wildly into one another's eyes; then Hod freed a hand from the line, picked up a short heavy hardwood club that lay on the gunnel, hauled off and let the halibut have it, twice, in the middle of his thick triangular head. The big fish stiffened and momentarily ceased his lashing. In that interval, the men hauled the rest of him in over the side. Hod struck him again as the fins began to quiver and the tail, as large as a small table-top, started to drum on the boards of the platform.

"Jeepers!" Donny said, staring with awe at the dead fish. "Look at his head. It wouldn't go into a bucket!"

"Go nigh a couple of hundred pounds, I guess." Hod sat down, exhausted, and pulled the cotton gloves off his blistered and bloody hands. "I guess you and Don'll have to haul the next few tubs, Willie. I'm pooped."

"How'll you swap now, Hod?" Willie said slyly, "say with some fat man's got a nice shiny office desk t' set to?"

Hod grinned. "Haul your trawls, you old bait-bucket," he said affectionately. "Or it'll be midnight before we get home."

Donny shared the pride and the excitement when the boat pulled up to the fish-wharf in the afternoon, and the other fishermen gathered around, bug-eyed, to see the big halibut.

There was no hint of condescension in their comments as they watched Nick Driver, the boss of the wharf, and a couple of his men haul the fish out of the dragger with a block and tackle.

"How'n hell did you manage t' land him?" Bill Pray said to Hod.

"Hauled him up and gafted him in," Hod said, briefly.

"Ayeh, but—wan't it a job?"

"Ayeh." Hod went back down the fish-wharf ladder and aboard his boat. The men, gathered around, wanted him to talk about it, he knew. But if he did, it would be only a matter of minutes before somebody made some kind of a sideways crack about him and Willie. That is, he thought probably someone would. It didn't bother him, but darned if he wanted to have to listen to it.

"My God," Bill Pray said, staring after him. "If I'd caught a halibut like that, they could hear me braggin clear over to Bellport. Hell, he ain't human."

"Hangin around with that Portygee, he's probly forgut how to talk English," Sam Grant said, winking at Bill. "Come on, le's go in and watch Nick put that damn thing on the scales."

"Biggest one we've had here in ten years," Nick Driver said, watching the arm of his weighing scales teeter to a balance. "Two hundred 'n fifteen pounds. Jeesiz, Willie, that's a good day's haul. Figger that out at—um—cents a pound, plus twenty-four hundred hake—" He scratched busily on a piece of paper with a pencil— "Hun'd 'n thirteen dollars. Come in the office, I'll give you the cash."

Willie came out of the office counting the money, and grinned at Donny, spreading the fat roll like a fan. "You sure ain't no Jonah, Don. Guess you'll have to come along again, bring us luck, hah? Here's yours." He held out a ten-dollar bill.

"Oh, gee," Donny said, awestruck. "I never earnt that much. I had too good a time. I don't—"

"Take it," Willie said. "You earnt it fair, all the work you done for us. How bout next Sat'd'y, if it's weather, and Mis Mackay can spare ya?"

"Oh, sure," Donny said. His face broke out into a wide grin and he took the money, folding it carefully into his pocket.

He ran most of the way home, but at the Mackay driveway he slowed to a dawdle. He thought suddenly of how swell it would be if he could have stayed with Hod and Willie—gone home with them to their house, kept on with the companionship that wasn't talk, but just having a good time because somebody you liked was there.

Maybe he'd go down later on, if he wasn't too tired, and tell Artie Osgood about the halibut and the way Hod caught it. He wouldn't tell Mis Mackay. Going in through the kitchen door, he realized that he was so tired he could hardly stand up. She'd be at him in a minute about forgetting the sweater and the dinner bucket, and there were all those chores to do before night.

She could ask him until she was blue in the face, but as long as he lived he'd never tell her one word about that halibut.

PART

II

ANN FREEMAN heard her mother call dinner and answered
absently. She went on typing for a few moments longer. The
scene she was working on had tried hard to crystallize all morning;
now she was beginning to see it dimly, and she wanted to get down
on paper at least enough outline so that the morning's work
wouldn't be lost if she stopped now.

She had been home nearly two weeks, doing her best to settle
down to the business of writing a book. The work had not been
going well; but she hoped it might, as soon as she got accustomed
to the sounds of a lively family racketing through the house and
to her father's resentment. Now that he had started to cut his
winter's supply of firewood, he seemed to have stopped, at least
temporarily, his worrying about the amount she burned up in the
woodshed chamber. She almost wished he'd go back to it; for what
bothered him lately was the fact that she'd come home without
either being married or having a steady job.

To him, these two things represented the world's achievement.
Without marriage or regular money coming in, a woman was wast-
ing her time.

Ann was typing her last few sentences when she heard his voice
bellowing up the back stairs.

"*Ann!* Your mother hollered *dinner!*"

"Okay," she answered. "Coming."

She scrabbled her papers hastily together, evening their edges on the table-top, and weighted them down with the corner of her portable typewriter.

It would be nice if she could wait to eat till she felt like it. She certainly wasn't hungry now, with that scene bubbling around inside of her. But one of her father's arguments of a lifetime had been that when a meal was called the entire family ought to drop everything and be on hand to eat it.

Coming into the kitchen, she saw that dinner wasn't quite ready, that she could have taken a little more time. Her mother was only beginning to dish up the vegetables from the kettles on the stove.

Polly, the eleven-year-old, was in the corner fiddling with the radio, and Sam, her brother, fifteen, was curled up on the wood-box with a comic-book. Her father, however, was already in his place at the table.

"It's five minutes past *twelve*," he announced, glowering at the ample kitchen clock on the shelf over the stove.

"That clock's ten minutes fast," Polly said. She had the radio turned to some fast dance music and was practicing a step by her-self in the corner.

"That's right," said Myra, dumping a kettle of carrots into a colander to drain. Her red face emerged momentarily from the cloud of steam. "And you needn't split a guzzet, Paris, till dinner's on the table."

Without a word Paris pulled out his big flat gold watch. Finding it confirmed what Polly said, he stared at the clock as if by looking at it he could set it back ten minutes. "What's the idea havin the clock fast?" he demanded.

"Sam and I set it ahead." Polly danced across the room and slid into her place at the table. "It makes *all* the difference."

"What for Godsake about?"

"Helps us to get up on time," said Sam, emerging from his seat on the woodbox. "We like it that way."

"Yes," said Polly. "We always know we have ten extra minutes. It helps an awful lot, especially getting up mornings."

Paris gave a moan of disgust. He pushed back his chair with a long scrape and started for the clock.

"Don't set it back now, for he'm's sake!" shrieked Myra, slipping the bowl of carrots on to the table. "You'll make it strike wrong, and somebody'll have t' strike it clear around the dial."

Paris opened the glass door of the clock and, referring to his watch, set the hands at two minutes to twelve.

"Now don't any of you let me hear any more of this damn foolishness about settin the clock ahead," he announced, coming back to the table. "Kiddin yourselves that you've gut ten minutes more time than there is!"

He picked up his carving knife and began whacking thick slices off the roast. "Just like this blasted daylight savin time we git in the summer. You don't think you have t' git up early or git somewhere till an hour later than you're sposed to. All you got t' do is frig with the clock!"

"Well, pass the plates so's I can help the vegetables," Myra said. "Don't just set there cuttin off meat."

"That clock stays *right*. See?"

As if to put a period to the announcement, the clock resoundingly struck one.

"But now you'll be an hour ahead of yourself all day," said Ann. She knew she ought to keep still, but she couldn't resist.

Paris gave her a black look, but at that moment the telephone in the sitting room rang, and he stopped to listen. It was the Freeman ring, two long and three short.

"Blast it all, when do they think a man eats his dinner? I never set down to eat in my life without I hat t' git up to answer that cussid thing!" Paris stalked into the other room, and his family heaved a collective sigh.

"There, now, somebody's gut t' take the time to strike that clock around," Myra said resignedly. "Why didn't you kids keep still? If you hatn't told him what you done it for, he'd have let it alone."

"Yes, Sam," chimed in Polly. "What did you have to tell him for?"

"You could ha' kept your own trap shut," said Sam, shrugging. "You was the one 't told him first."

Paris came back full of the telephone call. "You been buyin firewood of Hod Stilwell?" he demanded of Ann.

"Why, no," said Ann, puzzled.

"Hunh, I *told* Sam Grant he was crazy. He said he had two cords a stove lengths on his truck for you and where did I want it put. Seems he picked it up down on Spoonhandle this mornin. Said Hod Stilwell boated it across from the island and hired him to bring it up here to you."

"Oh," Ann said faintly. If Hod had done that, he must have meant the wood as a gift. Someone—probably her mother when he had brought up the suitcases—must have told him what a fuss Paris was making about her heating the woodshed chamber.

It occurred to her suddenly that the gift, if that's what it was, was one of the nicest she had ever had—a subtle one, too, reminding her of the talk in Bellport about taking chances, and letting her know that Hod remembered it and was backing her up with encouragement and sympathy.

Oh, darn dad, she thought. Aloud she said, "What did you tell Sam?"

"Well, he asked to talk to you, but I said *I* hatn't ordered no wood," said Paris importantly. "I told him what anybody else would have, to take his load back to Hod and tell him what he could do with it. Them Stilwell boys, both of em's nutty as a fruit-cake, and by gorry, Ann, I don't want t' hear tell a your havin anything t' do with either one of em."

"Seems to me you might let me answer my own phone calls," Ann said.

"*Your* phone calls!" Paris put back his head and stared at her. "Who in hell are you, the star boarder?" He sawed angrily with his carving knife at a tough piece of gristle and plunked a thick chunk of meat on to a plate.

"Oh, never mind. Skip it," muttered Ann. Oh, dear, she

thought, why did I bother to say anything? "That's too much meat, if it's for me," she went on. "I'm not very hungry."

"For the love of God, eat what's set in front of you." Paris made no move to mitigate the helping of meat, but thrust the plate out at Myra for vegetables. "It seems to me when your mother and Polly do all the work and you set up there like a lady waitin for *phone calls*, the least you could do would be to eat what's cooked for you."

He poked a goodly forkful of meat and potatoes into his mouth and sat chewing, his face set in lines of righteous melancholy.

Paris Freeman was a big man, loose-hung and so spare of frame that his clothes, no matter how much Myra took them in to fit, hung on him in wrinkles. The lines of his face and body all seemed to tend downward—drooping auburn mustache, creases at the corners of his eyes and mouth, even the folds of red sunburned skin on the sides of his neck. At fifty, Paris was already stoop-shouldered. When he walked, the weight of his long lean arms seemed to pull his body forward, as if he were reaching toward the ground.

It had been years since any member of his family had thought him lovable or attractive. Sam disliked him, and even Polly, whom in his rough, cross-grained way, he adored, privately thought him an interfering old bore. Myra, if anyone had asked her whether she loved him, would have been a little shocked at such a question—a woman was supposed to love her husband, wasn't she? Actually, Paris was only a habit. His entire family put up with him because they had to.

His trouble was that the world owed him a debt that it showed no sign of paying. He had been brought up to believe that if a man worked hard, paid his bills and provided for his family, sometime, some day, he would have his reward. There was no doubt in Paris's mind as to what the reward would be—money enough to quit working, sit back and enjoy himself. He had never stopped to think how this money would materialize in the hands of a lobster-fisherman who, in all his life, had barely made enough, week by week, to keep his family going. As a young man, his philosophy had been simple. At a certain time of life, the money would be there and he would have a comfortable, mellow, long-lasting old age.

Now, at fifty, Paris's mind was something like that of a child who has been promised and not given a piece of candy. Here he was, an honest deserving man—worked hard all his life with nothing to show for it. It was the fault of the times, of the cussed rich, of the damned Democrats and of his family like a weight around his neck. Growing old, Paris caught glimpses of reality as it is for the poor of the world and did not like what he saw. Life was a sell. The schoolbooks had lied to him, the minister in church had lied, and all the folks at home older than he was when he was a boy. He had opened the door to the world expecting to see sugar angels and there was only the boogie-man.

He drove his children toward success to make up for his own failure, demanding that they be the best-behaved and the smartest children in the school. Yet when one of them, Ann, showed signs of being about to make an impression in the world, resentment ate at him like acid. A woman ought to marry and make a home; she ought not to come around all the time showing her own father what he had failed to make of his life.

A good man, without his just deserts, whom nobody appreciated, Paris let himself go stoop-shouldered and reached for the ground.

"You'd think good food growed on bushes, the way you turn up your nose at it," he went on fretfully. "By God, if you hat to git up before daylight these cold mornins and haul a hundred traps with the ice freezin on your mittens, you'd appreciate how the money's made that buys a dinner like this."

His family, who had heard this speech before and did not deny the truth of it, went on eating in silence with the exception of Sam. Sam was experimental, with a tendency developed beyond his judgment for seeing how close he could come to edges without tumbling over. He also had a fifteen-year-old's keen sense of justice.

"Ann bought this roast," he said, his eyes dancing.

"Hah?" His father turned on him a pair of watery eyes. "Well, for cripes sake, one roast! The' ain't rocks enough on the beach t' count the number a roasts *I've* bought, but when somebody else buys one, I have t' hev my nose rubbed in it. You clean out that plate, young man!"

"Okay, okay," said Sam hastily. "I'm eatin."

"And this afternoon I want t' see you down in the wood lot with your ax, not rantin round the Bellport hall with them hoodlums."

Sam was a star forward on the Bellport High School basketball team. Seeing today was Saturday, with a big game coming up the following week, the team was planning to put in the afternoon perfecting their plays. Sam cast a quick look of alarm at his mother. Myra shook her head reassuringly; but there was warning, too, in her glance, not to carry the argument further.

"If your sister's goin t' burn up all the wood in the shed with a fire we don't need, so that the neighbors have t' send us in charity wood, some of us have gut t' give up some spare time to cut some, I guess." Hod Stilwell's wood had brought back the old grievance into Paris's mind. He glanced reproachfully at Ann and was infuriated to see that she hadn't even heard him. If she had, she gave no sign of it. Like most ineffectual tyrants, nothing made him so mad as disinterest in what he had to say.

"Well, answer me!" he bellowed suddenly. "Or can't you speak when you're spoken to?"

Ann jumped. She had been thinking that after dinner she would have to go down and see Hod and explain what had happened about the wood. She'd been trying to make herself believe she was annoyed at losing an afternoon's work. But taking a walk down the Spoonhandle seemed a very pleasant prospect for the afternoon. While she had been woolgathering, she saw, her father had got himself roaring mad about something. "What?" she asked.

"You listen t' me when I talk, young lady! If you're comin home here and turn the whole house upside-down without doin a lick a work, the least you could do is to have the manners t' listen to what's said t' you. Or hev you gut too big-feelin to care?"

"I'm sorry, pa," she said, trying to stem the tide. "I guess I was absent-minded. I try to leave my work upstairs, but sometimes it's hard to. You're right, it's rotten manners. What did you say?"

"Work!" spluttered Paris. "Work, you call it! In my day, work for a woman was washin dishes and scrubbin floors. You'd be a damn sight better off if you done some of it around here, too!"

"Look, pa," Ann said patiently. "We had that all out awhile ago, didn't we? I pay you board and help buy the food, and don't help out with the work because I need all my time. I thought you and ma said that was all right with you."

"Oh, God!" Paris groaned with disgust. "Why don't you get married, the way other girls do?"

Now we've got that again, Ann thought. Oh, well. Aloud, she said, smiling, "I can't just go out and ask some man to marry me, can I?"

"What's the matter—somethin wrong with you?"

"I shouldn't be surprised." It was useless to argue with him. She'd only get mad and he was too far gone now to care what he said. He was at the point where he was casting about in his mind for ugly things to say.

"Well, I'll be goddamed if I wouldn't be ashamed t' admit it," he bawled. "If you ain't no good, you might's well go jump off the wharf."

"Paris, you stop right there!" said Myra. Her face was red with embarrassment. "Before the children, shame on you!"

Paris paid no attention, but he did change the subject. "Work, you call it, and what is it? Settin up there thinkin of nasty words t' write down?"

Ann felt the little cold lumpy sensation in her chest that meant she was going to get mad. They had been through this before too, when her father had read her first book. He had been inflamed over some words she had used in an attempt to do what she hoped would be an honest piece of reporting. They had obscured everything else in his mind. He must be, she had thought, at least a little proud of the book because it was hers, yet in speaking of it he had never yet mentioned anything but that a daughter of his had written down the word "goddamn" for all the world to see.

"Oh, why don't you let people alone?" she said. "I don't mix into your business. As for nasty words, if you'll think back you'll find that you've used some nastier ones in the last few minutes, and a nastier idea, too, than I ever put into a book. If you want me to go somewhere else to live, I will, but while I'm here you've got to let me handle my own business."

Paris pushed back his chair and rose to his feet. For a moment he stood looking at her, in an offended, lofty silence, intended to reproach and shame. "That's a fine way for a girl to talk to her father," he said.

"You said much worse to me before I ever opened my mouth," Ann pointed out. "And I'm just as closely related to you as you are to me."

He turned and stalked out of the room, slamming the door. The slam made his exit, intended to be dignified, seem only peevish. In a moment, they saw him go past the window, headed for the wood lot, his ax and bucksaw over his shoulder.

His feelings, Ann knew, were really hurt, as they always were when any member of his family stood up to him. He would get mad and say what he liked—and he had a kind of genius for bearing down on the sensitive places—but if anyone talked back to him he couldn't bear it and would have it over and over in his mind for days.

"Oh, dear," Ann said.

Polly, who had been listening to the row with wide-eyed enthusiasm, suddenly decided to duff in and see if she couldn't make it last just a minute longer. It was too bad to have such a lovely fight over so soon.

"You hadn't ought to talk that way to papa," she began unctuously; "now he won't have a good time the whole rest of the day."

"And neither will anyone else," said Ann, between her teeth. "Polly, don't be a smug little brat."

"Why!" Polly's large brown eyes puddled up. "Mamma, she swore at me!"

" 'Brat' ain't swearin," said Myra decisively. "You stop it, Polly, I know you. Hustle them dishes off the table now."

"I've *got* to practice today, ma," Sam said, hauling his windbreaker over his head. He had lately taken a freak of getting into it without unzipping it. "The game's next Friday night."

"Oh, my land!" Myra put both hands to her temples, one on either side. "Well, kite along then, before he remembers what he told you and comes along back here. I'll fix it with him if I can, but if I can't you may have t' take a lickin, Sam."

"Okay." With sublime faith in her as a fixer, he went leaping toward the door. From the entry, out of his mother's sight, he looked back at Ann, clasped both hands over his head and shook them heartily.

Something about the gesture made her want to put her head down on the table and cry. She did like Sam; he was her favorite part of the family, and sometimes she didn't know what she would have done without him. Yet he didn't actually care that his father was a weak and disappointed old man—perhaps he didn't see it, his natural sympathy overlaid by the way his father treated him. You couldn't blame Sam; but about most other things he was intelligent and kind, and he had a good deal of sensitive insight when it came to people's feelings. It was only that his reaction was a kind of symbol of the way they all felt about Paris.

"Maybe I'd better do a lick of work for once and help you and Polly with the dishes," she said, getting up from the table dispiritedly.

"No, you don't!" Myra said quickly. "I don't care what your pa says, Ann, I'm perfectly satisfied with the way we fixed it. You don't cause no extry work, and that little bit a money comin in every week's a godsend. He ought t' have a talkin to for some of the things he said to you. That ain't no way for a man to speak to his daughter, and she as pretty a girl as you are, Ann. I expect t' tell him so, too."

"Oh, you'd better leave him alone, ma. He's hurt enough as it is."

"Well, he ought t' be. Polly and I'll do these dishes, now. Three of us'd only be in the way. Kite along out of here. If I was you, I'd go and hunt up Hod Stilwell. You know, I think he meant that wood as a present for you, Ann."

"I expect he did. That's what I'll do, I think."

*

Out in the wood lot, Paris morosely hacked away at a stubborn tree.

A man could git t' be fifty years old, he told himself, and not hev one damn thing to show for it except a pack of ungrateful kids, who et him out a house 'n home; and then when he tried to tell them a few things for their own good, they come right back at him with a mouthful of sarse.

Times had changed some, he thought, feeling the tree give a little under his ax, what with the Democrats in office forever and no chance now for a good man to rise to the top, and kids runnin their parents into the ground. His own father, if a kid of his had talked like that t' him, would of taken a stick to her.

And that's what I ought t' done, learn her that I'm the one that wears the pants in my own house, even if she thinks she can. I ought t' left marks on that bottom a hers that'd put it right back into a dress, where it b'longs.

Yet he could never touch her, he knew, with a stick or anything else. Not now. The world away from him had put a covering over her, sealing her away from his authority, his protection and his understanding.

Lonely, and full of the corrosion of his thoughts, Paris gathered up his ax and saw and stood back while the tree lifted from its stump with a satisfactory crunching and splintering sound, and toppled to the ground.

Needs a damn good lickin, he thought, helplessly harking back to the cure-all for the parents of his generation. By God, she'll git it, too!

*

The afternoon, from a gray lowering morning, had turned out sunny and warm. Walking through East Village toward the Spoonhandle, Ann first threw back her leather coat, finally took it off and carried it over her arm.

She had not been down in East Village since her return home, and she saw with a sense of surprise and shock that it had changed since she had gone away. Not the spruce woods and the pastures—they were as she remembered them, the ragged outline of the trees following the humped contours of the ground, yet somehow making a pattern finished and neat; the red granite ledges thrusting out between patches of nibbled turf like tough backbones from under the land. It was the hayfields and the houses that were different. The long grass had been left uncut, bleached a clear silvery tan by sun and frost; gables peeled paint, roofs spilled shingles. In the old days, East Village had been as immaculate as snowy paint and taut shingles could make it. And each year the hay had been cut and stored under barn roofs.

Hard times were a long while getting to an out-of-the-way, almost self-sufficient place like East Village; but once they got there, they stayed. It looked as if everybody at once had just decided to let things slide.

Myron Osgood's house needed new clapboards. The back of the building he used for his store was gray and scaly from the weather. Myron, she remembered, had long ago given up farming and fishing to try a grocery and gas station. He couldn't have done very well, from the looks of things. Nick Driver, too, no longer worked his land. Nick had gone into the lobster-buying game; his buildings looked rickety and down-at-the-heel. The Mackay place still was neat, but some upstairs blinds were loose and the hayfields that had been old Bob Mackay's pride and joy were choked with long grass and new-growth alders. Bob, though, was dead and his sons gone to the city. Very likely Mary Mackay, living there alone, couldn't handle the place by herself.

As Ann passed the Mackay house, she saw a boy, a skinny tall one, come out of the barn, bent over and running stealthily, as if he wanted to get past the kitchen windows without being seen. Out of range of them, he came into the road with a flying leap, straightened up and skidded to a stop before he plowed into Ann.

"Hi," she said, dodging a little. "You're in a hurry, I guess."

He looked like a nice kid who'd been up to something, a smudge of dust across the freckles on his nose, the sweat from his run starting out on his forehead. Ann had often seen Sam in just such a state; but Sam's reaction was usually a shrug and a grin. This kid's furious inimical glare startled her. He hesitated only an instant, then took to his heels and vanished in the thick bushes on the other side of the road.

My hat! Ann thought. What could he have been up to, I wonder?

Mary Mackay's front door opened and shut with a firm click, and Mary herself in shawl and rubbers came down the driveway.

"Hello," she said. "Oh, it's Ann Freeman. I heard you was home. Did that young limb of Satan come out this way?"

"Who?" Ann asked. "There was a kid—"

"That's him," said Mary grimly. "Which way did he go?"

"Why, I—I didn't notice. Up the road, I guess."

She was astonished at what seemed to be the change in Mary Mackay. The Mary she remembered had been a kind motherly soul, with a firm, tolerant hand over her turbulent brood. About this woman, there was something implacable, and to Ann, accustomed to the sparkling misdeeds of Sam, it came as a shock that a grown woman could be so icily and deeply angry at a boy.

"Whose boy is it, Mary?" she asked. "I don't seem to place him. Has he been pestering you?"

"He's that Mitchell boy I took to board for the State," Mary said, her lips tight. "He'd done nothing but pester me ever since the day he come."

"Boys that age are little hellions," Ann said sympathetically. "Sam drives us crazy sometimes."

"Crazy!" Mary said. "Sometimes I think that's just what I'll be."

It was helping her, Ann saw, to air the grievance, so she said nothing and listened.

"I told him he could take a job down to Willie Stilwell's," Mary went on, "if he didn't soldier on his chores for me. What does he do but spend every spare minute he's got down on that island. He never has time to do *nothin* for me, not even his reg'lar chores. Last Sat'd'y, he went out fishin with Willie, and this week he planned t' go again. Only I warned him Wednesd'y that he couldn't go if he didn't do his work, and he never. So early this mornin, I up 'n told him that he couldn't go today. He started to put the sarse t' me. If the's one thing I never could stand from a kid, it's sarse."

"I don't blame you much," Ann said.

"I grabbed him right by the collar and walked him up into the woodshed chamber and locked the door. I guess I couldn't of done it," Mary went on, "without me bein so mad and him so surprised. I told him he could stay there till he made up his mind to mind me. He's that stubborn, I never heard a thing out of him all the forenoon. Then what does he do, just now, but climb out the shed window and shin down the dreen-pipe. I see him go by the winder, all hutched over, and I guess, if I could of gut my hands on him, I'd of shook the daylights out of him." Mary pulled herself up short. "There!" she said, looking a little sheepish. "I swore I wouldn't git mad at him again, but I guess I can't help it."

"It does anyone good to get mad once in a while."

Mary nodded doubtfully. She felt better, Ann saw. "Maybe so, but not if you're mad three-quarters of the time. I was goin t' put out after him, but I swear, I'm weak's a kitten. I ain't seen you for a long time, Ann, and all I do is stand and blow off my troubles. Come int' the house and set awhile, won't you?"

"Well, I will sometime," Ann said, smiling. "I was going down the Spoonhandle to see Hod Stilwell, but if he and Willie have gone out today, I might as well go back home and do some work."

Mary gave her a surprised look. "Oh," she said. "I guess they never went out, for some reason. Their boat's to the moorin. I see it a few minutes ago, from my upstairs window."

Her voice sounded a little distant, and Ann was puzzled for a moment. Then she saw the light.

"Well, I'll go on down then. I have to see Hod about getting some firewood. I'm running an extra fire up home, and I hate to ask pa to cut the wood for it. He's got enough on his hands, as it is."

Mary's face cleared at once.

That had been it, Ann thought, with an inner chuckle that still wasn't quite amusement. I've been away too long. I'll have to watch my step.

For a single woman to go hunting up a single man, unless she had a good solid business reason, was still questionable behavior here at the island. A social reason wouldn't do.

"Good-by, Mary," she said. "I will drop in, sometime soon, though."

"You do that," Mary said. "I might's well go back and wait for that little limb to come home. I've made up my mind I'm goin t' take a good strong stand with him. He'll mind me, or he'll go back where he come from!"

The scamp, Ann thought, plodding thoughtfully down along the Spoonhandle road. He's got her so wrought up she's about ready to fly.

She was sorry for Mary, yet her real sympathy kept swinging perversely in the opposite direction. The Mitchell boy didn't look like a mean kid. As a matter of fact, he looked like a pretty decent, intelligent one. He had looked, Ann thought, coming out into Willie's clearing above the bar, more desperate than anything else.

In the half-mud, half-ice of the clearing, she could see the tire-marks of a truck which she guessed to be Sam Grant's, and on the bank Hod's two cords of wood had been dumped in an uneven windrow. Sam, it seemed, hadn't bothered to unload it in a pile. He had simply tilted his dump-truck and driven off, letting the wood trail out behind.

Oh, damn! Ann muttered. If it had been Pete's wood, Sam would probably have taken it off the truck stick by stick and tiered it up with his hands. Hod wasn't anybody, so why bother?

Willie's buildings, she saw, looking across the channel, had about them none of the slack discouragement that marked the other houses in East Village. Neat in their white paint, the weathered shingles tight on the roofs, house and barn and sheds stood securely and at home against the water and the trees. It was as if they belonged steadfastly to the land they were built on, and looking at them Ann felt a little clutch at her heart.

Since coming home, she had been wondering with growing uneasiness why on earth she had come; why she could have been such a fool as to believe that, having been so long away, growing up so different from her people, she could ever find common ground with them again. She was aware of their shyness and their modesty —their reticence with outsiders was more than half made up of the fear that they might not say or do the proper thing; that they might, in some way, let themselves be vulnerable. Yet she could not remember when she had lived among them that she had looked upon everybody outside her own townspeople with contempt—a contempt that seemed born of envy and all mixed up with it.

Six years—a century. It was hard to remember feelings she had had then, except the fierce longing to get away. But in the city, sometimes, the longing had been almost as fierce to come back. Six years had softened the bleak outlines of the stubborn land and people, so that when she finally had come, she was still homesick, finding the reality and not the dream.

Now, looking at Willie's island, she seemed to see for a moment, dimly, something of the harmony, the quietude, she told herself she remembered.

As she watched, Willie himself in his old hat and faded dungarees came out of the barn and down the path to the water. "You want to come over?" he called.

"Why, yes," Ann called back. "I guess I do."

She watched him as he pushed the light boat into the water, and rowed it stern-first across the channel. He was older than she remembered him, a tall, quiet man, thin almost to gauntness, straight-shouldered and powerful. His face was leather-brown, unlined except for two deep creases between the lean flat cheeks and the thin, slightly flaring nostrils. As the punt beached and he jumped out lightly on the pebbles, she saw that he moved easily and gracefully, as if the muscles flowed without effort under his skin.

"Willie Stilwell," she said, holding out her hand, "you look more like a red Injun than I remembered."

Willie grinned. "I am, part of one," he said. "Or so they always told me. But you don't remember me."

"Of course I do. You pulled me out of the mud-flats the year I was ten."

"That's right. I did. A mess you was, too. I never did find out whether your ma tanned you for it."

"She didn't, but pa did. He said no little lady would care whether there were eels under the rockweed or not."

"You found out, though," Willie said. "I see you a day or so afterwards, not ten feet from the place you mired down before, turnin over rockweed faster'n a blue her'n." He held the punt while she stepped in. "Only that time you was barefooted, not in a pair of rubber boots four times too big for you."

Ann laughed. "It was those boots that got me," she said. "Every time I lifted a foot, the mud sucked them off and I kept thinking what would happen if I lost pa's boots."

"That blue clay's worse'n flypaper," Willie said, dipping his oars. "You step in a soft patch of it, you're lucky it don't suck your feet off, let alone your boots. Hod's taken a load of traps off aboard the boat," he went on companionably. "He'll be right ashore."

There was no suggestion in Willie's voice of the half-ribald, half-self-conscious kidding, with which any other island man would have told her where Hod was. Willie just said, simply and directly, what he guessed she wanted to know. She decided she liked Willie a lot.

"We didn't go out today," Willie said. "Hod hated to miss a good chance, the weather'll break most any time now, but I had a shipment of hens and rabbits come, and we had to go over to Bellport this mornin to git em. I was just takin em out of the crates and puttin em in the henpen, when I see you over there on the shore."

He slid the punt neatly alongside a shelving rock on the shore of the island and got out, holding out his hand to help her make the step ashore.

The narrow path from the landing up to the house was worn down and sunken below the grass roots, its bare dirt smooth as a dark metal. Willie went ahead of her along it and turned off toward the barn. "I guess I better keep right on," he said. "Them critters been nailed up in them crates quite a while."

"Oh, sure. Don't let me bother you."

Willie looked back at her and grinned. "Wouldn't let nobody do that," he said. "Come on, too, if you want to."

Ann followed him into the barn. An ancient, scrawny hen, who seemed to be pacing the barn floor, said "Cra-a-w," ill-naturedly, and flounced past her with bristling feathers.

Willie chuckled. "That's Bertha," he said.

"She seems a little annoyed," said Ann.

The hen had stopped just outside the barn door, and was regarding her rigidly, with a malevolent bright eye.

"She don't like company. And I guess she don't know quite what t' make a these fellers, here. I d'no's I do, either."

Five big crates had been set in a row in the middle of the barn floor. From four of them came emotional clucking sounds, and white tail feathers and yellow bills replaced each other with feverish haste in the slatted openings. The fifth crate had a screened front, behind which three fat white rabbits sat and looked out with placid big pink eyes.

"I don't worry about them fellers," Willie said, jerking his head toward them. "But them hens been in there bout long enough."

He picked up a claw hammer with which he had apparently been working and began prying at the cover of one of the crates. The clucking intensified to a variety of squawks. The movement inside the crate became a white-feathered surge.

"I don't think much of the way they act," Willie said dubiously. "Seem awful nervous for hens."

The claw of the hammer caught and the cover came up slowly, all in one piece, with a loud screeching of nails. As it moved, the interior of the crate seemed to explode in Willie's face. Cackling and flapping, the pullets rose, as one, into the air, and dispersed. Some flopped out of sight into the cow's crib, others into the darkness of the haymow. But most of them went like bullets past Ann's head and out through the open barn door. One passed so close that she felt the slap of a sinewy wing against her cheek.

Peering after them she saw the flock rise into the air and come to roost in a yellow birch tree a hundred yards or so down the shore. Bertha, from where she stood on the barn doorstep, suddenly gave a hysterical squawk and fled out of sight into Willie's syringa bush.

"Godsake," Willie said. "I never see hens fly like that before. Did you?"

Hod, who had come past the corner of the barn just in time to duck, stood up and stared mystified at the door. "Jesus Christ, Willie," he said. "What was that?"

Still clinging a little drop-jawed to his hammer, Willie began to laugh soundlessly. "Sent me a lot of goddam pa'tridges, I guess," he said. "They even put Bertha on the run. Ann Freeman's here, Hod."

"Oh," Hod said. He stiffened perceptibly. "That so?"

Ann, dabbing at the helpless tears on her cheeks, couldn't stop laughing. She had to, she knew; Hod was probably mad about the wood, and having her see him dodge a stream of psychotic hens

quite likely hadn't helped much. "H-hi, Hod," she said, as soon
as she could speak.

"Hi," Hod said distantly. "What you doing down here?"

He sounded ungracious and hurt and she didn't blame him.

"I came down to explain about the wood," she said quickly, "and
to thank you for sending it. Pa got to the telephone before anybody
else—he always does, you know—and he told Sam Grant to bring
it back. You know how pa is. I'm sorry, Hod," she went on, seeing
his face begin to clear. "I could have wrung pa's neck and very
nearly did."

"So that's how it was," Hod said. In spite of himself, his breath
let go in a long-drawn sigh of relief. For an hour or so, ever since
he had seen Sam Grant over on the other bank dumping out his
wood, Hod had been nursing humiliation, in addition to feeling
like the fool of the world. He told himself he didn't care a hang
what was said in the village; but something in him had cringed at
the idea that people would be laughing, now, and having it over—
how he had sent Ann Freeman the silly gift of two cords of wood
and she had walked it right back to him. Sam Grant and Myron
Osgood's boy, Artie, who had been with him on the truck, would
see to it that everybody heard the yarn, with embellishments.

Worse than that had been the conviction that she hadn't under-
stood, perhaps didn't want to understand, why he'd done it. Look-
ing now at her clear candid eyes, friendly and full of approval for
him, his spirit soared upward. Of course she'd understood, and
what was more, she'd liked it.

"I don't know what I'm going to do with wood, though, until
pa cools off," she was saying. "Can I leave it there on the bank,
Hod, until I either get around him or find a place to work where
he can't fuss if I have it delivered?"

"Sure," Hod said. "Just let me know when you want it."

Willie, from the back of the barn where he was optimistically
beginning to open another crate, said suddenly, "Your pa makin
it hard for you, Ann?"

"Well, yes, he is. In a way," she said frankly. "I don't know that I blame him," she went on, anxious not to seem to criticize Paris too much. "He's set in his ways, and lazing around in front of a typewriter upstairs all day doesn't seem much like work to him."

Willie nodded. "I've known Paris a long time," he said. "He's one of these fellers that gits twitchy if all his womenfolks ain't busy around the house all day. Bothers you, don't he?"

Ann thought of the numberless times, since she had started to work in the woodshed chamber, that her father had interrupted her—coming to the foot of the stairs to ask her to find the grease for his boots, stamping up with an armful of the contested wood and dumping it in the woodbox with a crash, then to stand delivering a long harangue on how scarce wood was, how hard it was to cut. At first she had been touched when Paris had brought up wood for her. Now she knew that he only used it for an excuse to come upstairs, and as an opening for his opinions.

"He bothers me so," she said to Willie, "that sometimes I wonder if I'll be able to write at all."

"Well, I was thinkin," Willie said. "Hod, what shape's that old fishhouse of Bob Mackay's in? I bet Mary'd rent that, or even sell it, for little or nothin."

"I'll bet she would." Hod suddenly came to life. He had been watching a streak of sunlight that fell from the cobwebby old window in the peak of the barn on Ann's hair and the nape of her neck. The sunlight was golden and little motes of dust drifted across it. On Ann's hair it made sparkles of bright amber and turned to pale gold the soft short fuzz where the hair-line stopped and the velvety skin began. "I haven't been down there for a year or so, but the last time I walked by it, it looked tight, at least it had some shingles left. Might be pretty dirty, I guess, nobody's cleaned it out since Bob used to keep bait in there, but we could—" Suddenly aware that he was babbling, Hod let his voice die away in the middle of the sentence.

"You mean," Ann said slowly, "that there's a shack with a roof over it, around here, that I might get?"

"Sure," Willie said. "You remember Bob's fishhouse, down the cove, over on the other side. It's got a chimney, too; Bob used to build traps in there in the wintertime. Hod, why don't you take her down and show it to her? Maybe if you two'd git out from underfoot, I could spread out some corn and toll in some of them God's flyin angels them fellers upstate sent me. Damn a cussed fool like a hen, anyway," said Willie, grumbling. "I don't know why I bother."

"You want to, Ann?" Hod asked eagerly.

"Of course I do." She got up and started for the barn door, then hesitated. "Can't we help you chase the hens in, Willie?"

"Blast it, no. You'd have t' be the devil, a witch and a gale of wind. Things like them, they'll either have t' come of their own accord or they wun't come at all."

Standing in the barn door, he watched them go down the path to the shore. The thought came into his mind of his own father, the years of petty domineering, foolish interference, tyranny without good reason that a man could call to mind, and Willie's face clouded over.

What ails people, they can't let their kids alone, he thought, turning back into the barn. As if their kids was property they owned, and not livin breathin people.

The urgency of the cackling in the crates reached him again, and he began working on another cover, this time carefully, so that when a large enough opening was made, he could slide the crate up to the henhouse door and release its contents into the enclosure. He opened the remaining boxes this way without disaster, and then fetched a pan of cracked corn to scatter on the gravel in front of the barn.

"Co-ome, biddy, biddy, biddy," he called, rattling a few grains of corn left in the pan.

A step grated on the gravel by the side of the barn, and turning, Willie saw Donny Mitchell coming toward him.

Donny's jacket was torn and his face was smudged. A scratch across his nose had bled briefly and was smeared on his cheek where he had wiped the blood away. He had apparently waded across the mussel bar, for his shoes were mud to the ankles. But the expression in his eyes was what startled Willie.

"Lordsake, boy," he said. "What's wrong? What ails ya?"

"Nothin," Donny said. "I been waitin for *her* to get out of the way."

"Who, Ann? She's all right, Don. What's been botherin ya?"

"Mis Mackay wouldn't le' me come today," Donny said fiercely.

"We-el, we'll plan again. We didn't go out today, anyway." Willie laid down his corn-pan, and slid his arm around Donny's shoulders. "The'll be other days, Don."

"She says I can't come no more. She says I gut t' give up my job down here." The boy stood tensely, and after a moment Willie took away his arm.

"What she git mad about?"

"Oh, she says I don't do her work right. What does she expect —she don't pay me nothin."

"Ain't you been doin it good, Don?"

"She don't want to see me have any kind of a good time, that's all. She's bein goddam mean, if you ask me, that's all."

He wanted to tell Willie about the fight with Mis Mackay, how he'd spent the morning in the woodshed chamber, and how, sitting there alone, it had seemed as if he couldn't stand living in her house any longer.

But Willie's eyes on his were serious and thoughtful. "I can't let you come down here, Don, if she says no."

"Why can't you?"

"Because she's got the say. You and me both's goin t' be in awful bad if we keep on doin somethin she says not to."

Donny stood looking at him. "Maybe you're scared of her. I ain't."

"Hold on, son. I'll go see her again. Maybe we can talk her into it."

"But if she says I can't, you don't want me to come down."

"It ain't what we *want*. It's what we ought t' do. If you been scampin your chores, Don, she's right."

"All right," Donny said bitterly. "If you can stand it, I guess I can." He hesitated, then started out of the barn on a dead run. He charged across the mussel bar without stopping, though the tide had started to flow and the water was halfway to his knees.

Willie had been too surprised to stop him. He had been thinking hard what to say, seeing how upset Donny was, and how important it was that he should say the right thing. He did manage to call out, "Hey! Wait a minute!"

But Donny did not turn around. He ran on, out of sight into the woods.

Willie stood a moment gazing after him. Then, soberly, he picked up his pan and turned out to the gravel patch where he had spread out the corn.

But the half-wild hybrid chickens, whose tiny taut nerve-strands could not stand the stress of a few days' journey in a crate, still huddled unheeding in tree and hayloft and would not come down.

*

Nobody had used Bob Mackay's fishhouse since the day of his death, four years ago. Not many of his things were left there now —his boys had come home for the funeral and, among other things they had done in sadness for the dead, had been the clearing out from the fishhouse of their father's gear.

The small gabled building stood there now, on John Pray's land, by the shore of the tiny cove that looked off on Willie's mooring. In front of it a square cleared space, growing up to young spruce and alder, sloped down to a beach of pebbles and sand, with coarse marsh grass growing along its edge. The shack was open to the weather that came in through the loosely swinging door and broken windowpanes; and the small room smelled vaguely of long-gone lobster bait, tar and cold green spruce.

"Needs some fixing, I guess," Hod said, looking dubiously at the sour mess of old rope ends, rusty fishhooks and shavings that littered the floor.

Squirrels had used Bob Mackay's work-bench for a dining table. It was strewn with red-brown scales where they had chewed up spruce cones.

"If it was summer, you'd be set. I don't know how you'll keep warm in zero weather, though."

"It's just what I need." Ann's eyes shone and her hair stood on end where she had run her fingers through it. "There's a chimney —looks solid, too—and a place for a stove. I'll have to get some stuff in Bellport—a stove and a chair and some window-glass. I can scrub and paint that old bench for a work table. Hod, who'll I have to see to get it?"

"Well, John Pray—his father let Bob build the shack here when Bob had his weir down in this cove," Hod said. "You'd have to ask him, and then Mary Mackay owns the building."

"Let's go see them!" She caught him by the hand, pulling him toward the rickety door. "Oh, Hod, look at it!"

The afternoon sun on the harbor was a white, blinding glare, but in the cove it glinted yellow across the water's quiet browns and greens.

Hod grinned at her and did not let go her hand. "John wouldn't be home yet, he went out today. And I don't know's I'd better go along with you when you ask him, had I?"

Ann chuckled, too. She became aware that he was holding her hand and drew it away. "No, of course not. The whole island would gossip its head off. Single lady rents shack for immoral purposes, couldn't be anything else but. As it is, the Ladies' Aid will sew me into every infant's garment they make for the next six months."

"Wow!" Hod said. "You don't like em much, do you?"

"Sure, I do. I like em a lot. Only I can't stand the way they gossip. When will John be home?"

Hod looked at his watch. "It's about three now—an hour, I'd say. John'll let you have it, I think."

"If pa doesn't get wind of it first and slam the famous foot down," Ann said thoughtfully. "I'll have to do a little fast foot-work myself, I guess. You don't think John would sell me this piece of land the shack sets on, do you?"

"He might. Mary'd sell, I know. She needs the money."

"About what could I get it for?"

"M'm, that depends. A year ago, for little or nothing. Now that Brother Witherspoon's been nuzzling around, people are kind of feverish about land values."

"Oh." She looked disappointed.

"He's only after Willie's place, though. You can ask John."

"How long did you say? An hour?" She sat down on Bob Mac-kay's table and leaned back against the wall, bracing herself with her hands on the table top. "What'll we do for an hour? Anybody care if we chuck out some of this rubbish?"

"No, I guess not." He answered absently, his eyes on her face, seeing the deep glow of excitement behind her eyes, the color coming and going under the tanned skin of her cheeks. The light inside the shack was golden from reflected sunshine on the water, and it seemed to him for a bemused moment as if it might be she and not the sun who warmed and made luminous the rain-stained, furry walls.

"You don't seem a bit interested." She smiled at him companionably, lifting her chin, her head leaned back against the wall. "I think you're lazy. Expect a woman to do all the housework."

"No, I—" Hod saw the smile, the small pulse beating at the base of her throat. The words stuck and died away. He leaned and slid an arm behind her shoulders, and, for a moment, stood holding her, his eyes a few inches from hers. As she tensed, startled, he laid his other hand, palm down, across her throat.

Ann was too surprised to move. She couldn't anyway, she realized, caught off balance like that, damn him. Then, as his fingers, at once hard and gentle, touched her, she found suddenly that she didn't want to. Slowly, almost imperceptibly at first, a great wave of warmth spread from her throat downward through her body.

"Hod," she said in a whisper. "Let me go."

"All right," he said huskily. But he did not move for another long moment, and when he did it was to bend his head and put his lips against hers.

For an instant she let the sense of release, the drowning, wash over her, realizing with sudden humiliation and anger how similar this was to another time of drowning, just as urgent, and not so long ago.

Hod took his arms away and stepped back. "Ann—"

"I know," she said, not looking at him. "But go away now. Please."

"All right," he said again. Seeing her anger, he was as awkward as a schoolboy. "Please let me tell you. Ann, something's happened, I—"

"Oh, go away!"

Without a word he turned and went and she heard his steps, it seemed for a long time, thudding along the rocky path.

And this is how it is, she thought, furiously. Your body says to your mind—to your tough, intelligent mind that you're so proud of—go die. This is my province and I won't stand for nonsense from you. Something's happened.

Yes, her body said to her mind. Something strange and beautiful has happened.

And the answer to that was, Once before it was strange and beautiful, too. Wasn't it?

For a long time she stayed in the shack, hunched back on the table, her knees drawn up and her arms folded around them.

You fall in love, she told herself miserably, and at first it's hard to tell whether the experience is more beautiful to your body or to your mind. You have ideals about it. You're convinced that something that's so beautiful for the one must have loveliness and richness for the other.

She closed her eyes and instantly Cary Bennet was there, he of the rumpled hair and the impudent grin. The one who used to read aloud the poems of Dorothy Parker.

And thus they are, whose silly female dust
Needs little enough to clutter it and bind it,
Who meet a slanted gaze, and ever must
Go build themselves a soul to dwell behind it.

She remembered that quite well, and exactly how his voice sounded reading it. A little desperate, a little lonely—poor splendid wings—that was how he liked to have you think of him. A wanderer, sometimes drunk, with not a thing in the world—oh, my nothing!—in the way of security to offer to a woman. He suffered, but he wouldn't show it, his reading voice said, and it was nothing, anyway, that a little while in the back bedroom couldn't cure.

Oh, he'd studied her out and he'd been clever, offering her the things of the spirit she'd thought valuable, in coordination with the beauty of his body. And he hadn't let her find out the difference until the habits of her own body were conditioned, until to be without him was urgency and almost physical pain. When he was sure of that, the thing hadn't seemed worth while to him and he'd stopped bothering.

"You're a fool, Ann," he'd said, the last night she'd seen him. "For God's sake, let your body have some good healthy sex experience, and your soul will take care of itself."

And again, "God deliver me from a brainy woman."

So, all right, it had been her fault. If he wanted just an adequate body, there were places where he'd find exactly that, and let him go there. She'd said that to him and he'd answered with his half-smile, "But, Ann, dear, you're much safer."

But now that I know, how can it stay with me so long? she asked herself, watching the lines of the remembered face fade slowly from behind her eyelids.

Just how important the things of the spirit were she'd found out in those first few weeks when he hadn't come back. You'd give them up willingly, one by one—let him come back on his own terms, only let him come back. But after a while, the urgency had begun to die away, almost as if its own strength had devoured it; and lately she had begun to think about the old values again. They seemed, now that she wasn't blinded and stumbling around any more, to be the only basis for any relationship between any human beings. She was beginning to know again with certainty, as she once had, that the needs of the body and the needs of the mind were in balance, and must be, over and against the needs of body and mind in someone you loved.

Only, today, it hadn't taken much to make her remember the powerful potential in her body stirring to awaken, as if cracking through a tough, inviolate sheath. She remembered the fingers, tentative and trembling, against her throat. But not Hod Stilwell's fingers.

I ought to go away, she told herself forlornly. I ought to go home now and pack. He's different and he's nice, and if I went now he wouldn't fall in love with me. Oh, why didn't he know enough to leave things as they were?

The sun had set and the slow November twilight was coming down over the clearing when she left the shack. Her body felt cold and shrunken and she shivered a little as she started up the wood road. As she passed young John Pray's house, she saw him sitting by the window, and setting her jaw, she turned into the path to the door.

I won't be scared off, she told herself angrily. And I'll handle it somehow, too!

Young John, it seemed, would be only too glad to sell a piece of his land.

"Lord, yes!" he said, listening to her questions and turning to grin blithely at his wife. "Buy the whole of it, why don't you?"

"Wish I could," Ann said. "It's a swell place, John."

"Nuts! It's lonesomer than the tail-end of nowhere. Only reason Nell and I stay here is pa left us the house and land and now we got the kids we can't afford to move unless we sell. Why don't you buy it, Ann?" He winked at her. "We heard you was rollin, sold your book for a million."

John was Ann's age—twenty-five—and he had been one of hers and Hod's school generation. He had got married a year out of high school to a Bellport girl, and until John had inherited his share of the Pray property, they had lived in Bellport, both of them working at odd jobs around the summer estates. John hated fishing, he said, of any kind. What he wanted was a job like Earl Sprague's, a friend of his. Earl was year-around caretaker on one of the big Bellport places. He had eighty dollars a month, coming in steady.

"It ain't so much dough," John would say, earnestly expounding his ambition to his friends in the fishhouse. "But the thing is, in the wintertime when the rest of us is freezin down on the flats diggin clams for fifty cents a bushel, there old Earl is with his stockin-feet up on the stove, and his little old eighty dollars rollin in."

Now he looked at Ann expectantly, and Nell pricked up her ears, too.

Ann grinned. She was well aware that the gossip around the village had put her in the moneyed class. After all, a thing like a *book*, people said, you couldn't possibly get less than fifty thousand for it.

"That's all you know," she said to John. "You'd fall flat on your face if I told you writing was just like lobstering. You don't get your seed back."

"Haw!" John said derisively. "What d'you do it for, then?"

"Why—" Ann was taken aback. What *did* she do it for? "I think, a lot of the time, I work for the fun of it, John," she said soberly.

And once it had seemed like a rich kind of world to live in, she thought suddenly, the world of ideas and sentences, the words marching down the page, the hope, seldom more than that, that you'd said what you wanted to. It might come back if you worked hard and long enough. If only the ghost in her mind would go and haunt someone else, as, she thought, with what seemed to be a slight feeling of humor, it probably was, too, by this time.

"For the *fun* of it! Work?" John was obviously unconvinced. "My Lord, Ann, you must've gone kind a crazy, out to the west'ard, didn't ya?" He grinned. "But the' must be a little somethin in it. I notice you're loafin, now, and with some dough to throw away buyin Spoonhandle land, while every day I got *my* nose down on the grindstone."

"Loafing!" Ann snorted. "I'll swap jobs with you any day."

"Any time. I'll take the job *and* the income."

"Stop it, John." Nell, his wife, eyed him. "Can't you see she wants to talk business? Set down and have some supper with us, Ann. There's plenty."

"No, thanks. Ma'll have mine waiting."

"How about a can of beer, then?" John said.

"Well, I don't know but that would hit the spot."

Nell fetched the can from the shed, where she had it keeping cold, and put it down with an empty jelly glass at Ann's elbow. "Mag Snow's best. You haven't heard anything more about Mag and Aggie Stilwell, have you, Ann?"

"I haven't heard anything about them," Ann said mystified.

"Here we go," John said. "Lay off of them, Nell, or Ann and I'll never get to talk business." But he looked wise and knowing, and one dark eyebrow writhed upward on his smooth young forehead.

Nell was instantly agog. "*You* heard somethin, John! When you was in there, today! What was it?"

"Oh, well," John said resignedly. He was dying to tell the story, Ann saw. "Well, y'know, Ann, Aggie went in there to close Mag down single-handed, and the story was Mag turned a glass of beer all over her. You heard that much, a course. Well, the story is that Aggie went straight to Bellport to get the sheriff, and he wouldn't come."

"You don't say!" breathed Nell. "Had her arrested!"

"But I thought you said the sheriff wouldn't come," Ann said.

"Oh, he wouldn't," John said. "Said Aggie didn't have a case."

But Nell sat, a slightly dazed expression on her face, savoring the news. "What do you know about that!" she murmured. "Had her arrested."

"About that land, Ann—" John began.

"Well, what did Agnes do when the sheriff wouldn't come?" Nell was leaning forward, her mouth an O, ready to burst into laughter.

"Oh, my God! Went home, what'd you spose she'd do? I ain't got a doubt she told the sheriff what she thought, though. Poor Aggie, guess she's had hard luck with her temperance campaign. Now, Nell, that's all I know. If you want to hear any more, you'll have to go to the wimmenfolks. I don't doubt they got a good story all over town."

At this rate, Ann thought, I won't get a definite answer out of him all night. He might be stalling a little. She wondered if he were hesitating about what price to set on the land.

"Well," he said finally, "about that land. How about two acres for, say, two hundred dollars?"

"Oh, my Lord!" said Ann. "How about half an acre for fifty? That's about my limit, John, and that's not beating you down on your price."

"Why, I guess that'd be all right." He was disappointed, but he covered it up with a grin at Nell. "Guess we ain't ever going to get rid of it, Nell. Anyway, half an acre of the darned white elephant is somethin. But look, Ann, why not take an acre? That'd take you up to Willie Stilwell's beach and the town road. That road to the shack's only a private wood road, it ain't a right of way. I'll make you a price—seventy-five for the acre."

"Well, all right," said Ann doubtfully. "But I shouldn't, John."

"It ain't sensible, you know, not havin a legal right of way. You will have if you take the acre. You want a regular deed, or will a piece of paper do?"

"Better have it legal, I guess." She stood up. "Thanks a lot, John. Now if Mary Mackay'll only sell me that shack—"

"She'll have to, or move it off, if you buy the land," John said shrewdly. "Why, you could force her to—"

"Oh, I wouldn't want to do that!" Ann was shocked at the apparent ease with which he disregarded any feelings Mary might have in the matter.

"Well, if she won't, you let me know," John said. "I wouldn't have no compunctions about doin a little forcin, *before* I sell. Nell and me sure can use that seventy-five bucks."

*

Mary Mackay, however, was glad to be rid of Bob's fishhouse, which she had regarded as a dead loss anyway. At the end of the week, Ann found herself richer by an acre of Spoonhandle land with a rotting shack on it, and poorer by a hundred dollars.

The first day she went down to the shack to clean it out and estimate what she would need to make it into a habitable work room, she found the broken windowpanes replaced and puttied, the shingles patched, and the whole inside scrubbed and clean as a hound's tooth.

*

Hod had not planned, beforehand, to clean up the shack. He had just gone over there one late afternoon after he had got home from fishing, when he felt miserable and restless, with time heavy on his hands. She couldn't possibly be there, he told himself. If she were, he'd find out before she saw him hanging around, and go away. He didn't believe she'd want to see him. She'd made it pretty clear how she felt, the day he'd made the fool of the world of himself, and he didn't blame her. But the shack—the place where she had been, or, he thought, might just conceivably be this afternoon—drew him, as if by going there he might ease the unhappiness in his mind and the tumult of his senses that seemed to grow while the days went by and he did not see her again.

He'd sure made a fool of himself, he thought again, tramping down the road through the bleak woods. If he'd had the sense to wait, to keep his blundering hands to himself, until she'd got used to him, maybe understood better how he felt—but no, he'd had to go plowing in like a bulldozer the second time he'd seen her. She probably thought he'd acted like one of the fat-fingered fellows who couldn't keep his hands off a woman. Hod wished with all his heart that he had the power to put things back where they were in the first place.

For a moment, when she'd lain so still against his arm, he had thought she must understand how he felt. It didn't seem possible you could feel the way he had, and not have some of it, at least, get across. If a thing as strong as that grew up in you, for someone else, wasn't there any way besides words to make it known? The only words he'd had time to say had come stumbling out of him, wrenched—"Something's happened."

Oh, my God! he groaned, remembering with shame and a grinding embarrassment.

Yet suppose you did try to find words to sum up the sudden confused beauty you were caught in—how could you find them, what words would there be? She would know, maybe, words were her trade, but to him an unknown quantity, like a tool he hadn't had the knack to learn.

I don't know how to talk. Willie and I have lived alone so long. People think we're dopes and hermits. Maybe I could make you not think so. I've stayed by myself so much that sometimes I think I must be the only person in the place where I live.

Would that be it?

You . . . your hair is amber-colored, gold in the sun. If I could get close to it, I know it would smell like warm sand.

Not to do anything to hurt you, or that you thought was ugly. But would you think so if I touched you with my hands?

I haven't anything much to offer you. Not like what you're used to. It would be you giving everything to me. Unless, since I love you, that might be enough.

Would that be what you said?

No, Hod said to himself, striding out into the clearing. It might be what you felt, but you couldn't say it. Then . . . how?

There was no one at the shack. The door stood ajar and as he pushed it open a small terrified red squirrel darted between his feet and skittered out of sight into the brush. Hod hung around for a while, wandering about the clearing.

Then, unable to be aimless any longer and seeing some things he might do, he went home for tools and shingles, glass and putty, for soap and a bucket and Willie's long-handled steel brush. He worked on the shack until it was too dark to see, thinking hazily and hopelessly that what he could do with his hands might make plain, somehow, the things going on in his heart which he knew he couldn't find the words to say.

*

A few days after Donny had been down to see him, Willie slicked up and went to call on Mis Mackay. He would have gone before—knew he should have gone—but the fine weather kept on and he and Hod didn't want to miss any of it, knowing that soon it would break. He found that Mis Mackay had hardened her heart against him.

"Donny's got to learn to mind me," she said stiffly. "That's all there is to it. Besides, I need him here to help me."

"Well, I'm sorry," Willie said. "He's a nice boy and I've enjoyed havin him around."

"He must show you a side he don't show me, then."

"Why, I don't know why he would," Willie said slowly. "He's always tellin me what a nice home he's gut up here."

She made no reply, and Willie, after a moment, got up to go. He saw it was no use.

"You wun't change your mind?" he asked, pausing at the door. "I had a feelin he was gittin interested in learning about the boat and things. Kind of run of an idea you interest a boy, you'll have less trouble with him."

"No," Mary said. "I ain't felt 't was doin him a mite of good, I'm afraid. S' far as I can see, it's just made him more sarsy, if anything."

Donny, watching from an upstairs window, saw Willie walking slowly back down the road. He had just got home from school, and had been headed for the barn when he'd seen Willie coming and had ducked out of sight so as not to have to talk to him. It was pretty hard to face Willie when things were so wrong between them. But he had heard every word Willie said to Mis Mackay, listening tensely down the hot-air register in the floor of his room.

If he's so scared of gettin in bad with *her*, he told himself, I guess it's all right with me. Thinks more of what people'll say than he does of me.

Well, there it was. Willie hadn't even put up an argument. He'd just sat there and taken what she had to say. If he had, if he'd only just made a little bit of a fuss, Donny was all prepared to start over again—he'd even try harder with Mis Mackay's chores. He admitted to himself that he'd been kind of mean about that, and that she did have a little on her side. But the relief of admitting he'd been wrong was all obscured now by the realization that, after all, Willie didn't want him bad enough to fight for it.

I guess he won't miss me much, Donny thought, and as for my help aboard the boat, he can't figure that amounts to a lot either.

You couldn't trust anyone, not even if they said they liked you. For a while, being around with Willie and Hod, he'd begun to feel at home and liked again, the way he had with Uncle My. Now it was over, and he ought to have known better than to count on it.

Willie passed out of sight around a bend of the road and Donny turned away from the window. Tears came into his eyes, but he crushed them angrily away. He sat bleakly on the bed staring at his shoes. He'd planned on buying himself some new shoes with his own money, and he could have done it, too, with another week's work coming in. He could have done it out of his ten dollars if he hadn't had to replace *her* lousy old bucksaw.

He thought resentfully of the way she'd handled that—to get the most out of him she could, he told himself. The bucksaw he had busted had been older than God, worth about three dollars at the most. But did she let him pay her three dollars for it? She did not! She ordered a bran-new saw from Pete Stilwell, with a metal frame, that cost eight dollars, and she made him pay for that, the old skinflint. That left him two out of his ten-spot. The shoes he had set his heart on, a pair of brown buckskin ones—instead of the same old black brogans the State Woman always brought—cost three dollars and a half.

It's *her*, he said to himself. She don't want me to have a good time, or anything good at all. I bet she wishes I was dead. I sure wish she was.

Well, if she wasn't going to let him have a good time, or even a job, she better look out for her things. I'd take stuff from her quicker'n I could spit. Now she's lost me my job, she owes me money, and I'll git it out of her, too.

The first time, when he took the vegetable man's change a day or so later, he knew she hadn't seen him. The second time, she walked in through the door, just as he was putting thirty-five cents she'd left on the sideboard into his pocket.

Donny turned red. The sweat started out on his forehead and he stared at her, his eyes round with horror. But she didn't say anything. She just walked on by him and into the other room. For a while, he waited as if an ax were hanging over his head, and then, thinking he had got away with it again, it seemed to him that stealing to get your own back was as easy as taking candy from a baby.

As a matter of fact, Mis Mackay had been shocked to the depths of her heart at finding out that Donny stole money. The vegetable man had left sixty cents change on the kitchen table—she had seen it. When she went back to look for it, it was gone. No one but she and Donny had been in the house. Suspecting him, she had put the thirty-five cents on the sideboard, as if forgotten, and there it was—she'd caught him in the act of taking it.

Her first impulse was to telephone to the Welfare and have them, for sure, this time, take Donny away. After all, stealing money was a thing nobody ought to be asked to put up with. Other things were different; most everybody at sometime or other, innocently or otherwise, picked up this or that that wasn't his. But steal-

ing *money*, that really made you a thief. She'd call the State
Woman. It was true she needed Donny's board, but there must be
other boys and pleasanter ones to have around the house.

Halfway to the phone, Mary suddenly realized that she didn't
want them to take him away. If they did, she'd have to admit that
she'd failed with him.

Mary Mackay had been brought up to believe that there wasn't
a human being in the world who wouldn't respond in time to
kindness. To have to give up that conviction would have shaken
her to her foundations. She couldn't do it.

Heaven knows, she told herself, I don't care for him; he's the
most peculiar youngone I ever saw, but seems as though I could
make a decent man of him if anyone could.

She decided to give him a good talking-to; and then, when the
time came, she found she couldn't do that, either. There was some-
thing almost indecent in having another person know you knew
that he was a thief. She could scold him about stealing pie and cake
—that was different. But if you accused him of stealing money, how
could you ever look him in the face again? Every time he saw
you, he'd think of it; and in time he couldn't bear to stay with you
at all.

In the end, Mis Mackay did nothing. She took to keeping her
money in a locked drawer and her small change in her apron
pocket. It did not occur to her that if Donny had been her boy
Dave, she would not have thought him a thief at all, but merely
a naughty boy who had made a mistake. She would have charged
in, made known her wrath and her discipline, and speedily have
forgotten all about it.

Nor did she take into account the effect that keeping silent would
have upon her. Suspicious of Donny, watching his every move
when he was in the house, she lost the little respect and liking she
had for him and, in the end, the kindness with which she had
hoped to accomplish so much.

She gave up doing special things for him, like finding out what
he liked to eat, and cooking it. The cake-box and the cookie-jar,

from whose abundance he had taken many a between-meal snack when he first arrived, now, like as not, he would find empty. She no longer bothered to stretch her own scanty funds plus the meager board the State paid for Donny, to cover an occasional treat. The plain meals she cooked were wholesome, but the cheap cuts of meat were often tough and tasteless, with no cake or pie to take the curse off. Donny didn't like it—she could tell from the sullen disgusted way he looked at his food.

Well, what of it? she asked herself. She'd done her best for him, and he hadn't appreciated it, not one mite. He stayed in the house as little as possible; he never spoke to her now unless he had to. So far as she knew, he had given up going down to Willie Stilwell's after she had forbidden it, but he was off and away to other places whenever he could slide out from under her thumb. School nights, she managed to keep him in, doing his homework, but Saturdays and Sundays he often didn't even bother to come home to his meals. Lucy Osgood told her once that he and Artie were sneaking off and riding to Bellport on the bread truck whenever they could, but Donny denied it. Mary didn't press the matter. A few weeks ago, she told herself, she'd have had it out of him, but now, knowing what she knew, it didn't seem worth while to bother.

If anyone had shown to Mary Mackay the honest picture of herself which she could not see, she would not have believed it.

*

"For the love of a just God!" Paris Freeman said. "Will somebody kindly tell me what *this* means?" He was sitting by the lamp reading the paper that came every two weeks from Bellport. He always read the paper word for word, taking several evenings to it, including the items under *Transfers of Property.*

A man ought to know just exactly what went on under his nose in his own town, and there wasn't any way to find it out unless it was in the paper. Nobody, including his own women-folks, ever told him anything.

Now, Paris held the folded paper stiffly a few inches from his glasses, and stared at it as if he couldn't believe the words before his eyes.

"What what means?" Mending stockings under the other lamp, Myra had been thinking it was ten o'clock and time Sam and Polly got home from the roller-skating rink in Bellport, though she did hope they wouldn't come now, before their father went to bed. What Paris had said sounded so much like what he would have said to them, that she glanced involuntarily toward the door, almost believing that they'd come in and she'd not heard them. They hadn't, and now, she thought with a sigh, there'll be that to go through with. It certainly made him mad to have the kids stay out late.

"Why, here under *Transfers of Property*," Paris said, outrage sticking out all over his voice. "Listen: 'John Pray to Ann Freeman,' and by God, here's another one under it, 'Mary Mackay to Ann Freeman.' What's Ann doin, buyin up *property*? And what, for Godsakes, property's she bought? She never told me she was buyin up property!"

"Well, she told me," said Myra calmly. "She's bought that old fishhouse of Bob Mackay's and the acre of land it sets on."

Paris let his jaw drop. He stared at Myra, his head on one side, as if this were the last, heavy burden that ever a worried, harassed man had to bear. "What in he'm's name she want that for?" he demanded.

"She wants it to work in."

"Work in! What's she doin upstairs, for Chrissake? Ain't she satisfied with havin us all crazy, tiptoein around the house, so we won't bother her, has she got to go and get somewheres else to *work* in?"

"She ain't never said one word about nobody botherin her, and you know it, Paris."

"Well, she ain't goin down there, that's all! It ain't no place for a woman, off the main road like that, no tellin what might happen." Paris paused as some of the possibilities began to go through his mind. His eyes grew slightly glassy and he got up and made for the woodshed door. "I'm goin up'n tell her a thing or two!"

"No, you ain't, Paris. You let her be." Myra scarcely raised her voice, knowing he wouldn't listen. He kept on out through the shed and she heard his heavy steps pounding up the stairs to the woodshed chamber. Myra sighed.

Ann had been working, but she had heard the sounds of explosion coming from below, and she too sighed. She had closed the door to keep in the heat from the stove, but Paris drove his foot against it, sending it slamming back against the wall.

"What's your idea sneakin around and buyin property without tellin no one?" he demanded.

"Wait, pa," Ann said. "There's nothing to get mad about. I thought you'd be glad to have me get a workroom of my own, so I wouldn't cast a blight over the whole house."

All Paris needed was for someone to try to placate him. Then he was sure he had the upper hand. He strode across the room and shook a finger under her nose.

"You ain't goin down there, miss lady, see? Down in that lonesome place, with every man on the island startin in to traipse the minute they know you're there! What kind a works is that for a girl's been brought up as good's you've been?"

"But, pa—" Ann smiled at him. "Men don't like me. You said so yourself."

Paris brought up short. He tried, for an instant, to think of a comeback, but she had caught him too neatly. He opened his mouth, closed it and then said, almost in his normal voice, "Well, you ain't goin. You hear me?"

"All right."

This was more like. Paris hit his stride again. "And you can either sell that property back, or you can sign it over to me. To the menfolks in the fam'ly, where property belongs!"

"No. I don't believe I will."

"Who do you think you are? A man with a petticoat on? I'm sick and tired of you tryin to rule the roost in my house, actin as though you was the whole cussed, goddam works." He drew back his arm. "By God, I'll slap you so hard—"

"You lay a finger on me," Ann said, "and I'll pack my things and go down to my own place for good. For goodness' sake, pa, I'm not ten years old. Please stop acting so foolish," she went on, seeing the fury begin to die out of him and the old abused look take its place, "and think what it is you're saying. We could get along if only you wouldn't try to run me."

"I'd just as soon try to git along with a she-wildcat," Paris said, "and one that acts good deal like a she-cat, if you ask me." He tried to think of something else to say, but because she had talked back to him, his rage had left him high and dry, and he felt now only hurt and bewildered. "Sarse, sarse, sarse," he mumbled.

He started out through the door, but turned around and came back again. "I guess you know when your cussed works ketch up with you, you can come crawlin back to me and I'll be here," he said.

"I know," Ann said, trying to meet him halfway. She felt the lump start thickening in her throat. "I guess I'll always kind of depend on your being here, pa."

He went on, his scrawny neck stretching around the jamb of the door, his Adam's apple working. "What I come back for was to shet this door, so's the *queen* wouldn't be bothered by the *common people* moving around downstairs." Starting to close the door quietly, he changed his mind and slammed it hard.

*

One other person learned about Ann's venture into real estate with misgiving and disapproval. Pete Stilwell didn't have to wait to read it in the paper. He ran the grocery, and he got all the news hot off the griddle.

"You don't say," he commented to Bill Pray, who had the word from his brother, John, and had carried it around for quite a spell on the tip of his tongue. "Glad to hear somebuddy in this God-for-saken hole's been able to sell some property."

"How bout Willie?" Bill asked, eyeing him. "If he ain't hed a bite for his place, then he's hed a thunderin good nibble."

"You don't say." Pete did not look up from the column of figures he was adding. "That'll be two-seventy, Bill. Mean to tell me," he went on, taking Bill's five dollars and ringing open the cash register to make change, "that you've heard somethin definite bout that?"

"Godsake," Bill said. He grinned a little. "Thought you'd know about that, if anybody would."

"It's a smart man that p'tends t' know anything about Willie's business," Pete said. "He's a close-mouthed son-of-a-gun, but I do know Witherspoon's figgered it ain't worth his time. Kind of lost interest. Oh, I guess Willie'd sell if he gut offered a good price, but what's five hundred dollars? Smelt feed!"

"*Is* that a fact?" Bill looked at him, slightly open-mouthed. "Way I heard it was—"

"Uh-huh, you can hear anything, once the wimmen git t' havin it over. Five hundred dollars was what he offered and Willie told him what he could do with it. Don't blame him, do you?"

"Well, no. Don't know's I do."

"You know them summer people," Pete went on. "If they can git somethin for nothin, they will. If they can't, they lose interest."

"Hell, that's how they stay rich," Bill said, with the air of one who knew. "Darn me down, I was kind of hopin there might be a chance t' turn over some land, after all these years."

"I ain't heard of none." Pete turned away, picking his teeth with a match stick.

Bill gathered up his bundles. "Well, so long, Pete."

"So long. Only thing I've heard lately is that feller was here last month tryin to buy up spruce woodland for pulpwood," Pete said, just as Bill's back was disappearing through the doorway.

Bill turned around, pricking up his ears. "Who was that?"

"Oh, God, I've forgut. He never offered nothin. Not t' think twice about."

"Was that for the land or just the wood off'n it?"

"The whole works, land and wood, I b'lieve. God knows why he'd want the land, once the trees was cut. Some crank."

"You can't remember who 't was?"

"Hell, no. Wait, though. I d'no b't I did write down his name 'n address somewheres." Pete fuddled through a batch of loose paper scraps on his cash register. "Why *you* intrusted? You wouldn't sell your land for pulpwood, would ya? Damn if I would. Ruins the land. It's a crime what a gang a pulpwood cutters do to a wood lot."

"Well, I d'no. Kind of like t' know what he offered." Bill teetered a little in the doorway.

"Shucks. I told you last year I'd give you fifteen hundred for your wood lots," Pete said. "This fella don't offer nothin like that."

"I told ya nuts then, and I still say nuts." Bill grinned.

"Suit yourself. Yes, by golly." Pete came up with a crumpled rectangle of pad-paper. "I kind of run of an idea I wrote that name 'n address down. Joe King, Box 48, Bellport."

"Box 48, huh?"

" 'S right."

"So long." Bill shut the door. He opened it an instant later and stuck his head back in. "By the way, Pete, for the Lord's sake, don't sell my wife no more of them ellwives."

"Why?"

"They're rotten. She brought em on the table, I like to puked." Bill was gone, this time for good.

Pete stared after him speculatively. Now what did he mean by that? Well, the alewives had gone by a little, and maybe that was all he meant.

No other customer appeared, and after a while Pete went into his office. Unlocking his desk drawer, he took out and unrolled his map of Spoon Island, pegging the corners down with his ink bottle, two checkbooks and a plug of chewing tobacco. Laboriously, his tongue showing at the side of his mouth, he sketched in a tiny square just off the Spoonhandle road and labeled it "Ann Freeman."

"Goddam her," he muttered under his breath.

He looked for a blotter and not finding one, sat contemplatively while the ink dried. Then he rolled up the map and put it carefully away.

Got to git busy from now on, he thought, rising to go back into the store. He permitted himself a dry grin. Well, we'll wait a day or so and see what turns up in Box 48.

*

The next day Ann rode over to Bellport on the mail truck to shop for the furniture she needed for the shack. At the Furniture Emporium, she found a pocket-sized cookstove, which, the salesman said, the sporting trade used for summer camps.

"I only gut this one left," he went on, anxious to make the sale so that he wouldn't have to store the stove for the winter. "Lucky t' hev that. Last May I ordered twenty, and they went like fire in a brushpile in August."

He was, Ann realized, bearing down a little hard on the local idiom, deliberately flattening his voice and bringing out the words with a self-conscious twang. Either he thought she was late-season summer people or the habit was too strong in him. The Bellport merchants went to a good deal of trouble to preserve the rural atmosphere in their stores during the summer.

"Well, I'm not sure," Ann said dubiously. "I'd thought of a small airtight. How'll this be for heating in cold weather?"

"Heats like a son-of-a-gun," said the salesman, cheerfully, rattling off the stove covers. "Big firebox, see? Takes an ordinary-sized chunk of wood. You shut up the drafts, she'll keep a fire long's an airtight would."

Ann considered. It would be convenient to have something she could cook on, just in case she wanted to get a meal now and then down in the shack. And if Paris kept on, it was possible she might have to move down there to live. "How much is it?" she asked.

"Thirty-five dollars," said he glibly.

"For that little thing?" She looked at him, raising an eyebrow.

"Course, it's specially built."

Ann grinned. "Come off it," she said unexpectedly. "I *live* over on Spoon Island. I was born there."

The salesman looked taken aback. "That's the price," he said, without much conviction.

"Okay," Ann said, shrugging. "Let's see some airtights."

"The boss might be willing to come down, seeing it's a leftover from the summer trade, and we only got one. I'll ask him."

He vanished toward a cubby-hole in the back of the store and returned almost instantly. "He says he'll sell it for twenty-five."

"That's still too much."

The salesman let go his breath and relaxed. "Oh, take it for fifteen and get the damn thing out of the store."

"All right. Sold."

She bought as frugally as she could, but by the time she had paid for a straight kitchen chair, a studio couch and some saucepans and china to go with her cookstove, she realized she was spending more than she should have. She hadn't planned to buy the couch, but once the idea that she might have to go and live in the shack had come into her mind, it seemed to settle down and stay there.

I won't, of course, she told herself. It would about kill pa and even ma might think it was something pretty drastic.

But the more she thought of it, the more attractive it seemed. All that privacy—to come and go as she liked—no more listening to Paris's tempers and holding back her own because she didn't want to hurt him. In the end, Ann even added some sheets and blankets to the purchase of the studio couch.

The store, she found, had stopped truck delivery for the winter, at least to out-of-the-way places like Spoon Island. They would, however, take Ann's order down to the town wharf, where an island boat could pick it up.

As she came out of the store, she suddenly realized that she was glowing all over with satisfaction.

Gone quivery over furnishing a house? she asked herself, chuckling. Who'd have thought it?

Yet after all those years of living around in hall bedrooms and furnished apartments in the city, not caring a hang about surroundings, so long as they weren't so dirty or so noisy that her mind could not concentrate on ideas, why shouldn't she?

If I'm domestic, I come by it honestly from a long line of superdomestic mothers.

But it was more than that. The shack and the few meager sticks of furniture seemed to be feeding a subtle hunger, quieting a restlessness. Sitting in the rattletrap mail truck that made the afternoon's trip back to Spoon Island, Ann watched the bleak countryside unroll along the highway—the lonely gray sky, the glimpses of steely sea, the stern spindles of the spruces. It was the same countryside which had almost sent her into panicky retreat the morning she had got off the train at Bellport.

But now she thought, It's only winter countryside, and it's lovely to look at with all its ruffles gone.

*

The interior of the shack was going to be something to paint, Ann thought, impatiently tossing down the fat brush with which she had been trying to daub Inside Ivory on to the rough walls. Bob Mackay had figured that unplaned lumber was good enough for a fishhouse and now the splinters stuck out like hackles through Ann's paint.

She had patched cracks with putty and plastic wood, and the shack was tight—as tight as it could be, with rotting wood in places that would not hold nails. It was clean, too, from Hod's scrubbing —at least, she supposed Hod had done the scrubbing; she hadn't seen him since.

She didn't admit to herself that she was a little annoyed because he hadn't tried to see her. If he had come over to the shack while she was there, he would have found her friendly, but unapproachable. At least that was what she planned. She had laid out her course of action—he wouldn't be allowed to misunderstand again. But she was quite unprepared for the thump her heart gave when somebody stepped up on the flat granite doorstep and rattled the door.

She flew to open it. "Hi, come on in," she began cheerfully and stopped.

It was only Willie, with his shotgun tucked in the crook of his arm.

"Hi." Willie stepped neatly over the doorsill into the room. "How you makin out?"

"Fine," Ann said in a dashed voice.

Willie eyed her with a twinkle. "I was comin back from gunnin and I thought I'd drop by and see."

Actually, he had been over wandering around Cat Cove, hoping for a sight of Donny. It was Saturday, getting along toward evening —a gray gusty day with the sun once in a while poking out enough to make pale streaks on the gun-metal water. Just a day for ducks to fly. Willie had thought that maybe Donny might remember what Cap'n My had told him about a good duck day and come gunning. He missed Donny. But Cat Cove was deserted.

"How are the hens?" Ann asked. "You had any more explosions?"

"Sev'ral," Willie said with a chuckle. "If a spider so much as walks across the henpen ceilin, they go off like firecrackers."

"Nervous, I guess."

"That's right. Awful fighters, too. One of the roosters tangled with Bertha the other day. They like to tore each other apart. Only chicken, hen *or* rooster, I ever see willin t' tangle with Bertha."

Ann laughed. "I shouldn't like to tangle with Bertha myself."

"Me, neither," Willie said. "What you tryin to do, Ann, paint them boards?"

"I guess I'm not much of a painter," she said half-heartedly, indicating her afternoon's work.

Willie regarded it. "Looks like hell, don't it? What you want t' paint it for?"

"I don't know," said Ann disgustedly. "I got arty, I guess. I had an idea it might be cleaner."

"Well, I guess 't would be, and maybe kind of lay that old bait smell. M'm. . . ."

He stood his gun carefully in a corner, advanced on the wall and tapped it here and there with his knuckles. "That wall don't 'mount to much. I see where Hod patched it, it won't hold nails. Goin t' let in some cold this winter."

He had an air of absorption about him and Ann realized suddenly that he had forgotten her. He was running his long brown fingers expertly along the woodwork, probing here and there, searching out weak spots. She said nothing and watched him. Suddenly he stopped and turned to her.

"Know what I'd do? Them uprights is solid, it's only the boards and shingles that's rotten. I'd git some plasterboard and seal this room up tight. Then when you git to it, you can fix the outside without disturbin the plasterboard. It'd keep you comfortable this winter."

"Oh, Lord," Ann said. "I've already spent more than I should—"

"H'm. I gut some plasterboard over'n my barn chamber, left over from the time I fixed my house. 'T wouldn't take much, and Hod 'n I could put it on for you tomorrow."

"Oh, I couldn't let you do that."

"Why not?" He peered over at her seriously. "Old buildins— I don't know nothin I'd ruther do than fix one up. I don't know nobody's had more practice at it, either." Seeing she was about to protest further, he went on, "Little plasterboard, little work. Cost you, say, four dollars."

"Oh," Ann said. "But would that be enough, Willie?" It didn't seem right to let him supply her with materials and work for so little, though she could see the plasterboard would be the very thing.

"All I'd want," he said. "If you're walkin up the road now, I'll go along with you far's my turn-off."

She realized as they stepped out into the fresh cold evening that the shack had been damp and airless. She felt her chilled blood

start warmly through her veins, walking up the wood road beside
Willie, trying to match her steps to his effortless stride.

He moved along silently, absorbed in something again, she saw.
She was beginning to realize that Willie, behind his sealed brown
face and noncommittal eyes, lived a secret and intensely satisfying
life of his own.

"You know that Mitchell boy lives to Mary Mackay's?" he
asked at last.

"Why, no. At least, I've seen him, but I don't know him."

"He's been helpin me with odd jobs, off'n on this fall. I gut t'
know him quite well. He's a good little kid," Willie said.

This sounded different from Mary Mackay's story about the
same boy, Ann thought. She listened, waiting for him to go on.

"He ain't been down for quite a spell. He works for Mary, and
I guess she run of an idea he was spendin too much time with me."

"I'd think she'd be glad to have him spend time with you."

"Well, no," Willie said. "I live kind of apart. Not that I'm
diff'rent 'n anybody else, but if you live apart, folks git to thinkin
you are. I do it," he went on, "because I like to. I guess that don't
make sense, does it?"

"I think so," Ann said. "Do you really like to, Willie?"

"Yes. I do. Y'see, I ain't a violent man. The's somethin about
the pull an haul between people I can't stand. I found that out a
long time ago, so I come away by myself."

They had come to the narrow path that led down to Willie's
landing, and he stopped, shifting his gun from one arm to the
other.

"Hod's diff'rent, he ought t' be part of a town. He don't lay out
t' be sociable, but the way he's made, he ain't goin t' be very con-
tented until he learns how to be. Kind of wrings him outa shape,
living apart, and havin folks think he ain't like everybody else."
Willie grinned. "I ain't talked this much to anybody since I can
remember," he said. "What I started out to say, I think somethin
may be botherin that Mitchell boy pretty bad. He's a little bit wild
and he might quite easy be wilder. Mary Mackay's an awful good

woman, but she's like a lot of good women, a kid has to be her own before she can see that ordinary devilishness ain't a sign of a crim'nal."

"Could someone do something, you think?" Ann said, a little absently. She had been thinking over what he had said about Hod. If it were true, and she suspected it was, it explained a lot. It explained a kind of dissonance she had noticed in him.

"Might," Willie said. "I'd hate for Donny t' git into trouble. He ain't got a soul t' turn to, and he ain't what you could call bad. Right now, I run of an idea he could jump either way."

"I don't know what I could do," Ann said doubtfully. "I could drop by there."

"Wish you would, sometime." Willie turned and went quickly down the bank to his punt. He did not look back at her, but launched the punt and pushed away across the channel.

Maybe they think he's peculiar, Ann thought, but he's one of the kindest men I've ever seen.

He was one of the shrewdest, too, but she did not know that. She did not realize that Willie, according to his estimate of what a good trade should be, had just made one. He had, anyway, planned to offer her the plasterboard; and four dollars wouldn't begin to pay for it and for putting it on, if you were to consider prices.

But thinking about Donny, worrying about him, Willie had decided to ask something from Ann in return for his favor. He was convinced that something ought to be done, that somehow or other a hand ought to be held out; and he couldn't do it. Mary Mackay and Donny, himself, had seen to that. Ann might; and she was the only one he could think of who had the brains and the insight not to go at Donny with a steam shovel. So Willie, according to his lights, had made a deal.

*

Willie had been right—it didn't take much plasterboard to seal the inside of the shack, and only a few hours for Hod and him to put it on. By early afternoon, the shack was tight to the peak, covered with ivory-colored sheets, trimmed with neat brown wooden strips. Then Willie, still with a creative gleam in his eye, set Ann and Hod to putting on what remained of the paint. He himself painted both sides of the peaked ceiling. Finishing before they finished the walls, he went out and brought in some leftover plasterboard, which he nailed down over the boards of the rickety floor.

"That ain't much of a job," he said, eyeing the floor dubiously. "Ought t' hev new boards and rip them old ones up. But she'll do for this winter. Ought t' hev some kind of a carpet, though."

"Lord, Willie, you're a regular old woman," Hod said. So far, he had been silent for the most part, talking only about the job in hand. He might have been some unfamiliar carpenter's helper, hired for the day.

It would be nice, she thought, if he'd just go back to the way things were—just be natural and casual, the way Willie is. But apparently Hod didn't function that way.

"That's right," said Willie, grinning. "I've kept a neat house for a number of years, and I still say we ought t' hev a carpet."

"There's a roll of straw matting in our attic ma said I could have," said Ann, from the corner where she was doubled over brushing on paint.

" 'T ain't down here, though, is it?" said Willie regretfully. He tossed his hammer into his toolbox and began gathering up his other belongings. "I guess that's about all we can do then, Ann. Neat and cozy's the inside of a nutshell, ain't it?"

It was. The shack looked wonderful.

"It's worth a lot more than four dollars, Willie," Ann said, handing him the bills from her pocket.

Willie looked with satisfaction around the small, clean room. "We-ell," he said, "actual cash money, maybe. Might have t' pay more if you hired it done, I d'no b't. But Hod and me's kind of glad t' have a neighbor."

"That's right," Hod said unexpectedly. He had been cleaning out brushes in a battered tin can that held turpentine, and he came across the room wiping his hands on a paint-stained rag. "We haven't had what you could call a neighbor for a long time."

She caught a note of bitterness in his voice, and as he passed her she laid her hand on his arm. "Well, you've got one now. I honestly don't know how to thank you. It's a swell job."

"Don't thank me. I just fetch and carry for Willie on a job like this." He grinned at her, but his eyes under his straight brows were sober. She felt the lean muscle under her fingers tense briefly; then he moved away and scooped up the toolbox from the table. "Well, Willie, my son, what say? On our way?"

"I'm just payin you back for the times I've fetched and carried for you when you've fixed the enjun," Willie said quickly. "Darn son-of-a-gun, Ann, he makes a swab out of me when it comes to an enjun."

From the small side window of her freshly painted room, Ann watched them striding away up the wood road, Hod in the lead with his toolbox over his shoulder. Their two backs were almost identical—the same wide shoulders, narrow waists and hips, and they moved with the same slow grace, supple and sure over the rock-studded ground. Hod might be a little more powerfully built, but that was all.

They were not strange and eccentric, she thought, at least in the sense the village might think them so. They were only remarkable —two men with more than ordinary kindness, intelligence and strength. Because through the years Agnes Flynn had sighed her incessant, hypocritical grief for her "lost" brothers into the ears of the community, and Pete Stilwell had made people laugh with his dry drawling sarcastic comment, Hod and Willie had been pinned on one inexorable level in the eyes of their fellow-townsmen.

It was ironic, Ann thought, when most people knew that Agnes was an old tartar who would trample over anything for the sake of getting her way, and Pete, if you looked at him past the gear of town office, tradition and respectability, was a plain cheat and a swindler. Everybody knew that, and said so. Even the people Agnes trampled on and Pete swindled looked up to them because they were—what? Smart?

The Stilwells had been the island's great family for quite a number of generations. Now Agnes and Pete were the ones who made the most noise, who had the most money. Their grandfathers had set the temper of the town toward them and it would not change, any more than it would change toward weather signs and copybook maxims. A red sky at morning might not always be followed by a storm, and a rolling stone might sometimes gather moss; or the Stilwells who had the money might not be, now, in many ways, the best the town had to offer. People would know this, in reality. But it would not prove anything to them.

And even if you were intelligent and strong and kind, and these things were needed in the community, how could you defend yourself when the backbiting started? You never knew what people said about you or what they thought. You might sense it, dimly, but nobody was ever brave enough to face up to you and say, "Look, this is what goes on about you." Nobody ever gave you a chance to say a word that needed to be said in your own behalf.

Willie and Hod sensed it, she knew, and Willie, through the years, had built up his defenses and had built them strong. He was self-sufficient now, living the life he wanted, not too remote, because where he saw he could help he tried to, as in the case of Donny Mitchell. What he had achieved was his privacy. No man could seriously trouble it, and he had learned to live in it without loneliness.

But Hod had no defenses; in the end, he had nothing but anger and frustration. As Willie had said, Hod, for the good of his soul, needed to be a part of a town. He would never learn to live in loneliness. Yet there was something—she turned away from the window, wondering what it was she sensed in Hod, dimly, not yet to be put into words—some latent energy never allowed near the surface, a potential deep within.

*

Mary Mackay was sitting alone in her kitchen. After she had eaten and cleared away her dinner—Donny hadn't come home and she had no idea where he was—she had sat down in the rocker by the window, feeling lonesome and abused. For a while, she had knitted on the muffler she was finishing up for Dave's Christmas present. Dave had a milk route in Somerville, Massachusetts, and his wife Jory had written that a wool muffler would be just fine.

The muffler was done now and lay on the table ready for wrapping, along with the presents for Paul's and Benjamin's families. She'd had to skimp awfully to buy the wool for that muffler—the wool for Donny's red sweater had cost so much; and the rest of her presents she had had to make out of materials she had had in the house. It was a good thing she had that big box of tissue paper and ribbon she'd saved over from last Christmas, some of it hardly wrinkled a bit.

It certainly goweled her, she said to herself, rocking idly back and forth, her hands in her lap, to have to skimp on her own children's Christmas for the sake of somebody who wasn't even a relation. But she'd decided that if there was a time when you could win anybody over, it would be at Christmas. She'd made up her mind that Donny should have at least one nice present.

In a minute she'd get up and wrap her presents so they'd be ready for him to take to the post office when he went to school in the morning. She ought to get up right now and fix the fire, but there, she'd have to go out to the shed and bring in wood—he'd gone off without fetching a stick. The kitchen certainly was cold this winter, without any banking around the house; she'd been at him since November to nail the tarred paper on and to cut some brush to bank it with. So far, he had about ten feet done along under the front room windows where it didn't help the kitchen a mite. He was getting so he wouldn't do one single nameable thing.

She had said these things over so many times to herself that she could sit half-dozing, now, with the thoughts running querulously through her head. When a knock came at the door, she got up to answer it, still thinking as she turned the knob, Give a boy a good home like this, and still he don't appreciate it.

"My goodness, Ann Freeman," she said, coming out of herself with a jerk. "I certainly am glad to see you. I was settin here lonesome's an old goat, lettin the fire git down because I was too lazy to go git some wood for it. Take off your things and set down. I'll be right back."

She disappeared toward the shed. Ann heard her fumbling around in the woodpile, and presently she came back with a towering armload, which she dumped into the woodbox with a crash.

"Gracious, Mary!" Ann said. "You shouldn't try to carry so much. Let me bring in some."

"Oh, that's enough for now," said Mary, dusting off her hands and the front of her dress. "If I can git hold of that lazy boy I've got, for five minutes, I'll make him fill up the box tonight. No sense anybody else doin his chores for him. You been down fixin up your new house?"

"Oh, I've been having a wonderful time."

"I'm 'fraid it ain't much of a house." Mary peered into the stove to see if there might be a stray coal or two. Seeing the fire was black out, she poured in a generous dollop of kerosene from the can by the woodbox, dropped in a lighted match and hustled the covers on just as the oil caught with a puff and started a grand roaring up the chimney.

"You'll blow yourself up one of these days," Ann said, not because she thought Mary might, but because it was the customary thing to say when kerosene went off like that. Everybody built fires with kerosene. It was a good quick way.

"Oh, I guess not." Mary smiled. "At least, I ain't yit, and it's been a long time since I built my first fire with oil. How *are* you gittin along down there? I still feel kind of foolish, chargin you twenty-five dollars for that rotten old fishhouse."

"You'd never know it now. I've got it cleaned out and fixed up, and it's going to be the best workroom you ever saw. You'll wish you'd charged me more for it." Ann had started to tell about the plasterboard and the fine job Hod and Willie had done putting it on, but she decided not to. Mary herself wasn't the worst gossip in town, but it would be only natural for her to relay anything like that to the neighbors. In time word would, without doubt, get back to Paris that Ann was spending her time down in the fishhouse with Hod and Willie Stilwell. She knew the pattern of island gossip.

"So long's you don't freeze down there," Mary said.

"I don't expect I will. It was in better repair than you thought it might be. What lovely things!" she went on, looking at the presents spread out on the table. "Are those your Christmas?"

"Such as 't is," Mary shrugged. "I made em myself mostly. Dave's muffler there is the only thing new. I made that, too, but the wool's new. Them lace collars for the girls I cut out of an old crocheted bedspread I had."

"They're beautiful," Ann said.

The tiny medallions were crocheted out of fine creamy thread and Mary's own workmanship in cutting and hemming them was exquisite—little, almost invisible stitches.

"I couldn't find nothin like them in the catalog," Mary said, "and I spose it'll turn out that nobody's wearin anything like that now. But it was all I could think of, so I guess I'll send em. If the girls don't like em, they can stick em in the rag-bag. Money's short this year. I don't spose I should have, but I spent most of mine on some wool for a good thick sweater for Donny."

"Why, that's nice! I expect he'll like that, won't he?"

"I don't know whether he will or not. He ain't like most of youngones. But I thought I'd at least make another try." Mary took off her glasses and began polishing them slowly on her apron. Her eyes, without them, looked defenseless and bewildered. Ann was suddenly surprised to see how old she had grown. "He don't appreciate nothin. He's an awful difficult boy."

"How is he difficult? Is he tough, you mean?"

"No, he ain't tough. Not the way you expect them State boys to be. But then, his folks was from around here—you know, the Mitchells. It's just that he don't pay no attention to what I say, like I was talkin to a stone wall."

It was as if, again, Ann had loosed the waters behind a dam. Mary went on calling the roll of Donny's sins. She did not, however, say that he was a thief. That she had put away in her secret mind, and it lay there, deep buried and festering.

My goodness, Ann thought, she mustn't keep him here if she feels like that. It must be awful for them both.

"Why don't you let someone else take him, Mary?" she asked, sympathetically, as soon as she could get in a word. "Maybe you'd find another boy you'd like better."

Mary shook her head stubbornly. "I been wonderin if Christmas wouldn't bring him to his senses. Wait, I'll show you the sweater I made him. He ain't gut an idea in the world I've made it for him."

She went into the other room and Ann heard her unlocking something—a cupboard or a drawer. When she came back, she had the sweater, done up in snowy tissue paper. It was made of soft dark-red wool, thick and warm but not bulky, with a wide tan stripe running through its middle and across each of the sleeves.

"That stripe's kind of flashy," Mary said, "but I found out that's what boys want this winter. At least, they was a lot a them in the catalog, and I see that Artie Osgood wearin one the other day."

Ann nodded. "Sam's got one," she said. "Not half so good-looking as this, though. My, it's lovely, Mary!" She squeezed a handful of the resilient wool.

"Well, that's one thing I can do, make sweaters," Mary said. "I used t' make enough a them for my own boys. As a matter of fact, this is really Dave's sweater. Or it would be if I hadn't made up my mind to give it to Donny. If he don't appreciate it," she went on grimly, "after I've skimped on my own to give it to him—"

Oh! Ann thought. How can he appreciate it if she feels that way? She got up to go, feeling as if she were going to cry.

Footsteps sounded on the frozen ground outside the door, and Mary scrabbled the sweater out of sight under a pile of tissue paper. Donny himself came in, hesitating in the door as he saw there was company.

"This is Ann Freeman," Mary said abruptly. "I guess you ain't met her, have you, Donny?"

Donny said, "Uh," and ducked his head.

"We almost bumped into each other one day," Ann said, smiling at him. "I was hoping you'd come in," she went on. "I thought I'd take Sam over to Bellport on a Christmas party, next Saturday afternoon—movies and things. I asked him who he'd like to ask to go along and he said you. How about it? Can you make it, Saturday?"

Donny stared at her incredulously. "Sam? Sam *Freeman?*" He had already started edging toward the door which led upstairs, and he stopped dead.

"That's what he said." Ann nodded.

And that's a barefaced lie, she said to herself. I'd better hop home fast and square it with Sam, or I'll be on one hot spot.

"Why, I think that's real nice of you and Sam," Mary said with pleasure. "Of course you'd like to go, wouldn't you, Donny?"

"Well, uh," Donny said. He rubbed his chin against his collar, turning his head stiffly. "Thanks. I can't go this Saturday."

"You can't *go?*" asked Mary sharply. "Why on earth not?"

"I told a feller down to the wharf I'd help him shift some bait." Donny's voice was a mumble.

"Never mind, then," Ann said. "Some other Saturday, maybe. How about the next one?"

"Okay," he said. "I guess maybe I'll have to let you know. I ain't sure about that Saturday, either."

He was deeply embarrassed, Ann saw, anxious to get out of sight, and it seemed only kindness to stop talking and let him go.

"Fine," she said casually. "You do that."

He started for the door again, moving as silently as a ghost.

"Donny," Mary said, "you wait a minute. I want to talk to you."

"Okay." He paused in mid-stride, one foot a little in front of the other, but he did not turn around.

"I was only goin to say, while I had hold of you, that tomorrow night why don't you go down in the wood lot and cut us a Christmas tree? After school, I mean."

"*You* want one?" Donny said.

"Well, it would be mostly for you, I guess, seein you're the youngone."

"I don't want one."

"You don't?"

"N-nh. Not bad enough to bother to go cut one."

"Oh," Mary said. "I just thought it would be nice."

He waited to see if she meant to go on. When she didn't, he took a tentative step toward the door.

"And I think when people's nice to you, the least you could do is accept it."

"Okay." He opened the door and closed it behind him, and they heard him going slowly up the stairs.

"There," Mary said. "You see what I mean?"

Ann nodded. For a moment she was a little afraid to trust her voice. Then she said, "I see."

*

Sam, it turned out, didn't even like Donny.

"Oh, my Lord!" he said, turning to Ann a face of consternation. "What got into you, Ann?"

"Look, Sam! I know it was a dirty trick without asking you first. You've probably got your Saturdays planned up to the hilt."

"I've got basketball practice, that's what I've got. We work *every* Saturday afternoon. I couldn't take time off for movies, even if I wanted to. Besides, I wouldn't be caught dead—" He stopped. "Skip it, now," he said warningly, pressing his lips together in a stubborn line. "It's out, and that's all there is to it."

"What's the matter with Donny? Don't you like him?"

"Oh, he's all right," Sam mumbled.

"Well, what, for heaven's sake? He looks like a decent kid to me. Sam, are you being a snob?"

"You don't need to bother with him. He'll get tended to," said Sam darkly.

"Sam, I'll shake you—"

"Try it!" He whirled, caught her around the waist and shook her until she gasped. It was rather like being a shoe shaken by a puppy, and she could feel the affection under his rough grasp.

"Cut it out, you big lug," she laughed, trying to fight back. "Just because you've grown out of your britches, you think you can handle me! Time was, I could dust your diapers good and proper!"

His big, knuckly brown hands were like vises. At just the right time, she went limp.

"Sam, help me out, please. I know that kid's getting into trouble, and he hasn't got a soul to help him."

"Sure he is. No reason why we should stick our necks out, is there?" he growled.

"No reason why we shouldn't. Or can you think of one?"

"Plenty."

"What's he doing that's so bad?"

"Oh, I d'no." Sam looked stubborn. Then, looking at her, he suddenly made up his mind. "Well, look. A couple of times he's had stuff to peddle—like jackknives and gloves and, oh, stuff. New ones."

"Oh," Ann said. "Where would he get them?"

"Well, Artie Osgood had some, too. I asked Artie—you know, he never could keep his mouth shut. Don't tell, Ann, or the cops would be after them."

"No," she said, feeling a little cold. "I won't tell."

"Bellport stores. Shopliftin."

"Sam, no!"

He nodded. "I gave em both merry hell, last week. Said they

needn't bring their stuff around to me. Or any of my friends, either." He looked thoughtful. "I guess Donny must've thought it was pretty funny, me askin him to go to the movies."

"M'm. I guess so."

She was silent for a moment, thinking, and Sam said no more for a moment, either.

"Look, Sam. This is how it is." As briefly as she could, and hoping that, somehow, the story would reach him, she told him what she thought Donny's life at Mary Mackay's must be like, and she added some speculations of her own as to what his life must be like, anyway.

She needn't have worried. The story did reach Sam.

"Yeah," he said, looking embarrassed and downcast. "Yeah, I'm cryin. All right, I'll see what I can do." He couldn't get out of practice on Saturdays, he said, but he could make it some Friday night, maybe. "That do?"

"That'll be swell. You're my favorite brother, Sam."

"Ah, shut up," he said. "I ought to sock you in the puss."

They needn't have worried, as it turned out. Donny met Ann the next day, on the road to the shack, and said politely that he was sorry, his Saturdays were full up for the next few weeks. And, oh, yeah, it was too bad, but he guessed he was busy Friday nights, too.

*

On Tuesday morning, Hod and Willie went to Bellport for bait and they brought back Ann's furniture, landing it on the shore of her cove.

"I thought I'd better let you know," Hod said over the telephone to Ann. He had taken pains to call in the middle of the morning when he thought Paris might be out working in the wood lot, and he'd guessed right. Myra answered and called Ann to the phone.

"That's darned nice of you and Willie," Ann said. "I hope the time'll come when I get settled and quit being a nuisance to my neighbors, Hod."

"No trouble," he said briefly. "Glad to do it. So long." He hung up with a sharp little click.

Thoughtfully, Ann put her own receiver back on the hook and went to the hall closet for her coat. She was pretty much under obligation to Hod and Willie. She wished she could think of some way to pay them back. And if Hod were going to keep on doing things for her, he might be a little less reserved about it. "I've got to go down to the shack, ma," she called. "My stuff's come."

Myra came flying out of the pantry. "It has!" she cried excitedly. "Well, I certainly hope whoever brought it over put it some place under cover. If it was ever fixin to snow, it is right this minute. You be back to dinner?"

"I might not. That be all right?"

"Course it'll be all right. I'll fix you some sandwiches."

Ann planted a kiss on her plump pink cheek. "You're dusted over like a sugar muffin," she said, brushing with her finger at a dab of flour on the bridge of her mother's nose.

"Oh, I know it! I can't git within ten miles of a flour barrel without beglammin it all over me." Myra mopped vaguely, completely missing her nose and adding another spot to her cheek from additional flour on the corner of her apron.

Ann chuckled. "Don't bother about sandwiches."

"Now, Ann, I won't have you goin without your meals—"

"I won't. I had a notion, if I got my new stove set up, I might break it in. I was going to pick up some eggs and stuff at Myron's."

"Well—" Myra conceded regretfully. She hated to see one of her brood go out of the house unfed, but she wasn't one to fuss about it. "You mind you have something decent."

"I will. 'Bye!"

She ran down the steps and across the yard. From the sitting room window, Myra watched her go, standing a moment rubbing her hands against her apron. My! she thought, she's some crazy about that old fishhouse, and I don't know's I blame her. She ought t' have a place t' work in, where she can call her soul her own.

People would talk, Myra knew, about the shack. In fact, her

ear, sensitized through years of practiced listening, had already
picked up a few undertones behind the curious or wondering com-
ments of the neighbors, which meant that things were being said.
Not of course where any of Ann's folks could hear them.

But there! Them clapper-tongues, havin that over would keep
them from dreamin up somethin worse, and it would give them
that had little to do a way to while away their time. It *was* kind of
an unusual thing for a girl to do, and if it had been anybody but
Ann, Myra didn't know but she herself might have done a little
wonderin. Seein it was Ann, though, and you knew what she
wanted the shack for, of course it was all right.

I certainly am some proud of her, Myra thought, going slowly
back into her pantry. I wish I knew what ailed her though. I don't
b'lieve she's in love, unless it's with somebody away, but some-
times I think she acts like it.

She couldn't ever ask Ann, and Ann wouldn't say anything. If
it had been Sam, or Polly, Myra would have said without a
thought, "What's the matter, dear?" and either one of them would
have told her.

You can't get *to* her, she said to herself. It must be somethin
that bein away does to people.

You forgot how well you knew them, even if they did belong
to you, and you couldn't think of a way to say that you were right
there, in case they needed you.

Her mother was probably right about the weather, Ann saw, as
she walked down the road to East Village. The sky was lowery
gray, with a steeliness she knew of old was a sign of snow. The
grass under the culverts was still stiff with last night's frost and
the hard mud along the shoulders of the road sparkled with it.
The wind was damp against her cheek, smelling of cold and salt
and spruces.

But what made you think most of snow was the sense of waiting
in the air, in the trees, in the whole motionless and frozen coun-
tryside.

She had been working hard for the past week, with a kind of

dogged desperation. What she was turning out wasn't good. Sometimes it seemed as if she were working behind a thick sheet of clear glass—she could see what she wanted, but she couldn't get at it. The work itself seemed brittle as glass, inflexible, without warmth or color. But she'd kept at it. The thing, somehow, had to get itself done.

As she came out of Myron Osgood's grocery, her arms full of paper bags, a fine snowflake, hard as hail, bounced against her cheek, spiraled crazily into the road and lay there without melting.

I hope I'll be able to haul that stuff into the shack alone before it's buried, she thought. Some of it will be heavy, I guess.

Hod probably figured he'd done enough, getting the stuff over from Bellport and boating it ashore at the cove. She was a pig to want more, when he'd already done so much. But it would be nice if he'd come out of his shell a little. She could use some friendliness and companionship. Sam seemed to be the only one she could talk to, and he was busy, in and out of the house, absorbed in his own doings. Talking with Hod that day in Bellport had been fun.

I wish he'd had the sense to keep things the way they were. We could have stayed friends.

It was harder than she'd thought it would be, not having anyone to talk to. She could pass the time of day with her mother and Polly and walk warily around the armed truce with her father, though that was pretty profitless, for no one could tell just what would make him mad. So far the neighbors she'd seen had been pleasant, like Mary Mackay; but they'd have to turn her over in their minds and see her around for a few months before they'd feel free and easy. It took them a little time, always, to get used to anyone new.

It was taking her a little time to get used to them, too, she told herself ruefully. Outside of the general topic of the weather, there didn't seem to be much common ground to base talk on. Her mother and a neighbor could sit in the front room over their sewing all afternoon, with their tongues running like clappers. Through the closed shed-chamber door, she could hear the hum

that never seemed to stop. She'd often wondered what they found
to say so much about, but the one time she'd sneaked to the head
of the stairs to see, she'd heard Prilly Grant, Sam Grant's wife,
going on at a great rate about the grade school teacher.

"She never keeps one mite of order, spitballs flyin like *rain*, and
them big kids just rollin in the aisles. I says to Henny, I says, its
dis*cus*tin! From all I hear tell, though, the way she stays out late
and runs around with them Bellport fellers, *schoolin* around her
they are, she's too sleepy durin the day to—"

Ann didn't stay to listen to any more. She wasn't interested in
gossip, and even if she had been, she wouldn't have known enough
about anyone to talk.

So far, Hod and Willie had been the pleasantest people she'd
seen, and the most interesting, but now the work on the shack was
done, she didn't suppose she'd be seeing much of either of them.
Willie might drop by once in a while; but the way Hod was feel-
ing, she doubted if he would.

How was he feeling anyway? He knew, of course, that she'd
been angry with him that day at the shack, but, after all, nothing
very terrible had happened. She'd only made plain her feelings in
the matter. There was no reason, now, why they couldn't be friends,
like sensible people. Unless there were something else—

Oh! she thought, with a sudden pang, and brought up short in
the middle of the road. Suppose he thought she'd been listening
to talk since she'd got home, and was beginning to feel about him
the way the rest of the village did? He couldn't—he had too much
sense! But, living alone, the way he and Willie did, and being
sensitive anyway about such things, it might be he thought that
was why she'd been so angry. There was no way he could know
the real reason.

If that were so, it explained why he stayed so unapproachable.

Oh, dear, she thought. I've been too wrapped up in my own
troubles.

Coming out of the trees into the clearing, she saw with sudden
astonishment and pleasure that she wasn't going to have to worry

about help with the furniture. The assorted crates had been car-
ried up the twenty feet or so from the shore of the cove and set
conveniently outside the shack door. On the granite step, his big
shoulders relaxed against the threshold, a hammer and chisel be-
side him, sat Hod.

"Hello," he said. "I thought you might need a hand."

"Hello," Ann said.

Stacked by the door was a goodly pile of wood, and down by
the shore the rest of Hod's two cords had been thrown up on the
bank out of the tide's way.

"We boated it down last night," he said, his glance following
hers. "Willie's a pretty good weather prophet, and he said if this
should turn out to be a blizzard, we'd have a heck of a time shovelin
out the wood, so we brought it down."

"I don't know how I'll ever pay you and Willie back," Ann
said. She was, she realized, very glad to see him, and not just
because she needed help. He sounded almost the way he had the
morning in Bellport, friendly, interested, with casual mild humor
underlying the tones of his voice. His eyes, though, were unsmiling.

"Let's have that pack-load." He got up, deftly scooping the
paper bags out of her arms. "Where you want it put?"

"Inside, on the table, I guess."

"I'd have started opening crates, only it seemed kind of impo-
lite before the owner arrived," he said, coming back and picking
up his tools from the doorstep. "Guess we'll have to hustle if we
get things under cover before it snows. The stove first, maybe?"

Without waiting for an answer, he began ripping slats off one
of the crates.

He was being impersonal enough, Ann thought, and friendly,
the way she had hoped he'd be again. But she wondered, standing
a little uncertainly beside him, if he'd come because he wanted to,
or because he'd realized she'd have to have help.

"What can I do?" she asked. "You've swiped all the jobs."

"Wait till I get this open, you can have the tools while I set up
the stove."

No, there wasn't any way you could tell how he was feeling.

His strength was something to watch in action, and so was the precision of his hands. In spite of the biting wind, he had laid off his heavy sheepskin jacket, and under the faded blue flannel of his shirt, the flat muscles moved effortlessly and with grace.

"Couldn't I take one side of it?" she asked, as he lifted the small stove from its demolished crate.

"It's not very heavy—" He disappeared with it through the shack door, carrying it as if it had been a box of crackers. "Now," he said, coming back and fumbling around in the crate packing, "if you've only got the right lengths of stovepipe— Smart girl! Did you measure for it?"

"Yes, I—"

But he was gone again, with the stovepipe this time, and she heard him tapping and rattling it as he made adjustments to the pipe-hole in the chimney.

Ann picked up the tools and started to open another crate. She found she couldn't do very well in her mittens, and when she took them off the cold struck against her fingers like a stinging lash. It was a good feeling, something to put your mind on. She whanged away with the hammer. It was nice to have an active job of work to do, too. She felt, suddenly, as if she'd been doubled up for weeks.

"Why don't you come and look at this?" Hod asked from the door of the shack. "There're a couple of ways to set it up, and you might as well be sure it's the way you want it."

In the clean bare little room, whose only furniture had been Bob Mackay's bait table, the cheap tiny stove seemed to have taken on proportions and a grace that it hadn't had on the floor of the Bellport furniture store. It stood there with authority—with the dignity of a thing in its place—and Ann, looking at it, felt a sudden pride and contentment. "I thought it was homely when I bought it. But all at once it seems to have got quite beautiful."

"It put that on when I set it up," said Hod, and she flashed him a smile, delighted that he saw it too.

"How'd you like to build a fire in it? Place feels like an ice-box," he said, making a dive for the door. "Hey—look what the weather's doing!"

The northeast wind, having blown in half-hearted gusts for fifteen minutes or so, had decided to put some teeth into the business of making a storm. The distant island went out of sight in a snow-squall as if a wool coverlet had been dropped over them, and in the swift march of the blurred white line up the harbor, Spoon Island's western hook blotted out, the channel ledges went under one by one.

By the time Ann had gathered up an armload of excelsior and splintered slats for a fire, even the water of the cove had smothered out and inside the shack the windowpanes had gone white and blind.

The kindling caught at once, but thick smoke poured out of the covers and open drafts of the stove. For a moment, Ann's heart sank. It was going to smoke—maybe the chimney was clogged or something. No, there was a closed damper in the pipe. She opened it and the smoke cleared away. The fire poured up the chimney with a fine crackling sound. From the covers and the front of the firebox, a thin warmth began to rise that grew perceptibly as she spread her numbed hands to it. She stood warming them and listening to the pitting sound the snow made on the windowpanes.

What is there about building a fire that helps lonely people? she thought. The warmth, of course, but that's only a substitute. Maybe it goes back to times when a fire was about all the humanity people had.

It was good, too, this quiet and shutting away. You might be the only people in the world, everything else gone for now, whatever you might remember when the sun came out again. The way the land had looked this morning, still, waiting—you knew now what it was for. For covering up, release. In a little while the shoulders of stone, the dead leaves, the naked roads would be gone, drifted under a quietude as yielding as sleep.

I might be all right after a while. After enough of this, I might be rid of it. You could let go of a thing, I think, especially now you know it's nothing you want to keep.

The warmth of the stove grew and spread.

Hod bumped in through the door with an armload, his shoulders and collar powdered, his eyebrows fierce under a bushy fringe of white.

"That's food I've got in those paper bags," Ann said. "Would there be a well around within jumping distance where we could get water for coffee?"

"Sure. Remember the Fir Well?"

For a moment, straight out of childhood, a picture flashed into her mind of the small hidden spring under the bank down along the shore, its water bubbling out of sand and smelling of clean moss and spruce needles and coldness. "I haven't thought of it for years!" she said. "You mean to say somebody's bothered to keep it clear?"

"Willie likes to do things like that. He'd think 't was a crime not to keep a spring clear, even if it wasn't on his own land." Hod came over and stood beside her, spreading his hands to the fire. "Where on earth did you think you were going to get water down here?"

"I honestly hadn't thought. Not very practical, am I?"

"No. Not to notice." He looked at her, and for the first time that day his smile spread all the way to his eyes.

You couldn't meet a smile like that without returning it, at least partly in kind.

*

Paris Freeman told himself he didn't want to traipse the length of the Spoonhandle in a cussid, howlin blizzard. By God, it was bad enough to be out in it doin the afternoon chores, milkin the cow and luggin in wood that Sam, the lazy sod, ought to have been around to lug. What a man ought to be able to do after his day's work was go in the house where 't was warm, take off his boots, set down and read the paper. But no. Instid of that, he had to rig up and walk a mile and a half to make sure that crazy girl gut home all right.

This Paris told himself, stalking down the Spoonhandle wood road, humped over, his long petulant face thrusting into the driven snowflakes like the head of a melancholy sheep.

Actually, though Paris wouldn't admit it to himself, he was consumed with curiosity. He hadn't seen what Ann had done to the shack; he didn't know anything about what she was up to down there. You'd think a girl would invite her own father down to have a look, when she was fixin up a place, maybe ask him to help her out a little if there was any heavy liftin. But no, that wasn't Ann! If she was so keen on mindin her own business, she God and well could, for all he'd ever offer to help. He'd stay away from there. She wasn't goin to git the chance to call him nosy.

He wouldn't be goin down there this afternoon if he didn't think she might not need help, comin home through them woods in this storm. Not *him*.

He stepped up on the doorstep of the shack, stamping the snow noisily off his boots. It didn't occur to him to knock—probably Paris had never knocked before entering in all his life. His way, usually, was to turn the knob and open a door with a thrust of his boot. This time the knob didn't turn the way a knob should—somebody apparently had hold of it on the other side, and the door, when he kicked it, fetched up against a solid body.

The solid body was Hod Stilwell, who had just been leaving, and had stopped to talk with his hand on the door-latch.

In spite of the remarks Paris made when he was mad, it would never have occurred to him, actually, to suspect Ann of wrong-doing. These remarks were automatic; they meant nothing whatever. Now, confronted by a situation which, according to his standards, might contain possibilities, he was so flabbergasted that he could do nothing but stand and stare.

"Hi, Paris," Hod said cheerfully. "Come on in. Blows, don't it?"

"Hi," Paris said, responding mechanically to the customary greeting. He stepped inside, and Hod closed the door behind him.

"I was just goin." Hod hadn't taken his hand off the door-knob. "That is, unless you got something else you want done, Ann."

"No, that's everything. And thanks a million, Hod. I'd never have got that stuff lugged in alone. How'd you like the shack, pa?"

Paris's eyes had started to take in everything in the tiny room, but they had got no farther than the studio couch, and he was staring at that like a bird at a snake. "All right," he said stiffly. He swiveled his look and fastened it on her. "I come down t' git you, Ann."

"Why?" she asked, startled. "Is something wrong?"

"Why in the cussid hell should there be somethin wrong? I come down t' make sure you gut home. It ain't fit for me t' be out, let alone a woman."

"Oh. All right. Wait till I put on my coat. I was going to clean up the dishes, but they'll wait. I guess you'd like to go now, wouldn't you?"

"Dishes!" Paris peered nearsightedly at the table. By God, they'd been eatin together, and him tryin t' make out he was just in there t' help lug stuff!

"Yes," said Ann, putting on her coat. "We were starved when we got the stuff unpacked, and neither of us had any dinner. It's a slick little stove, pa. Heats and cooks just like a major. Want to have a look at it?" She made as if to open the door of the tiny oven.

"Hnh!" Paris grunted. "Like t' git home."

They walked along silently in single file, Paris stalking ahead. In the woods the spruces broke the force of the wind, letting the snow sift thickly down through their wildly lashing tops, but at the clearing where Hod turned off to go down to his punt, great clouds and waves of white poured horizontally off the land and out over the smothered water.

"So long," Hod said, stepping into the path, which was merely a white streak now through the tall grass, its smooth depression filled up with snow.

In his nervous irritation, Paris was ready to give advice to anybody. "You be careful, goin acrost there," he bellowed after Hod: "You misjudge, you'll blow to hellangone down the harbor."

"Nowhere to blow to but across to the island," Hod said composedly. He went down the bank and they heard the muted rattle of the pebbles as he pushed the punt across the beach. For a moment his blurred outline showed dimly as he rowed out from under the bank, then the whirling snow swallowed him.

"Ain't no day for man nor beast t' be out in a punt," Paris said fretfully. He strode along a few paces into the wind, and then turned about-face, so abruptly that Ann banged into him.

"What in hell you think you're doin, down there entertainin the neighborhood?" he wanted to know raucously. "And what you got a bed in there for, by God?"

The storm in her face had taken Ann's breath away. She felt, anyway, that if she had to talk now, answer Paris's useless questions, listen to his suspicions, she couldn't bear it. For a little while, shut away in the shack, with the snow blinding the windowpanes, and with Hod's good, quiet companionship, she had felt the first peace of mind she had known in months. She said nothing at all, but brushed on by and left Paris standing there, his mouth open to shout his empty accusations into the storm.

*

Word went around the village, traveling from door to door where the women visited, and over the party line where they didn't. Old Witherspoon wasn't interested in Willie Stilwell's place any more, and there wouldn't be a chance, after all, to sell off shore property at fat prices to the summer people.

The news was straight from the horse's mouth. Bill Pray had heard it from Pete; no, Willie himself had told somebody, just who it wasn't clear, but never mind. Or maybe it was Agnes who had said. After a while, it might have been anybody. But anyway, it was so. That is, it was so if Willie Stilwell had said it was. Pete or Agnes, you couldn't be sure, you knew *them*. But Willie!

Whatever else he might be, you knew about Willie. He never told a lie in his life.

People shrugged and said well, they never put much stock in the story anyway, and it would have been a good thing to have some property turn over, if you could get a good price. But there! You knew Spoon Island. Nothing ever happened there the way it did other places. They guessed they'd just live there until they shriveled up and the man came for them. Someone over in Bellport was buyin up spruce wood lots for pulpwood. Maybe there'd be somethin in that, but you knew them fly-by-nights, that nobody. ever heard of. Peddlers, that's all they were, and you hat t' watch em. Joe King, this one's name was, Box 48, Bellport, if anybody was interested to write. John Pray heard about him from Bill, who got his name from Pete. Or had Bill heard about it over in Bellport? After a while, nobody knew. But that was his address.

Box 48, during the week before Christmas, turned up two letters asking for information. One was from Bill Pray and the other from his brother John.

"Joe King" was actually a Bellport lawyer named Alec Staples whom Pete occasionally did business with. He had a law clerk working for him whose name was Joe King, but that was neither here nor there. Alec Staples turned the letters over to Pete the day Pete drove over from the island.

"H'n," Pete grunted, reading them. "You can offer John, here, nine hundred for his whole place. He'll take it, I think. As for Bill—" Pete's grin appeared and vanished. "Try two thousand for his twenty acres of shore wood lots. If he don't take it, go up to twenty-five hundred, and then we'll see."

So the Pray brothers each got a letter from Joe King, and young John snapped up the offer by return mail. In response to a telephone call, he went to Bellport the next day with his deed, and came back that afternoon with a bankbook, showing he had eight hundred and fifty dollars in the Bellport People's Bank.

"And there's the other fifty," he said to his wife Nell, hauling out a roll of bills. "Moving money, babe. Let's go."

It was as simple as that.

Bill Pray thought it over for a couple of days. He was a little more cautious than John, older, and he had been counting for years on getting a good price for his shore property, if the time ever came when the summer people moved in. This time he'd thought sure they would. In his disappointment, but mostly from satisfaction at getting five hundred dollars more than Pete Stilwell had offered him, he, too, decided to sell. He'd have twenty acres of good farm and wood lot left after the shore lots were gone. And it sure would give him a heave to go and wave that five hundred dollars under Pete's nose.

It didn't occur to Bill that there was anything funny about the pulpwood man's wanting the shore lots, because, after all, they were the ones that had the thickest growth of spruce. So Bill talked it over with Henny. They both had to admit that after a lifetime of living on what Bill made farming and fishing, that two thousand looked almighty big to them.

"It *will* seem funny not to own clear through to the shore, Bill," Henny said wistfully. "I declare, I've always gut kind of a satisfaction, seein them acres rollin back clear down to the ledges."

"Ayup," Bill said. "Me, too. Them acres been in the Pray family for a long time, Henny. Le's see." He figured briefly on a piece of paper. "My God, a hundred and sixty-nine years."

"My goodness' sakes!" She peered over to check up on his figures and convince herself.

"Well," Bill said. "You can't live on satisfaction."

And two thousand dollars!

So Bill Pray sold, too.

Word went around again, and this time it was more about the pulpwood man. He was really buying up land, and for once, offering real money for it. Bill Pray had sold some, and John had got rid of his whole place and was going to Bellport. Nobody knew how much they'd got, because the Pray boys hadn't said. But the word went around and it grew; on Thursday there were two more letters in Box 48. Sam Grant offered ten acres and Paris Freeman forty-five.

Sam got five hundred dollars and Paris three thousand from "Joe King."

And "Three thousand dollars!" the word went round again. Wasn't that an awful price for forty-five acres of that old busted-down land!

But it was a funny thing. When Nick Driver and Mary Mackay wrote, Joe King wrote back and said he was sorry, but for just now he'd bought up all the woodland he could use. It didn't occur to anyone that these properties didn't have outlooks facing the sea view; nor did anyone know that after these letters were received, Myron Osgood and Hallet Romer each sold two-thirds of their land.

Nearly everybody on the island wrote Joe King, except Willie Stilwell and Joe Sangor down on Spoonhandle. Willie didn't think twice about it; but Joe heard the talk up around the wharf, and he and Mary discussed selling. Because, Mary said, some day they must plan to go back to the Portuguese people in New Bedford. The children were getting old enough now to take notice of things; it was better to take them to grow up among their own kind. Joe agreed with her; but this strange man, this man buying wood lots for pulpwood, they did not know. It was better, too, not to trust anyone unknown, rather than to risk losing what they had.

"It's the Yankees again, Joe," Mary said. "We're better off out of it."

At the end of the week before Christmas, "Joe King," for a dollar and other considerations, transferred to Pete Stilwell nearly a hundred and fifty acres of Spoon Island eastern shore property. As a matter of fact, Pete paid him twenty-five dollars.

It was as simple as that, and satisfactory. And it left East Village ringed in tightly with new boundary lines that started only a few hundred yards away from the houses and barns.

*

Donny Mitchell's Saturday plans had nothing to do with helping any fisherman shift bait. At noon, he and Artie Osgood lay in wait for the big refrigerator truck that hauled bi-weekly loads of fish from the island to Ferriston—the nearest city of any size, forty miles from Bellport. Artie was friends with the driver, a hulking young man with pimples, who had given them the ride before. Donny wasn't friends with him, though he pretended to be. The young man, Paul Carter, was too nosy. He always wanted to find out things about you—who your folks were, what your business was and what you were going to do in Ferriston.

Artie didn't seem to mind that. All the way to Ferriston he and Paul talked and gossiped, while Donny sat silent, watching through the windshield the dirty ice in the road, the ruts and bare patches of concrete slide toward him and go out of sight under the truck's blunt nose. Artie was easy—he didn't seem to have to be on the watch all the time for fear he'd let on about things he didn't want people to know.

Donny was beginning to feel as if his mind held secrets too heavy to be told, but which might tell themselves if he didn't take care. And who his folks were, where he stayed and who paid for his board and clothes were his own business. Artie didn't have to watch that—people like Paul knew he was Myron Osgood's boy. Paul probably knew about *him*, too, Donny mused morosely, but he better keep his dirty mouth shut about it.

The trips to Ferriston didn't seem to bother Artie, either, or the stuff they had hidden away, or the money cached for what they'd sold. Artie was able to put all that out of his mind, until the time came to think about it again. He said he didn't care if they did get found out. Nothing bothered Artie, so he said.

The time would come, Donny promised himself, when he'd stop worrying too. Not about getting caught, that was your own lookout, that was a chance you took, but about what Uncle My would think if he was anywhere where he could know what Donny was doing. He'd always said he'd remember Uncle My as long as he lived. It seemed funny, now, to be trying so hard to forget him. His memory of the old man was already growing dim; sometimes, even if he tried, he couldn't call up into his mind what Uncle My's face had looked like.

As for Willie Stilwell, Donny didn't care what he thought, not now. The old ragbag, scared of a woman old enough to be his mother. By God, he thought, I don't care what anyone thinks. They can let me alone. When they're all rottin on dry fish and potatoes, I'll be ridin around in my Cadillac.

The truck pulled up at the town square in Ferriston, to let the boys off. Paul let her idle a moment in neutral, while he leaned out of the cab to kid Artie.

"What particular brand of hell are you two young baysters cookin up this afternoon?"

"Why," Artie said, his round fat face taking on a look of innocence, "we come over to get our Christmas presents, Paul."

Paul laughed, an explosive "Haw!"

"So, ain't it, Donny?"

"That's right," Donny said. He was sweating with impatience, wishing Paul would pull away and leave them alone, so they could go do what they had come for and get it over.

"Well, when you git your *shoppin* done, you want me to find you a nice piece, you come over to the market." Paul winked ferociously and drove away, enjoying tremendously his own mental picture of what two green kids like that would do with a woman.

"Damn him!" Donny said, between his teeth.

"Ah, shut up!" Artie glowered. Artie, too, was a little edgy over the afternoon's work to come, and besides, he considered it pretty naive to show that you were sore over a little kidding like that. "Come on," he said, jerking his head. "And see you don't turn green, like you done last time."

The boys went along the main street of the business section and loitered in front of a sporting goods store. Through the plate glass window, they could see there were three clerks in the store, all busy with customers. Going in, they stood idly by a counter, ostensibly waiting for a clerk to be free.

Artie let his eyes rove around the store. "Over there," he said, out of the corner of his mouth. "Them hunting knives? See?"

One of the customers picked up his package and went out and the clerk came toward them. "What can I do for you?"

"Like to see some rawhide laces," Artie said politely. "Long ones, please, for high-topped boots."

He was a nice-looking boy, if a little fat, neatly dressed in a blue windbreaker and dark blue pants. His pleasant round face and frank blue eyes generally made a good impression on people.

"This way, please," said the clerk.

Artie made quite a long business of choosing just the right quality and length of rawhide. "Got a good pair of leather-tops," he told the clerk, smiling shyly. "Want to fit em out right."

"Good idea," said the clerk. He was quite expansive and helpful in showing just what stock the store had in rawhide laces.

Donny had mooched along behind Artie and stood at his elbow. Then, as if understanding that his friend would be quite a while, he ambled off to another counter and looked at some sneakers. Idly, he watched the busy clerks, leaning back against a showcase, on which lay the hunting knives in their tan leather sheaths.

"Those'll be swell," Artie said at last, with the air of one who had been helped to make an excellent choice. He paid for the laces and stuffed the small package into the front of his windbreaker. As he waited for change, he turned around and jerked his head at Donny. "Hey, Bill, come on over here and look at the swell boxin-gloves."

Donny came, slowly, and stood looking, without seeing anything. He could feel a drop of sweat trickling coldly along the crease by his nose, but he did not dare to wipe it away.

Outside, they walked to the corner, turned around it and ducked into an alley.

"Get one?" Artie asked, as they broke into a run.

"Two," said Donny jerkily. "One apiece."

"Chee-*zis!* If you ain't the one," Artie panted back over his shoulder. "Me, I'd never of dared try for two."

On an obscure bench behind a bush in the city park, they wrapped the knives neatly in brown paper which Artie carried flattened be-

tween the back of his windbreaker and his shirt. They tied the
package with string, so it would look as if it had been purchased
in a store.

All afternoon they "shopped," in stores scattered widely in
various parts of the city, accumulating a variety of brown paper
parcels which they stuffed in the fronts of their windbreakers. It
was nothing unusual to see two boys loaded down with wrapped
bundles, in town shopping a couple of days before Christmas.

They ate at an obscure diner, when suppertime came, and took
the early evening train back to Bellport. Donny lay back on the
plush seat and closed his eyes. The plush smelled like old potato
peelings. It was funny, the cloth on a seat in a railway car smelling
like old potato peelings. He was so tired he couldn't hold the
calves of his legs from trembling, and his undershirt, beneath the
sleazy windbreaker, was clammy with sweat. He wished Artie
would shut up and let him rest. Maybe if Artie would stop talking
he could go to sleep. But Artie was on top of the world and it
seemed he couldn't stop talking.

"Hey," he said, giving Donny a poke in the ribs. "Look, there's
old Connie from the diner. Drunker'n a haddock!" He tittered.
"For cramp's sake, look at her. Rollin!"

"I don't care 'f it's Mrs. Roosevelt," Donny mumbled crossly,
but he opened his eyes.

Old Connie was coming along the aisle of the car, lurching
royally to the motion of the train. She was all dressed up in a long
black skirt and a man's brown tweed Norfolk jacket. On her head
she wore a rusty-yellow round turban trimmed with a full-blown
pink cloth cabbage rose. Connie had a basket full of neat, waxed-
paper wrapped sandwiches. She paused at each seat, resting the
basket on its wooden arm, and fixing the occupant with a bleary eye.

"San'wiches," she mumbled. "Have nice ham san'wich. Twen'
cents."

Some passengers were buying, but trade wasn't brisk. Most
people looked up, shook their heads and turned away with a wink
or a knowing grin.

"Hi, Connie," Artie said, as she came abreast and bumped to a precarious stop. "Ain't you a long ways from home?"

She peered down, obviously not too pleased to see someone she knew. The boys ate, fairly often, at her diner in Bellport.

"Hmp," she grunted. "It's you. Don't want t' buy nothin, I spose?"

"We just et," Artie said. "How's your feet?"

"Killin me," said Connie. She looked the length of the car and remarked in a loud voice to everyone, "My feet's killin me!"

The carload of passengers stirred. Heads came up, newspapers were lowered. People looked amused.

"They could drop off and rot here on this floor," Connie announced. "Nobody'd give a good goddam until they begun to stink. San'wiches?" She poked the basket at Artie, forgetting he had already refused to buy.

"Heck, I said no," he mumbled, sorry he had spoken to her in the first place. People, seeing his embarrassment, were beginning to snicker.

"Jus' like all the rest," Connie said stridently. "Young people jus' like old ones. Got their pants pockets sewed up so tight it'd take a charge a giant powder t' blast loose a dime." The train lurched and she stumbled against Artie, knocking his shoulder with the basket.

He leaned away, muttering under his breath, "Gwan, you ole fool! Git!"

"Wadda ya mean 'ole fool'?" she demanded belligerently.

Donny, in the half of the seat next the window, reached across and steadied the basket. "Hey," he mumbled, his face turning slowly red, "you want to seddown? You want my seat to rest a minute?"

Connie caught herself up, and the anger on her lined face changed to a good-natured grin. "Hell, no," she said. "You keep it, sonny. I gut work t' do. I'm earning my Christmas money. San'wiches?" she demanded, poking her basket into the face of the man across the aisle.

"Well, for Pete's sake!" Artie said, staring at Donny. "I spose you think I'd put up with givin half this seat to that dirty ole slut!"

"Aw, dry up, or I'll knock your face out the back a your neck," Donny said.

Artie opened his mouth to say something, but the look in Donny's eye suddenly impressed him and he shut it again. The rest of the way he was silent, while Donny looked out of the window.

They got back to Bellport in time to catch a ride home on the late mail truck, and hid the things in Artie's secret place—an oil-cloth-covered box under a brush-pile back of his father's garage.

Donny held out one bundle, tucking it carefully back in the front of his windbreaker. That is, he wasn't exactly holding it out, because Artie knew about it and was in on the joke. It was a Christmas present for Mis Mackay, something he had gone to quite a lot of trouble to get, hanging around longer than he should have to swipe it from the kitchen section of a big department store. She'd get the point of it all right, even if he gave it to her on Christmas, with a dead-pan face, as an honest-to-God present. It was a cookbook.

*

Pete was sitting in his office digesting his dinner on the day before Christmas, when he heard the car stop outside the store. He had not planned to keep the store open today, seeing it was Sunday. But Agnes and her son Stilwell, home from college for the holidays, were at his house. They had been invited for supper and Christmas Eve, but they had arrived at one o'clock and were still there. Agnes was agog because she knew Mr. Witherspoon was overdue—they had expected him yesterday—and she had everything ready for him to stay at her house.

So after dinner, Pete had gone down and opened up the store. He had an idea Witherspoon would come there first anyway and he felt it might be advantageous, just at first, to talk to him alone. By leaning forward and peering through his office door, Pete could see through the plate-glass window at the front of the store. It was Witherspoon arriving, all right, just climbing out of a big maroon-colored car, and another man with him.

Pete leaned back in his chair, spread a red bandana handkerchief over his face and began to snore. He was a picture of lazy content.

Witherspoon, after a short wait in the store and calling "Stilwell!" a couple of times, finally came back to the office door.

"Well, here he is!" he boomed heartily. "Hello, there!"

Pete removed his feet from the desk with a bang and sat up before grabbing the handkerchief away from his face. "Who t' hell's makin that cussid racket?" he growled, blinking as if bewildered. "Oh. For Godsake, it's Mr. Witherspoon!" His frozen glare melted into a sheepish grin. "Guess you caught me nappin."

Mr. Witherspoon advanced with outstretched hand. "Guess I did, and I don't blame you. How are you, Stilwell?"

"So-so," Pete said, flopping the hand up and down. "How's yourself?"

"Fine, couldn't be better." Mr. Witherspoon indicated the young man behind him. "This is Gerald Bundy, Mr. Stilwell."

"Relative a yourn?" Pete asked, eyeing Mr. Bundy.

"Oh, no. Gerald's my right-hand man."

"Hud-do." Pete flopped Bundy's hand, rather gingerly extended. His lawyer, I'll bet, he thought. Catch him taking any chances, without a lawyer along. Aloud, he went on, "Kind of cold in here. Guess my forty winks was long enough t' let the fire git down. You better keep your co'ts on till I drop in a couple chunks. I'd bout give you up," he went on, ambling over to the stove, "when you didn't arrive yistiddy."

"I was held up," Mr. Witherspoon said. "We ran into some snow."

Fumbling around in his woodbox, Pete unearthed a dusty butt of knotted yellow birch, which he maneuvered into the stove. "That so? I heard over the radio they'd had some snow t' the west'ard.

Funny we never had none here. Quite often we don't, though—it's the salt water."

"Is that so? Stilwell, I was wondering whether to send my chauffeur back to Bellport, or—" Mr. Witherspoon hesitated.

"Agnes'll put him up," Pete said. "If that's what you want." In Pete's voice was some doubt as to whether the great man would want his chauffeur sleeping in the same house. "Or he kin stay up home with me."

"Either would be fine. I'd appreciate it. Might need him, you know, need the car. Especially if we do any shooting. Gerald and I brought some guns along. We thought we might get a chance at some duck, this season of the year."

"All you want." Pete waved his hand in a circular motion, as if the air at any chosen moment could be filled with ducks. "Best gunnin on the coast over to Cat Cove. Matter of fact, me'n my family's havin coot stew for Chris'mus Eve dinner. My wife's cooked four-five extry, in case you folks was hungry."

"That was thoughtful. That was very thoughtful. You hear that, Gerald? We ate dinner in Bellport, but they'll taste mighty good, later on." The tip of Mr. Witherspoon's healthy pink tongue appeared briefly at the corner of his mouth.

Got him droolin over one thing, anyhow, Pete said to himself.

He pulled two chairs close to the stove, where the birch log was now crackling merrily. "You folks take off them co'ts and set. Or would you ruther go over't the house and wash up?"

"Oh, we're fine." Mr. Witherspoon laid his coat across Pete's desk and sat down, and the young man, Bundy, who so far had not opened his mouth, followed suit.

Pete was beginning to have doubts about Bundy's being a lawyer. He sure didn't act like one—more like some kind of a servant. Still, just as well not to take too much for granted.

He had placed the chairs facing the rope company calendar—put out by the Chesapeake Hemp and Manila Corporation, Mr. Witherspoon's firm—and Mr. Witherspoon was taking note of it, he was pleased to see.

Mr. Witherspoon, as a matter of fact, was thinking that the calendar was the one false note in Pete's otherwise irreproachable act.

I suppose he feels that's pretty subtle flattery, was his mental comment. Letting me know that my firm is well known even in this out-of-the-way place. H'm, it would be more surprising if it weren't. Well, I've known him and his kind for a long time. Smooth you down with compliments and feed you home cooking, but when it comes to purchase prices, they snap to like a rat-trap.

He decided not to mention the calendar.

"Well," he said, "I hope you've got everything arranged about the property, Stilwell. Gerald and I are pretty busy this time of year—shouldn't have taken even a Christmas holiday. But buying a place for my wife is—" he cleared his throat with a resounding *harr-umph!*—"is a matter of sentiment. I rather wanted to make the transaction on the spot."

If Pete's eyes were focused on anything, it was on the stomach of the raised-iron cupid on the side of the airtight stove. "Well, now, Mr. Witherspoon. I hope you ain't come all the way up here on a wild-goose chase."

Witherspoon glanced knowingly at Bundy and one of his neat eyebrows lifted slightly toward his hair.

"Your brother isn't prepared to sell for eight thousand dollars?" His voice held just the right amount of amused disbelief. "Surely he doesn't think he can get more?"

"William's a funny feller," Pete said, still looking at the cupid.

"I should think so."

"Place ain't wuth a quarter a that."

"I'm aware of it."

"Wouldn't pay that much 'f I was you."

Witherspoon shrugged impatiently. "I wouldn't consider paying a quarter of it if my wife didn't like the island. You know how women are—set their hearts on something. How about it, Stilwell? Let's get down to business. Will he sell for that or won't he?"

"I d'no," said Pete, "whether he will or not."

"That's rather a queer answer, isn't it?"

Pete got up, took the cover off the stove and spat into the fire. He replaced the cover and stood for a short moment with his hand on the lifter. Then he sat down again.

"Well, now I'll tell ya," he said. "I ben down t' Willie's place three times t' talk t' him since I gut your letter, but I ain't seen Willie. He ain't ben to home. I even sent him a letter through the mail. I ain't hed no answer."

As a matter of fact, Pete had done none of these things. On reading Witherspoon's letter and finding out, with bulging eyes, the latest price offered for Little Spoon Island, he had been sure that Witherspoon wanted the place pretty badly and thus would offer more. There was no doubt in his mind that Willie would sell for eight thousand; it just seemed too bad to Pete not to try for a bigger haul, under the circumstances. Knowing Willie, he'd been pretty sure Witherspoon would receive no answer from him. He now saw he'd guessed right about that. Willie would rather take a licking than sit down and write a letter.

"I see. You think he's avoiding talking about it to you?" Witherspoon asked.

"Might be. Willie's a funny feller, and he thinks a lot a that place. He don't want to sell it."

"Sentimental value, eh?" The sarcasm in Witherspoon's tone sounded a warning to Pete. Better not drive a willin hoss too far.

"You want t' go down and see him now?" he asked. "I shouldn't think he and Hod would go out haulin on Sunday, but then again, they might."

"Well, I want to settle the business. Gerald and I would like to enjoy at least a part of our holiday. I hope you understand, Stilwell, that I don't intend to put up with any more dickering. The way I feel now, I'm all prepared to buy elsewhere."

That's the talk, Pete told himself elatedly. He all but rubbed his hands together. That was the kind of a noise they made when they were all ready to go up on the price. They began to squirm on the hook, and it hurt like hell, but they went up.

"I guess you'll hev t' talk t' William," he said coldly.

Wouldn't do any harm to let the old prout think he'd got his back up a little, being talked to in that tone of voice. "You want t' drive your car down there, or do I have t' git out my truck? It's a pretty bad road, some places."

"Oh, we can take my car," Witherspoon snapped. He put on his coat without another word and led the way out through the store to his car.

Pete grinned at his wide, receding back, buttoned himself into a battered sheepskin jacket and followed.

"You see how it is, Gerald," Witherspoon said between his teeth, as they waited in the car for Pete to lock up the store. "The more you offer them, the more they want. I tell you, Gerald, the country's getting to be a nation of hogs."

"That's right, sir," Gerald said.

"The backbone of the nation," Witherspoon snorted. "With their feet in the trough."

Bundy nodded with an inward grin. It looked to him as if the backbone of the nation had the old boy over a barrel.

Pete came down the store steps and cheerfully jerked open the door to the front seat. "I'll set up here," he said, "and tell the feller how to go."

Doyle, the chauffeur, who had eaten poorly at Connie's diner and who had driven some three hundred miles that day, turned a polite, blank face to Pete's directions, and piloted the big car carefully over the bumps and ruts of the Spoonhandle road.

Willie was at home, Pete saw, as they pulled up in the clearing above the mussel bar. The big boat was tied up at the mooring, and Willie was out in the yard splitting wood. It was near high tide and the bar was covered, but Pete called across to Willie and Willie put down his ax and rowed across the channel in his punt.

"Mr. Witherspoon's come t' see you," Pete said, as Willie got out of the punt and came slowly up the bank. "This's Mr. Bundy and Mr.—" He turned to the chauffeur. "I guess I ain't heard your name, mister."

Pete felt it was a fine touch to introduce the chauffeur.

The chauffeur turned red and fidgeted with his feet, but Bundy said suddenly and irrepressibly, "Doyle. Mr. Doyle's his name."

Willie said, "Hud-do, Mr. Doyle," and shook hands. "Mr. Bundy. Hud-do, Mr. Witherspoon." He shook hands all around and then stood waiting, not looking at anyone in particular. There was a short silence.

Witherspoon said, "How are you, Stilwell?" and Willie nodded.

"I didn't get any answer from you about the proposition I made in my letter," Witherspoon went on affably. On the ride down, he had put away his ill-temper, enough, at any rate, so that his mind would be clear and sharp. He rather prided himself on his ability to control his temper. Bad temper had no place in the transactions of business.

"That's right," Willie said.

"Seems as though you could have sent him an answer, Willie," Pete put in.

"Seems as though," Willie agreed.

For an instant the eyes of the two brothers met, Pete's concentrated and sharp, Willie's clear, amiable and a little amused.

"I ain't no hand to write letters," Willie said.

"Well, no harm done," Witherspoon said, briskly, "since I'm here now and we can talk it over. How about it? If you're agreeable, we can go over to your house and complete the transaction. Where do you keep your deeds? Here, or in a safety deposit box somewhere?"

"Why, I d'no," Willie said. "What deeds was you talkin about? I ain't gut but one, to this place here."

"That's the one I mean, of course." Witherspoon's voice sharpened a little. He had to admit it, his patience was wearing thin. The way these people behaved, you'd think they'd never heard of him or of any offers he'd made. This fellow, with his noncommittal brown face and the disconcerting eyes, was cut off a different cloth from his brother. Witherspoon had been all set to deal with another edition of Pete. The difference threw him off balance a little.

Willie said nothing. He merely waited for Witherspoon to go on. He'd meant to read the letter sometime, but it had been out of sight behind the clock, and he'd forgotten it. Since Pete hadn't come around to pester him, Willie had hoped the matter of selling the place had gone out of everybody's mind. Apparently it hadn't. Here was Pete, agog, with that look in his eye Willie remembered from boyhood, when he'd had something that Pete wanted and, usually, had taken.

"I'd appreciate a definite answer from you, Stilwell," Witherspoon said. "I'm all prepared to make you out a check for the price I offered and if you'll get your deed, we'll drive straight to the county seat now and have the legal requirements fulfilled. You can have until next spring to move out. I want to start construction in April."

"I give you a definite answer last fall, Mr. Witherspoon," Willie said.

Mr. Witherspoon's mouth snapped shut and his jaw, rather craggy under the ears, thrust forward. "You mean eight thousand dollars isn't enough?"

"Eight thou—" Willie's voice failed. "Is that what you offered in that letter?"

"Good God! Didn't you get the letter?"

"Well, yes. I got it, all right. I meant to read it, but it kind of slipped my mind. Eight thousand dollars? You must be crazy."

"I'm definitely not crazy. That's my offer, which I'm ready to pay. Will you sell?" Witherspoon glared at Willie, the expression on his face one which, in his own office or in the business world where he was known, would have brought results.

Willie glanced over at the island. "No," he said. "I wun't."

"Holding me up, eh?"

"Willie," Pete said smoothly, "you better think that over, hadn't you?"

"No. I don't b'lieve so."

"All right." Witherspoon's voice was a little strangled. "What's your price?"

Willie merely shook his head. He was beginning to feel upset and sickened, as he always was at the spectacle of violence in anyone; and deep inside him a slow anger of his own was beginning to rise.

"Ten thousand!" said Witherspoon. "That straighten you out any?"

"Look, Mr. Witherspoon," Willie said. In spite of himself, his voice roughened a little. "I don't want t' sell my place."

"But I intend to buy it! Twelve thousand!"

Willie looked at him. "It ain't for sale."

"Fifteen!"

"Mr. Witherspoon," said Gerald Bundy, "hadn't you better—"

"Shut up, Gerald. These people are holding me up and they'll regret it!"

Behind Mr. Witherspoon's back, Gerald Bundy shrugged.

Willie Stilwell thrust his hands deep into his pockets. "You better go home and cool off, Mr. Witherspoon," he said. "You're crazy mad, and when you come to you'll find you don't want t' throw your money around like that. That kind a talk don't make no sense t' me." He went down the bank, pushed off his punt and got into her.

"Willie!" yelled Pete, stung to action. "Don't be such a stubborn goddam fool! *He means it!*"

Willie made no answer. He turned his back and pushed the punt stern-first across the channel. On the other side, he dropped her anchor on the bank and went into his house without looking back.

"I told ya m' brother was a funny feller," Pete said. He himself was furious, but he had fixed his face fast and now no one would have known it. "He'll come round when he's had time t' think things over. You just went a little too fast for him."

Mr. Witherspoon said "Really?" and stalked to his car. Over his shoulder he remarked, "I think you and he thought you might be just a little too fast for me, didn't you?"

In measured tones he directed Doyle to drop Mr. Stilwell back at his store, and for the entire ride he preserved an icy silence.

As Pete got out in front of the store, he said, "I'll go down t' see William again t'night."

"If you do," said Mr. Witherspoon, "you can tell him the deal is off. I've changed my mind."

Pete glanced at him uneasily. "Willie's got a way of makin people mad," he said. "You don't want t' let him—"

"Don't take the trouble, Stilwell," Witherspoon cut in. "I've listened to enough of it. Thanks for your hospitality, but I've decided to find a place to spend the night in Bellport."

The big car whirled away down the highway, leaving Pete standing. In fact, he had to step back a little to keep from being brushed by the fender.

He'll be back, Pete said to himself. But for the first time he wasn't quite sure. Up to a point, Willie had been sharp as a fishhook, pushed the old feller up to fifteen thousand as easy as rolling off a log. But to walk off like that and make him so mad was pretty poor policy. Or was it?

Pete reflected, turning the key in his padlock and closing the door behind him into the deserted store. The fire was out and a smell of dead fish hung heavily in the stale air. The thought entered his mind that he'd better find a cover for that box of smoked alewives. They had been badly cured and were getting rotten, but maybe he could sell a few more of them before anybody besides Bill Pray began to complain too loud. No sense taking any more loss on them than he had to.

He went out into the shed adjoining the store and poked about among empty crates for a cover the size of the alewives box. But after he found one, he stood absently holding it in his hand.

If that damn dumb halfwit has pushed him too far and queered my sales, he said to himself, I'll go down there and bury him under his own wharf.

The latch to the store door clicked and a lilting voice called, "Oh, Pe-eete! Are you here?"

Pete said Damn and blast! under his breath and went back into the store.

Agnes had on her fur coat, with a large bunch of artificial violets pinned to one lapel. The edge of a white silk scarf, tastefully arranged at her throat, showed the V neckline of a purple dress to match the violets. More violets shook and trembled on her hat, a crushed plush lavender turban she had bought a day or so ago for her own Christmas present at Millie Twitchell, Exclusive Hats, in Ferriston.

"Oh, there you are," she said gaily, as Pete came in. "I saw Mr. Witherspoon's car drive away, and I just had to come down. I couldn't wait any longer."

"You might's well of," Pete said testily, coming up behind his counter.

"Why, what—" Alarm almost instantly replaced Agnes's gaiety. "Oh, Pete, don't tell me Willie's spoiled everything again!"

"Spoilt everything!" Pete burst out. "That's a damn-fool female way to put it, if you ask me. He's not only ruined your prospects and mine, he's ruined the town for the next twenty-five years, that's what he's done, the stubborn son-of-a-bitch!"

In her agitation, Agnes did not even notice the swearing. "What happened?" she breathed. "Pete, what did he do?"

Briefly, he told her, and as the story unfolded, Agnes looked pale and sick.

"But, Pete, fifteen thousand dollars! I never *really* thought Willie was crazy."

"He's either crazy or he's a lot smarter'n we ever give him credit for. I never see a neater job of tradin, up to a point. Witherspoon'll either be back with a bigger order or he wun't, that's all."

Agnes took a deep breath. "You mean he's gone? Where's he gone? I couldn't tell when I saw him drive down the road, but I thought—"

"He's roarin mad at the lot of us. He's gone to Bellport to find a place t' put up."

"He won't be down to stay with me? Why, Pete, I've got everything ready—my upstairs front room all cleaned and aired and—"

"Well, you might's well pull the shades back down."

For a moment Agnes stared at him. Then two fat tears gathered in her eyes and rolled down her cheeks. For days, ever since Mr. Witherspoon had written asking if he could stay at her house, she had gone around in a happy dither of preparation. She had got in Tiddy Driver to help her and had cleaned her house from top to bottom, even the attic and woodshed. Although it wasn't the time of year, she had had Hallet re-wax every floor.

It had seemed to her that her years of planning and working on the house to make it beautiful were at last to be rewarded. Someone was coming who would be worthy to walk on her shining floors, eat off her hand-made doilies, sleep in her upstairs front bedroom whose crisp virgin-spotless chiffon trimmings had been waiting all these years for just this privilege.

Pete said nothing. He doubled his fist, feeling in his imagination the satisfying crunch of it into Willie's face; but after a moment he unclenched it, glancing down at the soft knuckles and pudgy fingers. There were other ways besides punching a man.

He carried the box cover over and put it carefully over his box of rotten alewives.

*

The sun set clearly, leaving a streak of colorless light, which deepened upward into pale yellow over the horizon. The sky above it was cold blue, infinitely high and remote, in which a single star shone with an icy glitter. In this clean brittle light, Witherspoon's big maroon car, the only object on the highway, sped toward Bellport.

Doyle, the chauffeur, tried not to let his smart whipcord shoulders sag from their accustomed soldierly stiffness at the wheel. He was bone-tired, with the deep muscle ache that comes from holding a fast car on the road for hours on end, and tonight, he felt, he was not so young as he once was.

He felt, too, a deep sense of outrage at the way the fellow Stilwell, in his ragged hat and dirty overalls, had talked to the boss. It was a bad thing, an unnatural thing, for such a person not to know his place. Particularly with a great and kind man, like Mr. Witherspoon.

He should be told, this omadhaun who had no better manners than to shake hands with a chauffeur, what it meant to a poor man to have Mr. Witherspoon befriend him. Doyle thought suddenly of the time when his own mother, that aged Irishwoman from the old country, had died, and he, her son, improvident as always, had not saved enough out of his chauffeur's wages to give her a proper wake.

Why, Mr. Witherspoon, seeing how downcast he had looked, had found out what the trouble was; and had he just shaken his head with empty sympathy? He had sent Mrs. Witherspoon herself to the mortician's, and she had picked out the finest coffin in Baltimore—a coffin of pure white, lined with satin, such satin as never a tired old Irishwoman had seen in all her life on the green earth, God rest her soul. Never had there been such a wake, with the fine priest and the Masses paid for, and Mr. and Mrs. Witherspoon themselves there, for all his friends to see. And this was only one of the things the Witherspoons had done for him and his family, through the years he had worked for them.

Doubtless it was a fine thing for a man to hold to that he held dear, above a potful of dollar bills. It might be something to have seen, if you did not know what you knew, if you had not had what you had. For a moment, Doyle straightened his shoulders, remembering the wild Irish independence he once had had, when he had been one of the best drivers ever to roll a truck-trailer combination over the transcontinental haul.

Gerald Bundy, the right-hand man, was tired, too, but his weariness came from brain tension. For two days now, in closer contact than usual with the boss, he had had to be watchful, say the right word, bring forth the proper reassurance at the proper time. Now he too was ready to slump, only on the soft cushions in the rear of the car. He thanked God he wasn't doing the driving—there'd been some talk of his driving the car on the trip, since Doyle had wanted to be at home with his family for Christmas; but at the last moment Bundy had felt justified in telling Old Pinky that he'd sprained his wrist slightly playing squash. After all, it was Doyle's job, not his, and why should he wear himself to a shadow?

Doyle, the poor devil, though, must be half dead. All the more reason to thank God it wasn't him. He liked Doyle—felt, sometimes, that they had a good deal in common. Of course he, Bundy, was a fifteen thousand dollar a year man now, with more to come if he handled things right. He'd worked his way up, too, mostly through pouring the old oil on Witherspoon.

Damn him, he thought, I hope it's been worth it.

Eleven years of life, spent year in and year out, except for his annual three weeks' vacation, catering to Witherspoon, humoring his whims, running his errands. Seeing a man in a ragged lump you could hardly call a hat, and a patched sheepskin jacket, stand up to the boss the way Stilwell had, made a fellow wish, in a way, that he himself had the guts to speak his mind once in a while. Gerald leaned back limply and closed his eyes.

He was roused a few minutes later by Witherspoon rasping something into the speaking-tube, and saw Doyle's deferential inclination of the head, his snapping to attention.

"What's got into you, Doyle? Be a little more careful of your driving. And you, Gerald, I'd appreciate it if you'd give me a little of your attention."

"Certainly, sir." Gerald felt an inward snapping to attention of his own.

"Tomorrow, Gerald, we're going exploring."

"Is that so, sir?"

"Ostensibly, we'll be gunning for ducks. Actually, we'll be searching every foot of that island for a building site. There must be other places as attractive as Stilwell's. I'll teach them a thing or two."

"You're through with the Stilwells, I take it."

"I am. They expect me to come back with a higher offer. They'll be unpleasantly surprised. Besides, if I buy another place, it won't be long before I can, if I want to, buy Little Spoon Island on my own terms."

"On the contrary," Gerald surprised himself by saying, "that fellow'll be pleased if you let him alone. He doesn't want to sell. It's only that precious brother of his with the itching palm."

"Don't be a damned fool," said Mr. Witherspoon peevishly. "They're both out for what they can get. All these people are. I only hope it doesn't get around that I went as high as fifteen thousand. That's one reason I'm determined to close a sale tomorrow."

Mr. Witherspoon leaned back and closed his eyes. He, too, it seemed, was tired.

In spite of himself, Gerald felt his jaws convulse and his mouth open in a nervous and noisy yawn.

*

On Christmas morning, Sam Freeman mooched, as he told himself he was doing, down through East Village looking for Donny Mitchell. He didn't think much of his errand. If it hadn't been for Ann, he be darned if he'd bother his head over a smart-alecky little heel who didn't have the sense to keep himself out of jail. But he and Ann had had a long talk last night. She'd told him of a scheme she'd worked out, and it sounded like a fairly good one. Sam had to grin at how bright it was. Something she'd said, too, had stuck in Sam's craw.

"If we know about it and don't do anything," she'd said, "and he goes to jail, we're just as responsible for it as he is, don't you forget it, Sam."

"I don't see why," Sam said morosely. "No skin off me."

For a little while she hadn't said anything, and then, looking at her, he was stricken to see tears in her eyes.

"Oh, Sam," she said, "Sam, *dear!* Don't grow up like most men feeling that a responsibility for defenseless people isn't any skin off you!"

So here Sam was, on Christmas Day, mooching down the East

Village road, looking for Donny. He'd stopped at Mary Mackay's, but she'd just said, looking at him dimly out of her faded old eyes, that she guessed Donny was down to the shore. Something was the matter with her, Sam thought, as he went down the driveway. She had some kind of a cookbook in her hand that she must have been looking at when he'd come to the door, and she'd been crying.

Down at the fish-wharf, one of the first people he saw was Donny Mitchell, all dressed up in a brand-new red sweater, leaning against the side of a building in the sun, and talking to Artie Osgood.

Well, that's all right, too, Sam said to himself. Kill two birds with one stone.

He paused briefly as he passed them, and spoke in a low tone out of the corner of his mouth. "Want to see you two. Meet me out on the end of the wharf, where no one can hear us."

"What for?" Artie said, eyeing him.

But Sam moved on, out on to the wharf away from the buildings, and sat down on the stringpiece at the very end. He grinned a little, waiting for them to follow him, as they did, presently, both agog.

"What's eatin you?" Artie wanted to know.

"Shut up and listen," Sam said. "There's a guy in my class got a cousin over in Ferriston, his father's one of the Ferriston cops." He saw that both Donny and Artie had frozen, staring at him in dismay.

"Before school closed Friday for Christmas vacation," Sam went on, "the cops had some storekeepers visit all through the Ferriston schools, to see if they could spot two kids who'd been shopliftin."

He waited, letting it sink in.

"They don't know what your names are, or where you live, but the storekeepers are on the lookout for you. They'll know you if they see you again." He got up. "That's all. I thought the least I could do was to tip you off."

"How'd you know about it?" Donny asked, breathlessly.

Sam jerked his head at Artie. "*He* told me. You ought to know by this time he can't keep his trap shut. They got the Bellport storekeepers primed too. Any two kids that come into any store, from now on, somebody'll have an eye peeled on em, and don't you forget it."

Artie was staring at him with a stiff face, but looking at Donny, Sam was amazed to see tears moistening the corners of his eyes and being sturdily crushed back.

"Thanks a lot, Sam," Donny said.

"Don't thank me," Sam said savagely. "You ought to know better than to lay yourself open to such a mess, you dumb little fool. Nobody but a dope'd take chances like that." He walked off along the wharf, his shoulders hunched. Halfway to the sheds, he turned around and looked back. "When'll you be comin to high school, Don?" he asked abruptly.

"Next—next fall. If I pass."

"Well, pass, then," Sam said. "You got a swell build for a basketball center, and we'll sure need some new blood on the team next year." He started on, then looked back again. "You two dopes!" he said witheringly. "You ain't so goddam tough."

This time he kept on until he went out of sight beyond the wharf buildings. He was, Sam discovered, as he took off on a run up the road, sweating, and he was glad it was over. He sure hoped it did some good, too.

The two boys left on the wharf looked white-faced at each other. "That stuff in the box," Donny whispered. "We better get rid of it. If anybody caught us with it—"

"Tonight," Artie said. "After it gits dark. We'll wrap it up in a bag with some rocks and borrow pop's punt and row it off in the harbor. Where the water's deep."

"Okay," Donny said. "I'll be around soon's it's dark."

It seemed to both of them that they couldn't wait for the long day to pass, that the stolen stuff in Artie's secret box must be sticking out of the ground like warts for someone to come along *today* and find it.

Sam and Ann Freeman both would have been astounded if they

had known how close their little scheme had come to what was actually true of the Ferriston police.

*

At noon on Christmas Day, Mr. Witherspoon, with Gerald Bundy following in his foot-tracks, came to Grampa Pray's old wood road which led down to the Spoonhandle. The two men wore hunting jackets and high-laced boots and carried shotguns. Gerald was sagging a little with the weight of his gun and the unaccustomed heaviness of the high boots. They had, since early morning, tramped along the entire eastern shore line of Big Spoon Island, following the contour of the coast. In a straight line, the distance would have been only some three or four miles, but Nelson Witherspoon was a thorough man. He had investigated every cove, every headland along the way. In some places in the woods, there had been snow to wade through, though in bare spots, it was easier. Gerald felt as if he had walked at least forty miles, he had a blister on his heel and he wanted his dinner.

"There's the car," he said with a gasp of relief, as they came out at the entrance to the Spoonhandle wood road.

They had left Doyle at the John's Reach bridge, with instructions to pick them up at the Spoonhandle at noon.

"So it is," said Mr. Witherspoon, barely glancing at it. "Let's see where this road goes."

Fresh as a daisy, he started off down the wood road. Gerald cursed under his breath. He left his gun in the front seat of the car and stalked disconsolately after him.

After some ten minutes of stumbling over the rocky ridges and roots in the path, he came up with Mr. Witherspoon, standing on the edge of a cleared neck of land, some hundred yards wide.

"This is wonderful, Gerald! Smell that salt air, and by jove, look at that view!"

"It is pretty spectacular," Gerald said. He took advantage of the pause to sit down on a gray outcropping boulder.

"Spectacular! Humph!" Mr. Witherspoon glanced at him. "I

don't know what ails you young people nowadays. Pure, unadulterated beauty in nature, or anything else, and you have some offhand adjective for it. Why don't you ever let yourselves go?"

If I did let myself go at this moment, Gerald reflected, it would be to pound the living hell out of you.

Aloud he said, "Well, other times, other adjectives, you know. They mean the same thing."

On the west side of the Spoonhandle, the channel ledges thrust red granite tops against the quiet harbor water. Behind them curled the dark arm of Big Spoon's western hook, and farther off the small spruce-covered islands were neat against the horizon. To the east, the tremendous blue plain of the ocean spread, empty except for three lobster boats, small as bugs in the distance, circling for traps under the pale December sky.

"Wonderful!" repeated Mr. Witherspoon. "We're getting somewhere, Gerald."

He plunged enthusiastically across the cleared space and out of sight into the woods on its other side.

And so it was that Nelson Witherspoon, bursting out of the spruces and followed by his unwilling henchman, came at last to the rocky headland where the small gray home of Joe Sangor huddled above the splendid sea.

*

Joe himself opened the door to Mr. Witherspoon's knock.

"How do you do," said Mr. Witherspoon. "Are you the owner of this land?"

Joe closed the door instantly. Another stranger, this time with a gun, looking for him as the owner of the land, could only be one who had something in common with those who had come for Mary's piano.

But Mary, smiling, moved past him and opened the door again. "Don't be a fool, Joe. It's probly no one important. See what he wants."

"Pardon me!" Mr. Witherspoon had heard Mary's remark, and

he spoke with dignity. "I merely wished to ask you some questions, for my information, about the land here. Nothing else."

"Come-a in, come-a in!" Joe said heartily, overdoing it in his eagerness to show Mary that he was not a fool. He swept his arm out in a wide gesture. "The house she is-a yours!"

Witherspoon stood tentatively just inside the kitchen door. His bigness seemed to fill the room, and inwardly Joe quailed. Who was this fine large man, and what did he wish of Joe Sangor? Behind him stood another man, not so fine nor so large, but with, alas, a small black mustache, like the salesman of pianos.

"My name is Witherspoon. This is Mr. Bundy."

"How you do," Joe said politely. The younger one, he saw, was looking at Mary with admiration. This, somehow, made Joe feel better. Any man who admired Mary could not be bad.

"Our name's Sangor," Mary said lazily, seeing Joe was not going on with the conversation.

Mr. Witherspoon bowed. "I've come in unexpectedly," he said, smiling. "I hope I haven't interrupted your Christmas."

His smile, he knew, had considerable charm, and his slight gesture included the Sangors' Christmas tree, which sat on a low table in the corner of the kitchen.

The Christmas tree leaned a little drunkenly and some of its colored balls were askew or broken, where the kids' hands had grabbed for presents. Wads of tissue paper and string lay around, mingled with toys in various stages of disrepair. Joe and Mary always let the kids tear at the tree and do what they liked with their presents. And Mary always waited until the next day to clear up; for Joe said that Christmas was the day when you ought to have the best time of the year.

"You ain't bodder us, mister," Joe said. "My kids, they have-a the Christmas four o'clock this morning—bang! smas! *toot!* So my head, ever since, she go bang! smas! *toot!* too. What I can do for you, me?"

"I'm always one to come straight to business," Witherspoon said.

"I've been in the neighborhood a day or two looking for property. Do you own this point of land and would you like to sell it?"

Joe and Mary looked at each other and then away. Joe's eyes had asked a question and Mary's had said, "Watch it!" Too many prosperous-looking gentlemen had come knocking at doors in the New Bedford Portuguese section, in Mary's childhood, with propositions to buy or sell. Their advent usually meant, in the end, loss of hard-earned cash.

This was evidently the man who had been buying up island lots for pulpwood.

Witherspoon saw and interpreted correctly their withdrawn expressions. "Of course you don't know me from Adam," he boomed. "But perhaps you've heard of me. I'm *Nelson* Witherspoon, and I own the big house on Catlett's Head, over at Bellport. I was in the Spoon Island Harbor on my boat last fall, talking with William Stilwell about buying his place."

"Oh, sure. Sure, I know." Joe's face cleared a little. "Hod he tell-a me about that."

"Well, I've decided not to buy Stilwell's place. I like this point better. What's it called?"

"She's-a called?" Joe repeated, not quite following.

"They call it the Spoonhandle," Mary said, fixing him with her clear, black eyes. "We own it, up to the other side of the cleared land, next to Pray's."

"About how many acres?" If Witherspoon found the direct, noncommittal stare disconcerting, he did not show it.

"Twenty, more or less, the deed says."

"Would you care to sell it for a fair price?"

Mary hesitated and again her eyes sought Joe's. He looked bewildered and a little flustered, and she saw, also, that he was getting mad because she was doing so much of the talking. She smiled at him and spread her long hands in a gesture of indecision. Poor Joe, she would have to guide him, he had no head for business, but he was the one to talk. "You'll have to ask my husband," said Mary.

"How about it, Mr. Sangor?"

Joe beamed and the bright color rose in his cheeks. "I think, me—" he began importantly. He stopped. This was something he and Mary would have to talk over when the man had gone. He did not quite know how to say this courteously. "Hnh?" he finished.

"If you care to sell, would you make me a price?" Witherspoon asked.

"I think he'd better make us an offer, don't you, Joe?"

"That's-a right. Make-a the offer," Joe said, relieved. His mustache flared and Mary saw he was all right again.

That was close, she thought. I ought to know better than to do that to Joe.

"H'm," mused Witherspoon. "I should think three thousand dollars for twenty acres might be a fair price, considering land values around here right now."

"Three thousand-a dollar!" The mustache fairly stood out at a right angle to Joe's face, and Joe collapsed into a chair. He raised his hands, palms outward, to a level with his ears and held them there, tensely. "We only give-a five hundred for her when we buy!"

"Wait, Joe." The light note of warning in Mary's voice caused Joe to drop his hands limply into his lap. "Land's gone up since then, you know."

Mr. Witherspoon bit his lip. He regretted his hasty offer; if he had waited, he might have got the land for two thousand, but it was too late now. Besides, his ample offer might end, once and for all, this everlasting haggling. "That's right," he said, affably. "Land's gone up. If you care to take me up, I'll be glad to drive you to the bank in Bellport tomorrow, and give you the cash."

"The cash?" said Mary slowly. For the first time the proposal began to have some reality for her. The man must be who he said he was, or he'd never dare go near a bank. And three thousand dollars! She and Joe could get back to New Bedford at last. If they could go back with that much money, it would be enough to buy a small house among their own people, with stores and friends near by, and children of their own kind for the kids to play with.

Mary said, "We might, Joe," looking at him; and Joe, seeing the go-ahead sign in her eyes, said heartily to Witherspoon, "Sure, we sell if you're on the level, mister."

"Could you be in Bellport, then, at nine in the morning, at the County Trust?" Witherspoon asked. "And bring your deed?"

"I guess so," Mary said. "Only I don't think we'll sign anything, Mr. Witherspoon, until we have the money."

"You'll have your money, all right," he said heartily. "Straight from the bank, in brand-new hundred dollar bills."

And so, on the day after Christmas, 1936, half of the narrow peninsula known as the Spoonhandle, bought originally from Massachusetts in 1765 for five pounds by an English sailor named Jonathan Pray, handed down by him to his sons and by them to his grandsons, carefully tended as farmland and wood lot for over a century and a half, and sold for five hundred dollars to a Portuguese fisherman, became the property of Nelson Witherspoon. As the deed read, for "a dollar and other valuable considerations."

*

Winter in a northern seacoast land is interlude. Day after day in the changing weather, high clouds soaring, storms driving low, the land huddles into itself. Salt water curdles into slush against the shore, then, slowly, into grainy pale-green ice, fissured by tides and flung in crumpled blocks up and down the beaches. The spruces crack and snap on a windless evening and let go their loads of snow, so that a wood lot in the cold seems to be talking to itself in a language of small stirrings, whispers and sighs. There is nothing people can do with land like that, bitten four feet deep with frost, secret and uncommunicative under snow.

Winter is a time of gear-overhauling in the fishhouses, snug with fires built in oil-drum stoves, of building traps and painting buoys, of mending the dragnet that the shark tore through. The shark himself is keen in the memory and the gaping hole he made is here and now. But the warm weather, the summertime, lost in the blizzard that drives the small drift under the windowsill, is as unreal as a ghost until it comes again. The talk above the tapping hammers is gusty and loud, but to a man going home to supper, walking through the snowy twilight is like walking through a dream, and the house looming in blown whiteness is a house of sleep.

Winter is the time of wood-cutting, the hollow *thung* of the axes like bells among the tree boles; the clean track of the wood-sled and the brown dung of the horses in the snow; the frosty maple-butt flying apart on the chopping-block at a touch of the ax.

In the early mornings, blue with snow and coming light, the deer comes to the orchard, digging with her cold hoofs for the frozen buried apples; and in the time after the gear is overhauled and the wood is cut and the boat is painted, content comes out or loneliness bites deep, depending on whether people are content or lonely.

PART

III

DONNY MITCHELL sat on the stringpiece of the fish-wharf, listlessly dangling his feet and looking off over the harbor. The weather was warm for the last of March, but the gusty little breeze that blew around the wharf buildings and made dark riffles off over the sunny water was chilly in quite an unpleasant way on the back of his neck. It made him wish he hadn't shucked his heavy underwear quite so soon. The thin summer stuff he had on under his pants and jacket sure did let the cold right through to his skin.

This morning when he'd got up to see the sun shining and the sky such a bright clear blue, he'd felt that winter was surely gone for good. If Mis Mackay'd been up and around, he wouldn't have dared to dig out his summer underwear. She'd have been after him like a ton of bricks, just as soon as she went up to make his bed and saw the thick union suit lying there across the chair.

But Mis Mackay was sick. She'd been in bed for two weeks with bronchitis, almost pneumonia, and Jory, her boy Dave's wife, had had to come on from Somerville to nurse her through it.

That Jory wouldn't give a hang if Donny walked out of the house start-nakid. She was just about the kind of tough skinny female you might expect Mis Mackay's boy Dave to marry. She made Donny think there were worse people in the world than Mis Mackay.

Jory ran the house and him, too, ragged. She kept after him to do things and to wait on her from the time he got up till he went to school, from the time he got home in the afternoon till he went to bed. Mis Mackay always had made a touse about him doing his school work evenings, but that Jory didn't even give him a chance to do that. She was always digging up a job.

It was pretty important just now that he do his school work, and a lot of it. All last fall he'd coasted along, not caring whether he finished eighth grade or not, and he'd got way behind the class. But since the day Sam Freeman had told him he had a good build for a basketball center, and implied that he might have a chance to get on the team if he got to high school, Donny had buckled down to make up work. He had an even chance to pass now, the teacher told him, if he did all right on the spring tests. They'd be coming up next month. And so, now, here was that Jory, yapping around Mis Mackay's house from morning till night, never giving him a minute's peace.

He'd got away from her today, though. It was Saturday, and he'd made up his mind when he heard her up in the night tending to Mis Mackay. She'd sleep later than usual, and by the time she got up, he'd be gone.

He'd hang around and see if he couldn't put himself in Sam Freeman's way, somewhere, either at the wharf or the stores. Sam had been pretty decent to him a couple of times during the winter, though being one of the older fellows, he didn't have much to spare for a kid like Donny.

He liked Sam now a lot better than he did Artie Osgood. Since Christmas, he and Artie hadn't seemed to get along very well together. Artie made him kind of sick, and he could see Artie felt the same way about him. Just seeing each other reminded them both of that narrow escape they'd had. They both wanted to forget the shoplifting business. And, besides, Donny couldn't get it out of his mind that Artie had told. It was true, Artie's telling Sam had probably saved their skins; but even so, the fact remained that they'd sworn to each other they'd never tell a soul.

Things had worked out pretty well for him this morning, Donny reflected. When he'd tiptoed down over the stairs, that Jory'd been sleeping like an old pig, snoring, too.

He'd come in his stocking feet through the sitting room, past Mis Mackay's bedroom door, and all of a sudden, not knowing just why he did it, he'd stopped and looked in. Maybe it was the sight of her thin wrinkled old hand lying on the white spread—the open door cut off part of the bed, and all he could see was that hand and part of Mis Mackay lying humped up and lumpy under the covers. Anyway, he'd thought, maybe there wasn't any love lost between them, but he hadn't seen her for over two weeks, and she'd been sick.

She was awake and she seemed pleased to see his towsled head stuck in through her doorway.

"Why, hello, Donny," she said. Her voice quavered like an old, old person's, and wasn't much more than a croak. "I was beginnin to wonder how you was gettin along."

"Pretty good," he said awkwardly. "How you feel now?"

"Lots better. I thought for a while there I was goin to hand in my checks, but I'm on the mend now."

He stood teetering from one foot to the other, wishing he hadn't come in, for now he was there he couldn't think of a word to say. He cast around for something that might please her. "The sun's kind of warm this mornin."

"Yes. Gittin spring."

"Well," he said, looking here and there, desperately. "Well—"

He's just *wishin* he could git away, Mis Mackay thought. She, too, couldn't think of anything. Except one thing—she hadn't planned to tell him so soon, but it was all she could think of to say. "Donny," she said abruptly, "the's somethin you'll have t' be thinkin about."

"What?" he asked, alarmed. Now what was coming?

"Jory thinks I ought t' close up this place and go back to Massachusetts with her and Dave. I hate to give up, but if I do, they'll have to find another place for you to stay."

"One place's good's another, I guess," Donny mumbled. He

looked at her with what she called "that dead-pan look," his face closed up tight. "You want anything, Mis Mackay? A drink, or—"

"No, I guess not."

"Okay, then."

He turned and padded out of the bedroom, and she called after him, "What you plannin t' do today, Donny?" but she guessed he didn't hear her, because he didn't come back.

Sam Freeman hadn't been around anywhere, so finally Donny had ended up down to the fish-wharf. He sat on the stringpiece and shivered in his thin underwear.

It's no skin off me, he told himself, trying to shrug. I don't care where I go.

The only thing was, Mis Mackay's was a place to stay. The Welfare, he supposed, would dig up somewhere else for him, but it was kind of too bad not to enter high school with the kids in his class whom he'd got to know. And the high school where he went might not have such a swell basketball team as Bellport.

He heard a slow step behind him and turned around to see Willie Stilwell sauntering along the wharf.

"Hi," Willie said.

"Hi."

Donny hadn't seen Willie, to speak to, since he'd run out on him last fall. He'd gone out of his way to avoid him. Once or twice during the winter, when he'd been on the wharf, Willie'd come up to him, but Donny had always managed to edge away before he had a chance to say anything.

At first, when he'd been so sore at Willie, he hadn't wanted to see him. Now, avoiding him had gone on so long, he felt embarrassed, not knowing what to say. Somehow, he didn't feel sore any more. But what of it? He'd be going away pretty soon.

Willie sat down on the stringpiece near him, folding his long legs, his bony knees sticking up under his chin. "Cold, ain't it?" he volunteered.

"Ayeh," Donny said. He went on talking before he thought. "I put on my summer underclo'es this mornin."

"You did?" Willie treated this as a piece of news. He grinned. "Y'know," he said confidentially, "I did mine, too. I couldn't resist it when I gut up this mornin. Felt like spring, smelt like spring. Now I wisht I hatn't."

"So do I," Donny said.

"How's Mis Mackay? Hear she's been quite sick."

"She's better." Donny leaned his head down between his own hunched-up knees and stared into the green, sun-flecked water that was making little slobbers up and across the slimy piles. Just being with Willie, he found, was all at once making him feel better, the way it used to. "She's goin away soon's she gits well," he said in a low voice.

"That so?" Willie nodded his head slowly up and down. "Well, she's gittin along and that's a big place for an old lady to handle. Dave's been after her to come and live with him, but she likes her home. She hated to leave it."

There was a silence on the stringpiece. Donny's head sank lower, and he leaned his cheek hard against his knee.

"That kind of changes matters for you, don't it?" Willie said.

Donny said, "Oh, I don't care where I go. One place is same's another."

"How'd you like to come down and live with Hod and me? Say we could fix it?" he heard Willie's voice say.

"Why, I d'no." He couldn't believe it; it was a voice saying something which might have meant a lot if it hadn't been just a voice.

"We'd like it fine," Willie went on. "We missed you when you didn't come down no more. You think it over." He got to his feet, unfolding slowly and silently. "Look's like Hod's got the bait loaded on, we'll have to be on our way. I'll see you later, Don."

Willie started down the wharf ladder, pausing with only his head in sight above the stringpiece. "Me, I've always wanted a boy of my own. I never thought I'd have the luck nor the chance to get Granville Mitchell's boy."

Hod was backing the boat out from under the bait-loading tub on the other side of the wharf. Willie waved to him and he rolled the wheel, swinging the big square stern around under the ladder, while Willie climbed agilely down the rungs, jumping the last four or five and landing on the deck as lightly as a cat.

"So long," he said, looking up. "You think it over, and you say the word go, we'll start things rolling."

Hod, looking up, too, waved a hand in laconic greeting. The boat shot away, flattening down like a rabbit as he touched the throttle. She left a long green-and-white wake, widening to a V as she roared down the harbor. Donny sat looking after her as she grew smaller and smaller.

She was a swell boat. Donny closed his eyes, picturing how it would be to live in the same house with Willie and Hod. Hod was pretty wonderful—it took a *man* to handle a two-hundred-pound halibut, and he was just the one who could do it. He liked Hod a lot. But Willie, he thought, and suddenly he realized clearly just what it was Willie had said, Willie was somebody you could feel about the way you used to feel about Uncle My.

A car drove up and stopped just the other side of the wharf sheds. Its doors banged shut and heavy steps started down the wharf. Two men came past the sheds on one side and two others on the other, walking fast. Three of them were strangers, but the fourth, Donny saw, glancing around, was Myron Osgood.

"There he is, the little hellion," Myron said. "Don't let him get away."

The four men spread out and bore down on him. Donny gave a wild look around. There wasn't anyone else on the wharf. It was him. They were after him. He darted over to the corner where the big piles extended up beyond the stringpiece, and stood there with his back to the tough wood, panting and staring.

"This here's Mr. Morrison, the Chief of Police over to Ferriston," Myron said. "You can tell him how you gut my boy Artie to go over there with you and steal all them things out of the stores last Christmas time."

"I don't know nothin about it," Donny said sullenly.

"We'll see whether you do," Myron spluttered. He was so mad he was sweating, and his face was a dirty-gray color. "Artie never would of, I know that, without you to egg him on. You take him along, Mr. Morrison, and we'll see what he says when he faces Artie."

In the front room of Myron Osgood's house, Artie was sitting on the sofa, crying. Across the room from him was his mother, rocking back and forth in the rocking chair, and she was crying, too. Artie's face was globbered with tears. He needed to blow his nose. When he saw Donny, he burst out into sobs, and for a moment he couldn't speak.

"There, you see how bad he feels," Myron said. "You can tell by lookin at him he ain't nothin like this tough young devil."

"He gut me into it," Artie sobbed. "He said he'd knock my head off if I didn't."

Donny's glance at Artie was blank and impersonal, and Artie burst out with louder accusations.

"He stole all the things, too. You ask them men in the stores. They'll tell ya that all the time I was in there I was busy buyin somethin. It was him took everything."

"How about that?" the police chief said to Donny.

"I d'no," Donny said. "I wasn't there."

"He's lyin," Artie said. "He was, too, there, and he stole all the stuff."

"Look here." Morrison took hold of Donny's shoulder and whirled him around. "This boy was over to Ferriston this morning and one of the storekeepers recognized him when he walked past the window. Don't you think he'll recognize you as well? Artie, here, may get out of it because he's owned up. You don't know what may happen to you if you don't."

But Donny merely shook his head and closed his mouth tight.

"All right. We may as well be on our way. You'll hear from us in a few days, Mr. Osgood."

"I'd like t' hev it kept as quiet's possible, Mr. Morrison," said

Myron distractedly. His normally good-natured face was drawn with anxiety. "After all, I'm second selectman of the town, and if this got around— It ain't as if Artie was a real bad kid. He ain't to blame. He was egged on."

"Well, the storekeepers'll be decent about it, I think," said Morrison, "especially if you make up the money they lost on the stolen stuff. First offense, and all, I don't think they'll prosecute. You'll have to bring your boy over, though, to the hearing."

"I guess you can understand I'll be awful grateful for anything you can do." Myron began fumbling awkwardly in his pockets.

Morrison grinned. "Okay. When the time comes. There's always a time and a place for gratitude, you know. Under the circumstances, I guess we can keep the hearing a private one." He slipped a stubby hand under Donny's armpit. "Come on, son."

"I hope," said Myron vindictively to Donny, "that you go to jail. I hope they—shove—you—just—as—far—as—the—law—allows." He brought out each word with harsh and separate emphasis, his outraged voice bearing down harder as he went along.

"You don't need to worry about that," Morrison said. "The State don't take no funny business from State wards. They figger if the kids can't behave, after all that's done for them, it ain't no use to fool around. They slap em straight into reform school."

"Well, I'm glad to hear it," Myron said. "That's where any kid ought to be that goes around makin crim'nals out of honest people's children."

He opened the door for the officers of the law, and closed it instantly after them, as if by doing so, and staying out of sight, he could conceal from the eyes of his neighbors what kind of a procession was coming out of his house.

The strange thing was that Myron Osgood wasn't a mean or a violent man. He was a decent man, in most things kind, respected by his neighbors; he had never done a harsh nor a cruel thing in his life. A comprehended emergency, however serious, would not have overtested his courage, for he was no coward and he could have met it with fortitude. But the alien thing, the evil from "away," creeping up on him and threatening everything he had, had shaken him to his foundations. For a terrifying moment, something called "crime" had stolen in from the outside world and touched him, personally—not somebody you read about in the paper over your morning coffee, somebody in a far-away, unregenerate city—but *him*. It was as if a submerged monster, its grim outlines trailing down into the green water as deep as the eye could see, had suddenly reached up into his safe, familiar boat and drawn a slimy tentacle across his hand.

And so, unstrung and unbelieving, Myron had lashed out, not at a thin-faced boy, but at the only part of the horror he could see.

He turned back to the sitting-room to meet the sobered eyes of his wife and the bugged-out, horrified ones of his youngest son. "Artie," he said, "you git upstairs to your bedroom. In about five minutes, I'm comin up and lam the hide off of you."

"Myron," Lucy said, "what'll they do? They can't put Artie in jail, can they?"

"I don't know what they'll do." Myron went to the sideboard drawer and took out his razor-strop. "All I know is, I hope to God I can scrape up enough cash so they won't do nothin. But by God, Lucy, puttin them State kids, the cussid little crim'nals, into a town and lettin em run wild, is more than a decent man ought t' hev to put up with, and somethin he ought t' be able to use his vote aginst."

Upstairs, he wrote his fright and his insecurity in no uncertain symbols on Artie's shrinking bottom.

*

The State's welfare worker drove over from Bellport that afternoon to see Mary Mackay. Mary was feeling better and she was sitting up, rocking by the window, her shoulders wrapped in a winter shawl of soft white wool.

"Oh," she said, smiling a welcome. "It's the State Woman. Come in and set down. I expect you've come about Donny's spring clothes. I d'no where he is, he ain't been home today. I been sick, as you see."

The welfare worker was surprised and shocked at the change in Mrs. Mackay, just since last fall.

The poor old thing, she thought, she must have been awfully sick.

Mary looked thin and feeble, and her face as if it had fallen away. But what startled the social worker was the fact that Mary was garrulous. In all the times before, when they had conversed about Donny, Mary had had only a few, essential words to say. Now, in her quavering voice, she seemed to be going on and on.

"I've had kind of a time with bronchitis, I guess for a while they thought it was pneumonia. It's took it out of me so they tell me I ain't fit to live alone any more. Jory, my son's wife, she's here now, she wants me to come to Massachusetts to live with her and my boy Dave, and I do hate to give up my place, I'll be lonesome up there, but I d'no b't I'll have to go. Now, about Donny, I want to be sure you find a nice place for him to stay with nice people—"

The welfare worker hadn't been at all sure she knew how to say what she had to say. She was feeling unhappy about what had happened to Donny—he'd been one boy on her list who was well-placed and contented, and she was pretty sure this nice old lady was fond of him.

"You do know of a nice place, don't you?" Mary asked anxiously. "I'd have to be sure it was a good one, or I won't feel right about leavin him."

Well, there was nothing for it. She'd have to blurt it out. "Mrs. Mackay, Donny was picked up this morning by the police. He'd been shoplifting in the stores over in Ferriston. They've been after him all winter." She stopped, her eyes on Mary's face. "I'm sorry. There didn't seem to be any other way to tell you."

Mary said nothing for a moment. She went on rocking back and forth, noticing, as she often had before, that the rocking chair was letting go a little somewhere in its underpinnings. You could feel it give now and then, and it had a soft little creak. But, after all, it was an old chair.

The State Woman wasn't telling her one thing she hadn't known before. Now, it's caught up with him, she thought, and I can't say I'm a bit surprised. It was out of her hands now, there wasn't a thing she could do. And suddenly, she realized, the relief was tremendous.

"Well, I must say," she said aloud, defiantly, "you could knock me over with a feather! Donny's been a good boy, awful nice to me. I've never noticed one thing off-color about him in all the time he's been here."

"Yes," said the welfare worker. "It happens that way sometimes. It's always hard for us to understand it, too."

"Them policemen must be awful foolish men. They've made a mistake," Mary said. "That boy ain't got an evil bone in his body."

"No. There's no mistake. The whole thing's been proved. Some of the Ferriston storekeepers have identified him."

"He own up to it?"

The welfare worker shook her head. "He's very stubborn," she said.

"Well, there," Mary repeated. "You could knock me over with a feather."

Of course he wouldn't own up to it, she told herself. I might just as well have give up from the first, because there never was anything anybody could have done.

"They'll put him away, won't they?" she asked.

The welfare worker looked hangdog. She could feel the expression come out all over her face as definite as pimples. "I'm afraid they will," she said. "There doesn't seem to be anything else to do."

"There ain't no way I can git him out of it?"

"No. What you say about his character may help, though."

"Well, you tell them he's an awful good boy," Mary said. "You tell them I said so, and I ought t' know."

"All right. I'm sorry, Mrs. Mackay."

"Never mind," said Mary Mackay. "What will be, will be."

"I'll have to take his things—"

"Oh, yes. Jory'll show you. Jory! *Jor-ee!*"

"Er—we're keeping it quiet, Mrs. Mackay. He won't be in reform school forever, and he might want to come back here sometime."

"I'll never tell a soul. Jory," Mary went on, as her daughter-in-law came in from the kitchen. "The State people have found a nice place for Donny to stay, and this lady's come for his things. Will you show her where his room is—I mean, was?" She leaned back in her chair, smiling up at them her dim, faded smile.

Jory came back downstairs and settled her lean flanks into a chair. "Well, ma," she said, "I guess that takes care of that. I didn't know, though, you'd notified *them* you were breaking up housekeeping."

"I hadn't. They just found a good place and took him there. The people wanted him quick."

"I guess they must have. Seems as though they might have said ah, yes or no to you first, but I guess that's the State for you. I ain't kicking, though. That gawky slob around the kitchen was driving me out of my mind. You feel all right, ma?"

"Yes," Mary said. "I feel fine. I don't know but I could eat somethin, Jory."

"Well, 'tis suppertime. I'll fix you something nice."

Jory got up and went out to the kitchen. Mary could hear her clattering the pots and pans, and humming as she worked.

Well, Mary thought. That's over for good and I'm glad. He was like that and it would of took more than me to handle it.

Now her mind was free, she could give up with good grace and go to Massachusetts. It would be hard to leave the home she and Bob had made and lived in so long. But it would be lovely to see Dave every day.

She didn't believe she was going to get along very well with
Jory though. Jory was kind of sharp.

But there, of course, Jory wasn't her own.

*

On the first day of April, Hod Stilwell took five hundred dol-
lars to Bellport and made Josh Hovey a second payment on the
boat. It was the bulk of his and Willie's winter savings. Together
with the three hundred Josh had allowed them on Willie's old
boat, it left only four hundred still to pay.

Josh took the bills and riffled them through once, looking Hod
up and down. "Smell the fish-scales on these, all right," he said.
"Looks like you ain't done s' bad with that gold-brick I stuck you
with."

Hod grinned. "You know it wasn't any gold-brick, you old
faker," he said. "I still don't know why you did it, when you could
probably have got more dough, quicker, from someone else."

"My ways is difficult t' fathom," Josh said, shrugging. "Come
int' the office, I'll give ya a receipt."

Bent over his battered roll-top, his tongue sticking briefly out
of a corner of his mouth, Josh scrawled something illegible on a
receipt blank with a protesting pen. "There ya are. Frame it."

"What good is it?" Hod turned the paper upside down in a
mock attempt to decipher the writing. "Looks as if the cat had been
walking on it."

Josh leaned back, tilting in his swivel-chair. He stuck a chubby
hand inside his shirt and resoundingly scratched his stomach. "Ain't
a bank in the state wouldn't honor that signature," he observed
comfortably. "So what are you kickin for? I see by the paper where
Spoon Island's turnin into a boom-town this spring," he went on.
"Why ain't you'n I in on some a that cash 'ts bein throwed around
over there?"

"Would you want to be?"

"Hell, yes. I ain't no goddamed eye-dealist. Pete, he kind of put
one over on the folks, didn't he?"

"People got to wondering if he hadn't," Hod said. "At the time he clipped around and bought in their land from the pulp-wood man."

"Hell, didn't you?"

"Sure. I still do. I still can't figure how he worked it."

"What you gittin sand in your craw for? Man sees a trade, chance t' buy somethin cheap and sell it high, fool if he don't, ain't he? Ain't no crime."

"No," Hod said. He regarded Josh with a knowing grin. "That's pretty tough talk, coming from you to me. After the fool's trade you made with me on my boat."

Josh looked embarrassed. "Wan't what I ast ya," he said.

"No, you asked me was it a crime to make a good trade. You know it ain't. Unless it's a case of swindling your neighbors."

"Mean t' say it's worse t' swindle your neighbors than 't is strangers?" Josh cocked an eyebrow at him.

"You know what I mean."

"Ayup. Guess I do." Josh sighed, letting his bulk settle deeper into the chair, overflowing its arms and seat with ample rolls of flesh. "You know how 't is with me, I been swindlin strangers for years. Done good at it, too. But darned if I ain't always felt the' was a line to draw, even if they was summer people. Ain't that funny?"

"Nope."

Josh pulled out a wooden match and looked at it reflectively. After a moment, he popped one end of it into his mouth and began to flip it, with a good deal of dexterity, from one side to the other. "How come Pete felt he could git away with a thing like that?" he said.

"The thing is, what's he got away with?" Hod said. "People sold land, that's all, and Pete had the sense to go around and buy it. Now he's making money selling acreage to summer people. All decent and above board. What ails you?"

"You're sore's a peep about it, ain't you?"

Hod shrugged. "No skin off me," he said. "Willie and I, we

don't have much to do with the town. It just seems to me that people whose families owned the land for generations ought to have the benefit of the big sale-price, that's all."

"H'm," Josh said. "You know, there's one thing, if I don't find it out, seems as though I wouldn't live out my time."

"What's that?"

"Last winter Bill Pray was madder'n hell when he found out Pete Stilwell had got hold of the land he sold. Said he was likely to go kill him, slow and horrible. He never kilt him. How bout that?"

"That was easy." Hod grinned, but the grin wasn't a pleasant one. "The day the property-transfer news came out in the paper, Bill went in to Pete's all ready to tell him what he thought about it. Only the minute he went in through the door, Pete lit into him first."

"What about?" Josh's eyes goggled with excitement.

"He gave Bill holy hell for selling his land for pulpwood. Said any man who'd sell his birthright for a mess of—of—"

"Pottage," supplied Josh, hastily. "Pottage, for Chrissake. Don't you ever read your Bible? Well, go on, why don't you?"

"For a mess of pottage, well, a man like that was a heel, ought to be cut up and fed to the dogfish. You know the mess a gang of pulpwood cutters leave—they cut down everything, but they don't use anything less than six-inch stuff and they leave the tops and the brush on the ground to rot."

"Well, for he'm's sake," Josh said. "I know what a gang of pulpwood cutters leave. What you tellin me for?"

"I'm just tellin you what Pete told Bill—and the one or two members of the Ladies' Aid who happened to be in the store."

Josh suddenly slapped his leg. "By gosh, that was smart!"

"Ayeh." Telling the story, Hod could feel himself getting mad all over again. "Anyone who'd spoil land as sightly as the spruce lots on the east side of Spoon Island, ought to be hung. So in a day or so the Ladies' Aid and the Village Improvement Society took up the matter, and the story goes around that Pete's a public-spirited citizen who paid out a lot of his own dough to save the island's trees. Agnes had a claw in the dish—she helped convince em. You take it from there. You know as much as I do. I smelt a rat at the time, and I still do, but I'll be damned to hell if I know how he worked it."

Josh wagged his head, in unwilling admiration. For a moment he sat regarding the dog-eared, stained blotter on his desk.

"Ain't it a caution," he said at last, "what sheep people is if some smart feller figgers out the way t' make em so?"

"Oh, hell!" Hod burst out. The violence of his own feeling suddenly surprised him. "It's not only that Pete's smart. He's got the whole weight of what the Stilwells used to be behind him. He can cook up anything, just so he frosts it over and doesn't cook it too raw."

Josh said nothing. He merely cocked his head at Hod, and the match in his mouth took on a slightly faster tempo.

"Even the people who sold their land don't think anything of the fact that Pete's getting rid of it hand over fist to the summer people and making thousands of dollars. That's just incidental. Oh, they're sorry they were fools enough to sell, but they feel that was their own fault, they didn't have Pete's vision. What he's getting now is a good man's reward for being a good man."

"H'm," Josh said. "Seems t' me you show quite a lot of interest, for a man who don't have nothin t' do with his town."

"I can get mad, can't I?" Hod mumbled.

"I d'no. Your grampop, Joel Frame, would of bust the bejeezus out of a situation like that. Y'know, the' was always an awful lot of diff'rence betwixt the Stilwells and the Frames."

"So I've heard."

"Willie, now, he's the spittin image a old Joel Frame. Or would be, if Ame Stilwell hadn't took the gimp out a him when he was a boy. So're you."

"Could be."

"Up till you took a chance buyin that boat, though, I never

figgered you had Joel's guts. Figgered you was a kind of a weak sister, 'f you know what I mean."

Hod was taken aback, and for a moment he was mad. He didn't like personal discussions, and he couldn't see that this one was leading anywhere. Besides, Josh had put his finger on a very sore spot. For months now, trying to bring himself to the point of telling Ann Freeman he loved her and not having been able to, Hod himself had come to the conclusion that people were probably right—he guessed he was a weak sister.

"Changed my mind," Josh went on, before he could speak. "Man's privilege. Ain't it?"

Hod got up. "Well, so long, Josh. Thanks for the credit on the boat. If things go all right, we'll have the rest of it for you this fall."

"Hold on, for Godsake," Josh said. "You're more'n sixteen years old, ain't ya? Bout time you begun t' git the right idea of what folks think of you. Ain't it? You was high-line, fishin out of Spoon Island, all last fall. Come winter, when the rest of the boys hauled up their boats, you went offshore all through the tough weather. Men knows their business fishin, they respeck that kind of a thing. Right now, it wouldn't take nothin t' knock out some a them theories Agnes and Pete's been promulgatin about you and Willie all your lives."

"Okay," Hod said, between his teeth. "You done, Josh?"

"Hell, no, I ain't done. The's one thing I want t' know, that if I don't find it out, I doubt if I'll live out my time. How much, honest, did old man Witherspoon offer Willie for that island?"

Hod grinned suddenly and inwardly threw up his hands. It wasn't any use staying mad at Josh. "You're a nosy old weasel," he said. "I've got a good mind to go home and let you stew."

"Ah, don't," Josh said. "How much, honest?"

"Fifteen thousand dollars," said Hod. He waited for the effect and got it.

Josh's jaw dropped wide open. The match stopped dead still, clung for an instant to his exposed pink tongue, and fell to the floor. "*Is* that a fact?" Josh breathed. "And Willie turned him down!" He slapped his leg suddenly and let out a whoop. "Ain't that beautiful! Ain't that nourishin!"

"Well, don't tell the town about it. If people knew, they'd think Willie was crazy."

Josh sobered instantly. "Crazy! What in hell you talkin about?"

"Wouldn't they?"

"Some would," Josh agreed. "Pete would. Some here in Bellport, I don't doubt. But ask the fellers that sold their land here fifteen, twenty years ago, and now the money's spent and them and their fam'lies out workin by the day for the jeasly, ice-cold side a nothin. Willie crazy? For Godsake!"

"Well," said Hod, with a doubtful grin. "You wouldn't sound very convincin over on Spoon Island right now. Not with everyone sure of a job with big pay, working on the new summer cottages."

"Work started a'ready, has it? How many new houses 's the' goin t' be?"

"Six, counting Witherspoon's. But Pete's still selling shore property. Beats me how he does it."

"No trick to it," Josh said, "if you know how. He's been workin through a couple a Bellport real estate agents, I know about. Understand they wrote letters to a lot of names in the summer directory, all about this new place, ain't been spoilt yit, and gittin in on the ground floor. Used Witherspoon's name as a come-on. Oh, it's easy enough. By the way, you gut any idea who 'Joe King' is?"

"Who cares?"

"Well, you, for one. I gut interested," Josh went on reflectively. "Seemed kind a queer to me, someone hell-bent t' buy pulpwood last winter. In my business, buildin boats, I git t' know a lot bout the lumber market. Last winter, pulpwood was a drug on the market. Northeastern Paper Company hed a million cords, more or less, settin up in the woods, warn't even movin, and still ain't. What'd that mean t' you, I wonder?"

An idea clicked in Hod's mind and began turning over fast.

"Somebody wanted Spoon Island land, but not for pulpwood," he said slowly.

"Well," Josh went on. "As I say, I gut interested. Northeastern ain't gut no buyer named Joe King. Far's I could find out, the' ain't no lumber company 't has. The' *is* a kid named Joe King here in town, I know his folks well. Lives on North Main Street and works in Alec Staples's office. Know Alec?"

"The lawyer?"

"Ayup. Pete's lawyer. Ain't he?"

"Yes," Hod said, staring at Josh. "Yes. He is."

"Box 48 is Alec's box. I seen him git his mail from it a lot of times. I wondered bout that box number when Bill Pray mentioned it last winter, but I never thought to check up till I gut to thinkin bout Joe King." Josh grinned. "Bellport ain't a very big town. Not in the winter." He stood up, easing his awkward body out of the chair with a moan. "Kuhriced, I git stiffer every five minutes. Oh, I been through it all," he went on. "But let Spoon Island dream. Don't tell em that shovelin dirt is bout all the jobs left for local folks after outside contractors git through bringin in their own men. Later on, after the summer cottages is built, the'll be some jobs, emptyin slops and luggin away garbage. After they've sold their boats 'n gear, expectin t' live the life a Riley. In five years, you can tell Willie, the crazy man, he can run for selectman. Git it, too. Say the's any local gov'mint left by that time, that a common, ordinary man can use his vote for."

"For God's sake, Josh! What are you kickin about?"

Josh stopped and looked sober. "Sure, I know. I've done all right, myself. I hadn't ought t' squawk. Boomin up a town, lot of outside rich folks comin in, it's awful good for local business. The groceries and the hardware stores. My boatyard. The rest of the folks, they git a livin, too. Only, the thing is, once you git summer people, you gut to figger out a way to keep em, or the town goes bust. The's men here in Bellport, good, upstandin men, who make reg'lar goddam prayer-rugs out of themselves, all summer long. Over here in Bellport, we don't vote no more. We gut a kind of a king, tells us what'll keep the summer people happy, and we vote for that. If you don't, you can be damn well sure, it'll be rotten bad for your business."

"Maybe you think you're telling me something—"

"Oh, hell!" Josh exploded. "Go on home. If you had the sense your grampop had, you'd a gut yourself a town job when you was twenty, the way he did. Then your neighbors'd have hed an honest man they could a gone to for advice about sellin their land. Goddam it!"

*

Hod went thoughtfully out of the boatyard building and walked along the mud-ridden street toward Connie's diner. In the April sunlight, watery and thin, Bellport drooped like a hen that had been rained on. Half the plate-glass windows on Main Street were boarded up, the planks splintery and weathered. Along the streets, a few people moved slowly, walking along and stopping, still wrapped in their winter overcoats.

In two months, it would be different, the town shined up, the streets full of traffic, the smart, seasonal Fifth Avenue shops opened up again, their gleaming windows full of sporting goods and expensive tweedy materials.

Well, hell, Hod thought resentfully. Most towns never do wake up, even for four months of the year. What does Josh expect *me* to do? He didn't take a stand, himself, when things started to boom over here. He was right behind it.

The thing is, something in his mind answered him, Josh didn't know as much then as he does now. Knowing Josh, Hod realized he believed he would have done anything a man could, if he could have thought of anything to do.

All right, what *could* you do? What would you *want* to do?

It stood to reason that having a town build up, get more prosperous, with work and money for people, wasn't a bad thing. A man who set himself to buck that would be a crack-pot. That was nothing to take a stand against.

As for the time to come, when the cottages were built and the townspeople had settled down to what Josh called making prayer-rugs out of themselves to keep what they had, what could be done about that, either? It was plain economics, depression following a boom. Rich people were used to servants. If you didn't act like servants, they'd bring their own, and then where would the jobs be?

Besides, that was one of the things that insured their coming—people who might or might not be big frogs at home, but who in a little place with everyone making believe humble, could make a hell of a splash. You couldn't change that unless you changed human nature. People had to scrabble, dog eat dog, and prove that in some way they were just a little better than anybody else. Hell, that wasn't just rich people, that was everybody.

Suppose a man didn't? What happened? Hod saw the answer coming and felt his mind start to duck sideways trying to dodge it. If you didn't scratch and push and shove, then you got to be like he himself was, like Willie was—not much account in the eyes of your community, and always just a little ridiculous.

He wished Josh had kept his mouth shut. Especially since he must have known there wasn't anything to be done.

Hell, Hod thought, remembering something else Josh had said. I'm no goddamed idealist.

But it sure did gowel him, and it was goweling him more every day, to have to sit around and watch Pete getting away with murder.

*

Hod opened the door to Connie's diner and closed it behind him. Somebody in the back let go with a bellowing blast of greeting. It was Joe Sangor, he saw, standing up at his table and waving both hands.

"Hi, Hod! You eat with me, hnh?"

He went along to Joe's table, stopping to flap his cap limply on over a wall-hook. "Hi, Joe. Didn't expect to see you over here, today. Thought you'd be up to your neck, packing. When do you start?" he asked, sitting down.

"When the hens she is get up tomorrow," Joe said promptly.

He was jubilant, bubbling over with excitement, and Hod realized with a little start of amusement, that he could smell wine on Joe's breath.

"Celebrating?" he asked, grinning. Joe didn't drink, he knew. He had a poor stomach even for wine, and he took a glass only on special occasions.

"A little," Joe said, looking sheepish. "For the luck. Hnh? The truck she's-a load, but the engine she make *siss*. Too much, you say, heavy, all them table, chair."

"Where'd you leave her—O'Brien's?"

Joe nodded. "They fix."

"Why don't you let me look her over for you? Save yourself a garage bill."

"Hah!" Joe said. He was eating corned beef and cabbage, and he spoke through a lusty mouthful. "I got plenty money, me. I bum my frans? No! Not when I have-a the dough. See?" He pulled out a fat roll of bills from his pants pocket and slapped one end of it on the table. "Pretty, hanh?"

"Goshsake, Joe! How come Mary let you loose with all that on you?"

Joe grinned. "I jus' get. She's-a from the bank," he said. "Oh, I take-a home, all right."

"All the same, you bum, I wish you'd let me take a look at that truck. You've got a long drive ahead of you and the roads'll still be pretty bad."

"She's-a fine truck," Joe said sensitively.

"She's a second-hand truck," Hod said. "And you've got a heavy load."

"Nnh."

"Okay, then." He might as well give up, Hod realized. He ought to have known better than to go after Joe in just that way. The truck, which had seen a good many better days, was the pride and joy of Joe's heart.

Joe had bought it last January, after Witherspoon had paid him for his land. He and Mary figured that to drive down to New

Bedford with their household goods would be easier, in the long run, and cheaper, than to ship everything and pay railroad fares for the whole family. And then, too, Mary said, when they got there, Joe would have the truck. There were any amount of ways a man with a truck could make a living.

At first, they'd planned to go to New Bedford at once, but the weather had been bad in January, winter driving was dangerous, Joe said, especially with a big load like that. The kids and Mary might catch cold. The fact of the matter was, Joe hated to face being outdoors that long in the cold weather. The idea drove him behind the stove in a fit of shivers, and Mary, though she wanted to get away and the three months of winter on Spoonhandle seemed, this year, to be more unbearably lonesome than ever, humored him.

So they'd gone on living in the old house through the winter, until the building materials for Witherspoon's new house had begun to arrive, along with a crew of workmen to clean up the site and start construction.

Now Joe was ready to go. The weather was still not warm, but anyway not like winter. He was, Hod thought, watching him, like a big kid going to the circus. I only hope that damn truck holds together, he said to himself.

Hod was pretty sure that O'Brien's garage, in Bellport, who had sold Joe the truck, had seen him coming. He didn't know what Joe had had to pay, but knowing O'Brien, he could imagine it was plenty.

"Well," said old Connie, at his elbow. "You goin t' order, or do I hev t' stand here while ruggus mortuous sets in on you?"

Hod jumped a little, and grinned at her. "I'll have the beef stew, Connie. How've you been?"

"Lousy," Connie said. "What's it to ya?" She moved away, her feet making a shuffling, splatting sound on the floor, and Hod saw she had on an old pair of knitted bedroom slippers, flattened out, with leather soles.

"She's-a sick," Joe said sympathetically, wagging his head. "Me,

I think she's-a awful sick, Hod. Mi-God, I'm glad I'm Joe San-gor!" He straightened up, puffing out his mustache, and brought both hands, palm down, with a thump to his barrel of a chest. "My wife, my kids, my truck, little cash. Hah?"

"Mean to say you put your wife first?" Hod grinned at him. "Before that truck?"

Joe grinned back, a flash of white teeth in his brown face. "Som'-times," he said.

He had been ahead of Hod with his dinner, and now, finishing, he began to scrabble together to get up.

"You wait'll I eat, I'll walk along with you," Hod said. He had been wondering if Joe wasn't going to say good-by. If he hadn't happened to run into him here, Joe, apparently, would have gone merrily off to New Bedford without so much as a hand-shake. Why was that? Hod thought, puzzled. He was going to miss Joe.

"Nnh." Joe shook his head. He teetered a little beside the table. "We stay Mag Snow's tonight," he said anxiously. "You come around, Hod, say good-by? We go next week, we think, but those-a men, she's-a say hustle, get out, the house she's-a to be burn down. So we go tomorrow."

"You mean they put you out before you were ready?"

"Ne'mmind. We stay too long, anyway," Joe said cheerfully. "You come-a Mag Snow's? I get home early." He puffed out his mustache again. "Couple bottles *vino*, maybe? For you, not me. You bring-a your girl?"

"Sure," Hod said.

All winter Joe had persisted in calling Ann his "girl." It was true, they had been a few places together—Mag's to eat, some-times Bellport to the movies. But so far as her being his "girl" was concerned, Hod thought, he guessed he didn't know, himself, about that. He sure hadn't found out how she felt.

"I walk-a with you now," Joe said, "but Joey and Leon, she's-a wait for me, down in the truck."

"Your kids? Don't you ever feed em?"

"They sick to the stomick." Joe rolled his eyes. "Oh, mi-God, the ice cream, the candy. They eat, they eat. They puke, they puke. So me, I fix the mattress, the quilt in the truck on top them table, chair. They sleep. But I better go back now."

"Mary'll kill you, Joe, letting them kids eat themselves sick the day before you plan to start. Don't you know better?"

Joe grinned. "She be mad," he agreed philosophically. "Them kids, they have-a the fine time, though. See you tonight, Hod."

"Sure. See you tonight."

Yes, he was going to miss Joe. The sons-of-guns, Hod thought, putting him out of the house before he was ready. Still, of course, he'd had all winter, and you knew Joe. He wasn't very practical when it came to things like that.

Connie brought him his stew and bumped the bowl down on the table in front of him. She did look sick, but with Connie, you never knew whether she was, or whether it was a hangover.

"That big Portygee's some hyped up over leavin these parts, ain't he?" Connie said.

"Seems to be."

"Well, I would be 'f I was him. God, I'm glad I ain't a Portygee. Ain't two people in this town ever treats a guinea anything but stinkin. How you gittin along with that girl you had in here with you last fall?"

"Good," Hod said briefly.

"Oh, I know 't ain't none a my business. You don't hev t' say so."

"I didn't say so. I said 'good.' That covers it."

Connie smirked. "Oh. That's diff'rent."

If it weren't a hangover, it was what would be one tomorrow or the next day.

"I was goin t' say," she went on, "that if you was fixin t' marry her, you got my blessin."

"Thanks. What if she won't?"

"Then you gut my blessin, and she ain't. She ain't that big a fool, is she?"

"Could be," Hod said. He felt himself beginning to blush, but there was no way he knew about to stop Connie.

"If I was twenty, by God, she wouldn't git a chance at ya," Connie said. "If I was twenty, and I wish to God I was."

"Well, Connie, I wish you was," said Hod. "We'd get married tomorrow."

"We would?" Connie was charmed. "Just for that, you don't hev t' pay for your dinner."

"Guess I better, hadn't I?"

"No!" she said loudly. "What husband around here ever paid his wife a rosy red cent? I'll take it out a that fi'dollar tip your girl left in here that time. Remember?"

"She did!"

"Ayup. I like t' never riz up from it, too. This ain't me you see here, this is my ghost. Good-by," she shouted, as he got up to go. "You marry her 'f you kin. She's a nice girl."

"Mm-hm," Hod grunted, hustling to get out the door. "So long, Connie."

*

To watch for the small weathered peak of Ann's shack as he came up the harbor in his boat had become second nature to Hod. Throughout the long cold three months of winter, whenever he and Willie came in from fishing, he always managed to take the last turn steering, so he could watch unnoticed through the side-glass of the windscreen, the cove opening out and the shack slide into sight, gray against the black of the spruces behind it.

Sometimes he couldn't see it at all through fog or driving snow; sometimes the gray gable was streaked and black with rain. When he and Willie got held up and came in after dark, which often happened, fishing through the tough weather, he had watched for the light in the shack window. She always worked past early lamp-lighting time, though she didn't usually stay in the shack all night, unless it got too cold and blustery to walk home. Paris made a terrific racket if she did, she told Hod privately, and it seemed simpler not to, at least through the winter.

He liked to think that sometimes she might hear the thrum of the engine and come to the window to watch the boat's red and green lights going up the harbor in the dark. He didn't know for sure—she'd never said. He'd seen quite a good deal of her, off and on. Sometimes he dropped by the shack in the evening to walk home with her; after a snowstorm, he took his shovel and went over to keep the paths clear.

If she heard him moving around outside, she always asked him to come in—quite often they had supper together at the shack before he walked with her up through East Village to Paris Freeman's house. And then, there'd been, too, the occasional trips to Bellport to the movies, or over to Mag Snow's to eat and spend the evening talking with Mag and Uncle Til.

He and Ann were easy together now—friends, he knew. She liked him. Beyond, he couldn't guess. Since the first day at the shack, he had made no further attempt to show her how he felt. Sometimes, it seemed to him, the weight of his feelings was too heavy to bear, too strong to keep in. But, he kept thinking, suppose I say something, and then she wouldn't let me see her again?

Tonight, coming home from Bellport, as the boat passed the mouth of the cove, he saw her sitting on the step of the shack and she waved to him. The shack, which was silvery in the twilight, seemed to take on a rather special shine. It was past suppertime—he had waited late in Bellport hoping to get bait which finally hadn't come in at all—but he hurried to put the boat on the mooring, and then, instead of landing at Willie's wharf, he rowed the punt around the point into Ann's cove.

"Good," she said contentedly, as he came up the bank and dropped down on the step beside her. "I hoped you'd come over."

"You did?" Hod said, pleased. "I'd come oftener, only there's no way to tell when you aren't working. Why aren't you today?"

She was now on the final draft of her book, he knew, and was plugging hard to finish it.

Ann laid a hand on his knee. "You're a very considerate guy," she said softly. "Not to come barging in."

Hod sat perfectly still, feeling the light touch, and almost held his breath, hoping she wouldn't take her hand away. She didn't.

"Work!" she went on, with what was practically a snort. "Try and do it! It isn't enough to have Witherspoon's boys tramping and yelling through the woods with their silly toolboxes. Today they got a bulldozer stuck up here on the wood road."

"A bulldozer?" asked Hod, staring. "*Stuck?*"

"Oh, it broke down, or something. They all came trooping in here after water for it. I was so mad at having my train of thought busted up, I said I didn't have any."

Hod laughed. "You could have sent them down to the Fir Well."

"And have them tramp all over that lovely moss? I told them they'd have to go back to the village for it. They didn't like that. Some of them were quite fresh."

"They were, were they?"

Seeing him begin to bristle, Ann tightened the clasp of her hand on his knee.

"I won't be going out tomorrow," he said. "Couldn't get bait. I'll be over and knock some heads together for you."

"Oh, they weren't *very* fresh. Just annoyed. They acted as if I were obstructing progress."

"Weren't you?"

"Mm-hm. I don't like Mr. Witherspoon's works and ways. Know what they're going to do with that bulldozer? Widen the road down the Spoonhandle, and then push over Joe Sangor's house and burn up the pieces. Call that progress?"

"Ayeh. I know. Kind of too bad. The old Pray house has been there a long time."

"Bill Pray's great-great-grandfather built it, didn't he?"

"Yes, the main part of the house. Way back along."

"The foreman of this crowd—at least I suppose he was, he did all the talking—red hair and a horrible Massachusetts twang—referred to it as that 'hooraw's nest down there on the point.'"

"Joe's dooryard *was* kind of a mess. You'd have to know Joe."

"He also told me for my information that a lot of guineas used to live there. I just said would he quit bobbing in and out of my woods like a damned leprechaun. I don't think he liked it much. I was mad."

"Edgy, too?" he asked, smiling at her.

"Edgy as all get-out."

"Want to go to a party?"

"A party?" She stared at him. "Did I hear you say a *party?*"

"Well, in a way. I saw Joe over in Bellport and he asked us to drop around to Mag Snow's to say good-by. I expect it'll be kind of a party."

"Hod, I'd love to! It's just the thing."

"Come on, then. We can eat over there—" He got up, reached for her hands and pulled her to her feet. As they stood close together, she felt his fingers tighten on hers with a quick movement, almost like a reflex. At once they loosened, and he stood holding them lightly. She could have pulled them away if she had wanted to. His eyes on hers were intent, serious and questioning.

She stood beside him quietly, waiting to hear what he had to say. She wasn't sure what, actually, she hoped he would say. They were good friends now; and out of his companionship, through the winter, she had drawn sustenance and a content as secure and steady as if he had been a wall for her to lean against. She felt, now, a deep confidence in him, a trust that she didn't believe anything could shake. The trouble was, his confidence in her seemed to be only up to a point—beyond that she could always sense his withdrawal. If only he could break through his reserve and tell her, she thought, perhaps we could go on from there. The way it was now, everything between them seemed to have come to a standstill.

She waited, expectantly; but Hod only said, "You'll need your coat, Ann. It's chilly on the water."

"I'll get it." She turned aside from him and went into the shack. Putting on her coat, she realized that the backs of her hands and her wrists still kept the pressure of his fingers. The sensation seemed to linger a long time, even after they had rowed off aboard the boat and started for the town slip across the harbor.

*

A good many of the workmen on the new summer cottages were staying in Bellport, traveling back and forth daily by truck. But those who weren't had rooms at Mag Snow's, and her house was full to overflowing. In addition, she fed dinners and suppers to some thirty or forty men. Word about the quality of her food had quickly got around—it was better than the Bellport restaurants, one workman told another, and she didn't charge so much for it. So a lot of them ate at the Come On Inn before going back to Bellport for the night. Mag's business was booming. She had never seen anything like it, nor, she said to herself, at the end of each day, had she ever in her life finished up a day so tired.

She had been a little put to it to find room enough for Joe Sangor's family, when they had stopped by that morning. After all, they were neighbors, with little kids, too, and she didn't want them to have to go all the way to Bellport—and then, like as not, have trouble finding a place that would take them in. Bellport hotels, even the poorer ones, were pretty persnickety. Mag finally decided to let Joe and Mary have her own room, with some cots for the kids. She herself could sleep out on the living room sofa. It was only for one night.

And she was some glad she had taken them in, she thought, as she and Mary Sangor sat down to a late supper together alone in the kitchen. They'd waited supper, but Joe and the two older kids hadn't got back yet from having the truck repaired in Bellport. The two little kids and Uncle Til had gone to bed early. All day, Mary, seeing how rushed Mag was with her work, and having nothing to do herself until Joe got back with the truck, had duffed in and helped. It had been a seven days' wonder to Mag to see how much Mary could do without even seeming to turn her hand over.

"You've sure done me one good turn today," Mag told her

heartily, spooning out two generous portions of apple sauce. "I swear, I don't see how you done it. You can work rings around me."

Mary laughed. "Joe's always sayin how quick I am with my hands," she said.

My, she's a pretty girl! Mag thought. Mary had on one of Mag's big white aprons trimmed with pale blue braid. The color set off her black hair and the creaminess of her skin.

"Well, I certainly wish you was goin t' stay here," Mag said. "It'd make my life some simpler, I can tell you."

"Kids and all?" Mary looked at her, her head on one side. "You wouldn't want to add to your troubles like that, Mrs. Snow."

"Call me Mag, I feel better. Poo, what's a few kids?"

"Ours are devils," Mary said. "There's a lot of Joe in em. And, of course, a little of me."

"I'll risk em," Mag said. "But there, I guess it ain't no use speculatin. You're heaven-bent for home, ain't you?"

Mary nodded.

"Kind of glad to go, too."

"Well—" Mary shrugged and smiled.

"Good to git home when you've been away from it a long while. I remember how I felt when I come home here from Portland, even if I didn't have no folks left. You gut folks in New Bedford?"

"No. Not what you could call folks. But Portuguese people, like us. We've missed havin friends."

"I'll bet," Mag muttered under her breath. "I wish we'd lived on the same side a the harbor," she went on. "But I'm kind a tied down with the business and with Tilburry. I ain't much of a neighbor to nobody, I guess." She stopped, embarrassed, wondering if Mary would think she was just talking, that she wouldn't have been a neighbor to a Portygee anyway, any more than the rest of the island people had, and it was all very well to talk, now that the Sangors were going away.

But Mary only said, "I wish you had." She pushed back her chair and got up. "These few dishes won't take a minute."

"Lord, let's stack em in the sink," Mag said. "Seems to me if

I see another dish today I'll bite a hole in it. Someone's comin,"
she went on, peering past Mary at the darkening window. "Must
be Joe and your other two kids. But I didn't hear no truck drive in,
did you?"

"No," Mary said, looking out. "It's Hod and his friend. Not
Joe."

"He's late," Mag said cheerfully. "Maybe it took the garage-
man longer'n he thought 't would to fix up the truck."

"Maybe." But Joe was a scalawag, Mary thought, not to tele-
phone, especially when he had Leon and Joey with him and was
keeping them out past suppertime.

"Hah!" Mag greeted Hod and Ann as they came through the
door. "Don't tell me *you* want to eat!"

"Fine thing!" Hod jerked his head at Ann. "She doesn't want
our trade, Ann. Let's go somewhere else."

"I ketch you!" said Mag. "You never hat t' go somewheres else
yit, did you? The's some chicken still warm, and some apple sauce,
if you don't mind eatin in the kitchen. The front part of the house
is full a them men. How're you, Ann? You ain't been over here
in a coon's age."

"I haven't been anywhere in a coon's age." Ann smiled. She
liked Mag. In Mag's house, she felt an easiness, a relaxation, that
she hadn't found anywhere else in the village. With Mag, you
had a sense of honest face values, of lack of pretense. No need to
be on your guard, nor to try to guess what Mag was thinking about
you. You knew.

Mary Sangor she didn't know so well. She had heard Hod and
Willie talk about Joe and Mary, and of course there had been a
good deal of gossip around the village when it finally became
known that Witherspoon had bought their place. In the fall, when
she had first come home, she had sometimes seen Mary at the
post office or the grocery; but when the winter weather really set
in, the snow was deep on the lower Spoonhandle road. Joe did the
shopping and took the kids over to the town slip in his boat so

they could catch the school bus. But Mary no longer came to the village.

Seeing her now, Ann smiled and said, "Hello, there," and Mary said, "Hello," and smiled back. But Ann sensed at once the deep reserve in her voice.

"Where's Joe?" Hod asked. "I saw him over in Bellport this noon, and he said to drop by tonight to say good-by. I thought I'd find him here waiting with a couple bottles of *vino*."

"The bum's not back yet," Mary said. "He's probably somewhere hunting up the *vino*. I'll fix him if he keeps the boys out late, when we've got to start so early tomorrow."

Her voice, speaking to Hod, had lost its reserve and was warm and friendly. It was a rather beautiful voice, Ann thought, not foreign, but with a slight lengthening out of vowel sounds and a huskiness that still wasn't quite native.

"Not back?" Hod knitted his brows. "Maybe O'Brien ran into trouble fixing up the truck."

"You think he might have?" Mary's eyes deepened. "I'd hate to be held up starting tomorrow."

"Could be. If he doesn't come rolling in pretty soon, we'll call the garage and find out what's keeping him." With Joe, Hod thought, it might be almost anything. He wondered if he'd better tell Mary about the boys eating themselves sick and decided against it. No sense worrying her.

"That's a good idea. I'm sorry about the *vino*, Hod." Mary smiled. "You could have had it with supper. Some would have gone swell with Mag's chicken."

"Oh, we'll make out. How about some beer all around, Mag?"

"Okay," Mag said. From somewhere she had produced two plates of steaming chicken stew, with vegetables and dumplings, which she set on the kitchen table. She opened the door of the big white refrigerator and brought out four bottles of beer. In the warm room, the sides of the bottles beaded up and steamed.

A car changed gears at the end of Mag's driveway and ground along in second for a few yards until the driver went back to high.

They were all silent a moment, listening, and Mary gave a little start and a quick run to the window. She was worried, Hod thought. He'd better go call the garage right away. His ear told him, even before the car lights flashed past the window, that it wasn't Joe's truck. From the quick glimpse of its outline he got, he thought it might be the Ford sedan belonging to the foreman on the Witherspoon job.

The car door slammed and someone ran, whistling, up the steps to the kitchen door. It was the foreman. He was a slight skinny young man, bareheaded, dressed in a brown windbreaker and khaki pants. Hod had seen him once or twice before at a distance; now, noticing close-up for the first time, the sharp, knobbly face, freckles and red hair, he understood, with an inner chuckle, why Ann had called him a leprechaun. He had, Hod realized, had a few.

The young man said "Hello" and his bright blue eyes took in the food and the four bottles of beer on the table. "Gee'sh," he said blurrily. "Tha' looks good."

"Ain't you et, either?" Mag asked resignedly.

"I had supper in Bellport," he said, with a lopsided grin at her. "But that was quite some time ago."

"Had a little somethin else, too, I guess," Mag said. "Well, haul up to the table. I'll stick on another plate. This's Mr. Bill Mahoney," she went on, introducing him with a sweep of her hand to include everybody.

The foreman was fairly steady on his feet, but the warm room was blurring him fast. He was now looking from the food on the table toward Ann and then toward Mary, with the slightly groggy air of one who has come out of darkness into too much light.

"You just drive over from Bellport?" Hod asked him.

"Yup."

"Didn't see a big truck loaded with furniture on the way, did you?"

"Nope. Wait—I may have. Passed some stuff, I know. Didn't notice what 't was." He sat down, thrusting his legs under Mag's kitchen table. "Hey," he said suddenly to Ann, "ain't you the young dame lives down in the God-forsaken camp on the wood road?"

"Mm-hm," said Ann, eyeing him coolly.

"Well, well, well. What you do run into!" he observed, with a pleasant, vacant grin.

"Look," Hod said. "Concentrate, will ya, fella? You sure you didn't pass a truck on the Bellport road?"

"I *yam* concentratin," Mahoney said, "only it's over here on the lady, bud. Pass anything?" He turned away from Ann as something seemed to occur to him. "Motor cycle cops! Lousy road was lousy with motorcycle cops." He giggled. "And me three sheets in the wind! Gawd, I drove like I was hatch'n out a hummin-bird's egg. Never looked right nor left all the way over. How'd I know if I passed anything?"

"Okay," Hod said.

"What's the idea?" Mahoney went on loudly, but still amiably. "Cops on a lonesome road where there ain't no traffic? We got more use'n that for our cops in Mass—Mass'shoosetts."

"Guess likely you have." Hod tried to keep his voice casual. He went on eating with an effort, feeling the cold start at the base of his spine and creep slowly to his shoulders. There were never any motorcycle cops on the Bellport road. If there were now, it meant some kind of an accident. Maybe the guy was seeing things, he thought. He's pretty drunk.

"Hod," Mary said, "would you call the garage now?"

He'd hoped she hadn't got it. But she had, he saw, looking up at her. She was standing by the sink, just out of range of the electric light over the table, but he could see her eyes glowing black in her white face. He pushed back his chair.

In the front room, where the telephone coin box was, most of the Witherspoon workmen were sitting around a table over a poker game. Hod had to crowd in behind them to get to the phone. He called O'Brien's Garage in Bellport, listened mechanically while the operator repeated the number and clicked her jacks. Someone on the other end of the line took down a receiver and bellowed, "Hullo!"

"What time did Joe Sangor leave there this afternoon in his truck?"

"Who? I d'no. Oh, you mean the big guinea. Bout six."

Six o'clock. That was two hours and a half ago. He should have been home by seven. God, nothing could be wrong with Joe. It wasn't possible.

"What was wrong with the truck?"

"Nuthin. We fixed it."

"Yes. What'd you fix?"

"Charlie done the work. He's gone home. *Hey, Ed! What'd Charlie do on the guinea's truck?*" There was a faint, far-off gabble, then the voice said again, "Sludgy carburetor. He cleaned that out. Oh, yeah. And fixed the steerin rod."

"He put in a new one?"

"Who t' hell *is* this? No, I don't think so. No. He didn't."

"Okay." Hod hung up. He pushed back past the poker table and went out to the kitchen.

"He left at six, Mary. He's probably broken down, somewhere along the road. I'll hunt him up." He tried to smile at her, aware of the stiffness of his lips. "Like to borrow your car," he said to Mahoney. "Okay?"

"Sure, sure." Mahoney gave him his foolish, amiable grin. "Glad to have a free hand to entertain the ladies."

Mag came across the room and put a capable hand on his shoulder. "You're goin t' bed, son," Hod heard her say as he closed the door. "Right now."

*

Hod saw it as he drove off the John's Reach bridge and around the sharp curve at the foot of the hill that led up into town. The car lights, swinging on the turn, picked up the black, twisted skeleton of the truck, glowing red in places, the charred, scattered pile of household goods, the smoke wisping up past the stiff branches of the spruce trees. Then the lights flashed past, and Hod brought the car to a stop, the brakes faintly squealing as he put them on too hard.

The state trooper, huddled up on guard by his motorcycle, looked up at the sound and came to the shoulder of the road. "On your way, bud," he said wearily.

"Okay," Hod said stiffly. "That truck belonged to a friend of mine. I'm trying to find him. Where is he?"

"Oh, good Gawd," the trooper said. He came closer and leaned, stiff-armed, against the side of the car, peering into Hod's face. "Sorry, bud. We been tryin to find out who he was. Him and two kids. It was a bad fire, by the time anybody got here."

"Any idea how it happened?"

"Can't tell for sure till she cools off some. Maybe not then. Far as we could tell, it looks like he couldn't hold her back on the hill with that load, and when he tried to make the turn, somethin give. She went off the curve and turned over."

"Ayeh," Hod said. He already knew that himself.

"The way we figure it, the feller wasn't hurt bad himself, but the kids was under the load. He was tryin to get them out when the gas-tank blew. Gawd, he must a been a giant. He had half that stuff unloaded when the fire caught him."

Joe would. That's just what he would do. Hod realized he was feeling numb all over, thinking of Joe as if he were still alive.

"If you know who he was, you better drive into Bellport and tell the boys," the trooper said. There was sympathy in his voice. He no longer sounded quite so impersonal. "We want to find his folks."

"Okay," Hod said.

"Want me to drive you?"

"No. Where do I go?"

He was aware that the trooper gave him some directions and that his mind registered them mechanically. He drove off down the highway.

*

The coroner's investigation of Joe Sangor's death was simple and didn't take long. The facts were open and shut, with no complications. It could hardly even be called an inquest—just an establishment of the immediate causes of accident, as required in cases of violent death to satisfy the law.

A not-too-bright Portygee fisherman, probably a little drunk—as witnessed by Ed and Charlie, the garagemen, who had smelt liquor on him—had dumped a second-hand truck that he wasn't used to driving anyway, off a curve at the bottom of a hill, killing himself and his two kids.

It might be true, as the coroner pointed out to Hod Stilwell, beforehand, that the state troopers had reported the truck's steering rod broken. For the purposes of the investigation, it seemed rather piffling to bring the matter up; nobody was to blame. There was nothing to show when the rod had snapped—before or during the crash. The man was a Portygee—you knew *them*—chances were he was drunk, they were all crazy drivers. An ordinary man with plain common sense would have known better anyway than to put that kind of a load on a junky old truck.

The Portygee's wife created a stir at the inquest, by standing up and saying that those who said her husband was drunk were liars; that more than one glass of wine made him sick; that he never touched any other kind of liquor. She had one of these husky voices that was low but carried all over the room. She was a damned good-looking woman, the way a lot of them Portygees were.

The sober, middle-aged Yankee town officials told each other afterwards that when they died they hoped their wives would have the decency to put on black for them, instead of a bright blue dress and a pair of yellow beads.

So, at the inquest, the immediate causes of the accident were established according to tradition and to due process of the law. Of other, less immediate, causes nothing was said; for with the blindness and inadequacies of closed human hearts, the law has no concern.

They buried Joe and his kids in sealed coffins at public expense.

Portygee-like, he'd had every cent he owned in his pants when he was burned.

Word went around that it must have been quite a wad, all that money Witherspoon paid him for his land—the little that was left of it, of course, for everybody said Joe'd been spending money like water. The Lord knew what his wife'd do, with no money and two little kids—be on the town, most likely, that was the way things like that ended up, for them kind of people. In fact, you could count on it.

Quite a few people went to Joe's funeral.

*

Hod drove back from the funeral with Mary and Ann and Willie in Mahoney's car. The little Irishman had been quite decent about lending his car during the past few days.

Hod kept his eyes straight on the road ahead. In the windshield mirror he had seen that Willie, in the back seat, had put his arm across Mary's shoulders and was holding her gently, and she had let her head droop wearily against him. Since Joe's death she had been like a sleepwalker, her face frozen over and dead white. She had spoken very little except to her children and, of course, the outburst at the inquest. There was something about Willie's gesture that hit Hod in a way that nothing else in the past few days had touched him—or maybe it was something that loosened up the tightness around what had already hit him hard.

In a way, you wouldn't have expected it of Willie, self-contained as he was; yet in another way you knew that the simple and the right thing was just what you could expect of him. It didn't occur to Hod that Ann beside him might be watching him or to care if she was. He suddenly felt as if something growing in him to break had let go. He let the slow tears trickle down his cheeks and drop off his chin on to the front of his good suit coat. When they turned into Mag Snow's driveway, he managed by some ducking and some quick work with his handkerchief to get rid of them.

Mary was staying at Mag Snow's, at least for a while, until she decided what to do. Mag said she wouldn't hear of her going. Not, anyway, until she was a little better off; and not then, unless she wanted to. Everything Mary had owned had been packed on the truck, even the clothes for herself and the children. What they had left was what they stood up in. Mag said not to worry, she'd manage things.

So far, Mary hadn't said anything but the low "Thank you" that seemed to come of its own accord from her stiff lips. She didn't seem to be aware of what was going on around her. She was carved silence, except with her children, Maria, the four-year-old, and Manuel, the baby of three. With them she was quiet and tender, even smiling, as if nothing had happened.

Hod parked Mahoney's car by the side of the house and got out to open the door for Mary. There didn't seem to be much, now, they could do—just leave her here with Mag. Mag would know, better than most, what needed to be done.

Mag opened the door and Mary's two kids came roaring out. They were delighted to see their mother, and she bent down to them, gathering them both into her arms.

"Mary," Hod said. "We're going, but we'll be around."

Mary didn't look up. They barely heard her soft "Thank you."

They went down the driveway in silence. Hod dug savagely in his pocket for a cigarette. He hadn't any, he knew. He'd left them in his other suit when he'd changed, thinking that going anywhere like a funeral, you certainly wouldn't want cigarettes. Now he wished he hadn't. He needed one and needed it badly.

"No cigarettes?" Ann said. "I haven't either. Have you, Willie?"

Willie shook his head. "I'll drop in to Pete's when we go by," he said, almost absently.

It had been months since either of them had been into Pete's— not since before the row with Witherspoon at Christmas time. No knowing what Pete might say or do to Willie, Hod thought. If he hasn't got over it, and of course he hasn't. He made up his mind he didn't need a cigarette that bad.

"Oh, never mind," he said impatiently. "I'll go up to Myron's when we get home."

Willie glanced at him as if surprised. "Might's well git some here," he said, starting up the steps to the store. "We all need one now."

Quite a crowd had come back from the funeral to gather at Pete's, Hod observed, as he and Ann followed Willie in through the door. Men in their Sunday suits and a few soberly garbed women were congregated in front of the counter. The talk ceased briefly as they all looked up to see who had come in, then resumed in a low clatter, which, out of consideration for its subject—a funeral and the events leading up to it—was kept to a subdued tone. Pete was behind his counter, and he had apparently foreseen the rush, for he had young Billy Grant, Sam Grant's boy, helping him wait on the customers.

Hod waited until somebody vacated a place by the counter, then slid into it. Pete was busy, waiting on Henny Pray, but he glanced up and seeing who it was, his eye took on a gleam.

"Well, well," he said. "Quite a stranger. Be with ya in a minute."

"As I was sayin," Henny said, apparently taking up the conversation where it had been momentarily cut off, "it was an awful thing, and it ought t' be a lesson to everyone that thinks about it."

"I can't help thinkin about that *poor* woman, though," Prilly Grant, on Henny's far side, put in. "Left like that, you might say, *destitute.*"

"That's why I say it ought t' be a lesson t' every one a the menfolks in this town," Henny said decisively.

Pete looked up from the column he was adding. "Well, I don't know, now, Henny," he drawled. "It might be more a lesson to some than to others. Most of us leaves the drunken drivin t' the Portygees, y' know. That'll be a dollar-ten. And sixty for the meat, I almost forgot it, less twenty cents for milk bottles. Leaves a dollar-sixty."

"I guess the' warn't no doubt he was drunk," Henny said. "That come out at the inquest, didn't it?" She fished in her pocketbook, hunting around for just the right change, which she laid beside Pete's hand on the counter.

Bill always told her to have just the right change, if she could, when she traded with Pete, because if you didn't watch him he was liable to short-change you.

Pete swept the money up and rang open the cash register. "Well, Hod, what you want? Yes, it did come out at the inquest," he went on to Henny, not giving Hod a chance to reply. "Drunker'n a hoot-owl, the way all them fellers git, the minute they lay their hands on a quarter. You give a guinea like that thousands a dollars, the way he had, and in five minutes the town'll have a crime problem. Only way t' do, by God, is keep em poor."

For a moment Hod stood quietly by the counter, his big hands gripping the raised brass rim that ran along its edge. His anger made a drumming sound in his ears, not loud enough to drown out what Pete was saying, but seeming, in a way, to be a background, so that the words coming out in the slow, cruel drawl, seemed clean-cut against it.

Suddenly aware of something electric in the atmosphere, Pete looked up. He started back a little and opened his mouth to go on; but Hod reached a hand across the counter and caught him by the smooth front of his shirt, twisting his fingers around in the limp black string tie. He heaved, and Pete rose up halfway across the counter, his feet dangling and his mouth gaping as the tie cut off his wind.

The talk around the counter stopped as if someone had cut a switch. There was a sudden, concerted movement as people whirled to stare, then, seeing what was happening, scrabbled to get away from it, stepping on each other's feet as they opened up a wide half-circle.

Hod heaved again and Pete came over the counter, his heels drumming on its linoleum-covered top. As he landed, kicking and half-sprawling, Hod let him have it with the open palm of his hand, first on one side of his face, then on the other. The slaps made heavy, meaty sounds in the silence, and presently other sounds were added, sustained gobbling squeals of pain.

Willie stepped out of the crowd and laid his hand on Hod's arm. "That's bout enough, don't ya think?" he said. "God, boy, he's had it comin for thirty years, but no need t' kill him."

"Okay," Hod said between his teeth. He delivered a parting whack and was pleased to see the congested face take on a purple tinge. Then he whirled Pete around, caught him by the collar and the seat of the pants and boosted him back over the counter. There was a scrabbling as Pete disappeared, then silence.

"Joe Sangor wasn't drunk," Hod said levelly to the popping eyes and open mouths around him. "I happen to know, that, as his wife said at the inquest, he couldn't drink without getting sick. What happened was, when Joe came down over Bellport Hill, his steering rod snapped. O'Brien at the garage told me over the phone that night, when we were trying to find out where Joe was, that his man Charlie had just repaired it. You can believe what you want to about the kind of a job was done. I went to look at the truck, and I know."

Hod leaned back against the counter, waiting, cold-eyed, for that to sink in.

"Some of you folks that's passing around the word 'drunk' so easy might like to know how Joe died. You can ask the state troopers, you don't need to take my word for it. He burned to death trying to get his two kids out from under a truckload of furniture. If he'd been willing to give up, he could have saved himself. That was quite a thing to do, for a drunk with a funny name, wasn't it?"

He turned to Billy Grant who was staring at him over the counter, white-faced and bug-eyed. "I'll have three packs of Chesterfields, Billy." He scooped up the cigarettes the boy hastily thrust at him, put down a dollar and waited for change.

"You ought to plan sometime to take your heads out of the sand," Hod went on conversationally. "It's kind of hard to believe that folks with funny names who ain't lived all their lives in the same place and in the same way you have can be decent human people, too. Or that somebody with a name like Stilwell, who growed up right here, could work a swindle on you to get your land cheap. You don't have to take my word for that, either. Some of you can hop over to Bellport and ask Josh Hovey." He picked up his change and stowed it in his pocket.

"Joe King," he said, "is a Bellport kid who works in Alec Staples's office. Box 48 is Alec Staples's mailbox, and Alec Staples is Pete's lawyer."

There were one or two exclamations from the men in the group, and Hod grinned.

"Figgerin out what that means, I see. Come on, Willie, Ann. Le's go home." He walked to the door and held it open for them.

"I'll probably go to jail for slapping the puss of your damned, public-spirited tree-savior, there," he said to the crowd of silent people, "considering the pull he has with the law. Pete's right in with the law. Pete, and people like him, half the time they *are* the law. If it'd start some of you to thinkin, though, I d'no b't I'd take a few months in jail and welcome. By the way, Henny, Pete cheated you ten cents on the groceries you just paid for."

He went out and closed the door, aware of the excited and hysterical gabble that grew in the store behind him.

They walked down the road to the shore, Willie slightly in the lead, striding along in silence. They were nearly there when Hod discovered that he had his arm tightly around Ann's waist, and that she was letting him keep it there. He helped her aboard the boat and sat down beside her on the stern seat, letting Willie cast off bow and stern lines, start the engine, and head the boat down across the harbor. He felt limp, he realized, and his heart was thumping in his chest like a drum.

"Hod," Ann said. Her eyes were almost black with excitement, and she had hold of his hand with both of hers and was rubbing it gently.

It hurt, he discovered, and looking down he saw with surprise that his hand was blue and puffy.

"Hod," she said again. "That was the most wonderful thing I ever saw."

Hod felt himself going red. "I couldn't stomach it," he said, his voice almost a mumble.

Willie, his back to them, steering the boat, suddenly spoke without turning around. "Well, I never could neither," he said. "I couldn't stomach it, so I cleared out where I wouldn't have to see it. God, I never figgered I was doin any worse'n most of honest folks do, only more so."

*

The morning after the slapping incident, Pete's store stayed closed. Sam Grant, going past early to the shore, observed that the padlock was still on the door, a thing that hadn't happened for years, since Pete was usually up at daybreak and open with the sun. Sam relayed the news, with a dry grin, to friends at the town slip and off on the gasoline scow.

"He probly warn't able t' open up," said Bill Pray. "My God, he was some sight when he went out a there last night. Did you see him? Swole up like a toad sculpin and two—I d'no b't three—of the hansomest black eyes you ever see. God, it done me good. I went home 'n et prit' nigh the whole of a pork roast Henny had in the sullerway."

"Didn't git a bellyache?" Sam asked, with interest.

Bill's digestion, as everyone knew, for the past three months had been delicate.

"Not one mite," said Bill, with relish. "I could've done it agin."

"Well, that's one way t' cure yourself," Sam said, grinning. "I guess likely 'f I'd been sick, what I seen last night would of cured *me.*"

"Cure ya!" Hallet Romer put in. "Thing like that would raise a dead man right out of his casket."

"You hear Agnes say anything this mornin?" Bill pricked up his ears. As Agnes's handy man, Hallet might be counted on for additional news.

Hallet wrinkled up his lip and sniffed. The sniff wasn't one of disgust or scorn. He simply had sinus trouble. People were used to the stuffed-up snort he gave every ten minutes or so, and would have missed it if he hadn't.

"Aggie's been flyin up and down the road between her house 'n Pete's since daylight," he said. "With a face like a meat-ax. She ain't speakin."

"It's a wonder she ain't been down with a razor-strop t' give Hod a goin-over," Nick Driver said.

"Hah! She better lay off of *him!*" said Hallet. "You spose Pete'll have him arrested, like he said?"

"I d'no," said Bill. "Likely to, I guess. But what I do know is, he God and well better not try it. This whole town'd go along with him to jail if Pete arrests him."

"That's right," Sam Grant agreed. "Jeepers, I never seen *nothin* like that, did you?"

"Ayup, I have. I've seen old Joel Frame fly into pieces just like that and trim up someone that needed it." Bill looked thoughtful. "I was thinkin last night it was kind of like old times. Ain't that so, Paris?" He jerked his head at Paris Freeman, who had just finished tying up his boat to the scow and had come aboard.

"Humph," grunted Paris. "I guess so."

"Well, you look pretty glum this mornin. Ain't you as tickled as the rest of us is?"

"Why should I be?" Paris came slowly across the deck, as if he had hardly the energy to lift his heavy rubber boots. "You can't beat thousands a dollars outa a man's hide, can you? Ain't one of us but took a worse lickin last winter than Pete did last night, if you ask me."

"Well," Bill said, "I been howlin spilt milk all spring, sheddin, you might say, tears a blood. But I can't say that this mornin I don't feel consid'rable better. He hatn't opened up the store when you come by, had he, Paris?"

"No," Paris said. "And I don't care if he never opens up his jeasly store. I ain't give him none of my trade since January, anyway. Not since I read in the paper who really bought my land.

Maybe the rest a ya was took in by that tree-savin business. I wan't. I see through him from the beginnin."

"That so?" said Bill dryly. "Too bad you couldn't of hed that kind of second-sight t' start with, warn't it? Saved some achin hearts."

"Yes," said Paris, glumly. " 'T was." Ordinarily, he would have got mad at Bill and clammed up tight or gone away, for Paris never yelled and ranted at his friends down around the shore the way he did at his womenfolks. But now he merely let his chin sag a little more and went on. "If I had, maybe I'd have money enough to take care a me the rest a my life, instid a landin in the poorhouse, the way we all probly will."

"Well," said Sam. "I d'no's I'm countin on that for some time t' come. What I'm lookin forward to is givin Myron some trade."

"By gorry, yes!" said Hallet. "Me, too!"

Nick Driver looked at him coldly. "You want t' watch what you shoot out a that mouth a yourn, Hallet," he said. "You know how word gits around."

Hallet looked crestfallen. "Oh, sure, sure," he mumbled. He swallowed and sniffed. "I guess you all know bout what I'll have t' do."

"Bout the same's we'll all do, in time, if you ask me," said Paris morosely.

Sam eyed him. "What 'n hell you talkin about?"

"Hah!" grunted Paris. "Who's hand-in-glove with the summer people? Who's goin t' know where all the jobs'll be, when the' is any? Who'll have the say in who gits em? You know who. You'll all be back tradin with Pete before you can spit, an you know it."

"By God, I don't have to!" Sam said. "I gut my boat and my lobster traps, and the' ain't no small-town, two-for-a-nickel Mewsolinni goin t' tell me where I git my job. Chrissake, Paris, hear you talk, anybody'd think you was clean out of the U.S.A. Go wan over to Italy and live, see how you like it."

"What's over in Italy?" Paris inquired, disinterestedly.

"Hah! You listen to your radio, read some paper besides the

Bellport Local Titter-Tatter, you'd know. 'T ain't no sense t' talk t' you."

"I spose you take in the Portland paper," Paris said with sarcasm.

"Sure I do. I read it, too. Lot of things in it a man can put his mind to. Good funnies." Sam grinned.

"Well, I can't afford a Portland paper," Paris said. He got up, slouched over to the side of the scow and let himself heavily down into his boat.

"Let ya have my old ones for a cent apiece," Sam called after him. "Or free, if you'll give em back after you've read em. Prilly likes t' have em t' line the cupboards with."

Paris made no response to this kidding. He cast off and a moment later his boat chugged away down the harbor.

His going seemed to leave no appreciable gap in the close-knit group aboard the scow, and the talk closed like water over his absence.

"Beats all about Hod, don't it?" Bill Pray looked thoughtful. "Nice quiet young feller, wouldn't of said he had nothin *to* him, all to once he gits right up on his hind legs 'n roars. Bright, too. Knows his way around."

Nick looked at him sourly. "Nothin new for my money," he said. "Just because he got up once on his hind legs and roared."

"Bout time somebody did," Bill said easily. "I wan't thinkin of a thing, except a few things bout old Joel Frame. There was an honest fella for ya." He got off the bait tub where he had been sitting and went across the deck to his boat.

"Guess I'll have t' do my tradin over to Myron's now," he said, looking up at the rest of them with a dead-pan. "Pete's closed down. Smart man like that, I guess he'll figger it ain't worth his while to open up again for quite some time."

*

Pete Stilwell did plan to stay closed down for quite some time. He was sitting up, this morning, in the big double bed in his bedroom, dressed in a blue striped cotton night shirt. His swollen face was wrapped in cold compresses to the eyes, and, as Bill Pray had said, it was hard to tell whether he had two black eyes or three.

He hadn't slept much the night before, because of the pain in his face, and he'd kept Minnie, his wife, pretty busy changing the compresses. But he felt better now, and he'd let Minnie lie down in the spare room to get some sleep. Agnes had been in a couple of times, her face a mask of horror. Her outrage and her exclamations had bored but comforted him.

Now, sitting up, he was examining, with minute attention to details, a set of architect's blueprints unrolled across his knees. His keen little eyes, with the blue-green swollen bags under them, went over the white lines, from sheet to sheet, taking in everything.

"They'll do," he said, almost aloud. "That's a damn good job."

He flopped back the covers and lifted his heavy legs, naked and hairy, out of bed. He felt around with his feet for his comfortable, flattened-out old slippers, and scuffed out through the hall to the telephone, kicking the half-closed hall door out of the way as he went along. There was no need to be quiet because Minnie was asleep. Minnie, for twenty years, had been as deaf as a post. She couldn't hear a thing that went on in the world, and the only way she could tell what was said to her was by reading lips. It was one of the minor blessings that had come to him that Pete thanked God for. So far as he was concerned, it didn't matter whether Minnie heard what was said to her or not.

He lifted the receiver, listened a minute, then depressed the hook and rang for central.

"Put me through to Ferriston," he said. "Eight-oh-four."

"Hullo," he went on, after a moment's wait. "Lancaster? Pete Stilwell. Them plans is okay. When can you start work?"

He pushed his underlip out over the upper one, listening thoughtfully to the far-away gabble on the line. "Fine," he said. "I'll be away for a month, maybe more, maybe less. Store'll be closed down, anyway. I want to give my wife a trip. She ain't had one, I ain't either, in God knows how long. . . . Where? Oh, California, I guess. Make a nice drive, wun't it? I'll leave everything with you. Glad you can do the job. Know it'll be a good one." He listened a moment longer, said, "Sure. Oh, one more thing, Phil. Like to be sure you use local labor. Makes me mad, these damn out a state contractors bringin in all their own men. I had my way, the'd be a law. . . . All right. See you do. G'by."

He hung up, scuffled back the way he had come, kicked off his slippers and crawled into bed. The blueprints he rolled carefully and put on his night table, picking up, as he did so, another roll of paper tied carefully with a string.

It was his map of Spoon Island, only different now, with new squares in fresh ink sketched in all over the eastern shore, showing where the wood lots had been sold and who owned them now. He had drawn the new boundaries in purple ink, to make them easy to see. The bright purple lines made East Village seem curiously cramped and shrunken in on itself.

Pete ran his finger, with its blunt nicked nail, over the northern-most boundary.

Farrel, he mused. Three acres.

Mr. Farrel was a New York man, who owned one of the big Bellport summer estates. What he was building on Spoon Island was really a nine-room sporting lodge, with a couple of small guest houses. Maybe a week-end place, maybe not. Hard to tell. Mr. Farrel was a family man—wife and four kids. They'd probly have quite an establishment over there, servants and all.

Whitcomb, he went on, sliding his finger to the next line. One acre.

Whitcomb was a painter, lived all over. Couldn't find out much about him, except he was pretty well-known, unmarried, lots of money. Over in his Bellport place, he entertained all summer. His new house was a good-sized one. It would be full of company.

Molino. Fifteen acres.

Pete's finger tapped the paper a couple of times before slowly tracing out the lines that bounded Molino's place. He'd prit' nigh made a mistake there, but, after all, it *was* kind of a funny name.

Man wasn't to be blamed. Mr. Molino had turned out to be the head of a Philadelphia machine-tool company, hell of a big firm, a very respected man and a millionaire, it looked like. He hadn't any Bellport place of his own, being fairly new there, but for the past two summers he'd rented a big house on the shore for his family and servants. His Spoon Island cottage would have fourteen rooms.

Yes, Pete mused, I like to made a bad mistake there, but as 't was, it turned out all right.

He hadn't made any mistake, though, about the man named Bergstein. By God, Pete said to himself, wincing, as he forgot and pressed his lips together, *he* warn't able t' buy nothin. *He* never gut in.

Washburn. Thirty acres.

Retired banker, Beacon Hill, Bellport. A ten-room house on what used to be Bill Pray's wood lots, plus some adjoining land he'd bought so nobody else could build near him. Washburn was going overboard, so his architect said, with lawns and rock gardens and landscaping. As soon as he could, he was going to sell his Bellport estate, and make Spoon Island his summer headquarters for good. That was a damn nice piece of business, the one with Washburn. Like all them Boston people, he had more relatives than Adam.

Jennings. Two acres.

Jennings was a friend of Witherspoon's, lived in Baltimore. Had a lot of money, didn't do anything for a living, so far as Pete could make out. Wife and two boys. Nine-room cottage. Kind of stand-offish, so far, but that was probly on account of Witherspoon. He'd come around, first time he wanted a few favors done. There were a lot of favors a man like Pete could do in a place, to make a man like Jennings a little more comfortable and happy.

Witherspoon.

Pete sighed. Then, slowly, with his finger he traced the outlines, not yet put in in purple, of what had been John Pray's place, which he, Pete, now owned. It stood to reason that Mr. Witherspoon would someday, maybe soon, want the rest of the Spoonhandle.

And that, he thought, would be all right, too. The old son-of-a-bitch. He'd come around, in time.

Well, there was the lot. That is, those were the owners of the six new cottages now being built and most of which would be done by July. It would still take some time after that to finish work on the grounds. But, by July, people would start coming. They wouldn't hold back any longer than they had to, when it came to starting living in their new houses.

Pete glanced at his list, neatly lettered along the bottom of the map, each name followed by a bracketed question-mark. Currie, Benson, Wakefield. Miles, Bannister, Matherson, Warren. Bannister was as good as sold. The others were still making up their minds, but they'd probly catch holt of the bandwagon, give them time. It had been a darned good idea, that one of making the place exclusive.

And that, plus the prospects, took care of all of the land, he thought, starting to stretch and not catching himself in time. The resultant sharp twinge of pain in his neck made him swear. "Ow! Goddam it!"

Rolling up the map and leaning back on his pillows, he said to himself, careful not to grin, Don't look as though I was goin to be too dependent, at that, on local trade.

And that reminded him—Mr. Molino had written him to be on the lookout for a housekeeper for him, from among the local women. Prilly Grant might do it—she was a nice neat woman—or Henny Pray. Maybe he'd offer the job to Henny. After all, he owed Bill a favor, maybe.

*

Henny Pray had been taking around a paper to all the people on the island. She was collecting subscriptions for a fund for Mary Sangor and her kids. It was surprising, too, how people had shelled out; or maybe not so surprising, seeing how the Sangors had been so misunderstood, and the way Hod Stilwell had talked the night before last, in Pete's store. To say nothing of what he'd done to Pete.

"My land," Henny had said to Prilly Grant afterwards, when they were walking up the road together and had thought up the idea of the fund, "wasn't that just wonderful the way he talked, and that change was ten cents shy, and I thought I give Pete just the right change, too!"

"You did give him what he asked you for," said Prilly. "I see it, when he made that addition, and I was goin t' tell you about it afterwards."

"Well, there! It just goes to show you!" Henny didn't believe for a minute that Prilly had seen the mistake. "You know, Prilly," she went on, skipping it, "I always thought Hod was good-lookin, but tonight it come to me he was just hansome!"

"So did it to me, you know it?" Prilly said.

Henny had nearly two hundred dollars subscribed for by the time she got to Myra Freeman's. It was just amazin! People hadn't given fifty cents or two dollars, the way they always did to the church fund. They'd dug. Some gave ten and fifteen dollars, and Myron Osgood had even come across with twenty-five.

But I guess *that's* understandable, Henny said to herself, with all the extry trade Myron's goin to git now!

"Well, there," she said, showing the list to Myra and gratified by the look of stupefaction on Myra's face. "It gives me back my faith in human nature, don't it you?"

"I think it's lovely," Myra said. "You better put Paris and me down for—" she hesitated—"for ten dollars."

"And me down for ten, too," Ann said. She had just been coming down the stairs and had overheard the conversation.

"Oh, Ann, that's fine!" Henny said. She was glowing all over with satisfaction—she couldn't remember when she had felt so good. "You been down there lately?" she asked inquisitively.

"Why, yes," Ann said. "I was down there this morning."

"How's the poor thing feeling, anyway?"

"It's hard to tell." Ann had been trying to get the picture of Mary's white, composed face out of her mind. She didn't want to talk about it.

"Well, I should say so, after all she's been through." Henny's voice took on a rich, pitying drawl. "The least we can do, I say, is give her this money. It'll pay her fare down to New Bedford, anyway, and see her through till she finds what she's goin t' do."

"She knows what she's going to do." Ann found it hard to keep the irritation out of her voice. Henny was a good soul, kind as they came, but it did seem as if she were getting a lot of pleasure out of being Lady Bountiful when there was very little about the situation, it seemed, for anyone to get pleasure out of.

Oh, dear, Ann thought. I'm mean. The money will be wonderful for Mary.

"What *is* she goin to do?" Henny pricked up her ears. "Ain't she goin to Massachusetts?"

Ann shook her head. "Mag Snow's offered her a job to stay and help run the Inn. Mary says she wants to do it."

"Well . . . tch!" Henny said. "You'd think she'd want to go back to her folks."

"She hasn't any folks."

"She hasn't! You mean she's all alone in the world?"

"Her folks and Joe's are all dead."

"Why, the poor, lonesome thing! It makes me come all over queer." Henny puddled up and fumbled for her handkerchief. She was warm-hearted, and it didn't take much of this kind of trouble to make her shed tears.

"I think," Ann said, "now that she's around on this side of the harbor and not stuck out of sight down on that point, she'll be easier to get acquainted with. Later on, when she feels better. She's a very nice woman, and I expect you'll enjoy knowing her." She went on, not knowing quite what had got into her, except that it was anger as she saw doubt appearing on Henny's face. "She'll be lonely, and she'll need friends. By and by, maybe you might ask her to join the Aid."

Myra, who had been listening from her chair by the table, drew in a quick breath, but she didn't say anything.

Henny said, "Why—why, yes, we'll have to think about it." She looked flustered and her lips opened and closed once or twice.

"Yes," Ann said, "you'd go around and collect money to offer her charity and pay her fare away from here. You'd cry over her troubles, even. But when you find she's going to be a neighbor, and it's a case of making friends or not, you'll have to think about it."

"Why, *Ann* Freeman!" her mother gasped.

"Well," Ann said angrily. "Isn't it so?"

Henny had turned red. She sat for a moment, speechless, while the color grew and faded in her plump cheeks.

"Well, Ann," she said at last, "I think you're absolutely right. I guess I'm ashamed that I had to have it pointed out to me." She got up. "I'll see about it, and I don't mean just 'think' about it."

"I'm sorry," Ann said. "I hope you're not mad, Henny. That came out all of a heap."

"You c'n be sorry for me if you want to," Henny said. "I guess if it came to a vote about takin Mrs. Sangor into the Aid, Myra, you'd vote 'yes'?"

"Yes, I would," said Myra instantly.

"Well, there's two of us. That's a beginnin, ain't it?" Henny said thoughtfully. She smoothed out her subscription list on the table and folded it neatly, making the creases with her fingernails. "I've got just a few more calls to make," she went on, getting up to go. "I'm just wonderin how much Agnes is goin to give, ain't you?"

*

Henny went briskly down the walk, along the road past Sam Grant's, and turned up the concrete steps that led to Pete's house. She hadn't planned on asking Minnie Stilwell for anything, considering what had happened; but all of a sudden it had occurred to her that there was no reason why she shouldn't. There was just a chance, too, that Agnes might be in to Pete's, and if she was, it would save Henny a long walk down to Agnes's house.

The real fact of the matter was, Henny, like everybody else on the island, was dying to know how Pete was taking things. Nobody had seen him since the night he and Hod had had the fight, and the consensus was that he was staying in his bed.

As she went up the steps, she was amazed to see a Ferriston construction company truck parked in front of Pete's store down the road, and a gang of men working at the side of the building, putting up scaffolding.

Now for goodness' sake, what can *they* be doing? she asked herself, stopping dead in her tracks. She couldn't suggest any answer to the question, so she went along to Pete's side door and rang the bell.

Minnie answered it and said, "Why, Henny, come in," in her colorless low voice. Minnie was tall and faded, indefinite like her voice. She had her hair in papers in the front, and in the back twisted up into a knob.

Henny said, looking straight at Minnie so she could see the motion of her lips, "How are you, Minnie? I can't stay a minute."

She always tried, talking to Minnie, to make her lip movements very plain indeed, and was sure that she had more success than most people in making the deaf woman understand. She would have been astonished to find out that to Minnie she always looked as if she were just standing there making faces, and that Minnie seldom got a word she said.

"I thought I'd come in to see if you and Pete wanted to join in on this," Henny said, producing her list. "And I thought if Agnes was here, I could kill two birds with one stone."

"Mm," Minnie said, reaching for the list. She saw at a glance what it was. Minnie could read, and often preferred to.

"Agnes?" Henny said, opening her mouth wide on the "a" and bringing out the "s" with a prolonged hiss.

"Oh," said Minnie. "Well, come in." She led the way into the front room, the list in her hand.

Agnes and Pete were sitting in the two big wing chairs beside the table, and, thought Henny, instantly rewarded for coming, he certainly did look a terrible sight.

He didn't seem to be making much of it, though. He just said,

"Hello, Henny, have a seat," as if nothing on earth had happened to him.

"Well," Henny said, taking a rocking chair. "This was the last place on my list, except you, Agnes, and I see I been able t' kill two birds with one stone." She felt a little foolish, saying right over again the same thing she'd said to Minnie, but there, she did feel nervous, and it *was* something to say. Minnie, she saw, relieved, wasn't looking at her. "Prilly and I've been gittin up a subscription fund for Mrs. Sangor—"

"For who?" Pete said.

Henny's lips tightened. "For Mrs. Sangor," she repeated, making the words very distinct indeed.

Pete ran his tongue over his back teeth. "Oh, the Portygee woman, hah?"

"Yes," Henny said. "People has just shelled out, too. I must say, I'm proud of my neighbors. I've got over two hundred dollars promised on this list."

"Is that a fact?" said Pete. "Quite a sum. Pay her way back to Massachusetts where she b'longs, wun't it?"

All right, Henny thought, setting her jaw. She'd show *them*. Maybe Pete thought he ran the town and Agnes thought she ran the Aid, but my gracious, they don't, not if the town and the Aid don't think so.

"Mrs. Sangor," Henny said, "ain't goin back to Massachusetts. She's stayin right here to help Mag Snow run her Inn." She paused a moment to let it sink in, and then went on. "The' was some of us thought it might be a nice idea to ask her to join the Aid, seein she's goin to be a neighbor now."

That got a rise, she saw, at least out of Agnes. Pete, to her surprise, merely grinned a little—at least, Henny thought it was a grin that appeared and vanished on his puffy lips.

"I'm sure the rest of the Aid will have something to say about that," Agnes said. "After all, it's always been just among us few friends, hasn't it?"

"I've asked them *all*," Henny said pointedly. "They're all for it, unanimous. Practically." She was lying like a rug, she thought, and she'd have to hustle right back around the village and prime the Aid. The Lord knew what they'd do. But she guessed, under the circumstances, they'd see things the way she did. After all, they weren't hypocrites, any more than she was.

"You mean you've asked everybody *first?*" Agnes said, turning bright red. "Without having a meeting or anything?"

What she meant, Henny knew, was everybody *else* first. "Yes, I have," she said sturdily. "And the entire Aid is for it."

Agnes's mouth shut, thin-lipped and tight.

"You better string along, Aggie," Pete said. He was still looking amused. "Ain't nothin like a funeral t' set a town's sentiments sloppin over. After the Aid's smelt of her at a couple a meetins, you won't have no trouble votin her out again."

Henny got up and started for the door. "I'll be goin," she said.

"About that list," Pete said smoothly, "I guess you can put me and Minnie down for fifty dollars. And Agnes, too. You want to give that much, don't you, Aggie?" He looked over at her. "We wouldn't want t' be the ones to hold back, when the town's tryin t' help a poor woman out. Would we?"

Agnes met his bland gaze and she jumped a little. "No," she said stiffly. "Put me down for fifty, too, Henny. But I think we'd better have an Aid meetin before we make any off-the-record decisions."

"It's up to you," Henny said icily. "I thought you'd just like to know how we all feel, that's all." She put a warning note into her voice, thinking as she did so, that the president of the Ladies' Aid was, after all, an elected office, not one you just held all by yourself for the rest of your life. They needn't think they could smooth her down, either, by subscribing four times as much as anyone else. Wherever it came from, it was money, and Mrs. Sangor could use it. Henny wrote down on her list, with firm little jabs of her pencil, the Stilwell names and the amounts they offered.

Pete himself got painfully to his feet and came to the door to see

Henny out. "Feel as if I'd stopped a cannonball with my nose," he said jovially, swinging open the storm door for her.

The Ferriston construction company truck was just pulling away from the curb, loaded with workmen bound home for supper.

"Havin that old buildin tore down at last," Pete said, jerking his head at it. "Bout time, too, the old eyesore."

"What!" gasped Henny. "You're havin the *store* tore down!"

"Ayup," Pete nodded. "Havin her tore down." He teetered back and forth on the balls of his feet for a moment, enjoying her flabbergasted face. "Havin a new one built," he went on. "Modeled after Griswold's Supermarket, over in Bellport. Got to keep up with town progress, you know."

"Well," Henny said feebly, "I guess that'll be an improvement. It'll certainly be an improvement to the town." The thought entered her head that retracing her steps over the village wasn't going to be such a chore as she'd expected. Not if she had news like this to tell. A store like Griswold's—why, Griswold's was a summer people's market! Common folks hardly so much as ever showed their faces through the door of it, they couldn't afford to.

"Ayup," Pete said. "We'll have pretty swell folks comin here, from this summer on. Got to keep trade to home, you know, have a nice clean modern place, they'll want to trade to. Them's all Bellport workmen, too. By God, I put my foot down on outside labor. Guess Lancaster's gut a few jobs left for local boys, too, if they want em. Damn these Massachusetts contractors, I say!"

Henny felt bewildered. Later on, she'd think it all out. She'd tell Bill. My goodness, Bill had been roaring around the house for days about the summer cottages all being built with outside people.

"Speakin of jobs, Henny," Pete went on. "Meant t' ask ya, almost forgut it. How'd you like one, workin over to Molino's this summer? Fella wants a housekeeper."

"Oh, my land! I couldn't! I—"

"Sure, ya could. Them folks is crazy bout home cookin, and you're the best cook in town, Henny."

"But I don't know nothin bout them kind of people," said Henny wildly. "I'd be scairt to death."

"Mis Molino'd show ya. You'd git used to it quick. She's a darn nice woman, just like common folks, ya wouldn't know the diff'rence." He offered her a slip of paper. "Here's Molino's address. You might want t' write. Oh, the job pays sixty a month, maid's uniforms, and three meals a day. My Lord, Henny, it's a lib'ral education, just goin into one a them houses. You never see such hansome things in your life as them people's gut!"

"Well," Henny said distractedly.

My land! she thought, sixty dollars a month, all clear money, comin in steady. She never could do it, Bill would have a connniption, and how on earth would she manage takin care of him and the boys? And workin around them people, seein em every day— why, she was a fool even to think of it. But—

She took the paper from Pete, folded it and tucked it into her pocketbook.

*

Willie waited for some sign from Donny Mitchell, but when the days went by and he did not hear from him, he decided that his latest effort hadn't been any use and he'd only said the wrong thing again. Then, on the fifteenth of April, on the way up to Myron Osgood's and passing along the road by Mary Mackay's house, he saw that the front windows were boarded up.

Mary must've gone away, he thought. Now, that's funny. Seem's as though Donny would've come down to say good-by before he let em take him somewhere's else. But there, he mused, I d'no why I'd expect it, seein he ain't been near me all winter.

Willie had been puzzled, at first, as to why Donny had so completely deserted him. It had been true, of course, that Mis Mackay had forbidden him to come down to the island and that Willie had had to back her up. At the time, he hadn't seen anything else he could do. But since talking with the boy on the wharf, Willie thought he was beginning to see the light. Donny'd decided that, because he hadn't made more of a fuss about it, he didn't want him.

Thing like that'd cut pretty deep, I guess, Willie said to himself, considerin the way he feels about people not likin him. I wish I'd realized before.

Now, turning into Myron's, Willie wondered what kind of a place the Welfare had found for Donny, and if there'd be any way of getting in touch with him.

He passed the time of day with Myron while Myron was collecting and wrapping his groceries.

"See Mary Mackay's gone away," Willie commented.

"Ayeh," Myron said. "Went last Sunday."

"Wonder what she done with her boy?"

Myron didn't answer, adding up his column of figures. "Sent him back where he come from, I God and well hope," he said, turning the slip around so Willie could see the total. Myron was being pretty meticulous about his sales slips these days. "Dollar-three. That right?"

"M'm." Willie fumbled in his billfold for the money. "Your boy was kind of sidekicks with him, wasn't he? I was wonderin if he left Artie his address?"

He was unprepared for Myron's outburst. "No, he never! And Artie don't have no more truck with him, see?" Myron flushed a little under Willie's mild, inquiring gaze, and turned his back, rearranging some cans on the shelf behind him.

"He bother you bout somethin, before he left, Myron?"

"I don't want t' say no more about him. But I tell you this, Willie, any more of them State kids in this town, it's over my dead body."

"That so?"

"Yes, by God, that's so!"

Willie gathered up his groceries. "Didn't you go to school with Granville Mitchell?" he asked reflectively.

"That ain't gut nuthin t' do with it!" Myron said angrily. "That kid was wilder'n a hawk. What's more, the' warn't nobody to hold responsible, when it come to payin for any damage he might of done."

Myron was still smarting from the bill turned in to him by the Ferriston storekeepers, which had been quite a big one, and also from what it cost him to get Artie out of the mess with a whole skin. It had turned out, from what the storekeepers testified at the hearing, that Artie always *had* bought something when he was in a store, that the other boy had been the one to do the actual stealing.

There was plenty of doubt, Myron assured himself over and over, as to just how much Artie had been forced into it. But anyway, the whole thing had cost him money.

"Well," Willie said. "See you, Myron."

He went back down the shore road, carrying his bundles, and wondering. Funny for Myron to be so tore out. He wasn't usually unreasonable about kids' ructions. Must be that Artie and Donny had got into something that Myron had had to pay for.

Willie was sure something was peculiar about the situation, a week or so later, when he got a letter from Donny. It was written on a plain piece of tablet paper. Donny had apparently thought hard, writing it, because quite a lot of it was crossed out with heavy, inky scratches.

Box 5047, Ferriston.

Dear Willie:

I guess you will be surprised to hear from me, but I thought I would write seeing I didn't get a chance to come down and see you before I left. I am with some very nice people on a farm back of Ferriston. They are awful good to me—

He had crossed out something here, and holding the paper to the light, Willie was able to make out, under the scratches, "and they have a Cidilac car."

Now why would he want to scratch that out? Willie wondered. Say some farm folks back of Ferriston did have a Cadillac, which sounded kind of fishy, what would be the point of thinking twice about saying so? Could be Donny'd started out to make things sound better than they were and then had decided not to lie. Willie read on:

I am doing all right in school.

A long, scratched-out part followed, hard to decipher, but Willie, his curiosity sharpened, finally figured it out: "They are letting me finish up the eighth grade here, so I will be ready for high school work in the fall." After Donny had crossed it out, he had written:

I am most through the eighth grade now, so I guess I will enter the high school here next fall. I hope they will have a good basketball team, but I bet it won't be as good as Bellport. I wanted you to know that I would have liked it fine to come and live with you and Hod, and the only reason I didn't was—

The next few sentences were inked over so heavily that Willie had to give up on them. He finally went on reading the rest of the letter:

—because I couldn't, I guess these folks here wanted me awful bad. But I sure would of liked it fine. I am kind of lonesome here, they don't let you go out much. If you see Sam Freeman, say hello for me to him, will you?

Yours

DONALD MITCHELL.

Willie sat for a while with the letter in his hand.

"They don't let you go out much."

"They're letting me finish up the eighth grade here—"

Well, why in hell would there be any doubt about letting a boy finish up the eighth grade if they were nice farm people, somewhere out back of Ferriston? And Box 5047, that would be in the city, unless you marked it R.F.D.

Willie folded the letter into his pocket and went down the shore to his punt. He rowed around the point to Ann's cove, went ashore and knocked at the door of the shack.

"I'm botherin you," he said, with a smile, as she opened it.

Ann shook her head. "I've already been bothered once this morning," she said. "I haven't gone back to work yet. It's too nice a day. I'm glad to see you, Willie, so don't look as though you thought I wasn't. Come on in."

"Had company or somethin?" Willie asked. He stepped into the shack and sat down on the end of her studio couch, stretching out his legs comfortably.

She had it fixed nice, now, he thought, with the bright pillows around and the straw matting on the floor. It sure was a pretty little room.

"Mr. Witherspoon's in town, calling on the landholders. Hadn't you heard? He was around this morning to see if I wouldn't sell him my acre."

Willie grinned. "You and me can sympathize," he said.

"You know what he's going to do? He's bought the rest of the Spoonhandle from Pete, and he wants to put up a six-foot steel fence with barbed wire along the top to mark his line. He says if he can't buy my acre he'll have to fence me in on two sides, up to the town road. It'll cost him a lot more."

"That'd be too bad. Good thing you bought an acre from John, instid of half an acre, warn't it? If you hadn't, he could a fenced you in on three sides, and all the way you could git in here would be by boat. My, my!" said Willie. "What'd you tell him?"

"Well, I asked him why a fence—what was there to get in or get out?"

Willie grinned.

"He said that wasn't the reason. He said a fence just seemed to make things more personal. He was nice and polite about it, but he sure wants my acre. Likes this shack, too. Said something about using it for a study."

"Go'n t' let him hev it?"

"Oh, I don't know—I hate to, but who wants a six-foot fence around them? And my book's almost done now, Willie. I might be going away before very long."

"No," Willie said. "You ain't, are you, Ann?"

"I'm—not sure."

Willie was silent a moment. Then he said, apparently apropos of nothing, "Hod's doin some thinkin, off by himself, mostly, these days."

"Is he all right, Willie?"

"Ayeh." Willie smiled at her.

"I haven't seen him for—for a while. I wondered."

"He'll be back. I think he's settlin some things in his mind. Good thing, too. Don't worry, Ann."

"M'm," Ann said thoughtfully. She'd been feeling forlorn and deserted, wondering why she hadn't seen Hod for nearly ten days.

"Be kind of too bad to sell your acre if you want to keep it," Willie said.

"I know. You'll be glad to hear he doesn't want Little Spoon Island any longer, Willie. He's satisfied with what he's got—says his view's far the finest one on the island. One thing he's sorry about, though, he planned to change the name of the island, if he got it, to Witherspoon Island. Just to make it more personal."

"H'm," Willie said. " 'T would of, wouldn't it?"

"I said why didn't he change Spoonhandle to Witherspoonhandle, but he didn't seem to cotton to the idea."

Willie's twinkle showed her his appreciation. "Guess you don't like him much."

"The funny part of it is," she said reflectively, "he seems to be quite a nice man. Full of enthusiasm. Boyish. He's sure of his welcome, and he knows without a doubt that he's the best thing that ever happened to Spoon Island. Maybe he is, I don't know. But it shakes you a little. What's on your mind, Willie?" she asked, seeing him looking inattentive and thoughtful.

"Like to have you read this letter from Donny Mitchell," Willie said. "See what you make of it."

Ann read the letter once, and then, carefully, again.

"I don't know, Willie. I— Oh, there's something about it that makes me want to put back my head and howl."

Willie nodded. "Guess that's just it," he said. "Sam wouldn't know nothin, would he?"

"If Sam did, he'd have told me, I'm sure. Some of the kids have been wondering where Donny went so fast, without saying good-by to anybody."

"They was some trouble," Willie said. "Myron Osgood is mad enough at Donny to kill him."

Ann thought fast. "Willie, I haven't said anything—Sam and I said we'd keep it under our hats. But you know you asked me last winter to see if I could do anything."

He nodded, looking at her.

She went on quickly, telling him about the connection with Artie Osgood, the Ferriston stores, and the scheme she and Sam had cooked up at Christmas time. "Sam said he was pretty sure it stopped them. At least, he's been keeping his eye out, and if they'd started again, I think he'd know it. So far as he's been able to tell, they stayed away from Ferriston all winter."

"Mm-hm. I guessed 't was somethin of the kind." Willie got up. "Too bad it couldn't of been stopped before it begun. It'd been quite easy then." He folded the letter and put it in his pocket. "I'll go see 'f I can find out what happened and 'f the's anything to be done about it. Seems as though, fella like me, all he does is go proguein round the aidges, after it's too late."

"That's more than most people bother to do, Willie," she said. "I guess I didn't do much, either."

"Well," he said. He started out, then put his head back through the doorway. "Hod'll be around, Ann."

*

Josh Hovey was sitting at his roll-top desk making out his pay-roll, when Willie came in through the door.

"Willie, you old son-of-a-gun!" he bellowed. "I ain't seen you since Adam was a doll. How've you been?"

"Good," Willie said. "You're fatter'n a puffer, Josh."

"That's right, I *em.*" Josh looked down at his midriff. "I was thinkin maybe I'd build a house 'n barn on that. Save taxes. You're

the only man I ever known, Willie, whose hand I'd like to shake.
Except Hod, I'd like to shake his twice."

Willie grinned. "Well, I might let you," he said. "If you was
t' do me a favor, Josh."

"You can hev anything out a me you want," Josh said. "Except
my wife. And the hove-down way I've felt, the last month or two,
I d'no b't you c'n hev her, 'f you was to ask nice."

"No," Willie said. "You take time, you'd probly think twice on
that, Josh. What would the address of Box 5047, over to Ferriston,
be? You know?"

Josh grunted. "You think because I figgered out Box 48 I'm a
directory for the whole goddam state."

"Well, no," Willie conceded. "But you know your way around a
lot better'n I do, Josh. I figgered you might know how to find out."

"H'm." Josh pulled his telephone toward him and flipped the
receiver off the hook. "Gimme the post office," he said to the
operator, and then, "Want to talk to Greg Graham. The post-
master, you sog! Or don't you know his name? Hullo. Greg? How
would I find out an address for a box number over to Ferriston?
. . . What was that number, Willie? Five-oh somethin. Five-oh-
four-seven."

He listened a few seconds, nodded, and said, "Thanks, Greg.
Ayeh, they're goin t' put me over there. I just wanted t' find out
where 't was," and hung up.

"Well, Willie," he said. "That ain't exactly an unknown num-
ber you're talkin about. It's the box of the State Industrial School
for Boys, over in Ferriston Hills. Greg says the Bellport State
Welfare Agency sends quite a lot of mail over there."

"Mm-hm," Willie said thoughtfully.

"For Godsake, Willie," Josh went on. "What you want t' know
for? If you don't tell me, I doubt if I'll live out my time."

"Been quite a while since I asked you any favors, Josh," Willie
said. He went on talking, telling as briefly as he could the story of
Donny Mitchell, and ending up with the details of what he wanted
to do.

Josh listened glumly. "Don't that beat hell!" he said. "Granville Mitchell's boy, you say?"

"Ayeh."

"And you want to adopt him? *Legal* adoption? Willie, you're crazy."

"Ayeh."

"My God, Willie, they wun't let ya. They're carefuller of them State wards than if they was virgin maidens. I d'no, but ain't the' a law, I'd have t' look it up, a precedent, anyway, that you have t' be a married couple?"

"I d'no, Josh. That's why I come to you."

"Want me to use my pull, hah? I swear I'd never of thought it of you, Willie." Josh grinned.

"You know of any other way?" Willie said soberly. "I want you to use anything you can think of. If the's a couple of judges t' kill, I wouldn't want you to stop at that, Josh."

"Well," Josh said. "I'll do what I kin. I know Judge Elliot. He'll say if it's an impossibility. I couldn't promise nuthin, Willie?"

"Fine." Willie got up to go. "Soon's you can, Josh?"

"Might take a few months. Might cost somethin. Oh, blast!" Josh said, deep disgust in his voice. "You know well's I do what it takes to bury a pound of flesh. If I was t' have my life over again, knowin the hog-waller I was goin t' help to build up, damn if I wouldn't stay a little bit of a baby." He levered himself out of his chair and went with Willie to the door. "Willie, you old sog," he said affectionately, "come agin. Been an awful spell sence we went fishin on the Banks together, ain't it?"

Willie grinned. "Ayeh," he said. "It has."

"And you gi'me back my faith, by God, you do," Josh said. "I guess, by gorry, if you do want her, you can't have my wife. Er— August, Willie. Maybe September. I'll drop you a postal card."

Back at home, Willie sat soberly down at his kitchen table to compose, for almost the first time in his life, a long letter.

*

Little Spoon Island
April 22, 1937.

DEAR DONALD:

Hod and I are haking almost every day now and we about loaded the boat when we struck a streak for three days running out on the Otter Bank. That's a good ways off-shore. It's so far out that the land to the westard looks like a fogmull and a lot of times when it ain't quite clear you can't see no land at all. Theys good fishing there, if you know just where to set the trawls. I been wishing you was along with us, for with them big loads we sure have needed a third hand the last three days.

Last week Hod and I went up to Winker's Island after trap ballace; when we had her loaded we had to wait for tide so I walked round shore to a camp I used to go gunning to. The road had almost all growed up to blackberry bushes and I like to tore the pants off of me gettin through. I was thinking that someday it might be a good idea to go there with some hatchets and a scythe and clean out that road. That camp sure is handy to use if you want to go gunning and Winker's Island is an awful good place for birds. Theys a cove there that freezes over in the winter-time, and sometimes of a cold morning, early, I seen that cove so black with ducks you couldn't see the ice. The blossoms on them blackberry bushes was thick as freckles on a redhead's nose. It's going to be a good blackberry year. This fall I plan to go over there with my bucket and my gun. I hope by that time you'll be home here to go with me. Maybe we could talk it up to Sam Freeman to go too, and stay all night in that camp.

There was a lot more, of news about the town—about how all the new cottages were coming along and about various people Willie thought Donny might be interested in. Ann Freeman had told him that Sam said he thought the Bellport basketball team had a pretty good chance to win the state championship next year. Sam said to say "hello."

I don't want you to let this letter make you homesick but I thought you wanted to hear all the news and I dug up all I could think of so you could have it. I'm glad you got a good place and the people are nice people. But whenever you can, I want you to be good and darn sure you can come home here and stay with me. Hod and I missed you something

fierce and theys a lot of things we ain't done and a lot of things I like
I ain't had a chance to show you. We'll plan on them when you come.
I'm glad you want to come and stay with me. Now I know you do, I
can start the ball rolling to fix it with the Welfare people. When the
time comes.

Yours lovingly

WILLIE STILWELL.

It took Willie the better part of three evenings to write the
letter. Mailing it, he still wasn't sure he had said what he wanted
to say.

When Donny first got it, he tore through it once as fast as he
could to find out if Willie knew he was in the reform school. He
stopped when he read the sentence, "I'm glad you've got a good
place." Willie didn't know.

He felt an almost choking sense of relief; then the realization
began to come to him, slowly, that if Willie knew, he wouldn't
want him. The reform school was the worst thing that could
happen to you. If you were sent there, that was the worst there
was.

If the kids in a town got out of line, that was what they held
over you. In all the places Donny had lived, there'd always been
some bad kid or other who "ought to be in the reform school," or
maybe one about whom people said, with relish, as if they were
glad, "Well, he's in the reform school, and that's the end of him."

Willie'll change his tune when he finds out, Donny thought. He
won't be likely to want me then. Besides, even if he does, I got to
stay here.

The kid named Pope was a State ward. He was seventeen, and
he'd been here four years. He'd be here till he was of age, old
enough to be let loose on his own. No matter what you were in for,
even if it wasn't much, they didn't let you go if you didn't have a
family to go home to—someone who'd be responsible if you got
into trouble again.

When he'd first come, Donny'd been mad and sore all through,
mostly because Artie'd got off. His old man was a selectman of the

town, he'd paid the cops dough. From the first—from the time Artie'd thought up the gag of swiping stuff from stores—Donny had supposed that sometime they'd get caught and have to pay for what they'd done. He was willing, he told himself.

It hadn't occurred to him that he'd have to take it and Artie wouldn't. Artie had got out of it by lying and by not being the one who'd done the swiping and because his old man had had the dough to pay. The real reason Artie hadn't done any stealing was because he hadn't had the nerve to.

Well, that was all right. Donny wasn't mad any more. Now he just felt tired—as if he couldn't drag one foot after the other. He'd had trouble doing the work out on the school farm that they'd set him to do, maybe because it was hot weather, and he wasn't used to the weather in Ferriston Hills. It was so far from the salt water. They'd poked him around and sent him to the school doctor for medicine and stuff. They hadn't been mean. It didn't seem like a place where they were mean, unless you got out of line.

He did his work slowly, not thinking much about it, or about anything. After he got Willie's letter, he began to make pictures for himself about the things in it—the camp among the blackberry vines, the black ducks, so many of them sitting on the white ice in that cove. Sometimes he thought about the morning he'd steered Willie's boat out to Hazlitt's Rock and watched the sun come up out of the water. Sometimes it seemed to him that almost everything, even the things he was looking right at, seemed dim and far away.

*

Ann Freeman tied the last knot in the string on the brown paper parcel, pulling it tight with a vicious yank.

There! she said to herself. Damn you, you're done, and I don't know whether to drop you in the post office or in the ocean.

The book had been finished for three days, and for that long she had been, she supposed, dithering, wondering whether to begin at the beginning and write it over, or to wrap it and send it along to the publisher. It had been a lot of hard work, but that was about all you could say for it.

She had felt different when she finished her first book—there'd been a sense of achievement and satisfaction then. This time she felt empty-headed and empty-handed, with nothing in the world left to do. It was a jolt, after you'd been busy for months, wishing there were twenty-four hours in a day, and then suddenly found yourself with nothing on your hands but idleness.

She tucked the brown paper parcel under her arm and went out. She'd go straight to the post office, drop the darned thing in the mail and stop worrying about it. She hoped.

And then what?

As she went past Willie's landing, she saw with surprise that Hod and Willie must be home—she didn't know why they would be, it was a fine, clear day and they'd been going offshore every day lately. She hadn't laid eyes on either of them for nearly a week. You'd think there was nothing in the world but fish. But today, the boat was on the mooring and smoke was coming out of Willie's chimney.

I'll bet they're eating, she said to herself. It was dinnertime, and she was darned hungry. On impulse, she went back to the landing and called out, and Hod, almost instantly, came to the door. Seeing her, he waved and came down the path to the punt.

"If you're having dinner over there," she said, eyeing him morosely, as he sculled up to the landing, "I want some."

"Sure," he said. "Hop in. You look as though you could eat a nice tack."

"You wouldn't know how I look," she told him nastily. "All buried up in fish."

"You are?" He eyed her with a glint of amusement.

"No. You are. At least, I suppose you must be. I haven't laid eyes on you for days."

"Willie and I struck a streak," he said cheerfully. "We found a place on the Otter Bank that must be hake-heaven. Know what we've made since I saw you last? Almost two hundred dollars. That's *fishing!* No bait, today, though."

"It sounds very dull to me."

Hod sighed. "Well, feed em first, talk to em afterwards," he said. "I always say."

She made no reply and presently he said, "What's in the bundle? Bring your lunch?"

"That," she said, "is my book. It's done, if you're interested."

Hod was in the process of hauling the punt up on the landing below Willie's house. He stopped in midstride, his rubber boots half in and half out of the water. "Why, Ann! Swell! Why didn't you say?"

"I don't feel like shouting it around. I just feel as if I'd swallowed a lot of snowballs."

"Well, goshsake!" He waded out along the side of the grounded punt, lifted her neatly off the stern thwart, before she realized what he meant to do, and started for the shore with her.

"Hod! For heaven's sake! Put me down!" She gasped, clinging with both hands to the suddenly precious parcel.

"Right here?" asked Hod. He stopped a few feet from the shore, where the water was still well over his ankles.

"You're pretty funny—" she began furiously.

But he merely bent his head and put his lips to hers in a long, thorough kiss. "That's for being a smart girl and finishing your job," he told her. "And this one's for me." He kissed her again, and this time, when he finished, he went the rest of the way to shore and set her gently on her feet. The brown paper package tumbled out of her hands onto the beach, and he stooped and picked it carefully up for her.

"It's a good thing for you that didn't fall in the water," she said grimly. "What on earth's come over you?"

He grinned. "I was wondering myself," he said. "I could describe it—"

But she fled along the path and up the steps into Willie's house.

*

Word went around that Pete and Minnie Stilwell had gone away. No one knew just where, but somebody saw them starting out in Pete's Chrysler, early one morning, all dressed up with the back seat full of luggage.

Someone else said it was because Pete couldn't stand the disgrace of bein beat up in public like that, and he'd gone away for good. But no, the town objected, that couldn't be. If he planned to stay away, he wouldn't be buildin a new store.

Finally, a week or so after he had gone, the matter was settled by a piece in the Bellport paper under the Spoon Island Items:

Mr. and Mrs. Peter Stilwell are enjoying a transcontinental motor car trip to California, where they will visit relatives in San Francisco. Mr. Stilwell, one of our outstanding business men, expects to return in time for the gala opening of his new up-to-date supermarket, on July 1st. Neighbors wish the Stilwells a pleasant trip.

"Neighbors sure as God do!" Bill Pray said dryly to Henny, reading the item. "I hope he drives off the top of the Rocky Mountains. Wonder what he plans to do with Minnie, accordin to this?"

The item caused a fairish ripple of amusement about the town, because everybody knew that Agnes always sent the Spoon Island news to the Bellport paper.

"What do you hear from Minnie and Pete?" Lucy Osgood asked Agnes at the next meeting of the Aid. "That's quite a trip they're takin."

"Oh, they're having the most *won*derful time!" Agnes said, with a gurgly laugh. "They've stopped off at the Grand Canyon, and on the way back next week they're hoping to see Yosemite National Park."

"M'm," Lucy said. "Makes it nice, doesn't it? I didn't know you had relations in California, Aggie."

"Oh, *we* haven't. They're some cousins of Minnie's. Quite distant, of course."

Yes, Lucy said to herself. Real distant, I'll bet. If any of *them* had relations in California, we'd all have heard about it before this time, you can be sure of that.

"They wanted to see Niagara Falls," Agnes went on. "But Pete isn't sure they'll have time. He's allowing an extra day or so, because he wants to be sure to make it back by the first to open up the new store."

"Well, Myron and I would've liked to had a trip this year," said Lucy. "But I guess we'll have to put it off till Myron sells some land."

There was an electric little silence, and then Agnes said blithely, "Well, there's lots of chance to, I guess, the way the summer people are trooping in. I guess that was what Pete had in mind when he decided to build his new store this year—all that new trade from the summer people."

Lucy flushed. That had drawn blood. Myron had been moping around for weeks, saying he'd be put out of business when Pete's new store was finished. He'd had splendid trade all through April and May from the local people. But there was no denying it, the idea of the new store had set everybody agog.

"Is it true what they say that it's modeled after Griswold's, over in Bellport?" Myra Freeman put in. She thought it was about time somebody said something, or Agnes and Lucy would have each other's heads torn off.

"Why, yes, it is," Agnes said "The architect's plans are just the same."

"Not quite so big, is it?" said Lucy.

Agnes bridled. "Well, no, not quite. This isn't Bellport. But I guess it'll be big enough to take care of Spoon Island." She paused to let Lucy get the effect of that, and then went on, "Oh, and one thing Pete told me before he left, he's going to have one whole end blocked off for a cold-room, to keep a big supply of meat and perishable goods on hand. My, won't that be convenient for everybody—things like that whenever you want them, not have to wait until the week's supply comes in!"

There was no denying it—the new store did sound impressive. Nearly everybody, by now, had seen the inside of Griswold's. Those who hadn't—and there were some who never had, because

Griswold's was too expensive—had made a point of going in there when they were in Bellport, to see what it was like.

It had a great deal of plate glass and steel, parallel counters down the middle so you could see everything, shining refrigerators for milk and butter, and a whole separate glass counter for different kinds of cheese. It certainly made you feel as if Spoon Island were coming up in the world, to have a store like that. Whatever you might say about Pete, he'd certainly been one smart man to think of it.

The men still might be mad at him, but when that store was opened, the women meant to see the inside of it or know the reason why. They wouldn't do all their trading there; of course for the bulk of it they'd stick to Myron. Pete needn't think he was going to have everything come his way—my goodness, not after what he'd done! But it would be foolish to go all the way to Bellport for things Pete carried that Myron didn't. There was no sense in taking a row to the point where you bit off your nose to spite your face.

The Aid was nearing the end of its sewing afternoon, and it felt, collectively, that it had had quite an exciting time. Not only had the sparks been flying between Lucy and Agnes, but they'd had a long discussion of Mary Sangor and they'd voted her into membership. Agnes and Sara Romer and Tiddy Driver had voted against it, and there had been one or two "doubtfuls," but the majority vote had been enough. They'd decided not to tell Mary or to invite her to a meeting for a few weeks; it seemed a little soon after her tragedy for her to be considering social affairs. But they'd voted her in, and there wasn't one of the ladies, putting away her sewing and getting ready to go home, who didn't feel a glow of satisfaction.

*

The screen porch of the Come On Inn was flooded with June sunlight. It turned Mag's climbing nasturtiums, the leaves just beginning to reach up past the porch rail, a rich green-gold, and it warmed Uncle Til's hands and the blanket across his lap where he sat in his wheel-chair letting the heat soak in.

The wheel-chair had been one of the first things Mag had bought when business had picked up, and Uncle Til, though he had scolded her for extravagance at the time, had to admit it was the most comfortable seat he had ever sat in.

"It ketches me in all the right places," he told her, "and that's more'n I can say for any chair I ever set in, even when I was well."

He was too lame and frail now to walk at all, even with his cane, but now he had the wheel-chair, he could roll himself around the downstairs rooms whenever he wanted to, and stop in front of any window he pleased. Every sunny day, either Mag or Mary managed to find time to take him on a ride outdoors, up and down the tar. It was the finest present, Uncle Til said, that a man ever had give him, and the best thing, bar none, that ever happened to him in his life.

He was waiting now for Mary to come and take him for his ride. He didn't know as he ought to let her today, he ought to make her rest. She and Mag had had an awful crowd to dinner—one of them "shore" dinners, too, with all them plates of different kind of food to lug around—workmen off the cottages, and summer people, too. It had been most three o'clock when they'd got cleared away. They were both lying down now to rest up before it was time to start a meal all over again. He should think they'd want to. He never in his life, he thought with admiration, had seen two women turn out so much work. It was an awful good thing for Maggie and him that Mary had decided to stay.

It did him good anyway, he said, to have someone so pretty moving around the house. Just to see Mary walk across the room made him feel like gittin out of that durn chair and hoppin like a colt. And it gave him a new lease on life to have them two nice little kids around. What if they did make a noise once in a while and wake him up out of his nap? He could always take another nap.

They were company for him, the kids were; they liked to talk

about the same things he did. In some ways, he told Mag, he en-
joyed them more than he did grown folks. He could set with them
while they played their games and did their bits of things, and the
three of them never interrupted each other one mite. It was nice to
have so much company around—made him feel rich.

"You know how 't is with us now, Maggie?" he said one day.
"We're *well-off* people."

The kids were out beyond the nasturtium bed now, playing some
kind of a game. Uncle Til could just see over the top of the railing
Maria's straight black bob and Manny's fuzzy curls. He had
promised Mary that he'd keep an eye on them while she rested. She
knew they'd be all right with him—he couldn't get up, but he
could always call someone, in case they got into trouble. Mary had
a horror of their getting out into the highway that went by the
front of the house. There was lots of traffic on it now.

By joppy, he thought with pride, that was one thing he could do
to help out, take care of the kids. It goweled him sometimes, a
grown man to be so helpless, with them two womenfolks working
so hard.

Course, Mary was a little nervous about going very far away
and leaving the kids with him. She stayed within call. He didn't
blame her, not after what she'd been through. Anybody'd be care-
ful, he guessed, with the ones they had left. She was resting now
on the couch just inside the open window that gave on the porch.
He didn't believe she was asleep. Now and then he could hear her
turn over and once he heard her sigh.

Well, Uncle Til thought, he himself had a pretty good idea
about how she was feeling. He'd felt froze over, just like that, for
a year after Neeley died. It was a funny thing—he'd got over it,
mostly, after that time, and in the years following he'd forgut how
it had felt. But, seeing Mary, all at once, lately, he could remem-
ber it as if it were yesterday. He wished he could let Mary know
somehow that the time would come when she wouldn't feel so bad.

There was a sudden flurry and the kids out by the nasturtium

bed came flying up the steps and in through the screen door, bang-
ing it behind them.

"Well," Uncle Til said, "what's it now?"

"It's a miny comin," Maria said, her black eyes blacker than ever.

"No, it's a fox comin," said Manny. He had been a trifle be-
hind his longer-legged sister, and the screen door, shutting on its
spring, had barely missed him.

"You look out, Manny," Uncle Til said. "That screen door
prit' nigh cleaned you out of your shoes. What's a miny, M'ri? I
don't recall seein one a them round here for a long time."

"Well," Maria said, looking at him with her head on one side.
"It's just got a long tail."

"Wag it?" asked Uncle Til, interested.

"Oh, yes!" Maria's eyes widened and darkened. "Wags it
somethin awful."

"Wags awful!" chimed in Manny, shaking his head.

"They don't hurt ya, though, do they?" Uncle Til asked
thoughtfully.

"They do if they catch you," Maria said. "They eat you into
little, tiny pieces."

"Foxes, too?"

"Oh, yes, they do, too."

"Oh, yes, they do, too," said Manny.

"Well," said Uncle Til. "You know bout the minys and the
foxes round this place, don't ya? I'd a told you, only I'd think
you'd know."

"What about em?" Maria came over by his chair, and Manny
followed her, lining up alongside.

"They don't 'mount to much around here. All you do is go
'Squee!' at em and they turn tail and run like a flock a turkeys."

Maria liked the sound of the word. She chuckled. "Squee!" she
said loudly. "Manny, say 'Squee!'"

"Squee!" said Manny. The word tickled him, too, and he began
to laugh.

"See?" Uncle Til said, soberly. "You've scairt the daylights out a every one of em. The' ain't one left on the premises."

"All right," said Maria. "Come on, Manny."

"Watch out for the screen door," said Uncle Til. "It'll take his tops'ls down. Where you goin now?"

Maria considered. "Well," she said, "I've got to go over to South America. There's a piano over there, only you got to have a license to play it. So I got to go over to South America 'n play the piano."

Manny said, "Wull, I'm goin, too."

"What you want to go way over to South America for, M'ri?" Uncle Til asked. "There's my piano now, right down by the nasturtium bed. You can play that any time, and you don't need no license here."

"All right," said Maria. She looked cheered up. "We won't go."

Manny said, "We won't go, Unc' Til."

Dear God, Mary thought, listening just inside the window. South America, Joe told them stories about that. But the piano—Maria *couldn't* remember it. She's too little to remember the piano.

I mustn't stay here with them, she said to herself. I must take them back, the way Joe and I planned to. With our own people, they'd forget things like the piano.

But Mag and Uncle Til were so kind, and there was a job here, a chance to earn money. How did she know what she could find to do if she went to New Bedford now? She knew a few people, yes, but there wasn't anyone who might know of a job. Most of them were all the time looking for jobs for themselves. And Mag was so kind. A friend. And she herself was useful here. If only she could be sure the kids could grow up happy. . . .

Mary turned her head listlessly on the pillow. It was time to get up if she didn't want Uncle Til to miss his ride. In a minute she would.

Someone was coming up the walk. Mary could hear the gravel crunching under feet. More summer people, wanting to eat or to stay the night? She lifted her head and peered cautiously out past the starched curtain. Callers. Prilly Grant and Henny Pray.

They were saying hello to Uncle Til, asking him where *she* was. What did they want to see her for? She'd been through all that, people coming to say how sorry they were. Of course, they'd given her all that money—it had been wonderful. She didn't know what she'd have done without it, and she hoped she'd made them see how grateful she was. But after that, she'd supposed they were through being kind—now that they'd got over being shaken by the terrible realities of death.

Mary got up, passed a comb quickly through her short black hair, slipped into a starched fresh dress and went out to the porch.

Henny and Prilly had come up on the steps, but not with the air of callers, for they were not sitting down.

"Well, hello, Mary," Henny said. "We can't stop a minute, we've both got to hurry home and get supper. But we wanted to ask you if you'd like to join the Aid. We voted you a member last month."

"Me?" Mary said, not letting her astonishment show in her face. "Why—why, that's nice of you. Why, of course I would."

"Well, then, the next meetin will be a week from Friday, at Prilly's house." Henny was flustered, and not at all sure she was saying the right things. "You just come. That's all there is to it. Now, Prilly, we'll have to run, or your menfolks 'n mine'll be home and not a mouthful to feed em."

The ladies retreated down the steps, both smiling, both starting to say at once, "Good-by. See you at the meetin."

Mary watched them go, still astonished, still feeling as if she had acted ungracious and tongue-tied. "Was I dreamin, Uncle Til?" she asked, "or have I been invited to join the Ladies' Aid?"

"You wan't dreamin," he said. "They did, an you said you would."

Mary turned and went in through the hall toward the kitchen. In the doorway she passed Mag, who had got up, hearing the voices, and had been unable to contain her curiosity. Besides, she liked to be on hand, these days, when people were around Mary, just in case. Mag wasn't taking any nonsense.

Mary apparently didn't see her, and Mag, looking at her curiously, went out to quiz Uncle Til.

"What ails her, Tilburry? It's the first time since her trouble I seen any expression on her face."

Uncle Til explained.

"My Lord of heavens!" Mag exclaimed. "I don't see nothin so very wonderful about that. You'd have t' pay *me* to make me go set for an afternoon with them old hens."

In the kitchen, Mary was thinking, "Maybe it'll be all right, after all. Maybe now I won't have to be scared all the time for my kids."

*

Ann Freeman's publisher had acknowledged the receipt of her manuscript almost at once. He was looking forward to reading it, he said, and would do so soon. Then for nearly a month she heard nothing, waiting and wondering with growing apprehension. It had been years since she had found herself with time on her hands. The days went slowly as if they were being doled out by someone who was unwilling to let them go, and for Ann, each one ended with the hour of mail-time.

She tried helping Myra around the house and for a while plunged into a whirlwind round of washing dishes and scrubbing floors that even Paris should have found exemplary; but Myra wasn't used to having help with the housework—she liked to do things as they came along and as she had to, she said. To have so much of the housework done up so fast and for such a long time ahead made her nervous and left her with time on *her* hands. To Ann's surprise, Myra actually seemed impatient about it.

"For the land's sake, Ann!" she wailed one afternoon. "I've had it in my mind to clean up that woodshed, for some day when I didn't have much to do, and here you've gone and done it! Now I'll just have t' think round and find somethin else, and what 't'll be I don't know! There, you're just raisin the Old Scratcher with my plans, and I wish you'd stop it!"

Knowing that her mother's seemingly erratic system of planning was, actually, quite methodical, Ann agreed that, strange as it seemed, she had something on her side. Myra didn't like housework very much, and probably creative planning was the only fun she got out of it. To have someone meddling in, with however good intention, undoubtedly *was* upsetting. So Ann gave up trying to do much except washing dishes and helping with an occasional meal, and she could see Myra was relieved.

Ann had thought, too, that she might get a belated word or so of approval from Paris, seeing she was at last buckling down and doing the work around the house that he thought so highly of; but Paris seemed hardly to notice, or if he did notice, he didn't say anything. He had the air, these days, of having given her up as a bad job; at least, that was what his aloof and occasionally disgusted glances seemed to convey. She hadn't listened to him when he'd talked; now he wasn't going to say any more. His attitude said that he was a beaten man—nobody appreciated him nor paid any more attention to what he said than if he was a hole in the wall. Though his family didn't doubt that he'd have plenty to say if any disapproved subject came up that he hadn't already worn himself out on.

Actually, since Paris had sold his land for a lot less money than he now realized he should have had for it, he was becoming more and more preoccupied with his own frustrations. The three thousand dollars he had got for the land he had put in the bank, where it remained untouched. The figures in his bankbook—the uncompromising "3," the fat, black zeros following it—were like symbols to him of all the good things life had promised and had cruelly withheld. There it was, money'd come, just as he'd always known it would. But it was just like everything else, something the matter with it. There wasn't enough and never would be, not if he left it sitting there collecting interest for the rest of his life. He was worse off, it seemed to him, than if he hadn't got any money

at all; for the knowledge of how near he'd come to reaching his
lifetime goal—enough, maybe, to take care of him through his
old age—brooded over him like a shadow, blacking out the rest
of his troubles. He was buried too deep in disappointment and
helpless resentment to bother much with his family. When he
came into the house from time to time and found Ann scrubbing
the kitchen floor, he walked around her without a word, usually
leaving muddy boot-tracks on the wet linoleum as the only sign
of his passage.

So Ann, with some regret and a little inner amusement at the
separate reactions of her parents, gave up and took to spending her
spare time down in the shack or taking long walks. It had been a
long time since she had wandered over the island, following up its
obscure and often forgotten wood roads, or climbing over its
beaches and craggy ledges. During the busy years, the wild and
solitary beauty of the eastern shore had almost gone out of her
mind—at least, it was still wild and solitary if she kept to the
stretches of shore line that remained where summer cottages
weren't under construction.

The land that had belonged to Paris, she had known, as a child,
every inch of—Apple Cove, with the sweet curve of its rocky
beach, High Head and The Head Cove, and the two black rocks,
just off the land, The Grinders, with their grim history. Wander-
ing along the shore, she could feel no reality in the fact that every-
thing was sold now, the acres which for so many generations had
belonged to the Freeman family. The place was the same—except
for the growth of the spruces and a few alder thickets which had
sprung up here and there, she couldn't see any change. She told
herself that she hadn't any right to feel at home here, but it didn't
do any good. The sense of at-homeness, of belonging, almost a
sense of possession, stayed automatically in the back of her mind.
Even while she walked along saying to herself, In a few months
there'll be a fat, ten-or-fifteen-room house *right here*, probably
showing a Georgian influence, and a tiled swimming pool dug into
Apple Cove beach—could be, with steam pipes to heat the salt

water, that was the kind of thing they did—even while her reason said this to her, the land, something else said, was the Freeman land and always would be.

It seemed absurd; but there it was—not actually regret that the land was sold, but more a habit of thinking, as if a feeling for land might be hereditary, transmitted as naturally as the color of eyes and hair, through chromosomes. She hadn't realized, before, that she'd feel like that. She would have thought she'd been away from the eastern shore too long. But, apparently, it was something you didn't get over.

She had gone, on a June afternoon, to spend some idle time climbing around High Head, thinking she might look at the foot of the cliff and see if the old wreck of a sailing ship's keel was there, as it had been through her childhood. It was. Wedged into a deep crevice in the rocks and anchored down by a blunt, heavy ledge that some northeast storm had shifted over it, the brown, wet, worm-eaten timbers looked, now, almost like a part of the rocks themselves. Barnacles and seaweed grew on them as naturally as on the ledges, and the bright-colored wrinkles and starfish apparently could tell no difference. Unless you knew where to look and what to look for, you wouldn't know that the misshapen objects had once been the backbone of a ship.

There was something comforting in knowing that anything so perishable as wood could be so timeless. I guess I must be old-fashioned and sentimental, after all, she thought. But everyone felt that way, of course; especially about things that, in childhood, had seemed exciting and romantic, and the wreck of an old sailing ship, lost too long ago to keep about it any memory of tragedy, had always seemed so.

She went along the steep side of the cliff, her feet following familiar footholds—the climb was easy if your feet remembered where they were. The knoll at the top was bare and grassy, as it always had been, but the spruces had grown up so that, now, you couldn't see the length of Apple Cove beach. It did seem strange that in all the time she'd been home, she hadn't been down here;

she thought, suddenly, that working so hard without a break, she'd let herself miss a great deal.

She kept on down the shore path to the cove, watching for the curve of the beach to open up beyond the trees. The curve was always lovely to see—white sand and gray pebbles and red granite ledges, and the blue line of the water lying softly against it. Scrambling down the face of the ledges to the sand, she did not see Hod Stilwell until she came face to face with him.

Hod had been gathering up flat, medium-sized rocks and piling them into a sort of cairn below high-water-mark. It was low tide now, and his punt was hauled up below on the beach. His boat was at anchor off in the cove. Hearing her scrabbling down, he stood arrested, a rock in each hand.

"Hello," Ann said. "You look like Chief Rain-in-the-Face about to start a massacre. Or was it the cave men who used rocks?"

Hod looked at her. "I *was* stacking up trap ballast," he pointed out. "But if you want, I can drag you around by the hair some." He tossed the rocks onto his pile and came purposefully toward her across the small space between them.

Ann retreated a little, until her back was against the slope of the ledges behind her, but he did not stop. He advanced until he stood quite close to her, and she felt herself blushing furiously. A few weeks ago, she would have felt sure of herself, and sure of him; but not since the day he had carried her up from the punt. That day she had ducked into Willie's house and all the afternoon she had stuck close to Willie, admitting to herself the turmoil she was in, making up her mind that she wouldn't be alone with Hod until it had quieted, and she could be sure what she might do. Hod had stuck around, too—but only for a while. Some time after dinner, he had picked up his cap and gone off by himself aboard his boat. She was pretty sure he had been angry with her; she knew she was angry with him for going. And to her chagrin, she hadn't seen him since.

Looking at him now, she dug hastily in her blouse-pocket for a cigarette and fumbled for a match. A cigarette, she knew from of old, was protection. She saw, from his ironic expression, that he knew it, too. He let her fumble for a moment, then pulled out a kitchen match, lit it with a flick of his thumbnail and held it to her cigarette.

"Where've you been all this time?" she asked hurriedly. "I haven't seen you for a long time."

Hod thrust his hands into his pockets. "I've been hanging around waiting for you to come to your senses," he said. He remained standing, with an air of permanency, in front of her. "Go on. Drag on it," he went on grimly, watching the cigarette. "I'll wait till you get through."

"What do you mean—come to my senses?" Ann took a pull at the cigarette, intending to make it a long, composed one, but she found her breath was coming too quickly for that. The drag, if it could be called one, emerged in a short, explosive puff of thin smoke.

"You know what I mean. At least, if you don't now, you soon will."

"Hod," she said shakily, "what's got into you? You're not like yourself. You're not—"

"I'm like myself for the first time, about, in my life," he said. "I've been a long time finding out what I am. But now I know. It hasn't been easy to think it through, either, and it took me a while. I love you, Ann. I think you love me. If you don't, I want to know. I don't recall how long I've hung around waiting to find out, but what I do know is it's too long." He put a hand on the ledge on either side of her, not touching her but imprisoning her between his long arms. "Now, dammit, you finish that cigarette!"

"I suppose you think I've been light-minded, letting you hang around," she said furiously. "Keeping you on a string—I haven't! Dammit, yourself!"

"I know you haven't," he said soberly. His voice was suddenly gentle. "It's all right, if there's still a reason. Is there, Ann? Now? Because, now, I have to know."

Looking at him, she knew, all at once and for the first time with certainty, that there was no reason now, and hadn't been for a long time. Her voice wouldn't come to tell him, not even a whisper, but after a moment her fingers let the unfinished cigarette drop to the sand. For a dazed, almost unbelieving instant, he looked at it lying there, before he took her into his arms.

The early summer sun blazed down the full length of the Apple Cove beach, dazzling on the rocks and sand, glinting against the blue water. They spent the afternoon hilariously poking around in the piles of bleached driftwood up and down the beach. It was a thing to do that both of them remembered with pleasure from childhood—going along the beach to see what had washed ashore. You seldom found anything that amounted to much, but you always thought you might. The sea had no discrimination. It floated anything ashore.

Today it seemed more bountiful, for some reason, than it ever had before; or perhaps the light through which they saw the gold and silver of the afternoon threw enchantment over the few commonplace things they put in their pile of salvage—a bait tub with a board missing from its bottom, an old oar, grayed with sun and salt and battered by the sea to furriness, an almost new two-by-four with a spike in it that Hod thought he might use sometime. And as the sun was going down and they were getting ready to go home, Ann stumbled on a round green glass toggle, lying like a clear soapbubble on a pile of sand.

"Oh, look!" she said breathlessly, and Hod came to look, regarding it as if it were treasure. Together they stood over the toggle, gloating for a moment before they picked it up.

"I'll bet it means luck," he said. "Anything so pretty couldn't mean anything else."

"I'm sure of it," said Ann. "We'll keep it, anyway."

"Remember," he said suddenly, "we said, once, we'd be beachcombers? Let's keep on being. Why, look, here's four good things we've found." He knelt to wrap the green toggle in his jacket for safe-keeping, and seeing her, standing there gravely and joyfully beside him, he reached out and took her hand and laid his cheek against it.

*

That evening, the Bellport telephone operator phoned Ann a telegram from her publisher. He was excited about her book, he said, wanted to print it at once; but there were a few things they wanted changed. Would it be convenient for her to come down to the city without delay? She took the train from Bellport—there was just time to catch it that night, and time for nothing else. On the train, she wrote Hod a letter. "I'll be back, darling," the letter said, "as soon as I can. Love, Ann."

*

Pete got home sooner than the town expected him, on the fifteenth of June. He drove in late in the evening and put his car in his garage. Nobody knew he was back; so Myron Osgood was surprised the next morning when the Chrysler stopped outside his store and Pete got out and came in.

"Godsake," Myron said. "When did you git back?" He realized he was being pretty stiff, and he didn't know's he cared if he was. At the same time a keen curiosity stirred in him. For some reason, Pete had come to see *him*.

"Well, I thought I'd never *git* back," Pete said. "Them deserts! Myron, did you know the U-nited States was more than half sand?"

"Why, no," Myron said. "I d'no's I did. Don't know's I ever give it a thought."

"I never knew it," Pete went on. " 'S enough to scare ya. She's sand halfway from the Mississippi River to the Rocky Mountains."

"Somethin to think about, ain't it?" Myron said. "How'd you like California?"

"I wouldn't give one plugged cent for the whole goldarn state," Pete said. "Houses all made out a that white plaster. Hotter'n hell, no rain all summer, and, they tell me, nothin *but* rain all winter.

Right now, she's dried up brown. Nothin but a lot a low hills the shape of a cow's bag without the tits, and prit' nigh the color of it. You wouldn't believe it, Myron, if I was t' tell ya that I never see one mite of green grass all the time I was there except on some-body's lawn, or in a park where they watered it."

"Hah! The' ain't no such place," Myron said.

"It's a fact."

"Well, now, you don't say!" Myron said, digesting it. His stiff-ness was gone, replaced by a deep sense of importance in hearing first-hand about a fabulous, far-off place. By gorry, Pete sure had traveled!

"I ain't done a thing but drink water ever since I come back," Pete said. He leaned from the packing case where he had sat down and squirted a rich stream of tobacco-juice out through the open door. "My gorry, I thought I'd never git soaked up agin. I was so dried-up when I left there that I'd burnt like a grass-fire, touch a match to me."

"Well, is that a fact?" Myron marveled. "That ain't what they tell ya bout it, is it? I always figgered it might be kind of a sightly place to go see. Kind of a fairyland."

"Oh, it's sightly," Pete grinned. "I wouldn't missed seein it. But it ain't no fairyland. It's a nice place t' spend the week-end, but I wouldn't want to live there. You know what looked the best to me on the whole trip? Spoon Island, and all that water, when I drove off the end a John's Reach bridge, last night."

"I'll be darned," Myron said, gratified. He guessed the place where *he* lived stacked up pretty good, when it come to the rest of the country. "But they got water out there, ain't they? They got the Pacific Ocean."

"Well, now, I'll tell ya," said Pete. "The Pacific Ocean, the part I see of it, along San Francisco Bay, don't smell good. They built their show highway along the east side a that Bay, and ridin along there the flats stink so it's enough t' kill ya. If we hed clam-flats stink like that, we'd hev the Board a Health out. Ayup. Well,

Myron, I d'no b't I come over to talk some business with you. You know it?"

Myron fetched up with a round turn. His suspicions of Pete, lulled by California, came back with a jump into his mind, and, he thought, he might have known. "That so?" he said coldly.

"I've started out on this new store, as you know," Pete said, paying no attention to Myron's manner. "And I find it's quite a proposition for one man to handle. What I need's some help, an experienced man who knows his way around in the grocery business. I don't know nobody I'd ruther hev than you."

Myron drew a sharp breath to answer him, and Pete held up his hand. "Now, wait," he said, "till I git through. I'll buy you out, your store here for a good, fair price. You can come over'n work for me, good pay—more'n you make stiddy on your own, I'd be willin to bet. You won't hev no responsibility for possible loss, and you'll have a job for the rest of your life."

Myron had started to get mad, but as Pete went on talking, the possibilities opened out for him. You never knew, with a little grocery like this, whether you'd break even at the end of the month or not. Often, you went behind.

"I'll take over all your outstandin bills, say they ain't too heavy," Pete said, "and pay you extry for your stock and good will. You think it over, Myron, and let me know. No hurry before the twenty-fifth. But I'm openin on the first of July, and I got to have somebody by then."

He got up to go. "Jeepers," he said, looking down the blue harbor, "I'm sure some glad to be back. You know, Myron, it's always easier t' work together than 't is to strain apart. Ain't it?"

That talk about the outstanding bills was what sounded good to Myron. He had a few—they weren't anything awful, but he didn't see how in thunder he was ever going to get enough ahead to pay them. And he couldn't help it, but the idea of being in debt all the time bothered him deeply. Myron had been brought up to feel that being in debt was a sin.

The other thing, the thing that had worried him from the beginning, was how on earth his store could keep going in the same town with Pete's new one. Myron knew his neighbors pretty well. They might be sore now, but they had short memories. First they'd say they'd do a little trading with Pete, only they'd watch him like a hawk; then, after a while, everything would die down—not be forgotten, just not bothered with. You couldn't blame people if they didn't want to take the trouble to be on the alert every minute.

He'd have to talk business, actual amounts of money—for steady wages, for the price of his store and good will; but the proposition, after all, didn't sound like a bad one. Unless there were a joker in it. Myron wondered, considering the idea.

But, he thought, if he did do it, it would be the first time in his life that he'd ever worked for anyone. All through his young manhood and youth, he'd been a lobster-fisherman, not making very much, but not having to take anything from anybody. Not having to do, with three-quarters of his time, what some other man said.

And standing there alone in his store, a feeling came over him of sorrow—a kind of grinding regret for something he'd had—or maybe not really had, but wanted and thought he might have. The feeling went deep, seemed to be almost like a pain gripping at his vitals. And when the next customer came in and he went back to work, it left him feeling, all day, uncertain and forlorn.

*

The idea of buying Myron out had come to Pete on the way home one night, driving across a long stretch of desert. He'd looked it over from all points of view, and in the end had come to the conclusion that it was a good business proposition.

It would cost something in the beginning, you had to expect that, and there'd be Myron's wages, too, a long-run affair. But, as he'd told Myron, with a store that size he'd have to have help—there'd be wages to pay anyway, and might as well have Myron as a less-experienced man. Then, too, he guessed likely he could cut Myron down in the winter, or even lay him off when trade was slow.

Myron might object, but there wouldn't be much he could do about it.

The thing was, by eliminating Myron's store, he could eliminate competition. Myron's was in East Village, closer to the summer people's places. You never could tell, the way the summer people were hipped on rural, country atmosphere, some of them might just possibly start a fad of trading at Myron's. There was only a slight chance, but he couldn't risk it.

Then, too, there was the matter of the local trade. Some die-hards, he knew, would never set foot in his store again, as long as they had Myron's to go to. But he doubted if they'd bother to lug their groceries all the way from Bellport for the rest of their lives.

So he guessed, all in all, the best thing to do was to buy out Myron—make it attractive enough so Myron wouldn't think twice about selling.

*

The first few days after Pete's return, nobody in the village saw much of him. Word went around that he was back, and there was, as might have been expected, quite a bit of speculation. But he kept to himself, spending a lot of time in Bellport, placing orders with wholesale house salesmen, figuring out, in one way or another, just what he'd need to stock the new store.

Selling suits of oil-clothes, work-gloves and kerosene all his life hadn't given him much experience in buying any kind of a luxury line, he knew that. Off and on through the winter and spring, he'd made the rounds of the big markets in Bellport, seeing what they had on their shelves and jotting down, as soon as he was outside, lists of a good many brand-names and kinds of merchandise. He'd improved his time on his trip, too, looking around in city stores.

Today, he was doing the same thing, only more thoroughly, for in the Bellport stores, in June, the summer stock was on the shelves. He'd spent as much time as he felt he could without being noticed, in Griswold's, making notes and keeping his eye peeled as to how they handled their trade. This morning, he felt he was about through; his orders, mostly, were in, and he guessed he had a pretty good idea of how to go about it. It wasn't so very much different from what he'd all along supposed it would be.

He thought he might buy something, just to take the curse off— he'd been hanging around in the store for quite a time—and he could have it to munch on, on the way home. He liked olives, and the store carried some dandies. Them great big ones, with the seeds. He moved over to a counter, where the young, tow-headed clerk at the moment wasn't busy.

"Like to have a pint bottle a them olives," Pete said. "And a half a pound of salted peanuts."

The boy lackadaisically got the olives down from the shelf, but halfway to the peanuts his hand stopped in mid-air, and he looked past Pete with a pleasant, welcoming smile.

"Good mornin, Miss Wiggs," he said, jerking his head up and down cordially.

A lady had come up to the counter, doubtfully holding out a cauliflower. "Now, Harry," she said. "You people must know these aren't worth eighty cents."

She had on a long, lightish summer skirt, a purple coat sweater and a white hat with a thin flimsy scarf tied around it. Even if Pete hadn't heard her speak, he would have known she was from one of the summer cottages.

"Them cauliflower, Miss Wiggs?" Harry said, as if he'd never seen one before. "Well, I d'no, we hed a turrible time gittin them. They cost us a lot and we ain't takin no profit on them. Handlin them more for the favor than anything else."

"But *eighty* cents!"

"I know." Harry was sympathetic. "But they ain't native, this time a year, ya know. We hev t' order em to the westard."

"Well, I'll take one," said the lady, crossly. "But it's highway robbery. They're never this much at home."

"Yes, ma'am. You want anything else, Miss Wiggs?"

"Excuse me," said Pete. "I thought you was waitin on me."

Neither Harry nor the lady looked up at him. Pete stood glaring at her elderly dignified back. "I said," he repeated loudly, "I was here first. You was waitin on *me.*"

Harry glanced briefly at his fingernails. "Be with ya in a minute, mister," he said indifferently.

"I'd like," said Miss Wiggs, producing a long list, "six cans of peaches, some sweet pickles, a can of—"

Pete stood fuming a moment, then he turned and stalked out of the store. His bottle of olives he left on the counter.

By God, he thought, they ain't goin t' git away with that with *me,* just because I happen to be from around here. The's plenty places a man can buy olives.

Muttering, he climbed into his car and drove toward home.

*

Myron Osgood had worked himself into a state. Go over Pete's proposition as he would, adding the figures with his glasses falling down on the end of his nose and his bald head sweating, he couldn't see the joker. He'd spent the whole afternoon that way, and the evening talking it over with Lucy. Looking at it from all sides, studying the sums of money Pete had offered, he still couldn't see where it wasn't a good proposition.

Now, lying in his bed in the warm June night, with only the sheet over him, Myron twisted and turned, unable to sleep. Lucy was against it, he knew, but it wasn't a matter of business with her. She just couldn't bring herself to see him working for Pete Stilwell. With Lucy, it was more the idea of knuckling under to Agnes. He couldn't say he blamed her. They'd been rivals, in a way, for years. Not that his business had ever come up to Pete's or given it much competition, except for the past two or three months; but there'd been enough independence connected with having their own store, so that Lucy could give back talk whenever she felt like it.

The triumph during the past weeks, everyone trading with him instead of Pete, had been sweet. He'd done well; but not well enough, Myron thought with a sinking feeling, to clean up all of those back bills. Now with Pete's new store opening up and the trade again divided, he couldn't see a single thing ahead but going in deeper. Unless he sold out to Pete.

There were his boys coming along, three of them in high school, Artie entering this fall. Just their clothes and shoes were a big item, even if you didn't consider all the extras that boys in school seemed to need. He couldn't begin to supply them all. But, heck, a man couldn't keep his boys too short. They had to have some-wheres near what the other fellows had, in the way of baseball bats and skates; otherwise they felt like small stuff and got left way behind. No knowing what a boy might do when that happened to him. Myron turned a little cold, thinking of the scrape Artie had got into last Christmas. Say what you would, if he'd had a little extra money to give Artie at the time, it never would have hap-pened.

His kids, Myron thought, twisting over again in bed, were as good as anyone else's—just as deserving as any man's of the things that were going the rounds. Why shouldn't they have a few base-ball bats, for God's sake, it wasn't any more than kids had the right to expect. So far, he'd managed to bring them up comfortable and decent, with as many extras on the side as he could possibly swing. They looked up to him, too, the way any kids ought to look up to their old man.

But the thing was, each year he kept going in just a little deeper. If a man kept on that way, the time would come as sure as little apples, when it would catch up with him. The wholesale houses weren't pressing; they never had. They knew that their bills would be paid eventually, as soon as Myron got around to them. But just suppose that right now all of them started pressing him at once? There wouldn't be one nameable thing to do but go through bank-ruptcy. Then how would your kids feel? Would they still look up to their old man?

There wasn't the slightest reason why the wholesalers should do that, and Myron didn't really think they would. Bankruptcy wouldn't have occurred to him if he hadn't, all at once, had to make up his mind. He didn't doubt he could go on, year in and year out, robbing Peter to pay Paul, making out just as well for a long time to come as he had in the long time gone by. But that didn't take emergencies into account. That one with Artie last winter had put him on the rocks for months. No, you couldn't get away from it—there was something about steady money comin in, money you could count on, that sounded kind of good.

It was funny, a man worked all his life, knowing each year as he went on that next year wouldn't be any better. That is, the figures in his books and his common sense told him so. But when it came right down to it, the figures and the common sense didn't amount to a hang. Something in your heart spoke up and told you not to be a fool, of course next year things were going to be better, and that was what you depended on. It was as if a little mainspring wound itself up inside you every so often, and that was what kept you going. You said to yourself, well, next year, maybe—and you worked just that much harder.

Well, the work was all right—a man expected that. He'd be lost without it. Only it did seem as if, as he grew older, that it might slack off a little; as if there might not be quite so much to keep on your mind and you could start to let down as you got tireder.

Myron flopped over again, and this time, Lucy, in the bed beside him, sat bolt upright with a jerk.

"For the Lord's sake, Myron, will you stop spinnin like a top and let me go to sleep? I bet my nightdress-tail is wore clean through with you wearin and tearin on it."

"I can't sleep," Myron mumbled. "I've gut to thinkin."

"Oh. Want some hot milk, dear?"

"Hot milk! My Lord, I'm sweatin, now."

"Well, go over 'n stand by the winder a minute. It ain't cold enough to catch cold, and maybe it'll cool you off so's you can sleep."

Myron climbed patiently out of bed and fumbled his way over to the open window. It was a fine clear night, he saw, the moon high, making a white glittering path across the harbor. The houses in the village were an almost unearthly white. Down by the shore, the gray wharf-sheds loomed black against the silver water, and he could even make out the separate piles of the wharf, the light was so bright and clear. Like a hushing sound from far away, he could hear the slow, soft rise and fall of the sea, moving lazily up and down the ledges.

An idea came into his mind, dimly, and he considered a minute, wondering what such a thing might mean, but try as he could he couldn't see any application for it, or how it might contribute to any solution of his problem. All it was, anyway, was a monstrous piece of bad logic.

"It beats all," he said, going back to the bed, "that when things around is so peaceful and pretty, humans couldn't manage to make themselves a little happier."

"Well," Lucy said, "I see you've made up your mind."

He hadn't thought so, but suddenly, he saw, he had.

"You're goin in with him, ain't you?"

"I'll only be workin for him, Lucy. Not goin in with him."

There was a long silence. "All right," she said, at last, "but I don't b'lieve I'm goin to knuckle under, Myron."

"No," he said. "It'll be all right, Lucy. I guess I can do the knucklin under for both of us."

"The thing is," she said, "Henny had a job offered her in one of the summer cottages, and she's took it. She says the's another one, helpin with the cookin. I'd like to try it, Myron."

"You ain't never had to go out to work," he said, slowly.

"No," she said. "And I don't have to now, Myron. Only, I'd kind of like to have us have a little extra."

"I guess it's up to you," he said. "If that's what you want, Lucy."

*

In the master's bedroom of his house in Bellport, whose big front windows looked out over the moonlit sea, Nelson Wither-spoon, too, lay awake and thinking. His cottage over on Spoon

Island was nearly done; there were some little matters of furnishing still left to attend to, and then he and his wife could move in. Nancy was having the time of her life. He'd wanted, having had the fun of buying the land and seeing through the architect's plans for the house, to let her have a good time choosing the furniture. She was; and to his way of thinking she was doing a wonderful job. The inside of the house was not only going to be comfortable; it was going to be merry.

In many ways, that little place over on Spoon Island had been one of the most satisfactory things he'd ever done in his life. He was glad now that he hadn't been able to buy Little Spoon Island. That had been only a symbol of security to him—the snugged-down, the quiet. He had even had it in his mind to name the house he might build there something like "Trail's End," or "Dunrovin" —a symbol to him that he had come at last to a peaceful place to spend the rest of his days there. His summers, that is.

But the cottage out on Spoonhandle, in the full track of the four winds and the open sky, was wild and free, like—yes, by Jove, it was like a hawk's nest. Might even be a good name for it. "Hawk's Nest." He must confer with Nancy. No place for a man of action, a sheltered island, with a place nestled down under trees. Spoonhandle, the naked end of the peninsula, the last outpost before the ocean, that was a better symbol.

The house had come out exactly the way he wanted it—unheard of, with architects being what they were—but from the beginning he had felt its auspices were good, that it was under a lucky star. Even more satisfactory, he felt, was his own effect on the village.

The mathematical precision of economics, he thought, watching the patch of moonlight creep slowly along his wall, was a strange and a beautiful thing. He had prophesied about Spoon Island, and then had sat back and watched for his prophecy to come true. Any student of economics could have made that prediction, though—first, the impact of money, then the slow gathering of forces, finally change unrolling with increasing speed.

It was a microcosm of the world, he mused—the world trade,

the international economics he knew so well—in a way, amazing, but inevitable, and most satisfactory to watch, even on so infinitesimal a scale.

You could see the effect already in Spoon Island—that big store of Stilwell's the first tangible sign. In the last analysis, he himself, and people like him, were the source of that store; they were the source of the sleepy village's awakening, the people's dusting themselves off, expectant, now of better things to come. And better things would come—work, wages, an upstanding town instead of an ingrown community headed slowly toward decay.

Whatever names those without foresight might call capital, this, in the end, was what it was: the mainspring in the clock-work of the world; and he who provided it was the one who kept the clock wound. Mr. Witherspoon remembered, with an inward chuckle, a joke he had heard once—an old joke—something about what a wonderful world God could have made if He had only had money.

Well, he thought, we're doing our best to help Him along with the good work. I only wish we got some of the credit He does.

He suddenly wished he could go to sleep. It must be late, and he wanted to feel fresh for tomorrow. There was something special in the way of a moon, tonight. Since he was awake, it might be a good idea to get up and look at it from the balcony. It might relax him, and a busy man didn't often get a chance to have an uninterrupted look at the moon.

He wrapped himself in a wool bathrobe—not because it was cold, but because it might be—and went out to stand on his balcony, to watch the sea whereon the moonlight fell in magic and magnificence.

*

Pete opened his store on July first, with himself and Myron Osgood waiting on the counters, and young Billy Grant hired for the summer to do chores and act as delivery boy. On the first day he did a good business, not only from the summer people, but from the local ladies and the kids. This was partly because Pete's was the only store in town now; and partly because, as the Fourth of July was coming up, he had filled both plate-glass windows with brightly wrapped fireworks.

He had sprung another surprise in the shape of a brand-new black Chevrolet delivery truck, with "Stilwell's" painted on the side in eight-inch-high fancy yellow letters.

Everything went pretty well; of course trade would pick up later on, when more cottages were finished and more summer people were in residence. You couldn't expect it all to happen at once. As it was, Pete was satisfied. The long, one-storied, neat stucco building might not be quite the size of Griswold's, but it had everything Griswold's had, and, according to the relative size of the towns, just as many customers.

The only fly in Pete's ointment had been that some hoodlums had sneaked up to the store in the middle of the night and had nailed a big sign up above the plate-glass windows. It was all of ten feet long, black letters on a white background, quite neatly done, and it read: SPOON ISLAND CO-OPERATIVE.

Damn kids, Pete thought. He'd have to use a stepladder to get it down. He'd set out to go out in the middle of the night when he'd thought he'd heard pounding sounds. He wished he had—with a shotgun.

He was right about the kids. Young Sam Freeman and a couple of the Pray boys might have known something about the sign if pinned down and made to tell. But not very many people saw it. Pete always got up early. It was only a little after daylight when he had the sign down.

*

The train stopping at Bellport in the early evening made connections at Portland with a through express from New York and Boston, and it was jammed. The cities were sweltering in end-of-July heat; summer vacation travel was at its peak. Ann Freeman, jostled down the car steps by a crowd of gaily-dressed, chattering people, thought of the remark Bellporters had made every summer since the time their town had become a resort: "New York and Boston's took a puke."

She had been gone nearly a month, sweating out in a hot hotel room the changes her publisher wanted made in her manuscript. He'd been right about them, she'd admitted without much objection. One whole early section of the book had seemed to him stilted and uncertain; he'd pointed out explicitly what he thought ought to be done. His suggestions, Ann saw at once, had sensitiveness and subtlety—as an editor, he knew his tools, too. So she had sat down and worked with a will, remembering wryly that the parts he didn't like were those she had written last winter, just before she had bought the shack.

Now it was done and she was home. Thank the Lord.

It was next to useless to look for anyone among the greeters on the platform, she saw, and she turned to pick out her suitcases from the mound of luggage. A week ago she'd written Hod the date when she expected to arrive, and had asked him to meet her— and there he was, standing with his back to her peering anxiously along the platform. He already had her suitcases, one in each hand, and her typewriter case tucked under his arm.

"Hello," she said, pushing through to him. "Let me have the typewriter, h'm? You've got enough without."

He shook his head, looking down at her, smiling. "Let's get out of here."

A block from the station the uproar was still audible, though muffled, in the still evening air.

"Just like Willie's new hens," Ann said. She felt tongue-tied, but only, she thought, because I'm so glad to see him. After an interval, she went on, to her amazement, "How—how are they?"

Hod glanced at her and chuckled. "The hens? They're fine. Except for a couple Bertha trimmed up, a week or so ago. Bertha's a down-easter, herself, and she finally lost her patience. They'll live, but not with the same feathers." He stopped. "So'm I," he said at last. "Fine, I mean. Now."

They walked on in silence down the path to the town slip. The boat was tied up at the float, her white paint gleaming immaculate in the fading light. The sun had set an hour ago; the long twilight was slipping into darkness. In the windless quiet, Bellport harbor was glassy black, the dark cut into yellow parallels by the arc-lamps along the shore.

Hod jumped aboard, setting the luggage carefully down on the scrubbed platform. Then he turned to her, and Ann, making the long step from the float to the boat's gunnel, found herself lifted down and whirled into the shelter of the coop. Her body in his arms felt weightless.

After a long time, he took his lips away from hers and laid his cheek gently against her cheek. "You'll never go away again," he said. He gave her a little shake. "Understand?"

She nodded, wordlessly.

"Say it!"

"I won't go away again."

"Say 'never.'"

"Never, darling." Her voice was a shaken whisper, muffled against his shirt, but he seemed to have no trouble hearing it. His arms tightened, almost crushing her breath out. Then, with a quick movement, he held her off at arm's length, looking her up and down. "You're a sight! Look at you! Traveling all the way from New York in a rig like that!"

"I thought I looked quite nice," Ann said meekly. She glanced down between his hands, which were on her shoulders, to her neat lightweight blue suit, silk stockings and summer shoes.

"I like you better in pants," he said. "You got any with you?"

"Mm-hm. In my suitcase. Lovely new ones."

"Brown?"

She nodded, her eyes on his face. "You look so—*dear*," she said softly.

"Never mind me." But he pulled her close to him and kissed her again, thoroughly. "Now you go below-decks and change. I'll bring down your suitcase. Which one?"

"I can't," she whispered. "If you don't hold me, I'll fall down! I—"

He gave her a little push. "Yes, you can. Which suitcase?"

"The big one."

She went down the short steps into the cabin, and he followed her, setting the suitcase flatwise on the locker.

"Put yourself into some decent clothes while I get under weigh," he went on, straightening up.

She sat on the other locker for a little while, hearing his steps moving around on deck while he cast off bow and stern lines and took in the fenders he had hung between the boat's planking and the float. She heard him bump the fenders down on the washboard, then, presently, the starter ground and the engine clicked over in its big white box at the end of the cabin. The reverse gear chunked; the boat moved backwards, then ahead. Outside on the bow, the water began to pour by with soft hushing sounds, and the engine picked up, settling into a smooth, creamy thrum.

When Ann finally came on deck dressed in the brown slacks and her new tan shirt, the Bellport lights lay well astern over the wake and the dark outlines of Hod's punt towing behind. The stars were out and the boat's hooded riding lights, low on the washboard, colored the curling-back waves from the cutwater pale green on one side, pale red on the other.

"Let me see," Hod said. He clicked on a tiny electric bulb set over the binnacle and shaded it with his hand so that the light focused on her. She could see the light, bright on the palm of his hand and the reflection of it in his eyes. The rest of him was in shadow. For a long moment he stood quietly looking at her. Then he turned off the light and pulled her into his arms.

"I know you better the way you look now," he said unsteadily.

She stood leaning against him while he steered, one hand on the wheel, the other arm around her.

"Look," he said, presently. He took his hand off the wheel and fumbled in his pocket for a slip of paper which he thrust into her fingers. "This is for you."

"What is it?" She held it up, but all she could make out in the darkness was its white rectangle.

He reached for the binnacle light, but she caught his hand. "Don't put on a light, it's too nice without. Tell me."

"Well," Hod hesitated. "You'll maybe think I went ahead without talking it over with you. It's a rent receipt. From Mary Mackay, for her house for a year. For us to live in." Then, as she did not speak, he went on eagerly, "It's a swell old place, Ann. Not modern, nor anything, but—"

"I think it's wonderful," she said. "I'll love living there—you know I will. How did you happen to think of it?"

"Willie's house is too small," he said, "and besides, Willie's going to get his boy, I think."

"Donny Mitchell? Oh, Hod, how swell!"

"Well, he had a card from Josh Hovey saying the judge was dead and to come over and see him next week. Willie seemed to think that clinched the matter. Anyway, while you were away, I wrote Mary. We don't want to live with anyone."

"No," she said. "We don't."

"I've been doing some thinking. A lot of it while you were away. I've got about what I want, with the boat, and with us living in Mary's house where we won't be apart from everything. But look, if you want me to, after a while, maybe next year, I could go somewhere and finish up my engineering course. It would take a little brushing up, it's been so long, but I could do it."

"Why should I want you to?" she asked, puzzled. "I'd only want that if you wanted it."

"Engineers make more money."

"So what?"

"You aren't marrying me for my money?" In the dark, she caught, dimly, the white flash of his smile.

"Are you marrying me for mine? I've got a nice fat royalty check, you know."

Hod chuckled. "You can keep it." He went on soberly, "I figure I can be more use staying around here, maybe shooting off my mouth about things in general, when it's necessary, than I can going somewhere and running somebody's Diesels."

"Good," she said. "That suits me, too."

"I met Agnes the other day, face to face in front of Mag Snow's," he said reflectively. "She had a lot to say. When she was through I found all I felt was kind of sorry for her. She seemed to me just like any other pin-headed woman, getting old and fat with no practical use a man could see. I don't know what's done it," he finished. "Maybe getting mad enough to cuff Pete down. Maybe finding out what people really think of me. Maybe you."

"Maybe you," she said. She waited for him to go on, but he said nothing.

"Look," she said softly, at last. "In New York I saw the man I was in love with when I came home last fall."

He did not move, except she felt his arm around her tighten. "That was it, last fall then," he said. "I'm glad you told me."

"I wanted you to know. Last fall. Not now. I found I could hardly remember his face."

The boat pushed steadily ahead its faintly-colored turmoil through the tranquil water. Now that it was full dark, phosphorus was coming out in the bow-waves, and the wake behind was a track of cold fire.

"Aren't you a little off course?" Ann asked presently. "I'm no one to say, of course, but the Bellport lights are over there. Spoon Island ought to be"—in the dark he saw the vague gesture of her hand—"somewhere thereabouts, shouldn't it?"

"We aren't headed for home," he said. "You mind?"

"No. Where are we going?"

"Don't distract the skipper with questions."

"The skipper's an old mossback. Won't take advice nor answer questions from nobody."

"Not from his womenfolks, anyway. Know where Winker's Island is?"

"Up the bay somewhere, isn't it?"

"A long ways up the bay," he said. "We're going ashore in the cove there and build a fire and cook two big steaks. I've got em below in a paper bag. The nearest people will be eight miles away."

"Horrors," Ann said. "I'm kidnaped. Hod, darling, I love you."

His body tensed a little against hers. "Mind saying that over again?" he asked slowly. "It's the first time I've heard you say it."

The cove at Winker's Island was small, almost landlocked, a tiny sheet of ink-black water, reflecting stars. The boat's wake and the churning propeller stirred up a tremendous green and silver conflagration. Shallow phosphorescent waves circled the cove with rims of fire, brushing up the beach in millions of golden sparks. White sand and the close-growing undersides of spruce branches lighted up briefly; then Hod cut the engine and the turmoil stilled. Ripples paled out, subsiding with a peaceful sound, and the ink-black shadows returned motionless and silent.

"Oh," Ann breathed. "Hod, look overboard at the anchor."

The anchor he had dropped into the shallow water lay clearly outlined on bottom with gold bubbles, and its rope was a limp gold strand leading upward to the bow of the boat. As they watched, the bubbles began leisurely to detach themselves, floating away in the black water.

It was too still to talk, Ann thought, trailing her fingers in the water from the stern of the punt as Hod rowed her ashore. He seemed to think so, too, for he said nothing while he grounded the punt, lifted out the basket of food and the blankets to sit on and carried them up the beach. She watched him go out of sight in the shadow under the trees. When he came back she was still sitting quietly in the punt.

"Want to get out?" he asked. "Want me to come and get you?" He kicked off his shoes, rolled up his trouser-cuffs and stepped into the water. "Mmm," he said. "It's warm. The sun's been shining on this sand all day. Air's not cold, either. Want to go swimming?"

She watched him come closer, his feet stirring pools of green silver in the water, felt his arms go around her as he lifted her out of the punt.

"Let's," he said, setting her feet on the sand. "Wash the city off you forever, Ann."

"You think it would?"

"I know it would."

His fingers moved at her breast unbuttoning her shirt, and she felt her clothes slipping down, unregarded, to the sand.

"Walk down into the water. I'll be with you there in a minute."

The sand, underfoot, was soft and warm. The water was cold at first against her ankles and thighs; then she lay on her back floating, and it seemed almost as warm as a few moments ago when she had trailed her fingers, coming ashore. She lay still, watching the pale bubbles gather on her hand. Then she heard the light splash around Hod's feet and saw briefly the tall white column of his body against the black shadows of the trees.

"Lovely stars," she said softly, looking up at them. "Millions."

He swam behind her and his powerful body touched hers, smooth and cold from the chill of the water.

"Lovely everything," he said, his lips against her ear.

He carried her up out of the water to the blankets spread on the sand, and as his lips, cold and salty, closed over hers, she felt the old known wave of drowning within her lift and topple like a long breaker thundering up a shore.

*

Paris Freeman was taking up his traps. He was taking them up for good, he told himself. This was the end of July, 1937, and the rest of his life he'd remember the date as the time when he sold his traps, sold his boat, and took a soft job ashore. He'd thought he was too old and busted-down ever to do anything else but go lobstering, and here was this summer man from Boston, Mr. Washburn, offered him a year-round job as caretaker on his place. Sixty dollars a month all winter, a hundred for four months in the summertime. It's all I need, by God, Paris told himself.

He felt somehow safe at last, as if, after a lifetime of battling to keep his head above water and going down for the next-to-the-last time, he had now come into a quiet haven. After he had decided to take Mr. Washburn's job, he felt himself relax all over. Now there'd be someone to tell him what to do. The grinding, uncertain business of making his own decisions was over forever.

Paris had thirty lobster traps piled up on the deck and platform of his boat. That was about enough of a load for his boat, he thought, even on a quiet morning. He had hauled all around Winker's Island, getting out before daylight in his eagerness, but he remembered two traps up by the mouth of the cove, and he guessed he could find room for them and not have to come back.

This is the last time, by God, I'll ever haul *you*, he told one of the traps, snaking it viciously aboard. It had two lobsters in it, he saw, both shedders, and he slammed them overboard, smacking them down hard on the surface of the water.

No sense havin traps down this time a year anyway, he thought, with every cussid lobster in the bay crawled away to shed his shell.

He ran up alongside the remaining trap buoy and was gaffing it in when he heard a boat's engine start up inside the cove.

Now who in hell could that be? he thought, craning his neck. No reason for anybody t' be inside there, this time or any time of day.

It was Hod Stilwell's boat. He made her out as she slid through the narrow entrance to the cove, and roared toward him, her bow wave streaking backwards and rolling up on the shore.

Hod had someone with him, and as they came closer, Paris saw with horror that it was his own daughter, Ann. He dropped the trap buoy as if it had been hot.

Hod ran up to within ten feet or so and reversed to a stop. Both of them, Paris saw through his fury, were leaning over the side waving to him and grinning like fools.

"For the love of a just God!" he shouted. "Ann, I'll take the hide off'n you. You been in there all night, by God?"

"Yes," Ann said. "And we cooked a steak for breakfast."

She wasn't one mite ashamed, the brazen little—

"We're headed for Bellport to get married, pa," she went on. "Want to come?"

"No, by God, I don't—" he began. Then he realized what she

had said, and the anger went out of him, leaving him weak. "Well," he said dazedly. "Well."

"We're going home first and get dressed up," Ann went on, smiling at him. "We'll collect ma and the kids and wait for you. Okay?"

"Well," Paris said again. He couldn't think of anything else to say. Then something occurred to him. "Hod, if you built a fire in on that beach, I hope you made sure 't was out. It ain't no time of year to start a wood's fire," he shouted irascibly.

"I doused it," Hod said. "Two buckets of water, Paris, don't worry. See you later."

He started up his engine and the big boat gathered speed in the water, leaving Paris staring after.

In a moment or so, he thoughtfully started up his own engine and followed them. He forgot all about that last trap he had in the water, and a day or so later, when he remembered it, he had to come back after all.

*

Young John Pray, with Nell and his two kids, had come back to the island. He came back, to everyone's surprise, in an old open-deck lap-streak boat, with a coughing, chugging, two-cylinder, two-cycle engine. He went straight to Pete Stilwell and asked him if he'd rent him John's old house, maybe sell it back to him, in time. Pete said he'd sell the house and four or five acres of wood lot around it. Witherspoon, of course, had bought John's Spoonhandle land, and what the shore lots Pete had left were worth was more now than John'd be able to pay.

John said okay, and he and Nell moved their stuff back into their old house. He sat around the fishhouse for the first few days he was home and told his friends, earnestly, why he had come back.

"Every job in Bellport that a man'd ever want to have," he said, "is sewed up tighter'n a bumblebee's blowhole. I hunted round for a month, and all I could find was diggin a sewer trench for some old rich poop's greenhouse. I whanged a pick and shovel up and down till my guts like to come out through my bellybutton, and one day the boss over there combed me out for bein ten minutes late gittin to work on time. I hove the pick and the shovel both to hellangone 's far's I could see em fly, and I took my week's pay and went down to the shore. Come night, I had nine trawls. The next day I found this boat and paid cash for her out a what I had left sellin my place. She ain't no good, old one-lunger you could shoot cooked beans through, but by God, I can haul trawls in her.

"I figger after I'm my own boss for a while, my guts'll go back where they belong, maybe, and I won't feel 's if I wanted to tear the livin daylights out of the first man that looks at me sideways."

"How bout Earl Sprague?" someone said. "Thought you was goin t' end up doin the same kind of a job he's doin?"

"Earl Sprague," John said, "can take his easy job and you can run of your own idea what he can do with it. Me, I'll dig clams, if I have to, and live on em, by God. Raw."

*

The date Josh Hovey had mentioned on his post card was the fifteenth of August. Willie took the boat alone that day and went over to see Josh. Hod was glad enough to have a free day to stay home. He and Ann had moved into the Mackay place. They'd decided to buy it when they found out that Mary was willing to sell, and there was a lot of repair work around the house that Hod wanted to get done.

So Willie set out by himself early in the morning, and he was over in Bellport just after breakfast time. The first person he saw, when he walked into Josh's office on the boatyard wharf, was Donny Mitchell, sitting in the chair beside Josh's desk. Josh was sprawled back in his swivel-chair, talking to him.

"Well, Willie, you old sog," he boomed. "I been showin this young feller around my boatyard. He can't make up his mind whether he wants to run a boatyard or skipper a vessel when he gits back a little meat on his bones."

"That so?" Willie said, quietly. He didn't like the way Donny looked, thin as a rail and with that unfocused look around his eyes, as if he weren't looking right straight at anything. "Well, there's plenty of time for him to make up his mind, Josh. Don't rush him."

"Ain't tried to," Josh said. "You and him'll have to go around to see Judge Elliot, Willie. Papers to sign, what-not. Matter of form, only. Everything's fixed."

Josh didn't say anything about the hard time he had had to get everything fixed, or mention costs, or the fact that he himself had gone sponsor for Donny, putting the whole weight of his own influence and money behind him. If he'd had his troubles getting "everything fixed," nobody was going to know it.

"Judge Elliot's in the Beatty Building," Josh said. "Number 6. Second floor."

"All right," Willie said. "Appreciate it, Josh. Come on, Don."

They walked the three blocks to the Beatty Building without saying anything. Donny strode along beside Willie, looking neither to right nor left, and Willie couldn't think of anything to say.

The Judge was businesslike. He seemed a little bored with the whole matter and he asked only a few questions. Everything, as Josh said, was fixed.

"About his name," the Judge said. "You want to change it to Stilwell, I suppose."

Willie glanced at Donny, but Donny was looking at the floor. "That's up to him," Willie said. "I'd like it if he wants to. If he don't, it's his business."

"How about it, young man?"

The Judge didn't care for Donny, Willie saw, and, well, that was all right with him. He himself didn't care much for the Judge. "It ain't a thing that's gut to be settled right away, is it?" Willie said. "I'll let ya know."

"Well, all right. Just so we get it down on the records," the Judge said.

What Willie wanted was to finish up the necessaries and get gone from there. He signed his name where he had to, picked up his copy of the adoption papers and stuck them in his pocket.

"That's all," said the Judge. "Now, young man, I don't want to hear any more of your—" he began, and Willie, seeing how Donny started as if he were stung and flushed up, cut in briskly.

"Thanks, Judge," he said. "We'll be on our way. Come on, Don."

"Well," the Judge said, surprised. "I just—"

"So long." Willie pushed Donny out the door, closed it behind them, and they went down the stairs to the sunny street.

"Thank the good Lord," Willie said. "That's the last you and I'll have t' do with them kind of men, Don. I don't think much of them clo'es you got on, for a hot day. They're too heavy. What say we go down the street here and git rid of a little money?"

"You don't have to spend money on me," Donny said. "Unless you want to."

"Oh, gosh, don't you want me to?" Willie let disappointment creep over his face. "Look, Hod and I are way ahead on payin.for the boat. Besides, every time we made a good haul this summer, I stuck away ten-fifteen dollars out a my share, thinkin to myself, 'This'll be for Don's new clo'es when he gits home.' Come on."

They bought a new dark blue suit for dress-up and Sundays, sweaters, shirts, underwear, shoes and overalls. Donny let himself be fitted at the clothing store without showing much preference. He did run his hand over the material of a tan waterproof wind-breaker, feeling its texture.

"How about it?" Willie asked. "You like that one?"

Donny shook his head. "It's eight dollars."

"What of it? Most a this stuff is just stuff you've got to have. I've saved out a few dollars for a comin-home present, somethin special, from me to you. You like that jacket, you can have it."

"It's airplane cloth," Donny said wistfully. "I—"

"All right, then. Stick it in the bundle," Willie said to the sales-man. "Why don't you put on a suit of them blue overhauls and a work-shirt? Likely we might end up fishin before we go home. Or would you ruther stay over here to the movies? It's a kind of a red-letter day, anyway, and I d'no b't we might celebrate."

"Maybe what you want, I guess," Donny said, without much

expression in his voice. He went into the dressing room to dress.

Willie was worried, though he tried not to let it show. It was likely the kid was still pretty upset. Maybe with good handling, he'd let out, in time, what was goweling him. He looked at Donny with approval when the boy came back dressed in the stiff new blue denims. "You look slick," he said. "Where's the suit you wore in here?"

Donny flushed. "In there," he said, indicating the dressing room. "I left it in there."

"Well, tell the man he can chuck the damn thing overboard," Willie said. "We don't want it."

He divided up the bundles with Donny and led the way through the Bellport streets to the wharf, where he had tied up the boat. He said nothing until they had cast off the lines and the boat was drumming down the harbor.

Donny stood silently beside him, leaning both elbows on the edge of the coop. He'd grown taller, Willie saw, and his face had lengthened some, maybe with his thinness, maybe with the change that comes with adolescence. He had a way now—at least Willie had never noticed it before—of biting his lips tight shut. Well, Willie thought. Give him time.

"How'd you like to take a run around to Cat Cove and see 'f we can dong us up a school of mackerel?" he said aloud. "It's kind of early in the season, but I hear tell they've been catchin a few in the weirs, here 'n there. Want to?"

"Ayeh," Donny said.

"Which d'you rather do—fix up the mackerel jigs and grind the chum, or steer while I do it?"

"I guess I'd like to steer."

He put his hands on the wheel, and Willie saw his shoulders straighten a little.

Maybe that'll fix it up, Willie thought. He kind of took to steerin the boat, that time he was out with us.

He went on talking while he dug the lines out of the locker and rigged the sharp, bright-leaded mackerel jigs to them. "All I got is some whole bait," he said. "Never had time to go to the sardine fact'ry for cuttings. But, you know, I always had good luck grindin up my own chum out of fresh herrin. I d'no b't mack'rel ought to like that better than that cooked stuff, anyway." He took a rusty old meat-grinder out of the locker, fixed it to a board over a bait-tub and began grinding the herring, letting the chum drop down into the barrel. The meat grinder had a rhythmic squeak, and presently Willie, seeing he couldn't think of any more to say, began to sing in time to it.

> Oh, we have a ship that sail-ed, upon the Lowland Sea,
> And she goes by the name of the Golden Vanit-ee,
> And we fear she will be sunk-en by the Spanish enemy,
>   As she sails in the Lowlands Low.

"You know that song, Don?" he asked.
"Yes."
"One of Uncle My's, warn't it?"
"Yes."

> Then up and spoke our cabin-boy and loudly outspoke he,
> And he said to our captain, "What will you give to me,
> If I'll swim 'longside of the Spanish enemy
>   And sink her in the Lowlands Low?"

> "Oh, I will give you silver and I will give you gold,
> And my own fair young daughter your bonny bride shall be,
> If you'll swim 'longside of the Spanish enemy,
>   And sink her in the Lowlands Low."

> Then the boy he made him ready and overboard went he,
> And he swam 'longside of the Spanish enemy,
> And with his bit and auger in her side he bored holes three,
>   And he sank her in the Lowlands Low.

> Then quickly he swam back, to the cheering of the crew,
> But the captain would not heed him for his promise he did rue,
> And he scorned his poor entreatins, though full loudly he did sue,
>   And he left him in the Lowlands Low.

Donny stirred suddenly at the wheel and hunched his shoulders. "Quit singin it, will ya?" he said in a strangled voice.

"Why, sure, boy," Willie said, quickly. "Hard to tell, anyway, which is me and which is the meat-grinder."

They made the remainder of the trip around the foot of Spoon Island to Cat Cove in silence, Willie sitting thoughtfully over his bait-barrel working the grinder. He stopped the boat just outside the entrance to the cove and dropped over the anchor.

"You want to be the one to keep the chum goin?" he asked. "Or will I?"

"I don't care."

"I will, then. Nasty job, anyway." Willie reached into the tub of chum, brought up a double handful, which he proceeded to wring out and mold into a ball. "You see this?" he proffered, hopefully. "It's kind of an invention of mine, known as a mack'rel bomb. You chuck two-three of these overboard, and they're heavy, see? So they sink down deep before the tide floats em off, and if the's a school a mack'rel around, deep down, it's likely to bring em up."

Donny nodded, without interest. He looked sick, Willie saw, white around the gills. "You want to go home, Don?" he asked.

"No. I'm okay."

They sat through the long afternoon, with time out for lunch. Willie ate heartily, trying not to notice that the boy only picked at his food. Willie was getting more and more upset. Something was pretty wrong with Donny, he was afraid. He thought maybe he'd better take him back to Bellport, maybe take him to see a doctor. He wondered what he'd better do, sitting mechanically throwing out his mackerel jig, letting it sink down, hauling it in again. For the most part, Donny sat hunched over his line, letting it dangle in the water.

Once or twice Willie jogged him a little about it. "God, boy, you don't never want to let a mack'rel jig stay still." But mostly he let him alone.

At four o'clock, Willie gave up. "Well," he said, "I guess either they ain't none runnin yet or the sun's still too bright in the sky. What say we go home? You tired?"

Donny suddenly looked up at him, and at the expression in his eyes, Willie realized he couldn't stand it any longer. "What is it, Don? Git it out a your system, boy, for God's sake."

"I been in the reform school," Donny said. His hands were clenched tightly on the gunnel of the boat. "I been thinkin how I could tell you."

"Why, I know that," Willie said slowly. "I knew it weeks ago before I wrote ya that letter. I found out by gittin Josh Hovey to look up that post office box number for me."

"Who else knows?"

"Josh," Willie said. "Myron Osgood and Artie—don't worry about them mentionin it, either. And me. That's all."

"Don't it make no difference to you?" Donny looked at his line, dangling limply in the water, and his voice was almost inaudible.

"Not in the way you're thinkin about," Willie said. "I'm sorry you had to go."

"I thought you wouldn't want me if you knew."

"Hell," Willie said forthrightly. "What you done was make a mistake. I don't say it warn't a bad one. It blew back in your face, and it wouldn't do to make it again, not now—not with you knowin, now, what a bad mistake it was. But look, Artie, he made the same mistake, didn't he? The difference was, he had the good luck of havin someone to stick up for him. You had to take what come. As for me not wantin you, I had a chance to back out when I found out where you was, didn't I?"

Willie would have gone on, but at that moment his line snapped taut with a zing. He let out an excited yell and a look of astonishment and exaltation came over his face. His fish, seeing he hadn't been holding his line taut, had got away; but Donny's line, the next moment, jerked out, and started to zig and zag through the water sending up a fine spray.

"Fried catfish into the Holy Land!" Willie gasped. "They've struck!"

He scrabbled excitedly around with his hands in the bottom of the chum-tub and sent a few shreds of herring flying over the side. Donny boated his fish, a bright-striped mackerel, eighteen inches long, and Willie moaned at the sight of it.

"If we ain't gone and donged up a school of big ones at the last minute when the bait's most gone!" His line zinged, and he hauled in, slatting off the mackerel and throwing his jig over again almost with the same motion.

For a few minutes the spray flew, the fish biting the jigs as fast as they hit the water. Then the chum was all gone and the school flashed away, following up-tide to find more abundant feed along its flowing track.

Willie, frustrated at seeing them go, suddenly picked up the empty chum-tub and with a heave sent it flying after them. The tub struck the water on its side, filled and sank at once, sending up a bubbling gurgle. Then, realizing what he had done, Willie stood astounded, watching it sink. "Godsake," he said. "That was a good tub."

Donny, in the stern, found himself laughing. He doubled over, shouting, his eyes filling with tears. Slowly, the look of astonishment left Willie's face, and in a moment, he laughed, too.

"Nothin like a school of mack'rel to git a man excited," he said. "How many'd we git, Don?"

"I think I got ten," Donny said proudly. "But I kind of lost count."

"Well, I caught seven, I know bout," Willie said. "I guess you wiped my eye out."

They gathered up the flopping fish from the platform, where they had been slatted off the jigs. But all they could find was fifteen.

"Maybe I only caught eight," Donny said.

"Could of been ten," Willie pointed out. "I always git too cussid haired-up to count, anyway."

Donny drew a deep breath. "Look, if you want to fill in my name the same as yours on them papers, it's all right with me."

"You sure? The name don't count much, anyway. Mitchell's a fine one."

"I been thinkin it over. I guess I'd rather."

Willie wiped his hands on a piece of engine waste, dug the papers out of his pocket and hunted around in his wallet for a short stub of pencil. He filled in the blank space with heavy block-printed letters. "Donald Mitchell Stilwell."

"There," he said, holding it up for Donny to see. "That looks kind of good, don't it?"

He let Donny start the engine and showed him how to kick her over slowly, so as to ease up on the anchor rope while he pulled it in.

"I know that song," Donny said, after a while, as they skirted past the foot of the island. "I don't care if you sing it."

So Willie sang the whole thing through again, and then they sang it through together. The boat droned homeward through the lengthening shadows of the afternoon to the tune of the doleful ballad:

So his messmates hauled him up, but on the deck he died,
And they wrapped him in his hammock that was so fair and white,
And they lowered him overboard and he drifted with the tide,
And he sank into the Lowlands Low.